Special Publication Number 1

Status and Conservation of West Indian Seabirds

SOCIETY OF CARIBBEAN ORNITHOLOGY

Special Publication Number 1.

Edited by

E. A. Schreiber and David S. Lee

The Society of Caribbean Ornithology publishes a bulletin, "El Pitirre", and "Special Publications" for papers too long to appear in the Bulletin. This publication has been made possible through the support of Ramsar Bureau, Gland, Switzerland, U.S. Fish and Wildlife Service, USA, and Seabird Research, Inc., Alexandria, VA, USA. The views expressed in this publication are not intended to represent those of the Society of Caribbean Ornithology. William Mackin, Univ. of North Carolina provided the maps for the publication.

The Society of Caribbean Ornithology is a non-profit organization whose goals are to promote scientific study and conservation of Caribbean birds and their habitat. Regular membership is $20, Institutional membership is $120. Send check or money order in U.S. funds with complete name and address to: Dr. Rosemarie Gnam, 13 East Rosemont Ave., Alexandria, VA 22301, U.S.A.

Copies of Special Publications may be ordered from the editorial office:

Dr. James W. Wiley
2201 Ashland St.
Ruston, LA 71270, USA

Telephone 318 274-2499.
Email wileyjw@ alpha0.gram.edu.

Cost including shipping: 1) within the United States $12.00 U.S., 2) elsewhere $17.00 U.S. Make checks, payable to "Society of Caribbean Ornithology".

Issued January 30, 2000
Society of Caribbean Ornithology, Special Publication No. 1, v + 223 pp.
Copyright © by the Society of Caribbean Ornithology, 2000.
ISBN 0-9677824-0-6 $12.00

STATUS AND CONSERVATION OF WEST INDIAN SEABIRDS

Edited by:

E. A. Schreiber
National Museum of Natural History
Bird Department MRC 116
Washington D.C. 20560 USA

David S. Lee
North Carolina State Museum of Natural Science
P. O. Box 29555
Raleigh, North Carolina 27626 USA

SOCIETY OF CARIBBEAN ORNITHOLOGY, SPECIAL PUBLICATION NO. 1.
2201 Ashland St., Ruston, LA 71270, USA

2000

TABLE OF CONTENTS

continued -

Table of Contents continued -

v

West Indian Seabirds: a disappearing natural resource

_____ ෪ ෪ ෪ ෪   ෨ ෨ ෨ ෨ _____

E. A. SCHREIBER [1] and DAVID S. LEE [2]

[1] _National Museum of Natural History, Smithsonian Institution, MRC 116 ,Washington D. C. 20560 USA, Email SchreiberE@aol.com._ [2] _North Carolina State Museum of Natural Sciences, P.O. Box 29555, Raleigh, NC 27626 USA, Email cbirds1002@aol.com._

Introduction

The Caribbean Islands are considered one of the world's "Biodiversity Hotspots", defined as an area of the planet that is critical to preserving the diversity of life on earth (Madre 1999). Twenty-five threatened regions were designated as Hotspots by Conservation International, representing only 1.4% of the land surface of the world, but containing over 60% of all plant and animal species. These 25 areas also contain 81.6% of the world's endangered bird species and high concentrations of endangered mammals and plants. All 25 areas have already lost 75% or more of their original vegetation. Five of the listed Hotspots are tropical archipelagos: the Caribbean, Madagascar and the Indian Ocean Islands, Polynesia-Micronesia complex, New Caledonia, and Wallacea (Indonesia). This points out the severe conservation problems suffered in the islands today and the continuing loss of biodiversity. We hope in this publication, by presenting the status and conservation needs of West Indian seabirds, to draw attention to the ongoing declines in these populations and the need for immediate conservation action to preserve these species.

In the early 1980s van Halewyn and Norton (1984) and Sprunt (1984) summarized the status of and conservation issues for seabirds of the Caribbean region. Since then, more detailed inventories have revealed that, for a number of species, population estimates made at that time were too high, and in a few cases where population monitoring has occurred, dramatic declines in the number of nesting pairs have been recorded. The original problems identified by van Halewyn and Norton (1984) have not been resolved (egg collecting, exotic predators, pollution, habitat destruction and disturbance) and several of them have become increasingly more severe over the last 15 years. Primarily because of the growing tourism industry, development of coastal habitats has increased and isolated cays and rocks, which were formerly relatively safe nesting sites, are now being developed or are visited by tourists seeking remote island experiences. Ironically, the seabird colonies themselves are becoming attractions for the ecotourism industry. Presently most of the species of seabirds nesting in the region are represented by tremendously reduced populations with aggregate numbers totaling only a few thousand pairs.

In August 1997, an International Seabird Workshop was held at the Society of Caribbean Ornithology's annual meeting in Aruba. Participants addressed conservation issues related to seabirds in the West Indies region (Fig. 1) and discussed steps needed to preserve seabird populations. All in attendance agreed that research and standardized monitoring had been largely neglected throughout the region, and that programs addressing these issues were vital to the long range survival of a number of locally breeding seabirds. Furthermore, with the general lack of

Figure 1. Key to the Island Maps Appearing in Each Species Account

Each chapter on species' status has a map that shows the locations of active colonies, colonies that were active years ago but from which we have no recent data, and known extirpated colonies. Owing to constraints on space, the maps appearing in the species chapters do not have the names on the individual islands. The numbered island names below correspond to those numbers on the following map for reference.

ISLAND NAME

1. The Bahamas
   a. Cay Sal Bank
   b. Bimini
   c. Grand Bahama
   d. Abaco
   e. New Providence
   f. Andros
   g. Eleuthera
   h. Exuma Cays
   i. Cat Island
   j. San Salvador
   k. Rum Cay
   l. Long Island
   m. Crooked Island
   n. Acklins Island
   o. Mayaguana
   p. Great Inagua
2. Turks and Caicos
3. Cuba
4. Caymen Islands
5. Jamaica
   a. Pedro Cays
   b. Morant Cays
6. Navassa Island (USA)
7. Haiti
8. Dominican Republic
9. Mona Island (Puerto Rico)
10. Puerto Rico
11. Culebra, Vieques, Cordillera Island: Puerto Rico

ISLAND NAME

12. United States Virgin Islands
13. British Virgin Islands
14. Anguilla
15. St. Martin
16. St. Bartholomew
17. Saba
18. St. Eustatius
19. Barbuda
20. St. Christopher and Nevis
21. Antigua
22. Redonda
23. Montserrat
25. Dominica
26. Martinique
27. St. Lucia
28. Barbados
29. St. Vincent and the Grenadines
30. Grenada
31. Tobago
32. Trinidad
33. Margarita Island (Venezuela)
34. Los Roques Archipelago (Venezuela)
35. Bonaire
36. Curaçao
37. Aruba

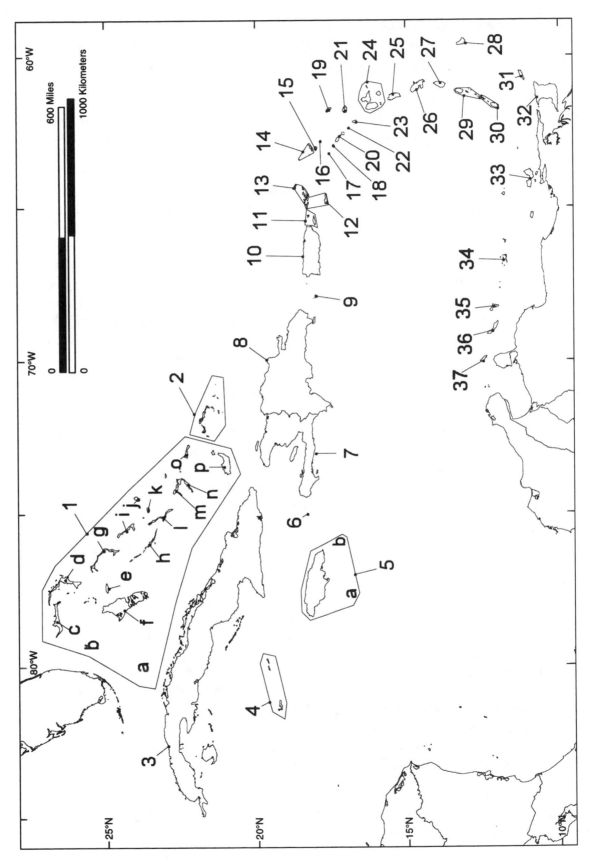

biology, distribution, conservation status and management needs was greatly needed. This publication is a direct result of these concerns. It represents the combined efforts of not only the authors of the chapters presented herein but also of a large number of biologists residing in the greater West Indies region.

The Bahama archipelago, Greater and Lesser Antilles, and Trinidad and Tobago (hereafter the West Indies region; Fig. 1) support an important assemblage of breeding seabirds. In former times, the relatively predator-free islands of the region sustained much more abundant seabird populations which were probably ten times or more greater than those of today (Pregill et. al 1994). Human habitation of the islands started about 7,000 years before the present and evidence suggests that the initial impact on nesting seabirds was devastating. With the arrival of man, seabirds became a common, easily obtained source of food, as evidenced by middens on St. Croix, the Bahamas, and elsewhere (Palmer 1962, Steadman et al. 1984, Pregill et al. 1994, Steadman 1997, Wetmore 1938). This exploitation was followed by a period of European contact where human predation on seabirds and their eggs continued, and continues today, but to a lesser degree. A variety of introduced mammals compounded the problem. This not only includes mammalian predators but over grazing by feral goats and sheep which is causing major erosion problems on some islands. Generally, seabirds were driven from nesting on the primary islands where human habitation and exotic mammal associates had taken over. For the most part, seabird colonies are now restricted to off shore rocks and cays, and inaccessible cliff faces.

It is difficult in modern times to fully appreciate the extent of pre-European contact, human reliance on seabird populations as a source of food in the West Indies. They provided an excellent, easily obtainable source of protein that was extensively exploited. The loss of seabirds from tropical islands is estimated to be about 90 to 99% (Pregill et al. 1994, Steadman 1985, 1989, 1995). In some cases, single species became a primary source for subsistence hunters and continual collecting over many years greatly depleated them. The following quotes from the 1600-1700s illustrate the extensive hunting of the Black-capped Petrel (*Pterodroma hasitata*), formerly an abundant species, but now in danger of extinction.

"It may be said that these birds are a manna that sends every year for Negroes and for the lowly inhabitants, who do not live on any thing else during the season.

After two or three hours of hunting I returned with my Negro to rest to cook some birds for dinner. I began finally to hunt alone. We reassembled at midday. The four Negroes had 138 diablotins. Albert had 43, and I had 17. Each of us ate two, and we left carrying the rest of our game.

"Those who read these memoirs will doubtless be surprised that we should eat birds in Lent; but the missionaries who are in these islands, and who in many matters exercise the power of bishops, after serious deliberation and consultation of a medical man, have declared that lizards and diablotins are vegetable food, and that consequently they may be eaten at all times (Labat 1724)."

"Its flesh is so delicate that no hunter ever returns from the mountain who does not ardently desire to have a dozen of these "devils" hanging from his neck (du Tertre 1654)."

Most tropical seabirds in the West Indies now exist at modest to relatively low densities. They normally feed at sea at great distances from breeding sites, and typically produce just one slow-growing chick per year. The combined result is that seabirds are more vulnerable on their breeding sites than most land birds because of the protracted period of nest occupancy and the concentration of complete regional populations to a few sites. Furthermore, populations are slow to recover from disturbance because of their low reproductive output. The entire populations of most seabirds nesting in the Caribbean consist of only several thousand pairs. To put the size of these populations in perspective with those in other regions, we point out that if all West Indian species were combined, the number would represent less than 20% of the total number of Leach's Storm-Petrels (*Oceanodroma leucorhoa*) from a single 6.3 sq kilometer nesting site off eastern Canada (Sklepkovych and Montevecchi 1989). In fact, of the 21 species of seabirds nesting in the West Indies, over half of these represent small populations whose conservation status is of current concern. Many of these are endemic species or races, and several are species with all or the majority of the world's population residing in the West Indies (see chapter "Action Plan for Conservation of West Indian Seabirds").

The Current Fauna

The breeding seabird fauna of the West Indies consists of three Procellariiformes (one of which, the Jamaican Petrel [*Pterodroma caribbea]* is possibly extinct, and another the Black-capped Petrel [*P. hasitata*] is highly endangered), seven species of Pelicaniformes (pelicans and their relatives) and 12 Laridae (gulls and terns). The Jamaican Petrel and Black-capped Petrel, Audubon's Shearwater (*Puffinus lherminieri),* White-tailed Tropicbird (*Phaethon lepturus),* Brown Pelican (*Pelecanus occidentalis)*, Cayenne Tern (*Sterna eurygnatha*) and Bridled Tern (*Sterna anaethetus)* are all represented by endemic subspecies. The Roseate Tern (*Sterna dougallii)*, is regarded as threatened by the US Fish and Wildlife Service with perhaps as much as 40% of the world's population breeding in the West Indies.

Nomenclature in this publication follows the American Ornithologists' Union Checklist (1998). Of a total fauna of 21 seabird taxa nesting in the West Indies (Table 1), 6 are endemic (Black-capped and Jamaica Petrel, Audubon's Shearwater, White-tailed Tropicbird, Brown Pelican and Cayenne Tern [subspecies of Sandwich Tern]). Five species and one subspecies (>20 %) are considered to be "Critically Endangered", 3 species are "Endangered", 4 species "Vulnerable", and 2 species "Near Threatened". Studies of the subspecific descriptions of most of these species have not been conducted and one or more of them could represent unique subspecies given the lack of inter-island movement of the populations. Fourteen of the 21 species nesting in the region are of conservation concern.

The Problems

Conservation of Caribbean seabirds has largely been overlooked. Most global assessments of areas said to be important to seabirds have been based on density and biomass figures, yet in the West Indies region seabirds were apparently so depleted prior to European contact and further depleted during the colonial period, that inventories are unavailable for primal populations. Because previously large populations of seabirds were not well documented in the literature, declines in West Indian species have not received the same amount of attention and concern as have some temperate and boreal seabirds. The serious conservation issues today are the continuing series of single event destructions of the small, seemingly unimportant relict colonies that remain. This site by site destruction has been spread out over time, not focused in

Table 1. Species list for West Indies and number of nesting pairs.

Common Name	Scientific Name	Number of Pairs
(Cahow Petrel	*Pterdroma cahow*)	now extinct in region
Black-capped Petrel	*Pterdroma hasitata*	1000-2000
Jamaica Petrel	*Pterdroma caribbea*	0-15
Audubon's Shearwater	*Puffinus lherminieri*	3000-5000
Red-billed Tropicbird	*Phaethon aethereus*	1800-2500
White-tailed Tropicbird	*Phaethon lepturus*	2500-3500
Brown Pelican	*Pelecanus occidentalis*	1500
Masked Booby	*Sula dactylatra*	550-650
Red-footed booby	*Sula sula*	8200-10,000
Brown Booby	*Sula leucogaster*	5500-7800
Magnificent Frigatebird	*Fregata magnificens*	4300-5300
Laughing Gulls	*Larus atricilla*	5000-10,000
Gull-billed Tern	*Sterna nilotica*	100-500
Royal Tern	*Sterna maxima*	450-800
Sandwich Tern	*Sterna sandvicensis*	2100-3000
CayenneTern	*Sterna s. eurygnatha*	10-100
Roseate Tern	*Sterna dougallii*	4000-6000
Common Tern	*Sterna hirundo*	50-100
Bridled Tern	*Sterna anaethetus*	5000-7000
Sooty Tern	*Sterna fuscata*	200,000-300,000
Least Tern	*Sterna antillarum*	1500-3000
Brown Noddy	*Anous stolidus*	10,000-18,000
Black Noddy	*Anous tenuirostris*	fewer than 100

any particular West Indian nation, or on any specific species, and for the most part is poorly documented.

Another problem, which has hampered seabird conservation, is that historically, ornithology in the West Indies region has focused on land bird studies, particularly on the zoogeography and conservation of island endemics. Seabirds of the region have been neglected over the years. Moreover, because seabirds now typically are confined to remote areas, where it is difficult or expensive to conduct research, little work has been done on them. As a result we have little knowledge about the status of most seabirds, and even less knowledge about their local natural history. This makes developing conservation criteria for them difficult. If we are to preserve seabirds in the West Indies, we must develop long-term plans for basic research and conservation and implement them in a regionally consistent manner.

The rapid economic growth of the entire area jeopardizes even the remote areas where seabirds now restrict their nesting activities. Growing tourism and other development in the Caribbean is directly threatening many remaining nesting colonies. Seabird nesting islands often have the exact characteristics desired by tourists seeking remote, isolated tropical retreats. In many cases the beauty and wildlife of the area draws tourists, but in the case of nesting seabirds, because of their intolerance of human disturbance, tourist's visits can easily destroy the resource they come to see. The increasing number of charter boats has brought man and his pets into repeated contact with isolated seabird colonies with devastating effects. Based on the timing of visits as it relates to the phenology of particular colonies, even a single visit by people unaware of the needs of seabirds can destroy an entire year's production of the colony.

This scenario is made grimmer by the fact that there has never been a complete inventory of the seabirds in the Caribbean and there have only been a few continuing studies of specific sites available to show population trends. Some important nesting sites believed to be of paramount importance to the regional survival of species have not been inventoried since the 1950s. Others have not been inventoried since the last century (Navassa Island, Cay Verde, Santo Domingo Cay, and others). Assessments made during the last 15 years (papers presented herein) show that the earlier inventories (van Halewyn and Norton 1984, Sprunt, 1984) erred in over-estimating populations. Additionally, populations of some species have declined dramatically during the past 15 years. Because the local populations are small, and condensed, the potential for the rapid disappearance of the few remaining major nesting colonies is alarming. The ability of tropical species with modest reproductive output to colonize or re-colonize areas once extirpated is minimal. Recolonization may not even be an option. Recent data show that, in some areas, seabirds rarely move between islands (Schreiber and Schreiber 1988). There are many examples of massive losses of seabirds from tropical island groups around the world (Steadman 1985, 1989, 1995; Wragg and Weisler 1994) and far too many examples of local extirpations and declines of species from particular islands in the Caribbean (Steadman et al. 1984, van Halewyn and Norton 1984 and papers in this volume).

Diversity in the Caribbean avifauna will be difficult to retain because of ecological imbalance and rapid development in a region with limited sources of income. Steps must be taken immediately to identify and protect areas important to seabirds. Local inventories and monitoring programs are greatly needed, but data gathering must be coordinated across the entire region. The difficulty in coordinating local inventories and long-term protection is exacerbated by the region's large number of independent political units (including mainland margins of the Caribbean, 28 different nations govern the region), languages, and currencies.

Seabirds will provide a valuable, natural ecotourism resource if they and tourists can be properly managed. Also, as a top-level predator of marine food chains, they provide us with a valuable yardstick to monitor the general health of oceanic systems. For example, seabirds collected off the North Carolina coast (many of which are of West Indian origin) have been used to document baseline mercury loads in the tissues of 27 species (Whaling et al. 1980), and growing incidence of plastic ingestion by pelagic species (Moser and Lee 1992). Yet, within the West Indies region we know very little about key foraging areas or seasonal variations of surface productivity and how they relate to the locations and success of seabird colonies. Coastal development and source pollution in wetlands throughout the Caribbean region is damaging marine nursery grounds. Some sea birds feed in these nursery grounds but more importantly they support the young of prey species, contributing to the productivity of pelagic habitats. Destruction of these wetlands, and the disruption of the natural processes which support them, will not only severely harm marine bird populations, but will also harm the marine related economies of the region.

While the number of endangered and threatened species of seabirds in the West Indies paints a rather bleak picture, there are several important regional conservation efforts which have been successful. Gochfeld et al. (1994) review case studies of four successful management programs: 1) Culebra, a Caribbean National Wildlife Refuge managed from Puerto Rico, 2)

Desecheo, an island off Puerto Rico where exotic mammals are being eradicated, 3) Jamaica with a successful seabird management program, and 4) Aruba where enforcement of existing wildlife laws, colony patrols and positive media coverage has allowed important larid colonies to recover. Barbuda, after a training program for wardens and tour guides, has set up a very successful eco-tourism program for their Great Frigatebird colony. These regional programs each serve as successful models that can be used elsewhere in the region. Consultation with the countries that have carried out successful programs can assist other countries in developing similar plans.

The chapters that follow are an outgrowth of a symposium held in Aruba at the annual meeting of the Society of Caribbean Ornithology in August 1997. During the meeting, seabird biologists and persons responsible for environmental programs from the West Indies and Bahamas were charged with estimating regional population sizes and developing of conservation priorities for the 21 species of nesting seabirds in the region. The general consensus of the participants was that seabird populations of the West Indies are lower than previously believed and that a number of species were of serious conservation concern. At that time West Indian seabirds were grouped into four conservation priority levels using the basics of the criteria developed by the International Union for the Conservation of Nature (see Chapter " Action Plan for Conservation of West Indian Seabirds"). The status review papers in this volume support these species priority ratings.

The Papers in this Volume

This volume is designed to serve as a guide to Caribbean nations in identifying regional seabird conservation issues and as a base line against which to measure long-range population trends of individual species. The volume also provides the necessary information to assist Government environmental managers in making the beginning steps toward conservation of seabirds. The chapters address the population status and conservation concerns for each nesting seabird species in the West Indies. Seabirds nesting in Mexico and along the Caribbean coasts of Central and South America are not covered specifically in this volume. Some authors do make a few brief comments about these areas for reference. In many cases, the current status of key colonies is unknown, and in a number of instances there have been no reports from colonies in the past 100 years. Where the data exist, we have tried to present details on exact colony locations as much as possible for comparison to future monitoring efforts. The distribution maps for each species are generated from a GIS system (see chapter on this by W. Mackin) and new information can be entered into this database as it becomes available.

E. A. Schreiber provides a chapter outlining current research needs for the region and a summary chapter discussing conservation priorities, listing species with ranking by degree of concern, and making recommendations for needed conservation action. A chapter outlining appropriate monitoring techniques is provided by Alan Burger. Paul and Francine Buckley discuss the use of helicopters to assess the status of seabirds over a large area. Also included is a complete bibliography of the seabirds of the region prepared by Jim Wiley. It is our hope that this volume will become a valuable resource for those working in the region who do not have access to much of the primary literature and that it will serve as a guide to the development of conservation action plans for the West Indies.

Acknowledgements

We thank the Society of Caribbean Ornithology and its members who have worked hard to provide data on the seabirds in their area and those who have written chapters for this publication, and the U.S. Fish and Wildlife Service for their support of the SCO and its annual meetings. We thank RAMSAR (Gland, Switzerland) and Seabird Research, Inc.(Alexandria, VA, U.S.A.) for providing funding to publish the results of this symposium. We are indebted to Will Mackin, Univ. of North Carolina who prepared the maps.

Literature Cited

American Ornithologists' Union, Check-list of North Am. Birds. 1998. AOU, Washington, D.C.

du Tertre, J. B. 1654. Histoire générale des Antilles, habitées par les François. Paris 2.

Gochfeld, M., J. Burger, A. Haynes-Sutton, R. van Halewyn, and J. Saliva. 1994. Successful approaches to seabird protection in the West Indies. BirdLife conservation Series no. 1: 186-209.

Labat, P. 1724. Voyages aux isles de l'Amérique. La Haye 1:1-360, 2:1-520.

Madre, A. S. 1999. Hotspots, earth's biologically richest and most endangered terrestrial ecoregions. Cemex, Mexico.

Moser, M.L. and D.S. Lee. 1992. A fourteen year survey of plastic ingestion by western North Atlantic seabirds. Colonial Waterbirds 15(1):83-94.

Palmer, R.S. 1962. Handbook of North American Birds. Yale Univ. Press, New York. 567pp.

Pregill, G. K., D.W. Steadman, and D. R. Watters. 1994. Late quaternary vertebrate faunas of the Lesser Antilles; historical components of Caribbean biogeography. Bull. of Carnegie Museum of Natural History No. 30.

Schreiber, E. A. and R. W. Schreiber. 1988. Great Frigatebird size dimorphism on two central Pacific atolls. Condor 90: 90-99.

Sklepkorych, B.O., and W. A. Montevecch1. 1989. The world's largest known nesting colony of Leach's Storm-Petrels on Baccalieu Island, New Foundland. Am. Birds 12:12-23.

Sprunt, A. 1984. The status and conservation of seabirds of the Bahama Islands. Pp. 157-186 in J. P. Croxall, P.G.H. Evans and R.W. Schreiber, eds. *Status and Conservation of the World's Seabirds*, Cambridge, U.K.: International Council for Bird Preservation (Tech. Publ.). 2.

Steadman, D. W. 1985. Fossil birds from Mangaia, Southern Cook Islands. Bull British Ornithol. Club 105:58-66.

Steadman, D. W. 1989. Extinction of birds in eastern Polynesia: a review of the record, and comparisons with other Pacific Island groups. Journ. Archaeo. Science 16:177-205.

Steadman, D. W. 1995. Prehistoric extinctions of Pacific island birds: biodiversity meets zooarchaeology. Science 267:1123-1131.

Steadman, D. W. 1997. Human caused extinction of birds. Pp 139-161 in M. L. Reaka-Kudla, D. E. Wilson, and E. O. Wilson, eds. *Biodiversity II: understanding and protecting our biological resources*, Joseph Henry Press, Washington, D.C.

Steadman, D. W., Pregill, G. K. and Olson, S. L. 1984. Fossil vertebrates from Antigua, Lesser Antilles: evidence for late Halocene human-caused extinctions in the West Indies. Proc. *Natl. Academy of Sciences* 81: 4448-4451.

van Halewyn, R. and R.L. Norton. 1984. The status and conservation of Caribbean seabirds. Pp. 169-222 in J. P. Croxall, P. G. H. Evans, and R. W. Schreiber, eds. *Status and Conservation of the World's Seabirds*,: International Council for Birds Preservation, Cambridge, U.K. (Tech. Publ.) 2.

Wetmore, A. 1938. Bird remains from the West Indies. Auk 55: 51-55.

Wragg, G. M. and M. I. Weisler. 1994. Extinctions and new records of birds from Henderson Island, Pitcarin Group, South Pacific Ocean. Notornis 41: 61-70.

Whaling, J., D.S. Lee, J. Bonaventura, and M. Rentzepis. 1980. The body burden approach of looking at natural mercury accumulation inn pelagic seabirds (abstract). 1980 Annual Meeting of American Ornithologists' Union.

Status of and Conservation Priorities for Black-capped Petrels in the West Indies

 G8 G8 G8 G8   &0 &0 &0 &0

DAVID S. LEE

North Carolina State Museum of Natural Sciences, P.O. Box 29555, Raleigh, NC 27626, Cbirds1002@aol.com

Introduction

The Black-capped Petrel (Pterodroma hasitata), a West Indian endemic, inhabits the western North Atlantic ranging at sea from Brazil to North Carolina (Palmer 1962, Lee 1977, 1984). It is essentially absent from the Gulf of Mexico, and uncommon at sea in the North Atlantic in areas not directly influenced by the Gulf Stream. Numerous records from coastal and inland North America result from tropical storms. Breeding is confined to the West Indies region (Fig 1). It is one of the few species of seabirds for which we know more about its biology at sea, than we know about its breeding biology. Like other petrels this species is highly pelagic, ranging at sea in the Caribbean and western tropical Atlantic (Morzer Bruyns 1967 a, b; Haney 1987). Evidence suggests that nesting birds regularly commute from their breeding sites in Hispaniola to forage off the coasts of Cuba (Lee and Vina 1993) and the southeastern United States as far north as North Carolina (Lee 1977, 1984).

This species is a winter breeder. Its phenology is poorly known but based on nesting habits of other similar-sized petrels, accounts from writers from previous centuries, a singe egg date (Smith 1959, in Palmer 1962), timing of molt, and the presence of vocalizing birds at nesting sites, most nesting activity is assumed to be between December and April. Based on the nesting behavior of Bermuda Petrels, it is likely that pairs regularly visit nesting burrows as early as November. Like other petrels this species is assumed to have a very protracted incubation and fledgling period. Labat's (1722) report of collecting birds (chicks?) from their burrows during Lent also indicates winter breeding. A recently vacated burrow found on 18 April 1996 by Williams et al. (1997) in Sierra de Baoruco, Dominican Republic, indicates nesting is completed by mid-spring. These birds are probably long lived and may not reproduce prior to their 5th to 7th year. They lay a single egg annually.

Status in the West Indies

In former times, the French islands probably supported larger human populations than were physically sustainable. People were protein deficient, and birds were considered a necessity as well as a great delicacy. Consequently, these birds were hunted constantly during the breeding season. Often, dogs were used to locate burrows (Labat 1722). Even the difficult and dangerous cliffs were scaled in pursuit of nesting petrels. It is now obvious that most populations did not survive this period of exploitation. On Hispaniola, where the only known extant populations still nest (Fig. 1), there is a documented decrease in petrel populations in the last 25 years. The fact that peasants living near colonies were unaware of any change in petrel populations in the early

1960's (Wingate 1964) is interesting, but certainly not conclusive, and I suspect Wingate's original discovery was of relict colonies. In addition to direct human consumption, other problems facing breeding petrel colonies include introduced predators, lights, lumbering, forest fires, and destruction and alternation of nesting sites. Fossil and sub-fossil material from caves in Haiti (Florida State Museum) suggest at one time these birds were extremely abundant and much more wide-spread in Hispaniola that they are today (Fig. 1).

Island by Island Status

Cuba: In January of 1992, Nicasico Vina (Univ. of Oriente) and I visited the area in the Sierra Maestra in southeastern Cuba where Black-capped Petrels were reported. In 1977, Vina collected six birds just a few kilometers off shore from this mountain range. This discovery was interpreted by others (i.e., Bond 1978, 1985, van Halewyn and Norton 1984) as evidence that the species nested in the Sierra Maestra. Lee and Vina (1993) found that, although this petrel was coming in at night to feed in a restricted area of strong upwelling adjacent to Cuba's southeastern coast, there was no indication that the species was flying inland to nest in the mountains. While their field work does not conclusively prove that Black-capped Petrels are not nesting in Cuba, it does show that there is no evidence, to date, to suggest that they do.

Hispaniola (Haiti): Wingate visited Haiti in November 1961 and found 11 Black-capped Petrel colonies located on forested limestone cliffs on the inland side of La Selle Ridge; one colony was 20 km from the sea. Colonies were limited to sites where soil was sufficient enough for burrowing, as there were no natural cavities for petrel use. He estimated a minimum of fifty pairs per colony and concluded that if the mountain ranges in the Dominican Republic were occupied as well, as many as forty colonies may exist. This does not appear to be the case (see below), but subsequent authors have used these figures to calculate population size. Only one additional colony has been discovered in Haiti since Wingate's visit (1984 Massif de la Hotte, Collar et al. 1992). Extensive follow-up visits in 1980 and 1984 to Massif de la Selle by Charles Woods (1987) concluded that at least some of the colonies discovered by Wingate had declined, some as much as 40%. There is no additional information on any of the Haitian colonies though detrimental human activities, even within the confines of La Visite National Park, have increased.

Hispaniola (Dominican Republic): A small population of Black-capped Petrels was discovered in the Sierra de Baoruco in 1981 (van Halewyn and Norton 1984), but their presence was suspected in the area prior to 1979 (Ottenwalder and Vargas 1979). This site is immediately adjacent to the location of the Haitian populations on the highest slopes of Lomo de Toro (2,250m). The population was surveyed in 1981 (Woods and Ottenwalder 1983), and in 1989 and 1990 (J. C. Haney and Lee, pers. comm.). Williams et al. (1997) visited this site in mid-April 1996 and heard calling birds and found one empty burrow. This breeding colony is apparently quite small and rather extensive searches indicate that the birds are limited to a single, steep 400-foot cliff about 7,200 feet in elevation. Most records of calling birds are from the winter period, although J. C. Haney (pers obser.) heard individual calling birds on 14 August 1989 suggesting some summer activity at breeding sites. It is probable that additional undiscovered colonies exist in the Sierra de Baoruco. The mountain is thinly populated, has little access, and, in contrast to neighboring Haiti, still extensively forested. Williams et al. (1997) however, point out that illegal selective logging occurs in areas adjacent to Haiti and charcoal-burning camps were found in the area.

Martinique: Most authors (e.g. Pinchon 1967, van Halewyn and Norton 1984) concur that on Martinique, the Black-capped Petrel was extirpated in pre-Columbian times by the Carib Indians who used the bird as a source of food. However, Wetmore (1952), in reporting a humerus of this petrel from Martinique (USNM 428289), points out another record from the 1800's when L'Herminier included this species on a list of species observed between 1827 and 1844. Wetmore concluded that the bone specimen is verification of this early report. The volcanic eruption of 1902 in Mt. Pelee is of speculative interest in that it may relate to the disappearance of Pterodroma on this island. The island has been heavily deforested and much of the available land has been converted to agriculture.

Guadeloupe: Bent (1922) and Pinchon (1967) reported rapid declines in the population as a result of an earthquake in 1847 and the use of adult birds for food and the greasy young for fuel. Nesting birds disappeared around 1850. The most recent information for the island was presented by Noble (1916) who was unable to locate any petrels. His guide stated that the diablotin had not been heard of for nearly 70 years. This island has also suffered from heavy deforestation.

Dominica: The species was numerous on Dominica (the designated type locality) through the early 1800's, and although its numbers certainly have been decimated, some suspect that a portion of this population is still extant. Based on early literature (summarized by Murphy 1936), it appears that historically the most significant West Indian population of this petrel once nested here. Petrels collected in Dominica in 1932 (Hobley 1932), and heard as recently as 1977 (van Halewyn and Norton 1984), provide no positive indication that the species is still nesting. Wingate (1964) visited the island in search for these petrels between 16 October and 10 November 1961. Conditions for field work were extremely difficult and nothing conclusive was learned. Although the last confirmed date of nesting is 1862 (Smith 1959, in Palmer 1962), a recent specimen from the island (Adolphus Christian per. com. 1990) provides further promise that the birds continue to exist.

Without evidence of nesting in Cuba, known breeding areas are restricted to the mountain ranges in southern Hispaniola where this petrel faces a number of conservation problems. The global population of Black-capped Petrels must be regarded as small and highly vulnerable. The recently discovered Dominican population (Ottenwalder and Vargas 1979) is quite small and apparently declining. Lee and Haney (pers. obser.) recorded no more than five pairs in January 1990, in contrast to 65 pairs estimated in 1981 (Woods and Ottenwalder 1983). Twelve colonies of at least 50 pairs each are known from Massif de la Hotte and Massif de la Selle in Haiti (Collar et al. 1992). Thus, we can assume a minimum of 600 pairs. Based on Wingate's field work in the early 1960's, various authors have considered the population to be from 2,000 to 25,000 pairs (e.g., van Halewyn and Norton 1984). People like to cite hard numbers yet Wingate (1964) notes: "It was extremely difficult to estimate the population when the nest sites were inaccessible and visited by petrels only at night. Flying birds could not be seen to be counted and individual calls could not be discriminated from the chorus." Furthermore these numbers are based on the assumption that there may be as many as 40 colonies, and at present only 13 are known from the island. A decline in number at known colonies has been reported (Woods 1987). In truth the size of the current population is unclear but, based on recent changes in Haiti, it is believed to range somewhere between 600-2,000 pairs.

Table 1. Known breeding sites of Black-capped Petrels in the West Indies

Location	No. of Pairs	Source
Cuba	0	contrary to earlier literature no indication of nesting in Cuba (Lee and Vina 1993)
Haiti	fewer than 2,000	2,000 to 25,000 pr.(Wingate 1964): at least 600 (Collar 1992) see text
Dominican Republic	5-40	Sierra de Baorunco two colonies 20 pr each Am Birds 36:334; one colony >5pr (Lee and Vina 1993); Bahoruco Range 40 pr Am Birds 35:866
Dominica	E	no longer present Prys-Jones 1982
Guadeloupe	E	none since 1847 (Bent 1922, Murphy 1936)
Martinique	E	none since pre-Columbian times (Pinchon 1967)
TOTAL	**fewer than 2,000**	

E - extirpated.

Conservation and Research Needs

Vermeer and Rankin (1984) list Pterodroma hasitata as one of seven endangered taxa of gadfly petrels. It is also included in the 1988 ICPB list of threatened birds of the world (Collar and Andrew 1988). Despite repeated attempts since 1990 to have this species evaluated for endangered status by the US Fish and Wildlife Service, no action has been taken. The reasons for this are unclear. The population size for this species is far below that of many other species (including seabirds) that are currently listed as endangered. The species regularly occurs in US waters and in areas where there are some major environmental issues (see below). Furthermore, the US military presence in Haiti would allow for some potential benefits directed toward the species or its nesting sites in that country. Minimally, endangered status increases the public awareness of the problems facing many seabirds and provides funding for much needed research. The only explanation for the lack of interest in consideration for listing has been that the USFWS is unclear into which regional office the species' management should fall. It would appear that the only way that a decision will be made regarding this species is if the FWS is directly petitioned to list it.

The areas of known nesting in Haiti and the Dominican Republic need to be surveyed in order to determine the current status of known populations, and the existence, if any, of additional ones. Because of recurring local reports the sea cliffs at Cabo Falso and Isla Beta, in particular, need to be surveyed. Risk to the 13 known Hispaniola colonies such as the extent of logging, human predation, and accessibility to nests by introduced predators must be determined. While probably not practical, conservation officers need to patrol ridge tops during the nesting season to curtail poaching activities. At least the national park areas in both Haiti and the Dominican Republic should be managed to provide protection.

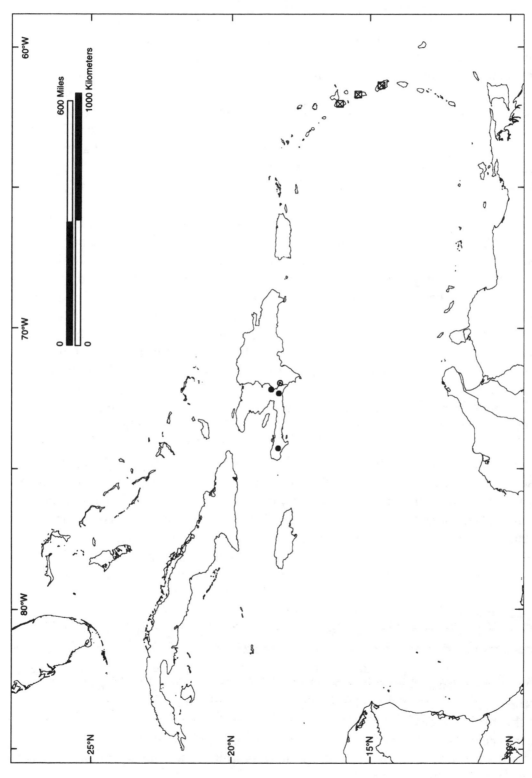

Figure 1: The status of known Black-capped Petrel breeding sites in the West Indies. ● = confirmed breeding location that has been surveyed recently. ⊙ = historic breeding location with no report that the colony has been extirpated. ⊠ = historic breeding location that is extirpated or thought to be extirpated.

Because of their secretive, nocturnal inland nesting behavior, the presence of unidentified breeding populations in the Bahamas, Greater Antilles and Lesser Antilles cannot be ruled out. Attention for surveys should first be directed to islands of known historic nesting. Extirpation from these islands has not been proven and relict populations of other globally endangered Pterodroma continue to be discovered in places where they were long considered extirpated. The fact that a few specimens have been found in the Lesser Antilles during this century suggests that the species still breeds in a few remote, yet undiscovered sites. While Dominica is certainly the most likely island to support unreported extant populations, Prys-Jones (1982) found no evidence indicating the species still survives on Dominica. Additional survey work in Hispaniola is clearly needed, and field workers should be aware of the possibility of additional populations in countries where nesting has never been documented. Surveys for petrels should be conducted in the winter (November to early April) when the birds are visiting nesting colonies and are most vocal.

Because the species occurs regularly, and is sometimes common off the North Carolina coast, and because of the relatively small numbers known to nest in Hispaniola, it seems reasonable to assume a large portion of the population forages off the coast of the southeastern United States. Lee and J. C. Haney (unpublished) estimated adult population size based on the extent of foraging areas and the petrel's densities off the southeastern United States. Collection of specimens off the southeastern United States shows the birds found there to be 68% adult males. Thus, the "at-sea" population estimate for the southeastern United States could be somewhat comparable to the actual minimal number of breeding pairs. After making a number of assumptions, Lee and Haney concluded the population foraging in waters off the Southeastern United States to be 2,000 to 4,000 adult males. While none of these figures, either from the breeding grounds or ones obtained at sea, provide real population estimates, it is important to note that the total number of known pairs appears to be only in the thousands, and may be far less.

The precise area off North Carolina where large numbers of these petrels concentrate, and the only area at sea where large numbers can predictably be found (often several hundred can be found in a few hours in a single small area), is currently under review for gas/oil exploration. Lee and Socci (1985) reviewed various aspects of this issue. There are environmental concerns in addition to problems resulting from potential oil spills. Ships stationed at this site could be detrimental to the survival of these birds. These petrels are known to be attracted to lights on foggy nights, and many could be killed on a single night when birds would fly into rigging and hulls.

Black-capped Petrels have the highest concentrations of natural mercury in their tissues of any species of seabird examined. These petrels have mercury loads 7- 9 times higher than most of the 27 species studied. Mean concentrations in the 22 Black-capped Petrels examined are 150g in muscle, 710 g in liver, 124 g in kidneys and 1098 g in feathers (Lee unpublished). Heavy metals are expected to be released into the water column in the area where these petrels concentrate off North Carolina if off shore drilling takes place. How this would effect the mercury loads in this bird is unclear.

Governments need to be made aware of conservation issues associated with the Black-capped Petrel. As it now stands, no country is accepting responsibility for the conservation needs of this very high profile, West Indian endemic.

Literature Cited

Bent, A. C. 1922. Life histories of North American Petrels and Pelicans and their allies. Bulletin U.S. National Museum 121, 325 pp.

Bond, J. 1978. Twenty-second supplement to the check-list of birds of the West Indies (1956). The Academy Nat. Sci. Phil. 20pp.

Bond, J. 1985. Birds of the West Indies. 5th edition. Houghton Mifflin Co., Boston.

Collar, N. J. and P. Andrew. 1988. Birds to Watch. The ICBP World Check-list of Threatened Birds. ICPB Technical Publication No 8. Smithsonian Institution Press, Wash., DC

Collar, N. J., L.P. Gonzaga, N. Krabbe, A. Madrono Nieto, T.A. Parker III, and D.C. Wege. 1992. Threatened birds of the Americas: the ICBP/IUCN Red Data Book. Cambridge, U.K.: International Council for Bird Preservation.

Haney, J. C. 1987. Aspects of the pelagic ecology and behavior of the Black-capped Petrel (*Pterodroma hasitata*). Wilson Bull. 99:153-312.

Hobley, C. W. 1932. Dominica "Diablotin". Jour. Soc. for Preservation Fauna Empire, New Series, part 17:17-20.

Labat , P. 1722. Voyages aux isles de l'Amerique. La Haye 1:1-360, 2:1-520.

Lee, D. S. 1977. Occurrence of the Black-capped Petrel in North Carolina waters. Chat 41:1-2.

Lee, D. S. 1984. Petrels and storm-petrels in North Carolina's offshore waters: including species previously unrecorded for North America. Am. Birds 38:151-163.

Lee, D. S. and M.C. Socci. 1989. Potential effects of oil spills on seabirds and selected other ocean vertebrates off the North Carolina coast. Occas. Pap. NC Biol. Surv. 1989-1. 64pp.

Lee, D. S. and N. Vina. 1993. A re-evaluation of the status of *Pterodroma hasitata* in Cuba. Ornitologia Neotropical 4:99-101.]

Morzer Bruyns, W. F. J. 1967a. Black-capped Petrels (*Pterodroma hasitata*) in the Atlantic Ocean. Areda 55:270.

Morzer Bruyns, W. F. J. 1967b. Black-capped Petrels (*Pterodroma hasitata*) in the Caribbean. Ardea 55:144-145.

Murphy, R. C. 1936. Oceanic birds of South America. Two vols. American Mus. Nat. Hist. New York.

Noble, G. K. 1916. The resident birds of Guadeloupe. Bull. Mus. Comp. Zool., Harvard Coll. 60:359-396.

Ottenwalder, J. and M.T. Vargas. 1979. Nueva localidad para el Diablotin en la Republica Dominica. Nturalista Postal 1976-79. 36/79:185-186.

Palmer, R. S., ed. 1962. Handbook of North American birds. Vol. I. Yale Univ. Press., New Haven , Connecticut.

Pinchon, R. 1967. Quelques aspect de la nature aux Antilles. Fort-de-France. 254pp.

Prys-Jones, R. P. 1982. A synopsis on the status and ecology of the birds of Dominica. Rondebosch, South Africa: Percy Fitzpatrick Institute of Ornithology unpublished report.

van Halewyn, R. and R. L. 1984. The status and conservation of seabirds in the Caribbean. Pp. 169- 222 in Croxall, J. P., P. G. H. Evans and R. W. Schreiber, eds. *Status and Conservation of the World's Seabirds*. Intl. Council of Bird Preservation, Techn. Publication No. 2. 1984.

Vermeer, K. and L. Rankin. 1984. Influence of habitat destruction and disturbance on nesting seabirds. Pp. 723-763 in Croxall, J. P., P. G. H. Evans and R. Schreiber, eds. *Status and*

Conservation of the World's Seabirds. Intl. Council of Bird Preservation Techn. Publication No. 2. 1984.

Wingate, D. B. 1964. Discovery of breeding Black-capped Petrels on Hispaniola. Auk 81:147-159.

Wetmore, A. 1952. A record for the Black-capped Petrel, *Pterodroma hasitata*, in Martinique. Auk 69:460.

Williams, R. S. R., G. M. Kirwan and C. G. Bradshaw. 1977. The status of the Black-capped Petrel Pterodroma hasitata in the Dominican Republic. Cotinga 6:29-30.

Woods, C. A. 1987. The threatened and endangered birds of Haiti: lost horizons and new hopes. Pp. 385-429 in *Proceedings 1987 Jean Delacour/IFCB Symposium on Breeding Birds in Captivity*. North Hollywood, California: International Foundation for the Conservation of Birds.

Woods, C. A. and J.A.Ottenwalder. 1983. The montane avifauna of Haiti. Pp. 607-626, in *Proceedings Jean Delacour/IFCB Symposium on Breeding Birds in Captivity*. North Hollywood, California: International Foundation for the Conservation of Birds.

Status of the Jamaican Petrel in the West Indies

——————   ෩ ෩ ෩ ෩   ෨ ෨ ෨ ෨   ——————

LEO DOUGLAS

Dept. of Life Sciences, University of the West Indies, Mona, Kingston 7 Jamaica.

Introduction

The Jamaican Petrel (*Pterdroma caribbaea*), a very little studied species, was said to have nested commonly in the Blue Mountains of Jamaica where specimens were collected up to 1879 (Collar et al. 1992). The species was considered abundant prior to mid-1800 and was hunted for food up to then (Scott 1891-1892). The last known collections of the species were made in Nov. and Dec. 1879. The last mention of the species nesting on the island was in 1891 when the Indian Mongoose (*Herpestes sp.*), introduced in 1872, was found in empty burrows of the species. Mongeese are believed to have caused the extinction of the petrels (Imber 1991). However dogs and feral pigs (the latter introduced at least 200 years earlier) may have contributed to its decline even before the advent of the mongoose (Godman 1907-1910; Gochfeld et al. 1990).

Breeding Biology

This nocturnally active species nests in burrows on cliffsides of almost inaccessible mountains, or in holes under trees in unfrequented woods at elevations of over 1600 meters (Carte 1866, Godman 1907-1910). Individuals fly out to sea to feed at dusk, returning to their burrows before dawn. Burrows are between 1.8 to 3 meters long, terminating in the nest chamber. Based on the time that museum skins were collected, the breeding season started in September (Imber 1991) with young hatching by February-March and fledging by May-June. Nothing is known about distribution of the species at sea except for James Bond's 1936 report of a possible sighting west in the Bahamian Islands (Collar et al. 1992). As with other species of *Pterodroma*, the Jamaica Petrel is thought to feed in pelagic oceanic waters where they are crepuscular and nocturnal feeders on various nectonic cephalopods (predominantly squid), fish and crustaceans which migrate towards the surface at night (Imber 1985).

Historical and current status

The species could well be extinct today as there are no recent reports of sightings, although there have been few systematic searches for it. The exact locations of the historical breeding sites were not recorded. However the following general localities have been gleaned from the literature (Fig. 1):

a) Location: Hilly interior of Metcalf, Blue Mountains
    Reference: Carte, 1866
b) Location: Near Cinchona Plantation, Blue Mountains
    Altitude: approx. 1600 meters
    Reference: Scott, 1891-1892
c) Location: Slopes above Nanny Town, Blue Mountains

	Altitude:	approx. 1200 meters
	Reference:	Thomas, 1890
d)	Location:	John Crow Mountains
	Altitude:	1050 at highest point
	Reference:	Scott, 1891-1892

Based on the given localities, historically the species appeared to have occurred along the full length of the Grand Ridge of the Blue Mountains and in the John Crow Mountains of the eastern end of Jamaica (Fig. 1). The localities also suggest that the species may have nested at elevations as low as 1,000 meters and not only "above 1600 meters" as stated by early writers. There are no reliable reports of sightings of Jamaican Petrels since the last birds were collected in the late 1800's, and empty burrows found in 1891. However, besides Bond's possible sighting, there are reports from individuals who are said to have heard the species calling at night in the John Crow Mountains, but no tangible evidence exists of the species' continued survival (Bourne 1965). However, it has been pointed out that it would be surprising if the Jamaican Petrel is indeed extinct (Imber 1991). This statement may be justified based on the following premises:

(1)   Gadfly petrels are well known for their ability to persist for decades and/or centuries in imperceptible numbers. A classic example being the Cahow (Bermuda) Petrel (*Pterodroma cahow*) which nested undiscovered on small islets for over 200 years despite the fact that Bermuda is among the most densely populated islands in the world (Bourne 1965).

(2)   While the introduction of the Indian Mongoose is thought to be responsible for the extinction of the Jamaican Petrel, Black-capped Petrels (*Pterodroma hasitata*) have survived in Hispaniola in the thousands despite the fact that the mongoose occurs on this island also (Wingate 1964a).

(3)   Much of the historical nesting range of the species has not been explored. It is covered by montane rainforest and elfin woodland, potentially providing abundant habitat but is rarely visited by humans.

(4)   The courtship, mating and pre-laying phase of the breeding cycle of the species, during which time they are most vocal, coincides with the peak of Jamaica's rainy season in October. Even the most dedicated woodsman rarely ventures far into the forested hills of the Blue and John Crow Mountains at this time.

"Lost species", particularly nocturnal ones, have a significant likelihood of surviving unnoticed for some time, and their re-discovery and conservation may simply await carefully prepared systematic searches. Leading authorities on *Pterodroma spp.* believe that the probability of survival of small colonies, or scattered pairs, of these long lived birds somewhere in mountains of eastern Jamaica is very high (Imber pers. comm., Bond 1965, Wingate 1964b). The related Gray-faced Petrel (*P. macroptera)* is known to live 30+ years (Imber pers. comm.).

After Scott's report, in which mongeese were found in empty burrows of Jamaican Petrels (Scott 1891-1892), no other written record exists of searches for the species until the early 1960's (Table 1). However, following Wingate's discovery of Black-capped Petrels in Hispaniola, a number of attempts were made to determine if the Jamaican Petrel still survived. The best documented search occurred on the weekend of January 25, 1969 (conducted by R. W. Smith, W. B. King and C. Kepler). The expedition lasted two nights and no petrels were seen or heard.

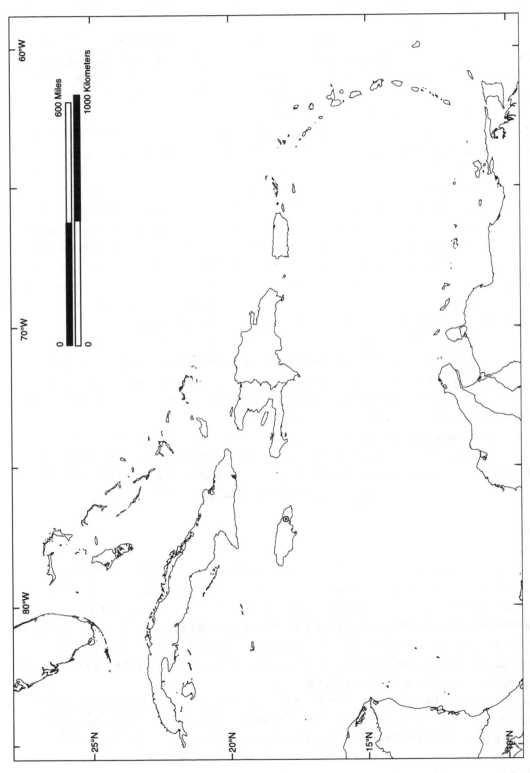

Figure 1: The status of known Jamaica Petrel breeding sites in the West Indies. ● = confirmed breeding location that has been surveyed recently. ⊙ = historic breeding location with no report that the colony has been extirpated. ⊠ = historic breeding location that is extirpated or thought to be extirpated.

These searches (Table 1) focused in the Blue Mountains and were apparently timed to take advantage of the relatively dryer conditions experienced between January and April. While these months may have proved more conducive to field work, it has been pointed out by Imber (1991) that "searches later than January, hoping to hear calls of the Jamaican Petrel will be futile" because the birds will be less vocal during incubation and chick rearing. James Bond suggested that the best locality for a search would be high in the John Crow Mountains. He did not believe any petrels still nested in the Blue Mountains (Bond 1965). Bourne (1965) reported that the birds were still said to call at night in the John Crow Mountains.

It must be pointed out that though all specimens of the species were obtained in the Blue Mountains, it seems to have occurred in both the mountain ranges. Many scientists have suggested the John Crow Mountains as the place where it may still survive (Scott 1891, Bourne 1965, Bond 1965, van Halewyn and Norton 1984). Collar et. al (1992) came to the following conclusion "several searches in the 1970's and early 1980's in the John Crow Mountains were unproductive". However, all searches mentioned in Jamaican ornithological literature occurred in the Blue Mountains. Van Halewyn and Norton (1984) made reference to the more detailed reports quoted in the Gosse Bird Club Broadsheet (1963-1983; Table 1) but these searches all took place in the Blue Mountains. Therefore, the documented searches of the past 35 years have, to the best of our knowledge, side-lined the John Crow Mountains, the area agreed by many to be possibly the last stronghold of the Jamaican Petrel. Indeed the only promising indication of the continued existence of Jamaican Petrels from the above mentioned searches has come from D. Wingate's 1971 visit to the John Crow Mountains during which he "thought they heard petrels" (van Halewyn and Norton 1984). The latest search undertaken by the recently formed Jamaican Petrel Research Group has focused on both an oceanic survey of Jamaican waters and offshore islands along with the historical breeding range of the species.

Collar et al. (1992) notes that it is conceivable that this species also nested in the mountains of Dominica and Guadeloupe since there is evidence of nesting black petrels in Guadeloupe and a 1905 report of Jamaican Petrels nesting in Dominica. However the records of such are unclear and no skins of the dark petrels from these islands are currently known.

Research Needs
Status Evaluation

There is an urgent need for a systematic search to determine the current status of this species (The examination of middens and remains in cave deposits might help determine the extent of breeding ranges). Searches need to be conducted to coincide with the courtship, mating and pre-laying periods from late September to December when the birds are most vocal and more easily located by their calls (Imber 1991). The following order of priority is proposed:
  (1) In Jamaica in the Blue and John Crow Mountains (above 1600m in the former) giving preference to John Crow mountain range.
  (2) On Dominica and Guadeloupe. Jamaican Petrels may have nested on these islands.
  (3) In current Caribbean Black-capped Petrel colonies. Imber (1991) suggested they might contain a few breeding Jamaican Petrels as the two would not interbreed.

Taxonomic Studies

The taxonomic position of this petrel has been a source of much controversy with many authors considering the Jamaican Petrel a dark morph or subspecies of the Black-capped Petrel

(Collar et al. 1992). Imber (1991) stated that the Jamaican Petrel should be treated as a distinct species based on biometric comparisons between the species which showed the Jamaican form to be smaller and presumably more closely related to the Cape Verde Petrel (*Pterodroma feae*). This has been downplayed because there is much apparent variation in the Black-capped Petrels (Collar et al. 1992). Imber's work has, however, been supported by a recent analysis of feather lice (Zonfrillo, 1993) which revealed that the lice of *P. caribbaea* and *P. hasitata* differ in three respects: 1) *P. hasitata* has a *Trabeculus* louse not found on *P. caribbaea*, 2) the louse species found on *P. caribbaea* is found also on *P. feae* but not *P. hasitata*, and 3) *P. hasitata* has an *Austromenopon* louse which is not on *P. caribbaea*. If these two species were races or color-phases of one another, their feather- lice should be identical. There continue to be skeptics and the issue perhaps will not be resolved until DNA studies have been done.

Table 1: Searches for the Jamaican Petrel[1]

Broadsheet # 4 (Feb. 1965)

Date of Expedition:	Dec. 1964
Team Members:	James Bond
Areas Visited:	Near Portland Gap, Blue Mountains.

Broadsheet # 4 (Feb. 1965)

Date of Expedition:	Not given.
Team Members:	R. W. Smith & M. Gochfeld
Areas Visited:	Judgment Cliff (Lower Yallahs Valley), Blue Mountains.

Broadsheet # 9 (Sept. 1967)

Date of Expedition:	March 23, 1967
Team Members:	W. B. King and Abbott T. Fenn
Areas Visited:	2 nights on Blue Mountain Peak & East Peak, Blue Mountains.

Broadsheet # 12 (March 1969)

Date of Expedition:	January 25 and 26,1969.
Team Members :	R.W. Smith, A.T. Fenn, D. Romney, W.B. King and C. Kepler
Areas Visited:	Crossed the Blue Mountain range from N. to S., overnight below Sugar Loaf Peak; "one night on West and Middle Peak."

Broadsheet # 22 (March 1974) & D. Wingate - pers. comm.

Date of Expedition:	Feb. 24,25 &27, 1971
Team Members:	David Wingate, A. W. Diamond
Areas Visited:	John Crow Mountains

---

[1] From the Gosse Bird Club Broadsheet, 1963-1996, Nos. 1-67.

Conclusion

The species is currently only known from a handful of specimens dispersed around the world, and no life history information is available. If a breeding population is found, a study of its breeding biology and ecology should be undertaken in addition to genetic studies. The area of nesting should be immediately protected from disturbance and attempts made to protect the birds from any introduced predators.

Literature Cited

Bond, J. 1965. A few problems concerning the bird life of Jamaica. Gosse Bird Club Broadsheet No. 4: 1 - 3

Bourne, W.R.P. 1965. The Missing Petrels. Bulletin of the British Ornithologists' Club 85: 6.

Carte, A. 1866. On an undescribed species of petrel from the Blue Mountains of Jamaica. Proceedings of the Zoological Soc. of London. 1866: 93 - 95.

Collar, N. J. et al. 1992. Threatened Birds of the Americas - the ICBP/IUCN Red Data book, 3rd. ed. P. 2. *International Council for Bird Preservation*, Cambridge, U.K.

Gochfeld, M., J. Burger, A. Haynes-Sutton, R. van Halewyn, and J. E. Saliva. 1990. Successful approaches to seabird protection in the West Indies. pp. 186-209. In Nettleship, D. N., J Burger and M. Gochfeld (eds.) *Seabirds on Islands – Threats, Case Studies and Action Plans*. Cambridge: BirdLife Conservation Series No. 1.

Godman, F. du C. 1907 -1910. *A Monograph of the Petrels*. London. 367 pp.

Gosse Bird Club. 1963 - 1996. Broadsheet Nos. 1- 67. Kingston.

Imber, M. J. 1985. Origins, phylogeny and taxonomy of the gadfly petrels <u>Pterodroma</u> <u>spp</u>. Ibis 127:197-229.

Imber, M. J. 1991. The Jamaican Petrel - Dead or Alive. Gosse Bird Club Broadsheet No.57:4-9.

Scott, W. E. D. 1891-1892. Observations on the birds of Jamaica, West Indies. Auk 8: 355-357.

Thomas, H. T. 1890. *Untrodden Jamaica*. Aston W. Gardner & Co. Kingston.

van Halewyn, R. and R. L. Norton. 1984. The Status and conservation of seabirds in the Caribbean. Pp. 169-222, in J.P. Croxall, P. G. H. Evans and R. W. Schreiber, eds., *Status and Conservation of the world's seabirds*. Cambridge : ICBP Tech. Pub. No.2.

Wingate, D.B. 1964a.Discovery of breeding Black-capped Petrels on Hispaniola. Auk 81: 147-159.

Wingate, D. B. 1964b. Does the "Blue Mountain Duck" of Jamaica Survive? Gosse Bird Club Broadsheet No.2: 1-2.

Zonfrillo, B. 1993. Relationships of the Pterodroma Petrels from the Madeira Archipelago inferred from their feather lice. Bol. Mun. Mus. Funchal Supp. No. 2, 325-331.

Status and Conservation Priorities for Audubon's Shearwaters in the West Indies

CB CB CB CB   BO BO BO BO

DAVID S. LEE

North Carolina State Museum of Natural Sciences, P.O. Box 29555, Raleigh, NC 27626,
cbirds1002@aol.com.

Introduction

Nesting populations of Audubon's Shearwaters (*Puffinus lherminieri*) are widespread in tropical seas with a few populations in the western north Pacific and western north Atlantic (north Bahamas and formerly Bermuda; Bradlee 1906) ranging into subtropical regions. Non-breeding individuals are, for the most part, confined to tropical regions, but in the western north Atlantic the species commonly and regularly ranges northward following the Gulf Stream and warm Outer Continental Shelf waters of the southeastern US to foraging in areas off Cape Hatteras. As a result of their relatively sedentary nature and high site fidelity, limited genetic exchange exists between populations. At least twelve subspecies, with considerable variation in overall size, are recognized.

In the Atlantic, they breed on islands throughout the Caribbean (Fig 1, Table 1), and the Cape Verde Islands; in the Indian Ocean Audubon's Shearwaters breed on islands in Arabian Sea, Mascarene Is., Aldabra, Seychelles, Amirante, Maldives and Chagos Islands. In the Pacific they breed on Galapagos Islands, Bonin and Volcano Islands, also Banks, New Hebrides and throughout the central Pacific.

Audubon's Shearwaters breed in a variety of habitats. The only common denominator to all breeding sites is the absence, or near absence, of terrestrial predators. They often nest in natural cavities, but will also dig their own burrows. The length of the burrows varies depending on the substrate. They also nest in the open spaces beneath rocks and coral rubble, under agavi leaves, and other forms of shelter. Nesting sites may be anywhere from just above the high tide line to higher elevations in the interior of islands. Both sexes incubate with each incubation shift lasting from 8 to 10 days (Palmer 1962).

Status in West Indies

The total population of Audubon's Shearwaters is unclear. Van Halewyn and Norton (1984) estimated there were about 5,000 pairs in the Caribbean region. However, the breeding distribution within the West Indies is not well known, and information on the size of the known colonies is scant, out of date, and typically little more than speculation. The current population (Table 1) is probably closer to 3,000 but actual numbers are hard to document.

Over 60 years ago it was believed that the numbers of these birds were diminishing throughout their range (Murphy 1936). Reasons for the decline have been attributed to domestic cats, introduced rats, human predation, human interference and perhaps to Barn Owl (*Tyto alba*) predation (Wingate in Palmer 1962). The mongoose is certainly a problem, but this has not been documented. In the West Indies population declines are difficult to address because there is little historical information available for comparison. Fossil and sub-fossil material shows that these

25

shearwaters were formerly abundant breeders on Mona (Puerto Rico), the south end of Abaco (unpublished records USNM, FSM), and Crooked Island (Bahamas, Wetmore 1938). The species has disappeared from Bermuda as a breeding species. David Wingate (pers. comm.) attributes this to the species vulnerability to predation by feral cats. Pre-fledglings come out of their burrows to exercise their wings at night and are easy prey for cats and other predators. He also believes that artificial lighting on Bermuda interfered with orientation of the adults.

In the late 1800's this species nested on small rocks off the windward shores of Barbados and Grenada (Feilden 1889, Lawrence 1889) but the Grenada population is now extirpated and only 100 pairs still nest off Barbados (E. Massiah and M. Frost, pers. comm., Table 1). Recent decreases have occurred on islands off Puerto Rico (Providencia Island, Naranjo 1979), where they have been extirpated from at least two islands. Guano deposits in caves on Mona (off Puerto Rico) indicate huge populations used to nest there. Thousands were reported to still occupy a small inaccessible cave on that island in 1937 (Smyth 1937) and their decline and extirpation may have been partly a result of earlier guano mining activities. The total size of the West Indian population is unknown but may be something on the order of 3,000-4,000. If the known extant colonies (Table 1) are the only ones in the region, then this estimate is probably too high.

Elsewhere in the Caribbean the species is known to nest in Curaçao, Bonaire, islands off Venezuela, Panama and Nicarauga (Wetmore 1959, Palmer 1962, de Schauensee and Phelps 1978, Voous 1983). Population sizes for these colonies are believed to be small. The population of *P. l. loyemilleri* , an endemic subspecies in the western Caribbean, has been stated by several authors (e.g., van Halewyn and Norton 1984) to be close to extinction. There has been little, if any, field work in this part of Caribbean to determine its actual status.

Table 1: Known breeding sites of Audubon's Shearwaters in the Bahamas and West Indies (Bermuda not considered part of West Indies).

Location	No. Pairs	Source
Bermuda	E	by 1981; Wingate, pers. comm.
Bahamas, Little Bahama Bank		
Tom Brown Cay, Abaco	?	NCSM chick specimen
Walkers Cay, Abaco	?	
Cay off S. Andros	B	Lee and Clark 1994
Cay Sal Bank	B	Sprunt 1984
Great Bahama Bank		
Washerwomen Cays	B	Sprunt 1984
Allans Cay, Exumas	200+	Lee and Clark 1994, M. Baltz, pers. comm.
Long Cay, Exumas	500+	Lee and Clark 1994
Noddy Cay, Exumas	B	Lee and Clark 1994
Malabar Cay, Exumas	B	Lee and Clark 1994
Little Cistern Cay, Exumas	B	Lee and Clark 1994
Sandy Cay, Exumas	B	Lee and Clark 1994
Twin Cays, Exumas	B	Lee and Clark 1994
Rocky Dundas, Exumas	B	Lee and Clark 1994

Table 1 continued –

Table 1 continued -

Location	No. Pairs	Source
Green Key	?	7 May 1884 USNM
Eleuthera	?	4 May 1889 USNM
San Salvador	15+	D. Lee, unpubl.
Conception Island	B	Sprunt 1984
Mira Por Vos	B	Sprunt 1984
Propeller Cay off Samana Cay	B	Buden 1987
East Plana Cay	B	Buden 1987
Turks and Caicos, East Cay	B	Buden 1987
Middle Caicos	B	Walsh-McGehee, *et al.* 1998
Providenciales	B	Buden 1987; Am Birds 38:968
Jamaica, Morant Cays	B	Douglas and Zonfrillo 1997
Navassa Isl.	?	van Halewyn and Norton 1984
Haiti	?	van Halewyn and Norton 1984
Puerto Rico (Providencia I)	E	Naranjo 1979
Culebra (Cayo Matoha)	E	Am Birds 39:965
Mona	E	J. Saliva, pers. comm.; "thousands" Smyth 1937
Monito	?	J. Saliva, pers. comm. 1998
US Virgin Is., Saba Cay	< 10	J. Pierce, pers. comm. 1998
Cockroach Cay	< 10	J. Pierce, pers. comm. 1998
Flat Cay	< 20	J. Pierce, pers. comm. 1998
Sula and Frenchcap Cays	< 10	J. Pierce, pers. comm. 1998
British Virgin Is., Anegada	E	J. Pierce pers. comm. 1998
Other islets	< 10	J. Pierce pers. comm. 1998
St. Martin	B	Voous 1983
St. Barts	?	van Halewyn and Norton 1994
Saba	1000+	M. McGehee, pers. comm.
St. Eustatus	B	Voous 1983
Barbados	100	E. Massiah and M. Frost, pers. comm.
Antigua	?	van Halewyn and Norton 1984
Guadelupe	200	van Halewyn and Norton 1984
Martinique	700	van Halewyn and Norton 1984
Rocher du Diamant	?	Bond 1956
Hardy I	500+	Pinchon 1967
Grenada	?	Lawrence 1889; still present?
Grenadines	E	van Halewyn and Norton 1984
Tobago	800	van Halewyn and Norton 1984
TOTAL	**3000-5000 pairs**	

B - breeds but no data available on numbers
? - bred historically and may still breed but no recent data
E - extirpated

Conservation and Research Needs

The most important need for this species in the West Indies is a systematic inventory of breeding sites. At this time it is not clear which specific islands, rocks and cays support nesting populations. Of particular interest is the line of keys off the north coast of Cuba. Audubon's Shearwaters are not documented as breeding in Cuba but it would be surprising if they do not nest on these keys. With the exception of the endemic West Indian petrels (*Pterodroma*) our knowledge is less complete for this species than any other western Atlantic nesting seabird. In combination with a region- wide inventory, we need an evaluation that addresses the long-range stability of populations. Information concerning protection of nesting sites, along with the documentation of the presence of exotic predators, needs to be compiled and updated.

The taxonomic status of populations of Audubon's Shearwaters off the coast of Venezuela also needs to be addressed. The relationships between and within Caribbean subspecies and those found elsewhere in the world should be investigated through DNA studies. Specimens collected off North Carolina are variable in size and plumage, and this is not age related. Variation in measurements in this series shows many specimens to fall below the ranges provided by Wetmore (1959) for the nominate race and within the range of *loyemilleri* and *boydi* (Lee 1988). However, there are few West Indies museum specimens from known nesting sites for comparison. Collection of modest numbers of specimens, or the salvage of dead ones, from various islands throughout the species range in the West Indies is needed. Presently, there are only a small series of specimens from a few breeding sites in museums. Documentation of breeding station morphometric and plumage variability and/or DNA studies are needed in order to address regional conservation priorities.

Despite the pantropical distribution of this shearwater, it remains one of the least studied species of seabirds in the world. A long-range banding study of an easily accessible West Indian population would do much to fill-in gaps in our knowledge of the natural history of this little known species. Even information as basic as the local breeding phenology of different populations is needed.

Presently there are plans for gas and oil exploration off the coast of North Carolina. The area under consideration is the same small area off Cape Hatteras where large numbers of various West Indian seabirds concentrate after the breeding season (Lee and Socci 1989, Lee 1995). While local densities of Audubon's Shearwaters are seasonally variable, and assuming the population estimate of 3,000-5,000 pairs is correct, up to 75% of the western Atlantic population summers at this specific site (Lee and Socci 1989). For example, 1500 individuals were recorded on a single offshore trip on 18 Sept 1988 (Am. Birds 42:299). Sixty eight percent of the individuals summering in this gas/oil lease site are adults (Lee unpublished).

Voous (1983) notes that Audubon's Shearwaters were being exploited by people in the Netherlands Antilles. These shearwaters are regarded as good eating. Adults, eggs and chicks have been traditionally collected for consumption throughout the West Indies region, and in the past, fat nestlings were collected, dried or salted, and sold on the open market. To some degree, these practices still occur. The extent that regional laws, regulations and enforcement protect this species is unclear. Local educational programs would help island residents appreciate the biology of these shearwaters and help them understand their conservation needs.

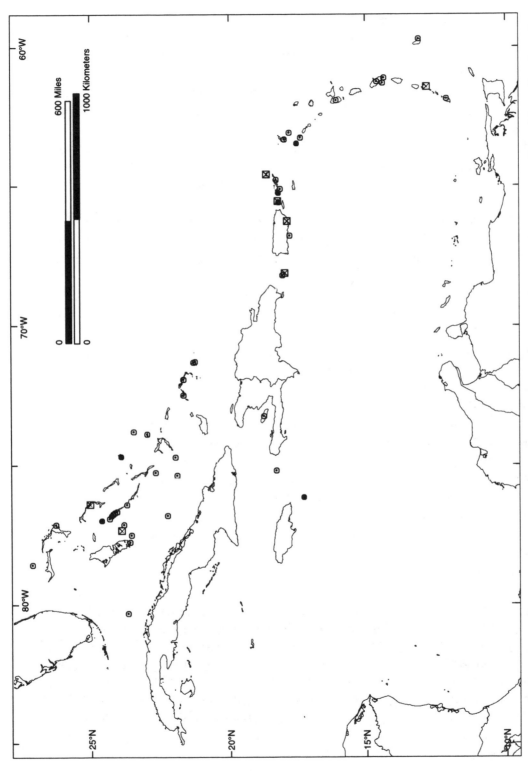

Figure 1: The status of known Audubon's Shearwater breeding sites in the West Indies. ● = confirmed breeding location that has been surveyed recently. ⊙ = historic breeding location with no report that the colony has been extirpated. ⊠ = historic breeding location that is extirpated or thought to be extirpated.

Literature Cited

Bond, J. 1956. Checklist of Birds of the West Indies (and supplements) The Academy of Natural Sciences of Philadelphia. Philadelphia Pa.

Buden, D. W. 1987. The birds of the southern Bahamas. B.O.U. Checklist No.8. British Ornithologists' Union.

Bradlee, T. S. 1906. Audubon's Shearwater and Peale's Petrel breeding in Bermuda. Auk 23:217.

de Schauensee, R. M. and W. H. Phelps, Jr. 1978. A guide to the birds of Venezuela. Princeton Univ. Press, NJ. 424pp.

Douglas, L. and B. Zonfrillo. 1997. First record of Audubon's Shearwater and Black-capped Petrel from Jamaica. Gosse Bird Club Broadsheet 69: 4-6.

Feilden, H. W. 1889. On the breeding of *Puffinus auduboni* on the island of Barbados. Ibis VI-1: 60-3.

Lawrence, G. N. 1889. An account of the breeding of *Puffinus auduboni* in the island of Grenada, West Indies, with a note on *Zenaida rubripes*. Auk 6: 19-21.

Lee, D. S. 1988. The Little Shearwater (*Puffinus assimilis*) in the western North Atlantic. Am Birds 42:213-220.

Lee, D. S. 1995. Marine birds off the coast of North Carolina. Chat 59 (4):113-171.

Lee, D. S. and M. K. Clark. 1994 Seabirds of the Exuma Land and Sea Park. Bahamas Journal of Science 2:2-9, 15-21.

Lee, D. S. and M. Socci. 1989. Potential effects of oil spills on seabirds and selected other oceanic vertebrates off the North Carolina coast. Occas. Pap. NC Biol. Surv. 1989-1.

Murphy, R. C. 1936. Oceanic Birds of South America. (2 vols.) The American Museum of Natural History, New York. 1245pp.

Naranjo, H. L. G. 1979. Las aves marinas del Caribe Colombiano. Taxonomia, Zoogeografia y Anotaciones Ecologicas. Tesis de Grado, Universidad de Bogota Jorge Tadeo Lozano, Facultad de Ciencias del Mar. 372pp.

Palmer, R. S. (ed.) 1962. Handbook of North American birds, Vol I: Loons through Flamingos. Yale Univ. Press. New Haven, CT. 567 pp.

Pinchon, R. 1967. Quelques aspects de la nature aux Antilles. Fort-de-France. 254pp.

Smyth, J. A. 1937. Audubon's Shearwater nesting on Mona Island, Puerto Rico. Wilson Bull 50: 203-204.

Sprunt, A. 1984. The status and conservation of seabirds of the Bahama Islands. Pp. 157-168 in J. P. Croxall, P. G. H. Evans, and R. W. Schreiber, eds. *Status and Conservation of the World's Seabirds*. Intl. Council of Bird Preservation, Tech. Publication No. 2.

van Halewyn, R. and R. L. Norton. 1984. The status and conservation of seabirds in the Caribbean. Pp.169-222. in J.P. Croxall, P.G.H. Evans, and R. W. Schreiber, eds. *Status and Conservation of the World's Seabirds*. Intl. Council of Bird Preservation, Tech. Publication No. 2.

Voous, K. H. 1983. Birds of the Netherlands Antilles. De Walburg Pers, Zutphen. 327 pp.

Walsh-McGehee, M., D. S. Lee, and M. J. Wunderle, Jr. 1989 A report of aquatic birds encountered in December from the Caicos Islands. Bahamas Jour. Sci. 5(3): 28-33.

Wetmore, A. 1938. Bird remains from the West Indies. Auk 55: 51-55.

Wetmore, A. 1959. Description of a race of the Shearwater *Puffinus lherminieri* from Panama. Proc. Biol. Soc. Wash. 72:19-22.

Status and Conservation Priorities for
White-tailed and Red-billed Tropicbirds in the West Indies

_____ ෆ ෆ ෆ ෆ   ഽ ഽ ഽ ഽ _____

MARTHA WALSH-McGEHEE

Island Conservation Effort, P.O. Box 599, Windwardside, Saba, Netherlands Antilles, Email tropbird@icanect.net

Introduction

Populations of both the White-tailed *(Phaethon lepturus catesbyi)* and Red-billed Tropicbirds (*P. aethereus mesonauta*) in the West Indies were undoubtedly much higher prior to human contact. This contact resulted in a loss of suitable nesting sites in the West Indies, the introduction of alien predators, and the taking of eggs and young for food. Present populations are primarily confined to predator-free cliffs on remote cays, and the number of nesting pairs is limited by the availability of suitable nest sites. There have been few surveys of tropicbirds in the West Indies, and most were incomplete and unreliable. The last published report on population estimates was in 1984 (van Halewyn and Norton 1984) and much of the data used in this report were from 20 to 100 years previous to its publication. Using recently published reports (post 1995) and information obtained from resident experts, a reassessment has been made for these species in the West Indies (D. Lee and M. Walsh-McGehee, unpubl. data). This reassessment indicates a dramatic decline in the numbers of White-tailed Tropicbirds in the past fifteen years. While the numbers for Red-billed Tropicbirds appear to have increased, the populations may actually be in decline since a disproportionately large extant colony was discovered on Saba and the number of known sites with confirmed breeding was more than quadrupled, yet the actual increase in the total number of pairs is slight.

Species Accounts
White-tailed Tropicbird (*Phaethon lepturus catesbyi*)

The White-tailed Tropicbird is the smaller and more common of the two tropicbird species in the West Indies (Lee and Walsh-McGehee1998). Tropicbirds occur on islands in the tropical Pacific, Indian, and tropical Atlantic Oceans. The Western Atlantic White-tailed birds occur on Bermuda, the Bahamas, and the Antilles, and are an endemic subspecies, *P.l. catesbyi*. Tropicbirds are highly pelagic and are seldom seen within sight of land except during courtship and nesting. They lay one egg on a cliff ledge, in a rock crevice or under vegetation. Most nests are inaccessible and thus censuses are difficult to carryout.

Van Halewyn and Norton (1984) estimated the total population of West Indies birds in the 1980s at over 10,000 pairs breeding at more than 30 sites. A review of recently published reports and consultation with people on most of the islands in the West Indies has resulted in a current estimate of a maximum number between 2,500 and 3,500 pairs (Table 1; Lee and Walsh-McGehee, unpubl. data), and actual population numbers may be 15-20% lower. Bermuda (not part of the West Indies) has the largest colony in the Western Atlantic: estimated at 3,000 pairs in

1950. The current population is down to 2,500 pairs and may be as low as 2,000 (Wingate pers. comm., Table 1).

The Dominican Republic and the Bahaman Islands have an estimated 500 and 1,000 pairs respectively. Combined colonies on Puerto Rico and Mona Island number 200-300 pairs. The remaining islands in the West Indies typically have colonies of 10 to 100 pairs, the majority

Table 1. Extant and extirpated colonies of White-tailed Tropicbirds and estimated number of nesting pairs in the West Indies. Bermuda is not considered part of West Indies.

Location	Number of Pairs
Bermuda	fewer than 2500
Bahamas	fewer than 500
Turks & Caicos Islands	82
Cuba	fewer than 50
Cayman Islands	60
Jamaica	80-162
Hispaniola	1000
Puerto Rico	200-300
U.S. Virgin Islands, total	40-80
Cas Cay Congo Cay	
Han Lollick Cay Brass Cays	
Water Island Misc. other cays	
British Virgin Islands, total	40-100
Fallen Jerusalem, Great Tobago B	
Guana Isl., Norman Isl. B	
Peter Isl., Round Rock, Virgin Gorda ?	
Dog Islands ?	
Anguilla	E
Redonda	5-15
Antigua	E
Barbuda	10-50
St. Martin	15
Saba	50-100
St. Eustatius	fewer than 10
Guadeloupe	68
Dominica	10-30
Martinique	fewer than 50
St. Vincent	?
Grenadines	?
TOTAL	**2,500-3,500**

E - extirpated
? - bred historically, no recent data to confirm present breeding

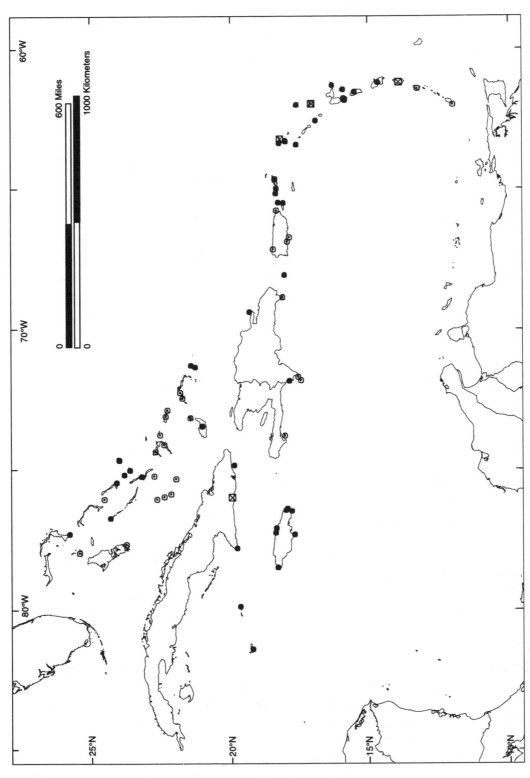

Figure 1: The status of known White-tailed Tropicbird breeding sites in the West Indies. ● = confirmed breeding location that has been surveyed recently. ⊚ = historic breeding location with no report that the colony has been extirpated. ⊠ = historic breeding location that is extirpated or thought to be extirpated.

having fewer than 50. There have been documented declines in Bermuda, Cuba, Cayman Islands, Puerto Rico, U. S. Virgin Islands and Jamaica. While the colony on Saba was estimated to be only a few pairs in 1984, there was a large population estimated at 300-400 pairs present in 1990. Local residents indicated that the birds were present in those numbers since the 1950s when they ceased to be taken for food. These numbers dramatically declined to between 50 and 100 pairs in 1998. It is believed that this decline is due primarily to nest site competition with the larger and more aggressive Red-billed Tropicbird, which breeds on Saba throughout the year (pers. obser.). There are fossil records from Anguilla where the species has been extirpated. Additional colonies throughout the area have historic records, but no recent information that confirms current breeding.

White-tailed Tropicbirds are not currently designated as globally threatened. The population on Christmas Island in the Indian Ocean (*P. l. fulvus*) has declined slightly, but is estimated at between 6,000 and 12,000 pairs. There are an additional 5,000 pairs in the remainder of the Indian Ocean (*P. l. lepturus*). The Pacific (*P. l. dorotheae*) is thought to have several thousand pairs and the South Atlantic (*P. l. ascensionis*) fewer than 3,000 (del Hoyo et al. 1992). The Western Atlantic subspecies (*P. l. catesbyi*) was classified as a species of no immediate concern with regard to conservation priority by van Halewyn and Norton (1984). A more detailed census and a documented continuing decline in the number of nesting pairs in the West Indian population has led us to designate this population as "Vulnerable" in the West Indies (see Chapter entitled Action Plan for Conservation of West Indian Seabirds).

Red-billed Tropicbird (*Phaethon aethereus mesonauta*)

The Red-billed Tropicbird is the largest and least numerous of the three tropicbird species. It occurs in the tropical eastern Pacific, Caribbean Sea, Atlantic Ocean, Red Sea, Persian Gulf, and Indian Ocean to the Straits of Malacca, ranging north to the Bay of California and Bermuda and North Carolina, and south to Chile. Birds found in the West Indies are *P. a. mesonauta*. Those breeding on Fernando Noronha, St. Helena, and Ascension Island are *P. a. aethereus* and those found in the Red Sea, Indian Ocean, and Persian Gulf are *P. a. indicus* (del Hoyo et al. 1992). Their nesting habits are similar to those of the White-tailed Tropicbird above. Because Red-bills are larger than white-tails, they can out-compete them for nest sites and this may be part of the reason the number of White-tails is declining in the Caribbean.

The endemic West Indian subspecies ranges from Puerto Rico east and south through the Lesser Antilles to islands off Venezuela and Panama (Table 2, Fig. 2). Its range overlaps that of the White-tailed Tropicbird from Puerto Rico to St. Vincent. They are absent from the rest of the Greater Antilles. Compared to the White-tailed Tropicbird, the Red-billed appears to be limited to more productive water (van Halewyn and Norton 1984).

Van Halewyn and Norton (1984) estimated the West Indian population at 1,600 pairs at 22 sites in the 1980s. After a review of recently published reports (post 1995) and consultation with resident experts in most of the West Indies, a revised estimate of 1,800 - 2,500 pairs was made. Populations and breeding locations for Red-billed Tropicbirds have been less well documented than those of the White-tailed because many of their breeding sites are not frequented by biologists. Inaccuracy in earlier estimates makes direct comparison with the data in van Halewyn and Norton (1984) and later publications difficult. For example, Voòus (1982) estimated Saba's population to number no more than twenty pairs. D. Lee and Walsh-McGehee (pers. obs.) estimated its population at 750-1,000 in 1996. Local inhabitants indicated that the numbers of birds had not increased substantially in that fourteen-year period. Given the disparity of Saba's estimate and the quadrupling of sites, the 1998 estimate should have been dramatically higher if populations at other sites were not declining. Furthermore, islands with Red-billed Tropicbirds have experienced the same loss of habitat, introduction of alien predators, and human disturbance as those with White-tailed Tropicbirds, and can be expected to have suffered the same deleterious effects. A breeding colony on Little Flat in the U. S. Virgin Islands

Table 2. Extant and extirpated colonies of Red-billed Tropicbirds and estimated number of breeding pairs in the West Indies.

Location	Number of Pairs
Puerto Rico, total	30±
U. S. Virgin Islands, total	225-300
Cockroach Cay Grass Cay	
Cricket Cay Carval Rock	
Hans Lollick Cay Brass Cays	
Mingo Cay Savannah Island	
Capella Cay Water Island	
Buck Cay Kalkun Cay	
Congo Cay	
Little Flat Cay	E
British Virgin Islands, total	fewer then 50
Great Tobago, Guana Island, misc. other isls.	
Sombrero	?
Antigua	50
Barbuda	50-100
Redonda	100
Anguilla	?
St. Martin	15
St. Bartholomew	?
Saba	750-1000
St. Eustatius	30
Montserrat	?/E
Guadeloupe	69
Dominica	10±
Martinique	50±
St. Vincent	?
Grenadines	?
Tobago	400
TOTAL	**1,800-2,500±**

E Extirpated,
? Bred historically, no recent data to confirm present breeding

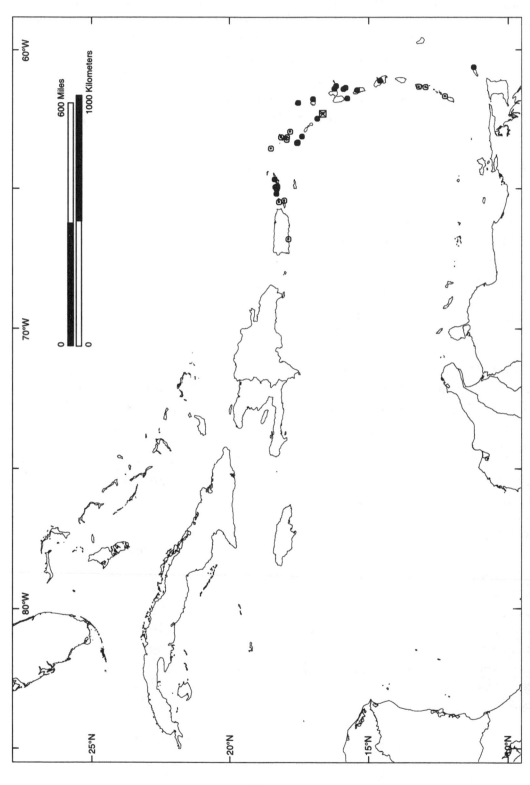

Figure 2: The status of known Red-billed Tropicbird breeding sites in the West Indies. ● = confirmed breeding location that has been surveyed recently. ◉ = historic breeding location with no report that the colony has been extirpated. ⊠ = historic breeding location that is extirpated or thought to be extirpated.

was extirpated and a historic colony on Montserrat is also thought to be extirpated (D. Lee and Walsh-McGehee unpubl.).

Red-Billed Tropicbirds are not classified as globally threatened at present. However, the global population may be under 10,000 pairs (D Lee and Walsh-McGehee unpubl.). Van Halewyn and Norton (1984) did list the West Indian population under "status to be monitored." I suggest that the status of this species be listed as "Vulnerable" in the West Indies (see Chapter entitled Action Plan for Conservation of West Indian Seabirds). It occurs in the West Indies, the Gulf of California, the Galapagos Islands and the Cape Verde Islands (persecution by fisherman in the Cape Verde Islands has reduced a population of fewer than 1,000 birds in 1969 to no more than 100 pairs in 1990) with a total maximum population estimated to be 3,200 to 3,700 pairs. Other subspecies have experienced similar declines around the world (del Hoyo et al. 1992). I believe that this species deserves global conservation consideration and that the West Indies supports a substantial portion of the world's population.

Research and Conservation Needs

Because tropicbirds in the West Indies nest primarily on inaccessible cliffs and remote cays, possibly to avoid predators and human disturbance, monitoring and research on these species is difficult. Apart from a study of the breeding biology and energetics on the White-tailed Tropicbird on Culebra, Puerto Rico done by Fred Schaffner (1988), there has been little other research done. A breeding biology study of Red-billed Tropicbirds is currently underway on Saba. Populations of White- tailed Tropicbirds on Bermuda have been well monitored by David Wingate, and Judy Pierce has monitored both White-tailed and Red-billed Tropicbird populations in the U.S. Virgin Islands. All tropicbird colonies, extant and extirpated (Table 1 and Table 2) should be surveyed during the breeding season and problems experienced by individual colonies should be noted (nest site competition, habitat degradation, predators, human disturbance, etc.).
Monitoring schedules should be established to determine fluctuations in population numbers and to determine rates of breeding success. Long term banding projects throughout the West Indies would yield valuable information on the age structure of colonies and on fidelity to colonies, specific nest sites, and mates. To date, there is little information on any of the breeding biology and ecology of these two species. DNA studies are needed to determine the degree of reproductive isolation between colonies at different locations.

The construction and placement of artificial nest sites could provide much useful information on nest requirements, and could attract pairs to sites where various aspects of their reproductive biology could be easily monitored. These nests could also be used as an environmental education tool. In more remote areas, artificial nests could be used to provide additional sites where natural nest sites are limited. Further conservation needs and monitoring plans are discussed in the Chapter entitled Action Plan for the Conservation of West Indian Seabirds.

Literature Cited

Blake, E.R. 1977. Spheniscidae (Penguins) to Laridae (Gulls and Allies). Manual of Neotropical Birds. The University of Chicago Press, Vol. 1. Chicago and London.

del Hoyo, J., A. Elliot, and J. Sargatal, eds. 1992. Pp. 280-289 in *Handbook of the Birds of the World*. Vol. 1. Lynx Editions, Barcelona.

Gochfeld, M., J. Burger, A. Haynes-Sutton, R. van Halewyn, and J. E. Saliva. 1994. Successful approaches to seabird protection in the West Indies. Pp. 186-209 in Nettleship, D. N., J. Burger, and M. Gochfeld, *Seabirds on Islands: Threats, Case Studies and Action Plans*. BirdLife Conservation Series No. 1.

Lee, D.S. and M. Walsh-McGehee. 1998. White-tailed Tropicbird *(Phaethon lepturus)*. No. 353. In Poole, A. and F. Gill, eds. The Birds of North America., Philadelphia, PA.

Stonehouse, B. 1962. The Tropicbirds (Genus *Phaethon*) of Ascension Island. Ibis 103b.

van Halewyn, R. and R. L. Norton. 1984. The status and conservation of seabirds in the Caribbean. Pp. 162-222 in Croxall, J. P., P.G. H. Evans, and R. W. Schreiber, eds. *Status and Conservation of the World's Seabirds*. Tech. Publ. No. 2.

Voous, K.H. 1983. Birds of the Netherlands Antilles. De Walburg Pers. Utrecht.

Walsh-McGehee, M., D.S. Lee, and D. Claridge.1999. A Review of the Distribution and Population Status of White-tailed Tropicbirds Nesting in the Bahaman Archipelago; including Recent Records from Little Bahama Bank. Bahamas Journal of Science.

Conservation of the Brown Pelican in the West Indies

————— ↄ ↄ ↄ ↄ   ↄ ↄ ↄ ↄ —————

By JAMIE A. COLLAZO[1], JORGE. E. SALIVA[2], and JUDY PIERCE[3]

[1] North Carolina F & W Research Unit, Biological Resources Division, U.S. G. S., North Carolina State University, Raleigh, NC 27695. Jamie_Collaz@ncsu.edu. [2] Caribbean Field Office, U.S. FWS, Boquerón, Puerto Rico 00622, Email jorge_saliva@fws.gov. [3] Department of Planning and Natural Resources, Division of Fish and Wildlife, 6291 Estate Nazareth 101, St. Thomas, U.S. Virgin Islands 00802.

Introduction

Brown Pelicans (*Pelecanus occidentalis occidentalis*) occur throughout the Caribbean and are often seen near shore, feeding. This subspecies is endemic to the Caribbean. Unfortunately, information on their status, population ecology, and conservation needs is scant. In recent decades the population was thought to be in trouble owing to the same factors affecting United States populations (e.g., contaminants, human disturbance; Schreiber and Risebrough 1972). Available data for the U.S. West Indies (i.e., Puerto Rico, U.S. Virgin Islands) and elsewhere in the Caribbean suggest that contaminants (e.g., DDT and metabolites, Hg) are not affecting their reproductive performance in the Caribbean (van Halewyn and Norton 1984, Collazo et al. 1998). Environmental contaminants, particularly DDT and its metabolites, induced eggshell thinning with concomitant reproductive failures in other areas of their range (Anderson and Hickey 1970, Blus et al. 1971, Blus et al. 1974a, 1974b).

Human disturbance and loss or degradation of roosting and nesting habitat is adversely affecting populations throughout the West Indian region (Collazo et al. 1998). Also of great concern in these islands is coastal degradation and how it may affect feeding habitats (Collazo and Klaas 1986). Pelicans are long-lived, hence, a long-term monitoring program is needed to better understand their population dynamics, and to identify and protect essential habitats.

Status in the West Indies

The Caribbean Brown Pelican is the smaller of two subspecies recorded in the Caribbean (Wetmore 1945, Blake 1977). *P. o. occidentalis* (Caribbean) is similar to *P. o. carolinensis* (mainland U.S.) but breeding plumage is usually darker on the undersurface and nonbreeding plumage is usually darker above (Blake 1977). The Caribbean Brown Pelican occurs along the Caribbean coast and offshore islands of Central America, and south from Venezuela to northern Brazil at the mouth of the Amazon (Blake 1977, van Halewyn and Norton 1984). In the Greater and Lesser Antilles, its range includes Bahamas, Cuba, Jamaica, Haiti, Dominican Republic, Puerto Rico, Virgin Islands, St. Martin, and Barbuda (Fig. 1, Table 1). This account adds Trinidad (G. Alleng, pers. comm.) to the range reported by van Halewyn and Norton (1984) and updates counts of nesting pairs of birds. An estimated 1500 pairs (Table 1, Fig. 1) nest within this area, and the species is considered Threatened in the West Indies.

Pelicans are long-lived (25-30 yrs) with deferred maturity, usually not breeding until they are at least three years of age (Schreiber 1980). Breeding in the West Indies has been recorded

39

throughout the year; peak nesting activity varies across its range (Collazo and Klaas 1986). In eastern Puerto Rico and the Virgin Islands they nest throughout the year and have two peaks of laying, September-October and March-April. In the other parts of Puerto Rico laying peaks in June-July. Clutch size is usually three eggs but can vary from one to three (Schreiber 1979). Productivity varies from year to year, depending on food availability and amount of human disturbance (Schreiber 1980), but averages about one young per nest (Collazo et al. 1998).

Concerns that factors affecting continental populations were also affecting populations in Puerto Rico and the U.S. Virgin Islands led to the designation of the species as endangered in this part of its range (DNR 1973, Philibosian and Yntema 1977). This designation prompted various research and monitoring efforts, generating perhaps the most extensive and detailed data base on their ecology outside the conterminous United States (Schreiber et al. 1981, Agardy et al. 1982, Collazo and Klaas 1986, Collazo et al. 1998). The mean number of individuals recorded during winter counts in Puerto Rico in 1992-95 (593) were 74% lower than in 1980-82 (2,289). Mean young per successful nest in the region was lower in 1992-93 (1.14) than 1980-82 (1.65). DDE, PCBs and mercury levels in egg samples, however, were low and did not adversely affect the species in either study period. The decrease in winter population counts from the 1980's to 1990's in Puerto Rico could be cause for concern because the 1990s counts were 32% (593/1840) of the expected mean winter count (Collazo and Klaas 1986). There was no obvious evidence that human disturbance was adversely affecting breeding or roosting birds during either study period but the birds are not well monitored and it could be a factor (Collazo et al. 1995). It is likely that roosting birds are often disturbed from beaches and this could cause them to leave an area.

The status of the species outside Puerto Rico and the U.S. Virgin Islands is hard to establish because data are scant, comprised mostly of notes or short-term surveys most of which were not done in recent years. Van Halewyn and Norton (1984) and Crivelli and Schreiber (1984) summarized this information and provided benchmark assessments of Brown Pelican status and conservation needs throughout the West Indies. Van Halewyn and Norton (1984) suggested that it was doubtful the species was in a precarious state outside of the U.S. West Indies, yet there are no real data on the number of nests. Brown Pelicans are considered common in Dominican Republic (Stockton de Dod 1981) and in Trinidad (5-100 seen daily, G. Alleng pers. comm.), but these could be roosting and wintering birds that are non-breeders. Data on number of nesting pairs and nesting success is lacking for the Dominican Republic. There are about 100 pairs nesting in Trinidad (Table 1) but we do not have data on their nest success.

Breeding populations in Mexico and Panamá (on both Caribbean and Pacific coasts) are believed to be large (i.e., 50,000+ birds Panamá and 40,000 pairs Mexico; Crivelli and Schreiber 1984) although there are no recent surveys. The number of individuals along coastal Venezuela and adjacent islands was estimated at 17,500 in 25 colonies (Guzmán and Schreiber 1987) but these data were not taken from recent surveys and the number of nests may be a fraction of this (2,000 pairs±). It is not known if there is genetic mixing of the birds through the Caribbean region or if there are separate sub-populations. There may be little to no interbreeding between West Indian and Mexican colonies, for instance.

Conservation Needs

Effective implementation of conservation measures depends on the availability of sound baseline information. These data do not exist for most colonies in the Caribbean basin. Pelicans are long-lived, and as such, reliable assessments about their demography and habitat requirements will only emerge from the implementation of long-term monitoring and research programs (i.e., 6-8 years; Schreiber and Schreiber 1983, Collazo and Klaas 1986). Basic data on population numbers, movement patterns, roost and nest site locations, and breeding productivity are needed to better understand the status of the species throughout its range (Schreiber and Risebrough 1972, Crivelli and Schreiber 1984, Collazo and Klaas 1986, Collazo et al. 1998). Conservation efforts should ensure the availability and integrity of essential habitats (i.e., foraging, roosting, and nesting), including restricting human visitation to colonies. Recommendations outlined by Anderson and Keith (1980) and Schreiber (1979) with regard to human disturbance and to promote pelican breeding productivity should be followed or used as initial guidelines. Organochlorines (e.g., DDT, PCBs) and other contaminants (e.g., Hg) known to have affected pelicans should be banned throughout the Caribbean basin. Mercury is suspected to be a problem in Venezuela (Guzmán and Schreiber 1987). Events such as oil spills need to be monitored. Mortality is not only recorded at the spill site, but due to its teratogenic effects, oiled adults can also cause embryo mortality.

Research Priorities

To determine the status of Brown Pelicans across its West Indian range basic information on their demography and factors that may affect their population health are needed. Particular attention should be given to estimating population numbers, survival and quantifying movement patterns. Mark-resight approaches were used in Puerto Rico and the U.S. Virgin Islands to document movement patterns (Collazo and Klaas 1986). Recent analytical advances provide an opportunity to obtain reliable estimates of population numbers and survival from mark and resight data (e.g., Pollock et al. 1990). Reliable estimates of population numbers, survival and breeding productivity, collected over 6-8 years, are needed to define a range of acceptable population parameter fluctuations for Caribbean Brown Pelicans. If such a research program cannot be implemented, Schreiber and Schreiber (1983) outlined procedures to assess the status of the species through a combination of minimum colony visits and population counts, albeit these data also need to be collected over 6-8 years. Contaminant evaluations should be conducted when available evidence suggest their presence (e.g., eggshell thinning, die-offs) or as part of a long-term monitoring program (e.g., every 10 years in the U.S. West Indies; Collazo et al. 1998).

The importance of understanding food availability patterns cannot be overemphasized. The population dynamics of this species is intimately related with this factor (Schreiber 1979, Anderson et al. 1982). Where possible, research efforts should focus on trying to understand factors such as prey species spawning patterns, habitat requirements and quality (see Murphy 1978, Yoshioka et al. 1985). Research efforts should ultimately provide an ecological basis to define what constitutes essential and high quality habitats for pelicans, and what factors undermine that quality.

Table 1. Extant and extirpated colonies of Caribbean Brown Pelicans in the Greater West Indian area, and minimum estimated number of nesting pairs:

Location	Number of Pairs
Bahamas, Turks and Caicos Islands	10±
Inagua	50-100
Cuba	B
Jamaica, St. Elizabeth	1-5
Portland Bight	?
Port Royal	15-25
Haiti	?
Dominican Republic	500±
Beata Island	?
Parque Nacional del Este	?
Puerto Rico (120-200 pairs)	
Montalva Bay	40±
Añasco Bay	E
Crash Boats, Aguadilla	25±
Conejo Cay, Vieques	100±
U. S. Virgin Islands (300-350 pairs)	
Dutchcap	100-120
Congo Key	100-120
Whistling Point, St. John	35±
Mary's Point, St. John	35±
Buck Island, St. Croix	35±
British Virgin Islands (160-180 pairs)	
Little Tobago	50-70
Guana Island	50-75
Norman Island	50 +
Lesser Antilles (150± pairs)	
St. Martin	B
St. Kitts, SE peninsula	B
Barbuda	2-10
Antigua	B
Trinidad	100
TOTAL	**1,500±**

? = bred historically but no recent observations
B = breeds but number of pairs and exact colony location is not available
E = extirpated.

Sources: van Halewyn and Norton (1984), Crivelli and Schreiber (1984), Collazo and Klaas (1986), Guzmán and Schreiber (1987), Collazo et al. (1998), A. Haynes-Sutton (Jamaica) J. Pierce (USVI, BVI), E. A. Schreiber (BVI), John Wilson (St. Kitts) pers. comm.

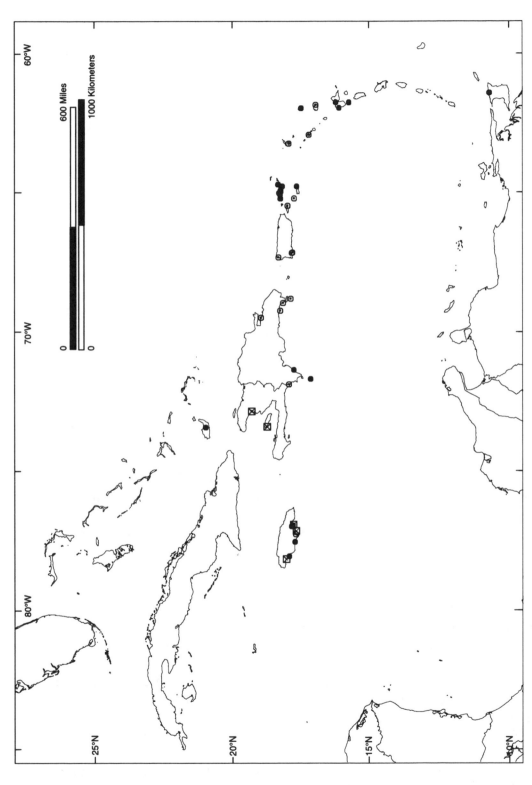

Figure 1: The status of known Brown Pelican breeding sites in the West Indies. ● = confirmed breeding location that has been surveyed recently. ⊙ = historic breeding location with no report that the colony has been extirpated. ⊠ = historic breeding location that is extirpated or thought to be extirpated.

Literature Cited

Agardy, M., R. L. Norton and R. H. Bouillon. 1982. Status of the Brown Pelican (*Pelecanus occidentalis occidentalis*) in the Virgin Islands. Final Report, U.S. Fish and Wildlife Service Federal Aid Program, Division of Fish and Wildlife, U.S.V.I. 37 pp.

Anderson, D. W., and J. J. Hickey. 1970. Oological data on egg and breeding characteristics of Brown Pelicans. Wilson Bull. 82:14-28.

Anderson, D. W. and J. O. Keith. 1980. The human influence on seabird nesting success: conservation implications. Biological Conservation 18:65-80.

Anderson, D. W., F. Gress, and K. F. Mais. 1982. Brown pelicans: influence of food supply on reproduction. Oikos 39:23-31.

Blake, E. R. 1977. Manual of Neotropical Birds. Vol. 1. The University of Chicago Press, Chicago, Ill. 674 pp.

Blus, L. J., A. A. Belisle, and R. M. Prouty. 1974a. Relations of the Brown Pelican to certain environmental pollutants. Pestic. Monit. J. 7:181-194.

Blus, L. J., B. S. Neely, A. A. Belisle, and R. M. Prouty. 1974b. Organochlorine residues in Brown Pelican eggs: relation to reproductive success. Environ. Pollut. 7:81-92.

Blus, L. J., R. G. Heath, C. D. Gish, A. A. Belisle, and R. M. Prouty. 1971. Eggshell thinning in the Brown Pelican: implication of DDE. BioScience 21:1213-1215.

Collazo, J. A. and E. E. Klaas. 1986. Recovery Plan for the Caribbean Brown Pelican in Puerto Rico and the U. S. Virgin Islands. Prepared for the U. S. Fish and Wildlife Service, Region 4, Office of Endangered Species, Atlanta, GA. 25 pp.

Collazo, J. A., T. Agardy, E. E. Klaas, J. E. Saliva, and J. Pierce. 1995. Population biology and status of Brown Pelicans in Puerto Rico and the U.S. Virgin Islands. Final Report submitted to the Caribbean Field Office, U.S. Fish and Wildlife Service, Region 4, Boquerón, Puerto Rico. 37 pp.

Collazo, J. A., T. A. Agardy, E. E. Klaas, J. E. Saliva, and J. Pierce. 1998. An inter-decadal comparison of population parameters of brown pelicans in Puerto Rico and the U.S. Virgin Island. Colonial Waterbirds 21:61-65.

Crivelli, A. J. and R. W. Schreiber. 1984. Status of Pelecanidae. Biological Conservation 30:147-156.

Department of Natural Resources (DNR). 1973. Rare and endangered animals of Puerto Rico: committee report. U.S. Dep. of Agriculture, Soil Conservation Service, San Juan, PR.

Guzman, H. M., and R. W. Schreiber. 1987. Distribution and status of Brown Pelicans in Venezuela in 1983. Wilson Bull. 99:275-278.

Murphy, G. I. 1978. Clupeoids. Pp. 283-308 in J. A. Gulland ed., *Fish Population Dynamics*. John Wiley & Sons, New York.

Philibosian, R., and J. A. Yntema. 1977. Annotated checklist of the birds, mammals, reptiles, and amphibians of the Virgin Islands and Puerto Rico. Information Services, Charlotte Amalie, U.S. Virgin Islands.

Pollock, K. H., J. D. Nichols, C. Brownie and J. E. Hines. 1990. Statistical inference for capture-recapture experiments. Wildl. Monogr.107. 97 pp.

Schreiber, R. W. 1979. Reproductive performance of the eastern Brown Pelican Pelecanus occidentalis. Contrib. Sci., Nat. Hist. Mus., Los Angeles. No. 317.

Schreiber, R. W. 1980. The Brown Pelican: An endangered species? BioScience 30:742-747.

Schreiber, R. W., and R. W. Risebrough. 1972. Studies of the brown pelican. I. Status of Brown

Pelican populations in the United States. Wilson Bull. 84:119-135.

Schreiber, R. W., and E. A. Schreiber. 1983. Use of age-classes in monitoring population stability of Brown Pelicans. J. Wildl. Manage. 47:105-111.

Schreiber, R. W., D. W. Belitsky, and B. A. Sorrie. 1981. Notes on Brown Pelicans in Puerto Rico. Wilson Bull. 93:397-400.

Stockton de Dod, A. 1981. Guia de campo para las aves de la República Dominicana. Editora Horizontes de America, Santo Domingo, R.D. 254 pp.

van Halewyn, R., and R. L. Norton. 1984. The status and conservation of Caribbean seabirds. Pp. 169-222 in J. P. Croxall, P. G. H. Evans, and R. W. Schreiber, eds. *Status and Conservation of the World's Seabirds*, Cambridge, U.K.: International Council for Bird Preservation, Tech. Publ. 2.

Wetmore, A. 1945. A review of the forms of the brown pelican. Auk 62:577-586.

Yoshioka, P. M., G. P. Owen, and D. Pesante. 1985. Spatial and temporal variations in Caribbean zooplankton near Puerto Rico. J. Plankton Res. 7:733-751.

Status of Red-footed, Brown and Masked Boobies in the West Indies

——————— ෆ ෆ ෆ ෆ   බ බ බ බ ——————

E. A. SCHREIBER

National Museum of Natural History, Smithsonian Institution, MRC 116, Washington, D.C. 20560.
SchreiberE@aol.com

Introduction

There is little information on the status of the three nesting booby species (Red-footed Booby, *Sula sula*; Brown Booby *S. leucogaster*; Masked Booby, *S. dactylatra*) in the West Indies. Visits to Caribbean islands by naturalists during the 1800s and early 1900s record the presence of these species on various islands but few to no data are given on the numbers of nests present or even if birds were nesting. Frequently large roosting groups of boobies were assumed to be at nesting colonies and these areas were reported as colonies, when in fact no nests were present. Some recorded visits were during the non-breeding season when no data on numbers of nests could be obtained. Thus it is difficult at this point to accurately assess what the status of these species was in most of its historical colonies. In recent years, few of the colonies have been visited by scientists. We do know that several colonies have been extirpated and others are often disturbed. Current existing colonies are shown in Figure 1 and numbers of nesting pairs in Tables 1-3.

Species Accounts
Red-footed Booby (*S. s. sula*)

This pantropical species (found in the Caribbean, and tropical Atlantic, Pacific, Indian Ocean and in the seas north of Australia) and is the smallest of the six booby species (Schreiber et al. 1996). They feed by plunge diving, eating mainly flying fish and squid (Schreiber and Hensley 1976) but little is known about where they feed. They probably feed at oceanographic features such as down-island eddies and current shears which produce an upwelling or downwelling and thus food concentrations (Schreiber et al. 1996).

They nest in trees in most cases, but will nest on the ground if trees are not available. Incubation lasts 43-49 days (mean 46; Nelson 1978) and chicks fledge at 91-110 days (Verner 1961, Amerson and Shelton 1975), taking longer in years of poor food supply. The fledgling continues to return to its nest each night for several weeks after first flying to be fed by it parents. The length of this period varies extensively: 78-103 days (mean 90) in the Galapagos (Nelson 1978) to about 1 month in Belize (Verner 1961). This points out the flexibility of chicks to adapt growth rate to food availability and thus survive bad years (Schreiber et al. 1996). The main nesting season in the northern Caribbean lasts from October through May (Nelson 1978).

Currently, I estimate there are a maximum of 8,200-10,000 pairs of Red-footed Boobies nesting on Caribbean islands (Table 1). Fourteen colonies are thought to exist (Fig. 1), although some of these may have been extirpated since the last visit by a scientist. There are only three

Table 1. Extant and extirpated colonies of Red-footed Boobies and estimated number of nesting pairs in the West Indies.

Location	Nmbr. of Pairs	Reference
Bahamas	1	Buden 1987
White Cay, San Salvador	2	D. Lee pers. comm., 1999
Cayman Is., Little Cayman	5,000	E.A. Schreiber unpubl. 1996
Jamaica, Pedro Cay	E	A. Haynes-Sutton pers. comm.
Navassa	300 +	Wetmore and Swales 1931
Puerto Rico, Mona	1,000-2,000	J. Saliva pers. comm.
Monito	200-400	J. Saliva pers. comm.
Culebra, C. Geniqui	4-5	J. Saliva pers. comm.
Desecheo	150 ±	J. Saliva pers. comm.
U.S. Virgin Islands, French Cap Key	175	J. Pierce pers. comm.
Dutchcap	12-16	J. Pierce pers. comm.
Cockroach Key, Sula Isl.	E	J. Pierce pers. comm.
British Virgin Islands, Great Tobago	1	E. A. Schreiber
Anguilla, Prickly Pear Cay West	2	ICF Kaiser
Redonda	1,000 ?	van Halewyn and Norton 1984
Guadeloupe, Grand Islet	1-3	Feldmann et al. 1999
Grenadines, Battowia Bullet	a few ?	Bond 1956
All-awash Islet	a few ?	Bond 1956
Grenada, 2-3 sites	E	van Halewyn and Norton 1984
Kick-em-Jenny Key	100 +	Bond 1956
Barbados	E	van Halewyn and Norton 1984
Tobago, St. Giles	100s	Dinsmore and ffrench 1969
Little Tobago	25 +	Dinsmore and ffrench 1969
TOTAL	**8,200-10,000**	

B = breeds in unknown numbers

E = extirpated

? = bred historically, no recent data are available

colonies with an estimated 1,000 or more pairs and seven colonies have 25 or fewer pairs. Data are badly needed for the colonies in Guadeloupe and the Grenadines, which could be extirpated. Several colonies are known to be extirpated: in the Pedro Cays off Jamaica, Cockroach and Sula Islands in the U.S. Virgin Islands, 1-2 sites in the Grenadines and on Barbados. The type locality for Red-footed Boobies is Barbados where Murphy (1936) reported them to nest in abundance, yet none are reported to nest there today.

The historic population is difficult to estimate as data are few, but I believe it could have been ten times or more greater than today's population. Little Cayman Island (Cayman Islands) appears to be the one place where the nesting population increased in recent years: from 2600 pairs in 1986 (Clapp 1987) to 5,000 pairs in 1997 (E. A. Schreiber unpubl.). This colony is a Ramsar Site and the fact that access is very difficult has helped to protect the birds over the years. Data for other colonies indicates that they are declining in size. On Desecheo Island, Puerto Rico, Wetmore (field notes, June 1912) counted 2,000 birds (no number of nests given). There are about 150 nests on Desecheo today, probably a decrease from what was present during Wetmore's visit. The number of nests in the U. S. Virgin Islands declined from 300 in three sites just 15 years ago (van Halewyn and Norton 1984) to fewer than 200 in 2 sites in 1996 (J. Pierce pers. comm.). Clark (1905) said it was reported to nest commonly on Battowia and Kick-em-Jenny in the Grenadines where recent reports of nesting indicate only a few pairs. All indications are that the population in the Caribbean is continuing to decline.

In the greater Caribbean area, colonies are reported on the Campeche Banks, off Mexico (1,400 pairs), on Half Moon Key, Belize (1,300 pairs), on several islands off Venezuela (Aves Islets 1,200 pairs, Los Hermanos Isles 100's of pairs, Los Roques Isles 2,000 pairs, and Los Testigos 100's of pairs), and on Little Swan Island off Honduras (a few). Other colonies may exist off Colombia (Albuquerque Cays, Ron Cador Cays, Serrana Bank, Seranilla Bank) but there are no data on the number of nests. Data are badly needed for colonies off Colombia and Venezuela some of which may be extirpated.

Brown Booby (*S. l. leucogaster*)

Brown Boobies are pan-tropical in distribution, occurring commonly with other booby species: this subspecies ranges through the Caribbean and tropical Atlantic. They feed by plunge diving and eat primarily flying fish and squid (Dorward 1962). They are thought to feed closer to shore than other boobies (Norton et al. in press). The nest is built on the ground and colonies are either on flat coral atolls or rock ledges and hillsides of high islands. Two eggs (1-3) are generally laid, and incubation lasts 42-47 days (Nelson 1978). Adults generally raise only one chick and the second egg is often considered to be an insurance policy in case the first chick dies. On Johnston Atoll (Pacific Ocean) about 0.5% of pairs raise 2 chicks (Schreiber 1997). Chicks fledge at 85-119 days (Dorward 1962, Nelson 1978) probably taking longer during bad food years, such as occur during El Niño events. They return to the nest to be fed by their parents for 1-2 more months (Nelson 1978) and have been known to do so for up to six months (Simmons 1967; study conducted during 1963-65 El Niño). Some nesting birds can be found in all months of the year on Great Tobago in the BVI but this may be due to nests failing and adults re-nesting. Goats destroy many nests so that adults probably relay quite often (Schreiber, unpubl.). Wetmore (1918) reports large young present on Desecheo, Puerto Rico during June 1912 which means the nesting season probably began in October-November. In the southern islands the nesting season is said to be from February through May (Clark 1905), but must be much more extended than that.

I estimate there are 5,500-7,800 pairs of Brown Boobies nesting on the Caribbean islands (Table 2). They are known to be extirpated from 6-8 colonies and the existence of another 11 is questionable (Fig. 2). Large colonies have been destroyed, such as the one on Desecheo Is., Puerto Rico which was reported to have 4,000-5,000 nests in 1912 (Gochfeld et al. 1994). There are only 15 current known colonies with more than 50 pairs and only one colony with more than 1,000 pairs (Southwest Cay, Pedro Cays, Jamaica, A. Sutton & C. Levy pers. comm.). Most colonies of this species are small (1-100 pairs) and could easily be destroyed. For instance, Great Tobago, British Virgin Islands (80-120 pairs) has feral goats on it which trample nests, directly destroying some, and causing severe erosion. The total number of nests in the U.S. Virgin Islands has been declining over the past 10 years from about 950 in 1987 to fewer than 200 in 1996 (J. Pierce, pers. comm.). Clark (1905) was told hundreds nest on Battowia and Kick-em-Jenny in the Grenadines and Grenada where they are suspected to be extirpated today. In the Bahamas, Cay Verde had 550 pairs and the Mira Por Vos group had 600 during a visit by S. Sprunt in 1979. Chapman (1908) reported 1,500 pairs on Cay Verde in 1907 so the population appears to have declined in recent years. Cay Santo Domingo, for which I can find no bird data for the past 100 years, had a large colony of Brown Boobies in 1859 (Bryant 1859). Van Halewyn and Norton (1984) estimated that about 2300 pairs nested in Puerto Rico and the Virgin Islands as recently as 15 years ago, and today only an estimated 1500 pairs nest there (J. Saliva and J. Pierce pers. comm.).

Another 4,500 to 7,000 pairs of Brown Boobies nest to the south and west of the West Indian islands on islands off Venezuela, Colombia, Honduras, Costa Rica, Belize and Mexico. The largest colonies are those on Albuquerque Cays, Columbia (1,000's of pairs), Seranilla Bank, Colombia (1,000's of pairs; van Halewyn and Norton 1984), and Las Aves Isles, Venezuela (1,000's of pairs; Phelps and Phelps 1959). There are essentially no recent data from these islands to indicate the current status of the birds. Most accounts of sightings of Brown Boobies do not include data on nesting. Paynter (1955) counted about 800 on Alacran Reef off the Yucatan with no notes on nesting. At the time, local lighthouse keepers said 1000's nested on two nearby islands (Islas Desterrada and Parajos), however, these reports are difficult to interpret. In 1986 only 20-50 pairs nested in the area, and only on Isla Desterrada (B. Chapman pers. comm.).

Masked Booby (*S. d. dactylatra*)

This species is also called White Booby and Blue-faced Booby. They are the largest booby species, weighing up to 2300 g (Anderson 1993, Schreiber unpubl.). They are pantropical occurring in tropical oceans throughout the world, frequently in colonies near or with other booby species; this subspecies is found in the Caribbean and tropical Atlantic. Masked Boobies eat mainly sardines (Galapagos), flying fish, jacks and squid (Anderson 1993, Schreiber 1997), in sizes which often overlap with those eaten by Red-footed and Brown Boobies. They feed in offshore, pelagic waters and are known to feed 65 km from the colony in the Galapagos (Anderson 1993) but feeding areas in the Caribbean are unknown. Masked Boobies nest on the ground and build no nest to hold the eggs. Two eggs are generally laid (only one chick is raised) and incubation lasts 38-49 days (Nelson 1978, Anderson 1993). Chicks first fly at 109-151 days of age and return to the nest to be fed by their parents until 139-180 ± days of age (Nelson 1978).

There are an estimated 550 – 650 pairs of Masked Boobies nesting in 8 known and 3-5 suspected colonies on Caribbean islands (Table 3, Fig. 3). Three colonies have been extirpated and five more may be. It is most likely that more colonies were extirpated prior to known written records. Masked Booby bones are found in pre-Columbian middens on St. Croix (Palmer 1962) indicating that they were eaten by early Indian inhabitants of the Caribbean. No boobies nest on St. Croix today. Owing to the small current size of most colonies (2 to 25) they could easily be extirpated by introduced predators or other anthropogenic factors. Only one colony has more than 60 pairs; about 250-350 pairs nest on Southwest Cay in the Pedro cays off Jamaica (A. Haynes-Sutton and C. Levy, pers. comm.). They have been extirpated from Middle Cay of the Pedro Cays in Jamaica where 440 pairs were reported as recently as 1986. The number of nests in the U. S. Virgin Islands has declined from 60 pairs in 1987 to 25 pairs in 1996 (J. Pierce, pers. comm.). In the Grenadines and on Grenada, Clark (1905) reported that a few were said to nest on

Table 2. Extant and extirpated colonies of Brown Boobies and estimated number of
  nesting pairs in the West Indies.

Location	Nmbr. of Pairs	Reference
Bahamas, White Cay	100+	D. Lee pers. comm. 1999
Cay Verde	550	Sprunt 1984
North Rock	600	Sprunt 1984
Booby Rocks, off Mayaguana	70-80	A. White pers. comm.
Turks and Caicos	B	Walsh-McGehee et al. 1987
4 other sites	E	A. Sprunt pers. comm.
Cayman Is., Cayman Brac	10-20	E.A. Schreiber unpubl.
Cuba: Cayo Piedras	?	Palmer 1962
Is. off north and one off south shore	?	Palmer 1962
Dominican Republic: offshore N	B	van Halewyn & Norton 1984
offshore NE	B	van Halewyn & Norton 1984
Beata	100s	van Halewyn & Norton 1984
Alta Vela	100s	van Halewyn & Norton 1984
Jamaica, Pedro Cays, Southwest Cay	1,000-1,500	A. Haynes-Sutton pers. comm.
Pedro Cays, Middle Cay & NE Cay	E	A. Haynes-Sutton pers. comm.
Navassa	?	Wetmore and Swales 1931
Puerto Rico, Mona	100	J. Saliva pers. comm.
Monito	500	J. Saliva pers. comm.
Culebra, Cayos Geniqui	75-200	J. Saliva pers. comm.
Desecheo	E	J. Saliva pers. comm.
Cordillera	?	J. Saliva pers. comm.
U.S. Virgin Isl., Cockroach & Sula Keys	150	J. Pierce pers. comm.
Cricket	B	J. Pierce pers comm.
Dutchcap	170	J. Pierce pers. comm.
Frenchcap Key	280	J. Pierce pers. comm.
Kalkun	70	J. Pierce pers comm.
British Virgin Islands: Great Tobago	80-120	E. A. Schreiber 1997
Little Tobago	20-75	J. Pierce pers. comm.
Redonda	B	van Halewyn and Norton 1984
Anguilla, Dog Island	690±	ICF Kaiser 1999
Prickley Pear Cay East	a few	ICF Kaiser 1999
Prickley Pear Cay West	100±	ICF Kaiser 1999
Sombrero	350-400	J. Pierce & RSPB pers. comm.
St. Barts	?	van Halewyn & Norton 1984
Saba	?	van Halewyn & Norton 1984
Dominica, Bird Isles	?	Nelson 1978
Guadeloupe, outlying islands	?	Noble 1916
Grand Islet	200-300	Feldmann et al. 1999
Martinique, Little Tobago	B	Nelson 1978

continued........

Table 2 continued.

Location	Nmbr. of Pairs	Reference
Grenadines, Battowia Bullet	E	Bond 1956
All-awash Islet	E	Bond 1956
Carriacon Isles	B	Nelson 1978
Les Tantes	B	Nelson 1978
Grenada, 4 sites	E	van Halewyn & Norton 1984
Kick-em-Jenny Key	E	Bond 1956
Tobago, St. Giles	B	Dinsmore 1972
Little Tobago (both isles)	300	van Halewyn & Norton 1984
TOTAL	**5,500-7,800**	

B = breeds in unknown numbers
E = extirpated
? = bred historically, no recent data.

Battowia and Kick-em-Jenny where a few may still nest. In the Bahamas, Bryant (1859) reported 20 pairs on Cay Santo Domingo. D. Lee (pers. comm.) found 6 pairs on White Key on a recent visit. There is good cause for concern for the continued existence of this species in the West Indies.

Another 4,000-5,200 pairs of Masked Boobies nest on islands off Venezuela and Mexico. Phelps and Phelps (1959) report for islands off Venezuela; Los Hermanos 100s, Los Roques a few, and Los Monjes a few. Boswall (1978) found about 50-60 nests on the Campeche Banks islands, off Mexico. In 1986 there were 4,000 – 5,000 nests present on four islands of the Campeche Banks (J. Tunnell and B. Chapman pers. comm.). The nesting season in the northern Caribbean is from about September through April (Schreiber, unpubl.), and in the southern Caribbean is from March through September (Boswall 1978). On the Campeche Banks nests may be found at any time of year (J. Tunnell and B. Chapman pers. comm.).

Research Priorities

Little research has been conducted on boobies in the Caribbean region. Verner (1961, 1965) did perhaps the most extensive work and that was on Red-footed Boobies. In order to determine their current status a survey of all historic colonies should be done during the breeding season. This survey should assess the problems birds are experiencing (predators, degradation of habitat, human disturbance). An annual monitoring program for seabird colonies should be established and colonies surveyed 3-4 times per year to determine how many nests successfully raise young (see Schreiber and Lee this publication). Population size and age classes should be monitored over the long-term. Because these species are long-lived (up to 30 years) lack of successful breeding can easily be missed for years if colonies are not monitored: The mere presence of a lot of birds in an area does not mean young are being raised each year. The subspecies of boobies are poorly described (Schreiber et al. 1996) and data on morphometrics and systematic relationships

Table 3. Extant and extirpated colonies of Masked Boobies and estimated number of nesting pairs in the West Indies (Florida is not included in West Indies).

Location	Nmbr. of Pairs	References
Florida Keys, Dry Tortugas	7	Robertson & Woolfenden 1992
Bahamas, White Cay	6	D. Lee pers. comm. 1999
Santo Domingo Cay	?	Bryant 1859
Cayman Is., Cayman Brac	2-8	E A. Schreiber 1997
Jamaica, Pedro Cays, Southwest Cay	250-350	A. Haynes-Sutton pers. comm.
Pedro, Middle Cay	E	A. Haynes-Sutton pers. comm.
Puerto Rico, Mona	55	J. Saliva pers. comm.
Culebra: on offshore islets	3	J. Saliva pers. comm.
Monito	50	J. Saliva pers. comm.
U.S. Virgin Isls., Cockroach and Sula Cays	60	J. Pierce pers. comm.
Frenchcap	40-50	J. Pierce pers. comm.
St. Croix	E	J. Pierce pers. comm.
Redonda	?	van Halewyn & Norton 1984
Anguilla, Mid Cay	1	ICF Kaiser 1999
Dog Isl.	20	ICK Kaiser 1999
Sombrero	40-60	J. Pierce pers. comm.
Grenadines, Battowia Bullet	a few, ?	Bond 1956
Grenada, Kick-em-Jenny Key	a few, ?	Bond 1956
TOTAL	**550-650**	

B = breeds in unknown numbers, E = extirpated, ? = bred historically, no recent data.

throughout their ranges are badly needed. Banding data indicate that boobies are philopatric and that there is very little movement between colonies (Woodward 1972, Amerson and Shelton 1976, Schreiber et al. 1996). There probably is little to no interbreeding between boobies nesting in the northern and southern Caribbean. If they are in fact, separate subspecies this has important consequences for conservation and will affect conservation priorities. A comprehensive study of the genetic relationships and morphology among Caribbean colonies is needed to adequately describe the subspecies. To assess subspecific relationships of Caribbean boobies, an adequate number of specimens should be collected from several locales on which genetic and morphological studies can be done. Together, morphological and genetic studies would allow, for the first time, an accurate description of subspecies. Additionally several hundred of each species should be banded in several colonies throughout the Caribbean range in order to determine movement patterns in general and if there is any inter-island movement of breeding birds.

Conclusion

All three booby species are in need of immediate conservation measures in the Caribbean.

Van Halewyn and Norton (1984) list Masked Boobies as "of special concern" and both Red-foots and Browns as "status to be monitored". With the population declines that have occurred since 1984, I believe the population status should be changed to "Endangered" for Masked Boobies and "Vulnerable" for Red and Brown Boobies (see Chapter entitled Management Recommendations for West Indian Seabirds). The trend of decreasing numbers for all the booby species indicates that close monitoring of the populations are needed. Further unnatural losses of colonies and individuals are expected to occur. Currently there are plans to build a rocket launching facility on Sombrero Island off Anguilla which would destroy this island as a nesting site for Masked (60-80 pairs) and Brown Boobies (400-500 pairs) as well as for other seabirds.

Literature Cited

Amerson, A. B., and P. C. Shelton. 1975. The natural history of Johnston Atoll, central Pacific Ocean. Atoll Research Bull. 192: 1-479.

Anderson, D. A. 1993. Masked Booby (*Sula dactylatra*). In A. Poole and F. Gill eds. *The Birds of North America*, Philadelphia, The Academy of Natural Sciences; Washington, D.C., The American Ornithologists' Union. No.73.

Bond, J. 1956. Check-list of birds of the West Indies. The Academy of Natural Sciences, Philadelphia, PA.

Boswall, J. 1978. The birds of Alacran Reef, Gulf of Mexico. Bull. B.O.C. 98: 99-109.

Bryant, H. 1859. A list of birds seen in the Bahamas from Jan. 20 to May 14, 1859, with descriptions of new or little known species. Proc. of the Boston Society of Natural History 7: 102-134.

Buden, D. W. 1987. The birds of the Southern Bahamas. B. O. U. Checklist No. 8. British Ornithologists' Union.

Chapman, F. M. 1908. A contribution to the life histories of the booby (*Sula leucogaster*) and man-o-war bird (*Fregata aquilla*). Papers from the Tortugas Lab of Carnegie Inst. 2:139-150. Washington, D.C.

Clapp, R. B. 1987. Status of the Red-footed Booby colony on Little Cayman Island. Atoll Research Bull. 304.

Clark, A. H. 1905. Birds of the southern Lesser Antilles. Proc. Of the Boston Soc. Of Natl. History 32: 203-312.

Cory, C. B. 1909. The birds of the leeward islands, Caribbean Sea. Field Museum of Natural History, Publ. No. 137, Vol. 1: 193-254.

Dinsmore, J. J. 1972. Avifauna of Little Tobago Island. *Quarterly Journal of the Florida Academy of Sciences* 35:55-71.

Dinsmore, J. J. and R. P.ffrench 1969. Birds of St. Giles Islands, Tobago. *Wilson Bulletin* 81: 460-463.

Dorward, D. F. 1962. Comparative biology of the white booby and brown booby, Sula spp., at Ascension. Ibis 103b: 174-220.

Feldmann, P., E. Benito-Espinal and A. R. Keith. 1999. New bird records from Guadeloupe and Martinique, West Indies. Journ. Field Ornithol. 70: 80-94

Gochfeld, M., J. Burger, A. Haynes-Sutton, R. van Halewyn and J. Saliva. 1994. Successful approaches to seabird protection in the West Indies. BirdLife Conservation Series no. 1: 186-209.

ICF Kaiser. 1999. Supplemental biological surveys on Sombrero Island and other Anguillan Islands. Arlington, VA.

Murphy, R. C. 1936. Oceanic birds of South America. American Museum of Natural History. New York.

Nelson, B. A. 1978. The Sulidae, gannets and boobies. Oxford University Press, Oxford.

Noble, G. K. 1916. The resident birds of Guadeloupe. Bull. of the Museum of Comp. Zool. 60: 359-385.

Norton, R., and E. A. Schreiber. in prep. Brown Booby (Sula leucogaster). In A. Poole and F. Gill eds. The Birds of North America, Philadelphia, The Academy of Natural Sciences; Washington, D. C., The American Ornithologists' Union.

Palmer, R.S. 1962. *Handbook of North American birds*. Yale Univ. Press, New York. 567pp.

Paynter, R. A. 1955. The ornithogeography of the Yucatan Peninsula. Peabody Museum of Natural History Bull. 9.

Phelps, W. H. and W. H. Phelps, Jr. 1959. La nidificacion de las aves marinas en el archipelago de Los Rocas. Boletin de la Sociedad Venezolana de Ciencias Naturales.

Robertson, W. B., Jr., and G. W. Woolfenden. 1992. Florida bird species: an annotated list. Florida Ornithol. Soc. Spec. Publ. No. 6. Gainesville, FL.

Schreiber, E. A. 1997. Breeding biology and ecology of the seabirds of Johnston Atoll, central Pacific Ocean: long-term monitoring. Report to Dept. of Defense, Aberdeen Proving Ground MD.

Schreiber, E. A., R. W. Schreiber and G. A. Schenk. 1996. Red-footed Booby (*Sula sula*). In A. Poole and F. Gill eds. *The Birds of North America*, Philadelphia, The Academy of Natural Sciences; Washington, D.C., The American Ornithologists' Union. No. 241

Schreiber, R. W., and D. A. Hensley. 1976. The diets of *Sula dactylatra*, *Sula sula*, and *Fregata minor* on Christmas Island, Pacific Ocean. Pacific Science 30: 241-248.

Simmons, K. E. L. 1967. Ecological adaptations in the life history of the Brown Booby at Ascension Island. The Living Bird 6: 187-212.

Sprunt, A. 1984. The status and conservation of seabirds of the Bahama Islands. Pp. 157-168 in J. P. Croxall, P. G. H. Evans and R. W. Schreiber, eds. *Status and Conservation of the World's Seabirds*, Cambridge, U.K.: International Council for Bird Preservation (Tech. Publ.) 2.

van Halewyn, R., and R. L. Norton. 1984. The status and conservation of Caribbean seabirds. Pp. 169-222 in J. P. Croxall, P. G. H. Evans, and R. W. Schreiber, eds. *Status and Conservation of the World's Seabirds*, Cambridge, U.K.: International Council for Bird Preservation (Tech. Publ.) 2.

Verner, J. 1961. Nesting activities of the Red-footed Booby in British Honduras. Auk 78: 573-594.

Verner, J. 1965. Flight behavior of the Red-footed Booby. Wilson Bull. 77: 229-234.

Wetmore, A. 1918. The birds of Desecheo Island, Puerto Rico. Auk 35: 333-340.

Wetmore, A., and B. H. Swales. 1931. The birds of Haiti sand the Dominican Republic. U. S. National Museum Bulletin 155. Washington, D.C.

Woodward, P. W. 1972. The natural history of Kure Atoll, northwestern Hawaiian Islands. Atoll Research Bull. 164: 1-318.

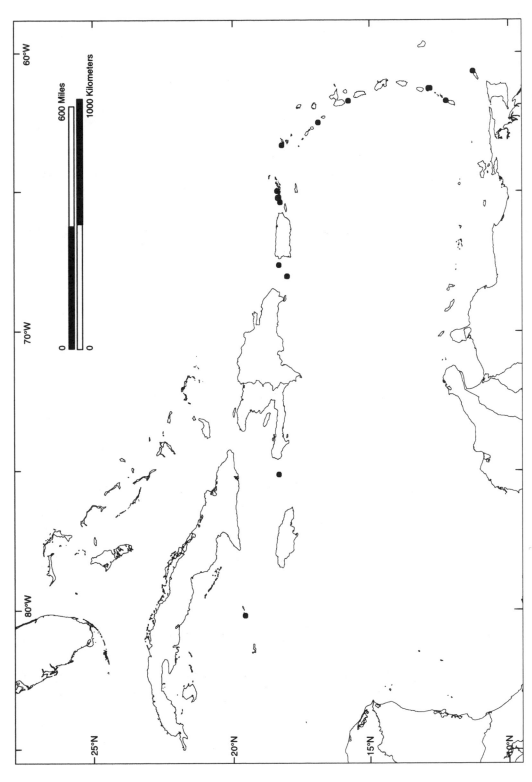

Figure 1: The status of known Red-footed Booby breeding sites in the West Indies. ● = confirmed breeding location that has been surveyed recently. ◉ = historic breeding location with no report that the colony has been extirpated. ⊠ = historic breeding location that is extirpated or thought to be extirpated.

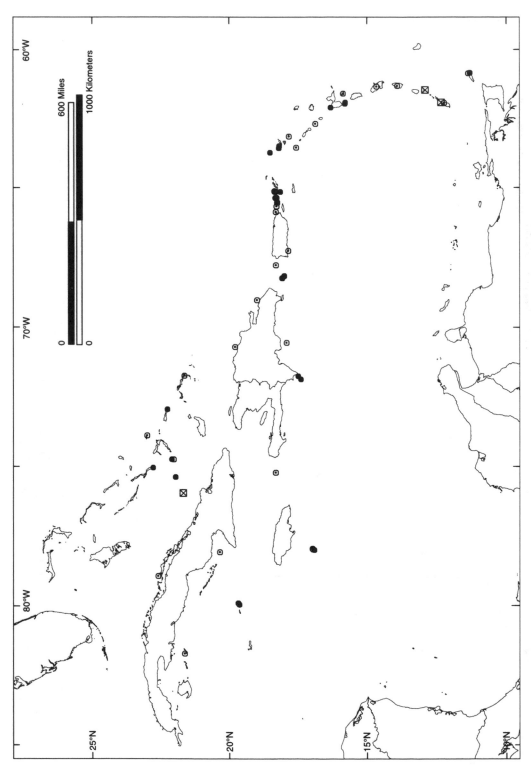

Figure 2: The status of known Brown Booby breeding sites in the West Indies. ● = confirmed breeding location that has been surveyed recently. ◉ = historic breeding location with no report that the colony has been extirpated. ⊠ = historic breeding location that is extirpated or thought to be extirpated.

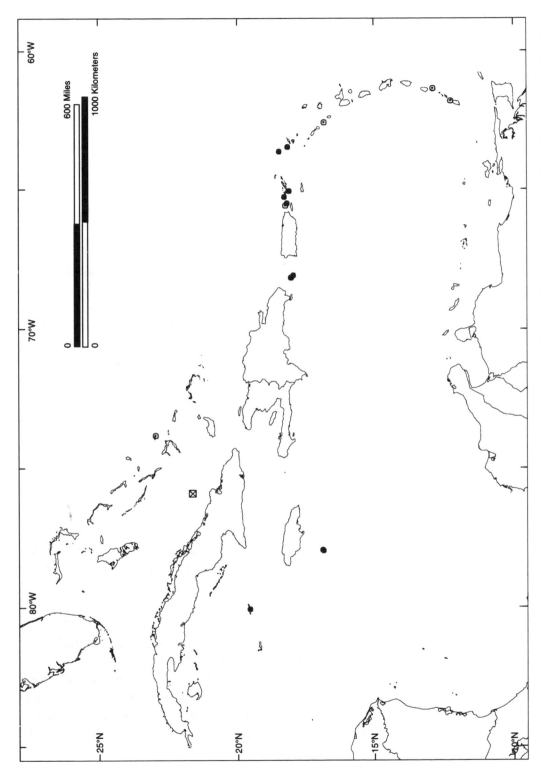

Figure 3: The status of known Masked Booby breeding sites in the West Indies. ● = confirmed breeding location that has been surveyed recently. ◉ = historic breeding location with no report that the colony has been extirpated. ⊠ = historic breeding location that is extirpated or thought to be extirpated.

Status of the Magnificent Frigatebird in the West Indies

C3 C3 C3 C3   80 80 80 80

KEVEL LINDSEY[1], BRUCE HORWITH[2], and E. A. SCHREIBER[3]

[1] *Island Resources Foundation PO Box 2103 St. John's, Antigua.* [2] *Island Resources Foundation, 6296 Estate Nazareth No. 11, St. Thomas, USVI 00802-1104.* [3] *National Museum of Natural History, Smithsonian Institution, MRC 116, Washington D. C. 20560* SchreiberE@aol.com

Introduction

Frigatebirds have some of the most extreme life-history characteristics in the bird world including an exceptionally long incubation period for their single egg and very long nestling and post-fledging care periods for chicks. With a wing span of almost 2.5 m and a body mass of only 1100-2000 grams they have the lightest wing-loading of any bird and are amazingly adept in the air. For such a spectacular bird they have been little studied and as a result we know very little about their population size and nesting colonies or their demographics. Their wide ranging habits make them seem ubiquitous around the Caribbean, as is certainly indicated in the literature of sightings. Yet, there are few colonies and most of these consist of fewer than 100 pairs of birds (Table 1, Fig. 1).

Magnificent Frigatebirds are probably one of the most threatened seabird species in the West Indies with fewer than 4,300-5,300 pairs remaining with 75-80% of these in five main colonies. The extensive development occurring over the past 200 years in the West Indies has caused the extirpation of many historic colonies. Additionally, storms destroy nesting habitat and introduced predators take eggs and young.

Distribution and Population Size

Magnificent Frigatebirds nest primarily on islands in tropical waters of both coasts of the Americas and on one or two islands in the Atlantic. They are seen hundreds of miles from their colonies when not breeding, and are usually in groups, often segregated by sex (possibly owing to different wing-loading between sexes: Harrington et al. 1972). In the West Indies the five main colonies are on Southwest Cay in the Pedro Cays, Jamaica (700-1000 pairs); Monito, Puerto Rico (200 pairs); Great Tobago, British Virgin Islands (500-600 pairs); Barbuda (2,000 pairs); Giles Is. off Tobago (500-900 pairs: Table 1, Fig. 1). A "large colony" is reported to be on Anguilla (van Halewyn and Norton 1984 and prior literature) but we can find no data on the exact name of this islet. Peters' (1927) visit to Anguilla during February, when the colony should have been active, reports only a few sightings of frigates, no nesting. A small colony of 40 pairs was found on Dog Island (ICF Kaiser 1999) in July 1999 which may be the one earlier reported and just be greatly diminished today.

Some historic reports indicate that current colonies may have been much larger in the past: i.e. Brown (1947) writes of thousands of nests on an islet off Tobago which as of 1969 (Dinsmore & ffrench 1969) only supported an estimated 500-900 nests. When Chapman (1908) visited Cay Verde in the Bahamas he noted the presence of 200-300 frigatebird nests. Today this colony has only 100 pairs (S. Sprunt pers. comm.). Some more current references to the presence of colonies appear to be cited from Bent (1922) and these data were from visits by others sometime previous to 1922. Thus, much of our information on locations of nesting colonies for this species is very out of date.

The only colonies for which we have good recent data (Table 1) are in the Dry Tortugas, just off the Florida Keys (Robertson and Woolfenden 1992, Stevenson and Anderson 1994), Bahamas (D. Lee pers. comm.), Jamaica (A. Haynes-Sutton recent visits), Cayman Islands (Schreiber visit 1997), Puerto Rico (J. Saliva visits in 1990's), U.S. and British Virgin Islands (Pierce, Saliva and Schreiber visits in 1990's), Sombrero (J. Pierce pers. comm.) and Barbuda (Schreiber visits 1996-1998). Data for other Caribbean colonies (Table 1) are mostly from visits 30 to 100 years ago. Given the level of disturbance in many Caribbean colonies, some of the other purported colonies may not still exist. At least twelve nesting sites have been abandoned within the century. The colony that existed on the Marquesas Keys off southern Florida is thought to have abandoned the island by 1990 owing to human disturbance (Robertson and Woolfenden 1992, Stevenson and Anderson 1994). The type specimen of Magnificent Frigate is from Aruba and today there are no colonies there. At one time Seal Key, Bahamas was reported to have over 1,000 pairs of nesting frigates (Bryant 1859). Today there are none (Buden 1987).

Colonies in areas south and west of the West Indies have suffered also. The Mexican population includes about 2,000-3,000 nests on islands offshore of the Yucatan and about 2,000 nests on the Campeche Banks. Data from islands offshore of the Yucatan are from many years ago and these colonies may no longer exist, or may be greatly diminished owing to human disturbance. The Campeche Banks are fairly remote from disturbance and data from the 1986 visit by J. Tunnell and B. Chapman (pers. comm.) are probably indicative of the numbers of frigatebirds nesting today. There is a colony of over 1,000 pairs on Half Moon Key off Belize and there may be more colonies in the string of islands offshore from Belize and Honduras though there are no reports from them in many years. Some of these islands are inhabited, however, and frigates could have been extirpated. There may be some nesting on islands off the eastern side of Panama (Bond 1956). In South America, Venezuela, Colombia and French Guyana are reported to have nesting Magnificent Frigatebirds. The total number of nesting pairs on the east coast of Central America and the Caribbean coast of South America is estimated to be 6,500-7,500.

Biology

Nesting in most Caribbean colonies begins in October-November with some egg laying continuing through January. Frigates generally nest in monospecific colonies but they may nest in colonies with pelicans, boobies, cormorants or other birds as they do on Redonda. Incubation duties are shared by both sexes and last for 50-60 days. Young first fly at 150-207 days of age. The major portion of the diet consists of flying fish and squid (Diamond and Schreiber in prep.), taken from the surface by hovering and swooping. However, in many Caribbean harbors frigate-birds are often seen feeding on discarded scraps from fishmongers or on food waste dumped into the sea. Frigates are also known to take nestlings of Sooty Terns (*Sterna fuscata*), Sooty Storm-petrels (*Oceanodroma tristrami*), and hatchling sea turtles (Schreiber 1996). They will eat the eggs and small young of their own species when adults have been disturbed from the nest.

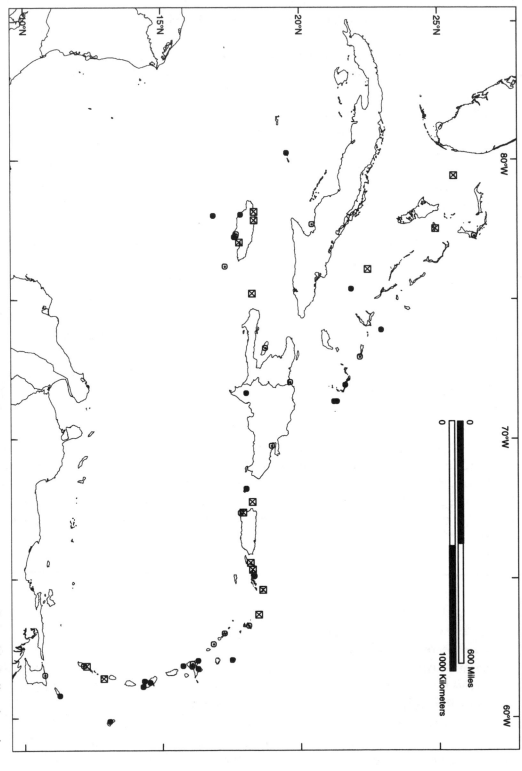

Figure 1: The status of known Magnificent Frigatebird breeding sites in the West Indies. ● = confirmed breeding location that has been surveyed recently. ⊙ = historic breeding location with no report that the colony has been extirpated. ⊠ = historic breeding location that is extirpated or thought to be extirpated.

Conservation Problems of Specific Colonies

The colony of about 2000 frigatebird nests on Barbuda is reported to be the largest in the Lesser Antilles (Schreiber 1996). It contains an estimated 28-40% of the total frigatebird population in the West Indies. The site has no legal protection (although this has been proposed to the Antigua government) and eco-tour operations have caused some disruption to the colony in the past. During 1998, E. A. Schreiber trained fishermen and tour guides to conduct eco-tours of the colony, allowing people to see and enjoy the colony without disturbing the birds. This should help ensure the continued survival of this colony. The colony on Great Tobago, British Virgin Islands is protected only by being difficult for humans to access. However, goats on the island are destroying the vegetation and allowing no regeneration of new trees so that eventually the frigatebirds will lose their nesting habitat. If forced to nest on the ground, nests and eggs will be trampled and by goats. The relatively small colony on Little Cayman, Cayman Islands is protected by law and is fairly inaccessible. A proposed new, larger airport adjacent to the colony may pose a threat in the future. On the Pedro Cays, off Jamaica, introduced dogs, cats and rats are a problem, as well as human habitation and probable poaching. Recommendations for conservation are discussed in the last chapter by Schreiber and Lee.

We have no recent data on the sizeable colonies in the Dominican Republic, Martinique and Tobago. These colonies could well be much smaller today. Recent surveys of the Guadeloupe colonies show that they harbors a significant proportion of the frigatebird population in the West Indies (Table 1). We do not know how well protected they are or if they have introduced predators.

Table 1. Extant and extirpated colonies of Magnificent Frigatebirds and estimated number of nesting pairs in the West Indies (Bahamas and Netherlands Antilles are not considered part of West Indies population).

Location	Nmbr. of Pairs	Reference
Bahamas, Atwood Key	10	Buden 1987
Cay Verde	100	Sprunt 1984
Booby Cay and Great Abaco	?	Bond 1956, Sprunt 1984
Turks, Penniston Cay	25	Walsh-McGehee et. al 1998
Grand Turk	B	Buden 1987
Seal Key	E	Buden 1987
Middle Caicos	100-200	Walsh-McGehee et. al 1998
Penniston Cay	50	Walsh-McGehee et al. 1998
San Salvador	10-15	D. Lee pers. comm.
4 other sites	E	van Halewyn & Norton 1984
Cayman Is., Little Cayman	120-150	Schreiber 1997 visits

continued -

Table 1 continued -

Location	Nmbr. of Pairs	Reference
Cuba, Puerto Escondido (Guantanamo Bay)	?	Palmer 1962
Jamaica, mainland	E	Haynes-Sutton pers. comm.
Southwest Cay, Pedro Cays	700-1000	Haynes-Sutton pers. comm.
Portland bight, Two Bush Cay	fewer than 200	Haynes-Sutton pers. comm.
St. Elizabeth, Parottree Pond	10+	Haynes-Sutton pers. comm.
Port Royal Cays	E	Haynes-Sutton pers. comm.
Haiti, San Lorenzo Bay	?	Wetmore & Swales 1931
Samana Bay	?	Bond 1956
Gonave	?	Wetmore & Swales 1931
Dominican Republic, San Lorenzo Bay	150+	Palmer 1962
Navassa	E	Wetmore & Swales 1931
Puerto Rico, southwest mainland	E	J. Saliva visits 1990's
Monito	200-300	J. Saliva 1994 visit
Culebra	E	J. Saliva visits 1990's
Desecheo	E	J. Saliva visits 1990's
U.S. Virgin Islands, George Dog	E	J. Pierce, J. Saliva pers. comm.
Dutch Cap	E	J. Pierce, J. Saliva pers. comm.
British Virgin Islands, Great Tobago	500-600	Schreiber 1996-7 visits
Anegada	E	Schreiber 1996-7 visits
Anguilla, Dog Island	40	ICF Kaiser 1999
Sombrero	E	J. Pierce 1998 visits
Barbuda	2,000	Schreiber 1997 visit
St. Kitts	B	Evans 1990, J. Wilson 1997
Redonda	?	van Halewyn & Norton 1984
Martinique	400-700	van Halewyn & Norton 1984
Guadeloupe, Grand Illet	440	G. Le Blonde pers. comm. 1997
Tillet	100	G. Le Blonde pers. comm. 1997
Saint Rose	150	G. Le Blonde pers. comm. 1997
Petit Canal	500	G. Le Blonde pers. comm. 1997
Grenadines, Battowia	?	Bond 1956
Grenada, 4 sites incl. Kick-em-Jenny	?	van Halewyn & Norton 1984
Tobago, St. Giles	500-900	Dinsmore & ffrench 1969
Trinidad	B	van Halewyn & Norton 1984
Barbados	100	Bond 1956
Bonaire, Kralendijk & Lac	?	Voous 1957
Curaçao, Macuacu Is	B	Voous 1957
TOTAL	**4300 - 5300**	

B = breeds in unknown numbers, E = extirpated,
? = used to breed and may still but no recent data

Conclusions

Magnificent Frigatebirds should be considered a "threatened species" in the Caribbean. With only 4,300-5,300 pairs remaining, and the majority of these in four colonies, the species could be easily extirpated from the region. Human disturbance, development, introduced predators and hurricanes pose continued threats to their survival. See the last Chapter, Management Recommendations for West Indian Seabirds, for specific recommendations on conservation for this species.

Literature Cited

Bent, A. C. 1922. Life histories of North American petrels and pelicans and their allies. U. S. Natl. Museum Bull. No. 121. Washington, D. C.

Bond, J. 1956. Checklist of birds of the West Indies. The Academy of Natural Sciences, Philadelphia. 214 pp.

Brown, L. 1947. Birds and I. Michael Joseph Ltd., London.

Bryant, H. 1859. A list of birds seen at the Bahamas, from Jan. 20 to May 14, 1959 with descriptions of new or little known species. Proc. Boston Society of Natl. History 7: 102-134.

Buden, D. W. 1987. The birds of the southern Bahamas. British Ornithologists' Union Checklist No. 8. London.

Chapman, F. M. 1908. A contribution to the life-histories of the booby (Sula leucogaster) and Man-o'-War Bird (Fregata aquila). Papers from the Tortugas Lab. of Carnegie Inst., Washington, D. C. 2: 139-150.

Diamond, A. W., E. A. Schreiber. in press. Magnificent Frigatebird, *Fregata magnificens*. In A.

Poole and F. Gill eds. *The Birds of North America*, Philadelphia, The Academy of Natural Sciences; Washington, D.C., The American Ornithologists' Union.

Dinsmore, J. J. and ffrench, R. P. 1969. Birds of St. Giles Islands, Tobago. Wilson Bulletin 81: 460-463.

Evans, P. G. H. 1990. Birds of the Eastern Caribbean. MacMillan Caribbean. 165 pp.

Harrington, B. A., R. W. Schreiber and G. E. Woolfenden. 1972. The distribution of male and female Magnificent Frigatebirds, *Fregata magnificens*, along the gulf Coast of Florida. American Birds 26: 927-931.

Noble, G. K. 1916. The resident birds of Guadeloupe. Bull. of the Museum of Comp. Zool. 60: 359-385.

Palmer, R.S. 1962. Handbook of North American birds. Yale Univ. Press, New York. 567pp.

Paynter, R. A., Jr. 1956. Birds of the Swan Islands. The Wilson Bulletin 68: 103-110.

Peters, J. L. 1927. Birds of the island of Anguilla, West Indies. Auk 44: 532-538.

Phelps, W. H., and W. H. Phelps, Jr. 1957. Las aves de Isla de Aves, Venezuela. Boletin de la Sociedad Venezolana de Ciencias Naturales 88: 63-72.

Phelps, W. H. and W. H. Phelps, Jr. 1959. La nidificacion de las aves marinas en el archipelago de Los Rocas. Boletin de la Sociedad Venezolana de Ciencias Naturales 90: 13-20.

Robertson, Jr., W. B., and G. E.Woolfenden. 1992. Florida bird species: an annotated list. Florida Ornithol. Society, Special Publ. No. 6. Gainsville, FL.

Schreiber, EA. 1996. Barbuda Frigatebird colony status report – Preserving birds as an Economic Resource. Report to the Organization of Eastern Caribbean States, Natural Resources Management Unit. 21 pp.

Sprunt, A, IV. 1984. The status and conservation of seabirds in the Bahama Islands. Pp. 157-168 in J. P. Croxall, P. G. H. Evans, and R. W. Schreiber, eds. *Status and conservation of the world's seabirds.* International Council for Bird Preservation, Cambridge, U.K. (Tech. Publ.) 2.

Stevenson, H. M., and B. H. Anderson. 1994. The Bird Life of Florida. Univ. of Florida Press, Gainsville.

van Halewyn, R., and R. L. Norton. 1984. The status and conservation of Caribbean seabirds. Pp. 169-222 in J. P. Croxall, P. G. H. Evans, and R. W. Schreiber, eds. *Status and conservation of the world's seabirds*, Cambridge, U.K.: International Council for Bird Preservation (Tech. Publ.) 2.

Voous, K. H. 1957. The birds of Curaçao, Bonaire and Aruba. In P. W. Hummelinck ed. Studies on the fauna of Curaçao and other Caribbean Islands. Vol. VII, Utrecht.

Walsh-McGehee, M, D. S. Lee and J. M. Wunderle, Jr. 1998. A report of aquatic birds encountered in December from the Caicos Islands. Bahamas Journ. of Science 5:28-33.

Wetmore, A., and B. H. Swales, 1931. The birds of Haiti and the Dominican Republic. U.S. National Museum Bulletin 155. Washington, D.C.

Status and Conservation Priorities for Laughing Gulls, Gull-billed Terns, Royal Terns and Bridled Terns in the West Indies

 C8 C8 C8 C8   80 80 80 80

JOHN W. CHARDINE[1], RALPH D. MORRIS[2], JAMES F. PARNELL[3] AND J. PIERCE[4]

[1] Canadian Wildlife Service, St. John's, Newfoundland, A1A 5B2, Canada, Email john.chardine@wc.gc.ca, [2] Department of Biological Sciences, Brock University, St. Catharines, Ontario, L2S 3A1, Canada, Email rmorris@spartan.ac.brocku.ca, [3] 6451 Quail Run, Wilmington, North Carolina 28409, Email jfparnell@worldnet.att.net , [4] Government of the Virgin Islands, Divs. of fish and Wildlife,6291 Estate Nazareth 101, St. Thomas, U.S. Virgin Islands 00802.

Introduction:

The species accounts for Laughing Gulls (*Larus atricilla*), Gull-billed Terns (*Sterna nilotica*), Royal Terns (*Sterna maxima*) and Bridled Terns (*Sterna anaethetus*) are combined since none of these species is experiencing a particular problem in the West Indies, other than that of all the Caribbean seabird species, human disturbance. Their populations are not considered endangered or threatened and the basic needs to ensure their future survival in the West Indies are the same steps needed by the threatened species. While the number of potential breeding sites for these species is unlimited, in actuality, most sites are often disturbed by humans in one way or another. They commonly experience failed nesting seasons in many locations and this is expected to increase as more boaters visit islands, more hotels and housing developments are built, and eggs continue to be taken for human consumption. Because they are often disturbed, the birds change colony locations frequently and it is difficult from year to year to say exactly where they are nesting. Thus recorded breeding on an island in one year, does not necessarily mean they will be on that island in following years. This makes determining population sizes difficult as not all islands are surveyed each year.

These four species are colonial, nesting in colonies of a few pairs to several thousand pairs. Colonies may contain mixed species which requires careful observation when nest counts are carried out. They all nest in spring and summer, laying eggs mainly during May.

Laughing Gull (*Larus atricilla*)

Laughing Gulls (the only gull nesting in the Caribbean) are not common in the West Indies with an estimated total population of 5,000-10,000 pairs. They have been extirpated from many colonies since the 1700's owing to development of nesting sites (Burger 1996). They breed along the Atlantic coast from Maine south through the Lesser Antilles and Caribbean (Nisbet 1971, Howell and Webb 1995). They breed on Aruba and Bonaire in the Netherlands Antilles, and along the coasts of South and Central America (Voous 1983, ffrench 1991). Within the Caribbean there are few surveys of the actual number of nesting pairs. An estimated 2,000-4,000 pairs nest from Puerto Rico east through Anegada (Table 1). Jamaica has 20 or more pairs (A. Haynes Sutton

Table 1. Number of nesting pairs of Laughing Gulls in the West Indies.

Location		Number of Pairs
Bahamas		50-100
Cuba		?
Jamaica, Port Royal		E
Morant Cays		5-50
Hispaniola		?
Navassa		10-20
Puerto Rico, total		1200
Culebra, La Cordillera, Mona, Monita		
U.S. Virgin Islands, total		1500-3500
Booby Rock	5-20	
Buck/Capella	50-100	
Current Cut	100-200	
Dog Island	200-400	
Flanagan Island	100-300	
Flat	200-400	
Frenchcap	20-50	
Henley	100-200	
LeDuck Island	50-200	
Little Hans Lollick Island	200-500	
Ramgoat	50-100	
Rata	20-40	
Saba	100-200	
Trunk	100-200	
Turtledove Cay	200-400	
British Virgin Islands, scattered islets, total		300-600
Anegada		?
Anguilla, Scrub and Prickly Pear East		a few
St. Martin & St. Barts		100±
Antigua & Barbuda		400-800
Guadeloupe		B
Grenada (many sites)		B
Barbados		E
TOTAL WEST INDIES		**5000-10,000**

B – reported to breed, no data on number of pairs
? – reported to breed in the past, no recent data and may be extirpated
E – extirpated

pers. comm.) but no thorough survey has been carried out and there may be more pairs. They are thought to nest on Cuba and Hispaniola but there are no data from recent years. Scattered other colonies occur in Jamaica, St. Martin, St. Barts, Antigua, Barbuda, Guadeloupe and Grenada (Fig. 1). The total number of nests in the West Indies is on the order of 5,000-10,000 pairs (Table 1). Colony sites may move from year to year, which could be related to the amount of human disturbance they receive from boaters, and eggs are commonly taken for human consumption (J. Pierce and E. A. Schreiber pers. comm.).

Pairs begin courting in April and most eggs are laid by the end of May. Colonies are located on sandy areas, in marshes, at the edges of mangrove swamps, or other appropriate habitat. They prefer some vegetation around them to provide visual isolation from neighbors and perhaps protection from the sun. They build a nest of grasses and seaweed (whatever vegetation is available) and generally lay 2-3 spotted eggs. Incubation lasts 22-25 days (Schreiber et al. 1979). They are fed by their parents until they are about 60 days old (Burger 1996). Laughing Gulls feed while walking along or swimming and do not plunge dive. They are scavengers eating crustaceans, fish, shrimp, insects and human garbage. They have learned to prey on eggs and small young of some of the tern species, particularly if tern eggs or young are left unprotected by the adults.

The greatest threats to the survival of Laughing Gulls in the West Indies are loss of habitat and human consumption of eggs. Protected and patrolled nesting areas are badly needed.

Gull-billed Tern (*Sterna nilotica aranea*)

This medium-sized tern is less restricted to the marine environment than most other members of the genus Sterna. While it usually nests in colonies along the coast, it may feed on insects, crustaceans, and even small vertebrates over freshwater or terrestrial environments. The Gull-billed Tern is widely but somewhat sporadically distributed, breeding at scattered sites in Europe, Asia, Africa, Australia and the Americas. In North America, *Sterna n. aranea* nests along the Atlantic Coast southward from Long Island southward to the Caribbean and Mexico. *Sterna n. vanrossemi* breeds in small numbers along the Pacific coast of North American in California and Mexico (Parnell et al. 1995).

This tern does not regularly dive for food in the fashion typical of a tern, but feeds on insects by hawking and on fiddler crabs, lizards, and even the chicks of other terns by plucking the prey from the surface with a steep swoop (Parnell et al. 1995). Gull-billed Terns are monogamous first breeding at 5 years old (Møller 1975, 1981) often arriving paired at the breeding sites. They usually nest with Common Terns (*Sterna hirundo*) and Black Skimmers (*Rhynchops niger*) on bare sandy substrates, usually upper beaches or small islands (Clapp et al. 1983) or in brackish marshes (Erickson 1926) along the Atlantic Coast of North America. Colony size is usually small, from a few pairs to a few dozen pairs (Clapp et al. 1983). Nests are usually sparsely lined with vegetation, or more commonly, with shell fragments (Parnell et al. 1995). Three eggs usually constitute a full clutch (Bent 1921) and both parents incubate during a 22 -23 incubation period (Witherbee 1941). Fledging occurs at about 28 - 35 days and young may remain with parents for at least 2 to 3 months after fledging (Møller 1975).

Breeding by the Gull-billed Tern in the Caribbean is sporadic and at widely scattered locations (Table 2, Fig. 2), and often mixed in with other species (Parnell et al. 1995). Norton (1982) reported a few pairs nesting at Anegada Island but this colony may be extirpated (J. Pierce pers. comm.). Van Halewyn and Norton (1984) reported possible nesting on Cuba and Hispaniola based on a personal communication from J. A. Ottenwalder. Sprunt (1984) reported 12 pairs breeding on Great Inagua in 1967 and 1972. He noted that the species was a summer resident at several other places in the Bahamas and speculated that additional small breeding colonies were likely present. Lee and Clark (1994) found an individual bird at Waderick Wells in late May 1991, and also speculated that there were likely small undiscovered breeding colonies in the Bahamas.

The limited evidence available indicates that this species nests only sporadically and in very low numbers in the Caribbean. We estimate that there are between 100 and 500 pairs nesting at five to seven sites (Table 2, Fig. 2). Initial needs are for surveys to verify the breeding distribution, to locate breeding sites and to determine nesting populations. Protection of nesting sites, and more effective enforcement of protective laws are suggested by Sprunt (1984). Public education to enhance awareness of this uncommon species is also needed.

Table 2. Number of nesting pairs of Gull-billed Terns in the West Indies.

Location	Number of Pairs
Bahamas, Great Inagua	a few
scattered islets	100-300
Cuba	?
Hispaniola	?
Puerto Rico	E
U. S. Virgin Islands	1-2
British Virgin Islands, Anegada	possibly extirpated
Anguilla, Sombrero	a few, sporadically
TOTAL WEST INDIES	**100-500**

? – reported to breed in the past, no recent data and may be extirpated

Royal Tern (*Sterna maxima maxima*)

This large crested tern is an inhabitant of coastal margins seldom seen inland and seldom wandering more than a few kilometers from land. The Caribbean subspecies occurs from Maryland on the Atlantic Coast of North America southward through the Caribbean (Fig. 3) and along the Atlantic Coast of South America to Argentina. Royal Terns feed on a variety of fishes and crustaceans caught by plunge diving, often from several meters above the water's surface (Buckley and Buckley 1972).

Frequently Sandwich Terns (*Sterna sandvicensis*) nest together with Royals, usually in smaller numbers. Individual nests are simple scrapes in the sand that become cemented into shape by the excrement of the adults. Nest densities often reach 6 to 7 nests m^2. One egg constitutes the normal clutch, although occasionally two are present. Incubation lasts about 30 days. Chicks leave the nests when less than a week old and form a mobile creche near the colony site, often

Table 3. Number of nesting pairs of Royal Terns in the West Indies (total does not include South American colonies).

Location	Nbr. of Pairs	Reference
Bahamas; scattered Cays (75 total pairs)		Sprunt 1984
Great Bahama Bank	50-100	Sprunt 1984
Cat Island	50	J. Parnell 1998
Rum Cay	5-10	J. Parnell 1998
Conception Island (South Rocks)	14	Sprunt 1984
Great Inagua	12-20	Sprunt 1984, Parnell 1998
Hawksbill Cay	27	Buden in press
Exuma Land and Sea Park	breeds	Lee and Clark 1991
Plus miscellaneous other cays	breed sporadically	
Cuba	?	van Helewyn & Norton 1984
Jamaica, Morant Cays	30-60	A. Haynes-Sutton pers. comm.
Pedro Cays	10-20	A. Haynes-Sutton pers. comm.
Puerto Rico, Culebra	50-155	FWS 1997
U. S. Virgin Islands, fluctuates, total	150-200	J. Pierce
Cockroach E		J. Pierce
Dog Cays 25		J. Pierce
Frenchcap E		J. Pierce
Flat Cays 1-20		J. Pierce
Kalkun E		J. Pierce
Pelican Cay 1-10		J. Pierce
Turtledove 10-80		J. Pierce
Anguilla: Anguillita & Scrub Islands	a few	ICF Kaiser 1999
French Guyana, Battures de Malmanoury	100+	van Halewyn & Norton 1984
Venezuela, Las Aves	?	van Halewyn & Norton 1984
TOTAL WEST INDIES	**450-800**	

E – extirpated

? – used to breed here but no recent data and may be extirpated

along a beach. Here they are fed by their parents until they fledge at about one month of age. Only a single brood is produced each year, although re-nesting may occur if nests are destroyed early in the incubation process (Buckley and Buckley 1972).

Royal Terns are present all year throughout most of the region. Birds seen during winter are often birds that nested along the south Atlantic coast of the United States and moved into the Caribbean for the winter. Many first-year birds also summer in the Caribbean (Van Velzen 1972). Populations counts since the 1950s are sporadic, and the lack of complete surveys does not allow us to estimate numbers with any degree of accuracy. There are probably between 450 and 800 pairs in the West Indies (Table 3). The largest colonies apparently are at Battures de Malmanoury off French Guyana and at Las Aves off Venezuela (van Halewyn and Norton 1984), and off Culebra Kepler and Kepler 1977). Fifteen additional colonies have been reported from the eastern Caribbean since 1950, but these apparently are small and irregular in occurrence (van Halewyn and Norton 1984). Kepler and Kepler (1977) reported about 155 pairs in the Culebra region in 1971. Sprunt (1984) reported small colonies in the Bahamas in the 1960s and 1970s on Great Iguana; the Schooner Cays, off Eleuthera; on South Rocks, off Conception Island; and on South Cay, southeast of Andros. See Table 3 and Figure 3 for details of location, numbers and dates.

Bridled Tern (*Sterna anaethetus melanoptera*)

The Bridled Tern is a small-bodied Asiatic and tropical American seabird that breeds on scattered oceanic islands in the subtropical and tropical Atlantic, Indian and western Pacific

Table 4. Number of nesting pairs of Bridled Terns in the West Indies.

Location		Number of Pairs
Bahamas, 20 + shifting sites		1000's ±
Cuba, on several cays		B
Jamaica, Morant Cays		1000 ±
Port Royal		10-25
Portland Bight		25-40
Pedro Cays		B
Hispaniola		B
Cayman Islands, Grand Cayman		20±
Puerto Rico, 10± shifting sites, total		500-700
Culebra cays	La Cordillera	
Mona	Monito	
Guajataca Cliffs		
Desecheo		
U. S. Virgin Islands, 15 shifting sites, total		400-1000
Booby Rock	5-20	
Caraval Rock	0-30	
Cockroach Cay	10-30	
Congo Cay	25-50	
Dutchcap, Flanging, Salt Cays	B	
Frenchcap	200-400	
Little Flat Cay	50-100	
Kalkun Cay	10-20	
Saba Cay	50-200	
Turtledove Cay	25-50	

continued ....

Oceans. Bridled Terns usually breed in association with Sooty Terns (*S. fuscata*) and other seabirds although usually in much lower numbers. At a distance it can be confused with the Sooty Tern as breeding adults of both species are black and white with a white forehead stripe that extends backwards above and behind the eyes, a broad black eye stripe, and contrasting black upper and white under parts. Key diagnostic features of the Bridled Tern are a dark head separated from a lighter back by a whitish collar-band across the back of the neck, grey back, and a white line that extends farther behind the eye than the Sooty Tern. In flight, the wing-beats of Bridled Terns are relatively slow and shallow compared to Sooty Terns, and the characteristic vocalizations of the two species at their breeding sites differ substantially. Breeding is seasonal between late April and early August throughout the Caribbean.

Nests are found in loose colonies in rocky areas, usually well under large boulders or rocks, or deep under overhanging ledges on the rock face, often on the periphery of the island. Nesting

Table 4 continued ...

Location	Number of Pairs
British Virgin Islands (no counts)	B
Anegada	a few
Carrot Rock, Cistern Point, Cooper Isl., Cockroach	B
Dog Isls., Fallen Jerusalem, Green Cay, Ginger Cay	B
Round Rock	B
Necker, Norman, Peter Islands	E
Anguilla, Prickly Pear Cay East	8-12
Sombrero	300-500
St. Martin	B
Saba	B
Guadeloupe, Les Angustins	30
Grand Illet	70
Pate	50
Tillet	170
Pointe des Chateaux	60
Desirade	85
Marie Galante	14
Dominica	B
Martinique	B
Grenadines	B
TOTAL WEST INDIES	**4000-6000**

B – known to breed here but no recent data
E – extirpated

under thick vegetative cover (as in LeCroy 1976) or in the open (as noted by R. van Halewyn on Aruba) is less common. Because of this nesting situation, the single egg is often difficult to locate. Bridled Terns are wary around their nest site and usually leave to sit on a nearby rock before an observer arrives. Consequently, the egg or chick can readily escape
detection. Eggs are more finely spotted and less variable in coloration than those of Sooty Terns, with a generally brownish background.

Bridled Terns nest on islands in the Bahamas and throughout the Greater and Lesser Antilles (Fig. 4), central America and Aruba off the northeast coast of Venezuela (Lee & Booth 1979, R. de Kort pers. comm.). Specific confirmed nesting of "several thousand pairs" of the Caribbean race (*S. a. recognita*) at 20 of 56 sites throughout the Bahama Islands are given in Sprunt (1984). Van Halewyn and Norton (1984) note that the Caribbean supports a large proportion of the total Atlantic population, and that the largest numbers of breeding pairs are on the archipelago of islands between Puerto Rico and the US Virgin Islands (1000-2500 pairs at about 30 sites; Table 4, Fig. 4). Population counts of Bridled Tern pairs on islands in the Culebra (Puerto Rico) archipelago ranged from 360 in 1971 (Kepler & Kepler 1977), 487 in 1982 (Furniss 1983) to 232 in 1989 (USFWS unpubl. data in Gochfeld et al. 1994), with declining numbers in recent years (J. Saliva pers. comm.). A colony of 300-500 pairs was recently discovered on Sombrero Island (J. Pierce pers. comm.). The populations in Guadeloupe have been recently surveyed by G. Le Blonde (Table 4).

There are few breeding colonies anywhere in the Caribbean of the sizes noted for Brown Noddies and Sooty Terns. Van Halewyn & Norton (1984) list the total breeding Caribbean population at 7000 plus pairs at more than 50 colony sites. We estimate that there are between 4000 and 6000 pairs (Table 4, Fig. 4). Stiles (1984) notes the Caribbean race (*S. a. recognita)* as a rare visitor to the eastern Atlantic coast.

The literature on Bridled Tern breeding biology, ecology and behavior is impoverished and Haney et al. (1999) offer the best summary of their biology and status. Much of the other available published information is found in articles dealing with other primary species, or in the general accounts found in bird guides. Comparative studies breeding biology and feeding ecology of Sooty and Bridled Terns at the same island locations would be particularly instructive. Diamond (1976) contrasted aspects of the breeding chronology of the two species on the Seychelles in the western Indian Ocean, and LeCroy (1976) compared Sooty and Bridled Terns on Los Roques in Venezuela. LeCroy noted that compared to Sooty Terns, Bridled Terns have a more varied vocabulary, nest beneath vegetation, show a different pattern of courtship behavior, have young that do not creche, and occupy elevated "sentinel posts" near the nest.

Bridled Terns from the Culebra National Wildlife Refuge had higher levels of lead and cadmium in breast feathers than either Sooty Terns, Roseate Terns or Brown Noddies at Culebra, and higher than terns on the eastern seaboard of North America (Burger & Gochfeld 1991). While no explanation was offered for these trends, the authors recommend study of metal levels in the foods of tropical seabirds during the breeding season.

Conservation Priorities
The main threats to all seabirds at their nesting colonies in the West Indies are habitat alteration by human activities and human disturbance in colonies. The presence of introduced mammalian predators is also a large problem. Gochfeld et al. (1994) review four case studies of conservation initiatives in the West Indies that note the importance of (a) annual censusing and

surveys to track changes in population numbers, (b) habitat protection, (c) wardening and enforcement, and (d) involvement of local residents. We would add to that, introduced predators need to be removed from nesting islands.

An up to date inventory of colonies and population sizes is needed. We need to know basic natural history information on patterns of breeding and factors that affect breeding success. A number of sources note that Laughing gulls, Bridled Terns, along with Sooty Terns and Brown Noddies, are referred to locally as "egg birds", and excessive egging of them continues today. There is a long tradition among many of the people living in the Caribbean to conduct annual collections of seabird eggs, and sometimes chicks and adults. Van Halewyn (in Gochfeld et al. 1994) notes that Aruban males consider tern eggs a delicacy that have aphrodisiac properties. Patrols of colonies by wardens and public education programs are needed to improve the situation.

Several general threats to seabirds are recorded in Gochfeld et al. (1994). These include direct threats at sea (oiling, drowning in fish nets), indirect threats at sea (commercial fishery development, over fishing, toxicant contamination), and direct threats at the breeding colonies (introduced exotic or alien animals, natural predators, egging, human disturbance, tourism, habitat destruction). Some natural predators also help limit tern populations by taking eggs and small chicks. Predatory land crabs (*Gecarcinus ruricola*) are known to drag live tern chicks away from unattended nests (Burger & Gochfeld 1988). Laughing Gulls are notorious for taking eggs and small chicks of unattended tern nests.

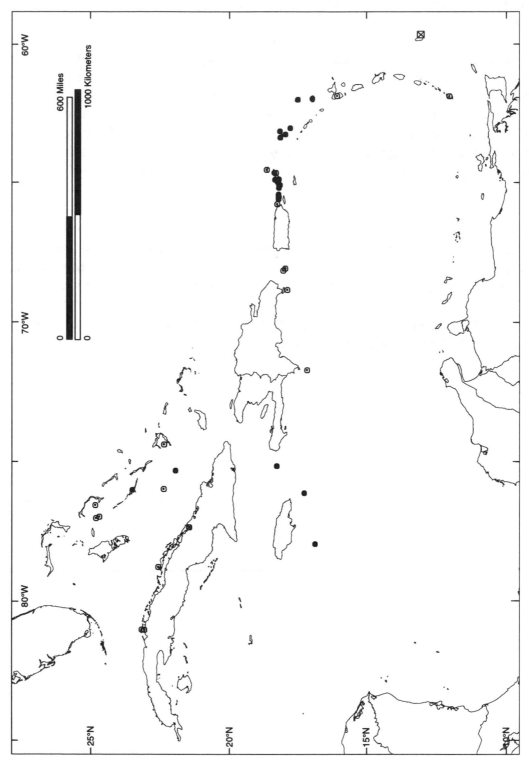

Figure 1: The status of known Laughing Gull breeding sites in the West Indies. ● = confirmed breeding location that has been surveyed recently. ⊙ = historic breeding location with no report that the colony has been extirpated. ⊠ = historic breeding location that is extirpated or thought to be extirpated.

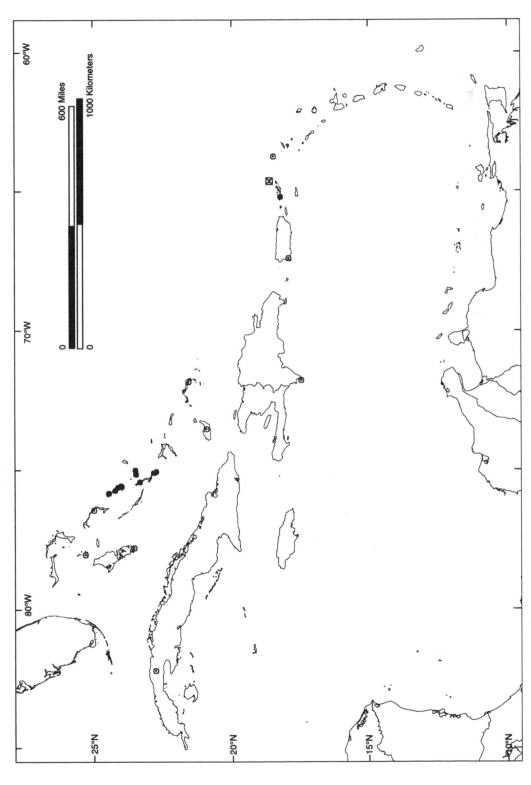

Figure 2: The status of known Gull-billed Tern breeding sites in the West Indies. ● = confirmed breeding location that has been surveyed recently. ⊙ = historic breeding location with no report that the colony has been extirpated. ⊠ = historic breeding location that is extirpated or thought to be extirpated.

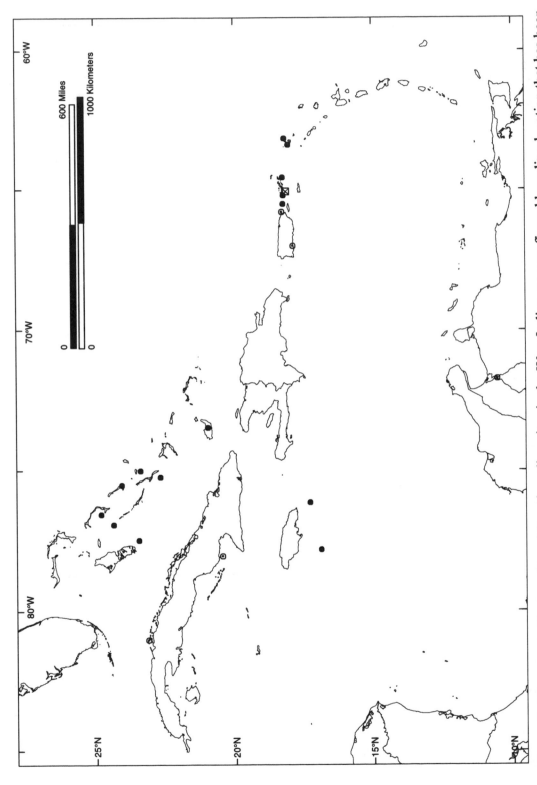

Figure 3: The status of known Royal Tern breeding sites in the West Indies. ● = confirmed breeding location that has been surveyed recently. ◎ = historic breeding location with no report that the colony has been extirpated. ⊠ = historic breeding location that is extirpated or thought to be extirpated.

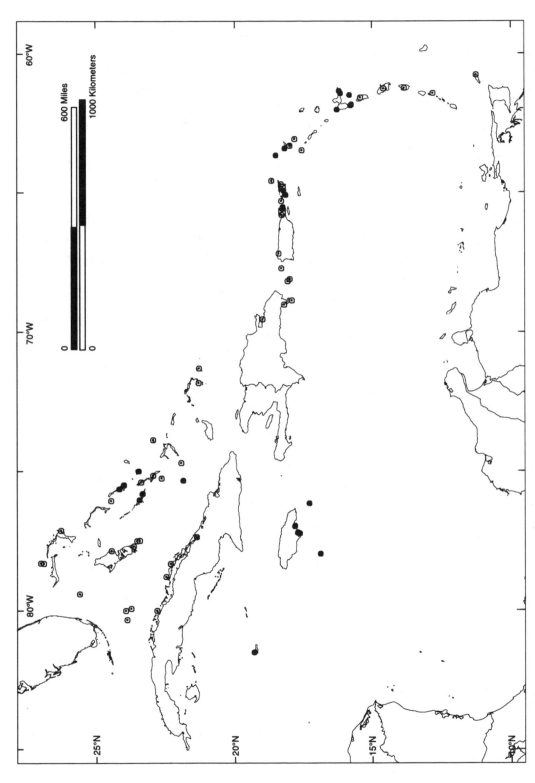

Figure 4: The status of known Bridled Tern breeding sites in the West Indies. ● = confirmed breeding location that has been surveyed recently. ☉ = historic breeding location with no report that the colony has been extirpated. ☒ = historic breeding location that is extirpated or thought to be extirpated.

Literature Cited

Buckley, P. A. and F. G. Buckley. 1972. The breeding ecology of Royal Terns *Sterna* (*Thalasseus maxima maxima*. Ibis, 114:344 - 359.

Burger, J. 1996. Laughing Gull (*Larus atricilla*). In The Birds of North America, No. 225 (A. Poole and F. Gill, eds.). The Academy of Natural Sciences, Philadelphia, PA, and The American Ornithologists' Union, Washington, D. C.

Burger, J. & M. Gochfeld. 1988. Nest-site selection by Roseate Terns in two tropical colonies on Culebra, Puerto Rico. Condor 90: 843-851.

Burger, J. & M. Gochfeld. 1991. Lead, mercury, and cadmium in feathers of tropical terns in Puerto Rico and Australia. Arch. Environ. Contamin. Toxicol. 21: 311-315.

Clapp, R. B., D. Morgan-Jacobs, and R. C. Banks. 1983. Marine birds of the southeastern United States and Gulf of Mexico. Part III: Charadriiformes. U. S. Fish Wildl. Serv., Division of Biological Services, Washington, D. C. FWS/OBS-83/30. xvi and 853 pp.

Diamond, A.W. 1976. Subannual breeding and moult cycles in the Bridled Tern Sterna anaethetus in the Seychelles. Ibis 118: 414-419.

Erickson, W. J. 1926. Gull-billed Terns breeding on the coast of Georgia. Auk 43:533-544.

Erwin, R. M. 1995. Responses to human intruders by birds nesting in colonies: experimental results and management guidelines. Colonial Waterbirds 12:104 - 108.

ffrench, R. 1991. A guide to the birds of Trinidad and Tobago. Rev. ed. Cornell Univ. Press, Ithaca NY.

Furniss, S. 1983. Status of the seabirds of the Culebra archipelago. Col. Waterbirds 6: 121-125.

Gochfeld, M., J. Burger, A. Haynes-Sutton, R. van Halewyn & J.E. Saliva. 1994. Successful approaches to seabird protection in the West Indies. Pp. 186-209 in Nettleship, D.N., J. Burger & M. Gochfeld (Eds.). Seabirds on islands: threats, case studies and action plans. Birdlife Conserv. Series 1, Birdlife International.

Haney, J. C., D. S. Lee, and R. D. Morris. 1999. Bridled Tern (*Sterna anaethetus*). In Poole, A., and F. Gill, eds. *The Birds of North America*, Inc. Philadelphia.

Howell, S. N. G., and S. Webb. 1995. A guide to the birds of Mexico and northern Central America. Oxford Univ. Press, Oxford, UK.

ICF Kaiser. 1999. Supplemental Biological surveys on Sombrero Island and other Anguillan Islands. Arlington, VA.

Kepler, C.B. & A.K. Kepler. 1977. The seabirds of Culebra and its adjacent islands, Puerto Rico. Living Bird 16: 21-50.

Lazell, J. D. Jr., 1964. The reptiles of Sombrero, West Indies. Copeia 1964: 716-717.

LeCroy, M. 1976. Bird observations in Los Roques, Venezuela. Amer. Museum Novitates No. 2599: 1-30.

Lee, D. S. and M. K. Clark. 1991. Seabirds of the Bahamas Land and Sea park, part 2. Bahamas Journal of Science 2:15-21.

Møller, A. P. 1975. Sandternens (*Gelochelidon n. nilotica* Gm.) Ynglebiologii Danmark (The breeding biology of the Gull-billed Tern {*Gelochelidon n. nilotica* Gm.} in Denmark; English summary). Dan. Ornithol. Foren. Tidssk. 69:9-18.

Møller, A. P. 1981. Breeding cycle of the Gull-billed Tern (Gelochelidon nilotica) especially in relation to colony size. Ardea 69:193-198.

Nisbet, I. C. T. 1971. The Laughing Gull in the northeast. American Birds 25: 677-683.

Norton 1982. West Indian Region. American Birds 36:1019-1020.

Parnell, J. F., R. M. Erwin and K. C. Molina. 1995. Gull-billed Tern (*Sterna nilotica*). *In* The Birds of North America, No. 140 (A. Poole and F. Gull, eds.). The Academy of Natural Sciences, Philadelphia and the American Ornithologists' Union, Washington, D. C.

Schreiber, E. A., R. W. Schreiber, and J. J. Dinsmore. 1979. Breeding biology of Laughing Gulls in Florida. Part I: nesting, egg and incubation parameters. Bird-banding 50: 304-321.

Sears, H. F. 1978. Nesting behavior of the Gull-billed Tern. Bird-Banding 49:1-16.

Sprunt, A. IV. 1984. Seabirds of the Bahama Islands. *In* Status and conservation of the world's seabirds (J.P. Croxall, P.G.H. Evans, and R.W. Schreiber, Eds.). ICBP Tech. Publ. No. 2. Pp. 157-168

Stiles, F.G. 1984. Status and conservation of seabirds in Costa Rican waters. Pp. 223-229 in Status and conservation of the world's seabirds (J.P. Croxall, P.G.H. Evans, and R.W. Schreiber, Eds.). ICBP Tech. Publ. No. 2

van Halewyn, R. & R.L. Norton. 1984. The status and conservation of seabirds in the Caribbean. *In* Status and conservation of the world's seabirds (J.P. Croxall, P.G.H. Evans, and R.W. Schreiber, Eds.). ICBP Tech. Publ. No. 2. Pp. 169-222

VanVelzen, W. T. 1972. Recoveries of Royal Terns banded in Virginia, Pt. I: The Caribbean. The Raven 43:39-41.

Voous, K. H. 1983. Birds of the Netherlands Antilles. Walburg Press, Netherlands.

Witherby, H. F. 1941. The handbook of British birds. Vol. 5. H. F. & G. Witherby, London.

Status and conservation of Sandwich and Cayenne Terns in the West Indies

_____ ‏ଔ ଔ ଔ ଔ   ଜ ଜ ଜ ଜ _____

ROBERT. L. NORTON

Alachua County Environmental Protection Dept., Gainesville, FL 32601, USA, Email rnorton@co.alachua.fl.us

Introduction

The genetic relationship of Sandwich (_Sterna sandvicensis_) and Cayenne Terns (_S. s. eurygnatha_ or _S. eurygnatha_) is not well understood and some authors consider them to be one species with separate subspecies while others consider them to be two species (Shealer 1999), a fact which clouds the history of their population sizes. Currently they are regarded as one species (AOU 1998, Shealer 1999), and some limited interbreeding apparently occurs (Junge and Voous 1955). I will give separate accounts of them here since both breed in the West Indies and they are distinguishable from each other. Interim forms are seen occasionally at colonies in Puerto Rico and the Virgin Islands (mottled yellow and black bills) indicating interbreeding (Shealer 1999). _S. sandvicensis_ has also hybridized with _S. elegans_ in southern California. Little is known of the current breeding locations or status of either Sandwich or Cayenne Terns in the Caribbean region owing to a lack of surveys and confusion about identification of tern species. They have been subject to various types of disruption and exploitation in the last century and their continued long-term success in the Atlantic tropics could well be in doubt.

They eat mainly small marine crustaceans, fish and squid, feeding along coastal areas (Shealer 1999). They generally feed in small flocks with other species of terns or with frigatebirds and boobies. Prey are caught by diving from the air. Often they are found nesting in colonies with Royal Terns, Roseate Terns and Laughing Gulls (Shealer 1999). Both species nest on bare sandy areas of islands near borders of vegetation, avoiding rougher, shell covered substrate. Laying takes place mainly in May in the Caribbean and the 1-2 eggs are laid in a depression in the sand which may be lined with seaweed or bits of shell. Incubation lasts from 23 to 25 days and chicks fledge at about 25-28 days, although this may take longer in poor food years (Shealer 1999).

General Distribution and Population Size

Sandwich Terns. Audubon reported Sandwich Terns from Florida in May, 1832 to be new to the list of North American birds. He had never seen it at any other location between the Florida Keys and Charleston, South Carolina, and presumed that it originally arrived from Europe. North American populations have been documented since about 1908 when northward movement of breeding birds as far north as Maryland (Clapp at al. 1983) was reported. They breed on the Atlantic coast of North America in Virginia, North Carolina, South Carolina and Florida, along the Gulf coast from southern Texas east to southern Mississippi , Alabama and Florida. In the Old World they breed from the British Isles and southern Scandinavia south to the Mediterranean, Black and Caspian Seas.

Table 1. Location of nesting colonies of Sandwich Terns and number of nesting pairs.

Location	Number of Pairs	Date of Survey
Bahamas, Great Bahama Bank	400	July 1977
Exuma	250-350	1997-1998
Ragged Island	?	
Bird Rock	?	1979
Hogsty Reef	150	May 1979
Great Inagua	100-150	1998
Miscellaneous other islets	B	
Turks and Caicos, West Caicos	suspected	
Jamaica, Pedro Cays	10-20	1997
Cuba, Los Canarreos	?	
Puerto Rico, Culebra,	fewer than 50	D. Shealer pers. comm. 1998
southwest	465	D. Shealer pers. comm. 1998
British Virgin Is., Anegada	E	June 1997
Green Cay	50-80	June 1997
Beef Island	E	June 1997
U. S. Virgin Is., scattered islets, varies		
Cricket Cay	E	June 1997
Dog Islands	100-800	1994-1997
Flat Cay	28	May 1978
Hans Lollick	E	1994-1997
Pelican Cay	50-300	1994-1997
Turtledove Cay	50-250	1994-1997
Anguilla, Sombrero	?	May 1980
WEST INDIES TOTAL	**2100-3000**	

B – breeds in unknown numbers
? – used to breed but no recent reports
E – extirpated

The first colony in the West Indies was found in 1965 (Buckley and Buckley 1984). In the Caribbean they breed on various islands in the Bahamas, probably off southern Cuba, off Jamaica, on islets in the Virgin Islands, possibly on Sombrero (although none were seen breeding in 1998; J. Pierce pers. comm.), off Yucatan (Cayo Arcas, Alacran Reef), off Belize, on Curaçao and on Trinidad. Sandwich Terns were formerly more widespread in the western Caribbean off Belize, but are now considered extirpated there. One of the earliest estimates of this species in the Bahamas (Sprunt 1984) is from Great Inagua: 150 pairs in 1967 and 125 pairs in 1972. In 1971, 735 pairs were reported on Culebra, Puerto Rico (Kepler and Kepler 1978). This estimate remained fairly consistent a decade later in 1982 and 1983 but had dwindled to fewer than 50 pairs by the 1990's (D. Shealer pers. comm., Table 1). Southwestern Puerto Rico is reported to have about 465 pairs during the 1990's (D. Shealer pers. comm.). They have been extending their range northward in the Caribbean during the past 20 years (Norton 1984; Table 1, Fig. 1). A small number of Sandwich Terns nest at Aruba and Bonaire. The entire Caribbean population may total no more than 2100 - 3000 pairs.

Cayenne Terns. If Cayenne Terns bred in the West Indies before 1962, their populations were overlooked as they were not reported in the literature (Buckley and Buckley 1984). Currently a large portion of the world population breeds in the Netherlands Antilles which van Halewyn (1985) has estimated at over 9000 pairs. This number may be declining as a result of egging and pollution (Table 2). Murphy (1936) noted that this species has an extensive range along the Caribbean and Atlantic coasts of South American. They currently nest in Puerto Rico (Culebra Island), the Virgin Islands (sometimes paired with Sandwich Terns), in the Netherlands Antilles, on islands off the coast of Venezuela (Las Aves, Los Roques), on Soldado Rock off northern Trinidad (sometimes considered to be Sandwich Terns), off Guyana, and along the coast of Brazil (north to Espirito Santo) and southern Argentina (LeCroy 1976, van Halewyn and Norton 1984, Gochfeld et al. 1994, Tostain et al. 1992, J. Pierce pers. comm.; Table 2, Fig. 2). The size of the West Indies population is not well known but probably numbers between 10 and 100 pairs. There may be more nesting sites of Cayenne Terns but owing to confusion with Sandwich Terns, they have not been recognized. Because the two species apparently interbreed, observers need to carefully record plumage and bill characteristics of the birds.

Table 2. Location of nesting colonies of Cayenne Terns and number of nesting pairs in the West Indies (Netherlands Antilles and Venezuela not included in total).

Location	Number of Pairs
Puerto Rico, Culebra	a few
U.S. Virgin Is., Pelican Cay	a few
British Virgin Is., Anegada	a few
Trinidad, Soldado Rock	a few
Netherlands Antilles, Curaçao	1600
Bonaire	fewer than 4000
Aruba	3500
Venezuela, Las Aves & Los Roques	100's
Margarite Island	1000
Guyana, Battures de Malmonoury	1200
Connétable	200-800
WEST INDIES TOTAL	**10 - 100**

Conservation Status and Research Needs

There are many threats to the Caribbean population of Sandwich and Cayenne Terns. The taking of eggs for food remains a problem in many places (Schaffner et al. 1986, J. Pierce pers. comm.). The presence of rats and other mammalian predators on nesting islands causes the loss of many eggs and young. Avian predators on their eggs, such as Laughing Gulls (Larus atricilla) and Oystercatchers (Haematopus ostralgus), often nest on the same islands preferred by Sandwich and Cayenne Terns. There is a continuing conflict between human interests (fisheries, tourism, development of beach areas) and the birds needs (safe nesting sites). This may be the greatest threat to the survival of both species. The development of and disturbance of beach sites is a threat to many seabird species. The impact of curious boaters landing on isolated islands is a threat no matter how well intentioned a visit might be.

Another threat is that from pollution, either from direct oil spills or hydrocarbons passed on through the food chain. The largest colonies of these species are located very near oil refineries of the southern Caribbean. Feeding and nesting requirements of these Sterna species, and other seabirds, leave them vulnerable to diminishing resources resulting in ever smaller populations. Pollution is not as great a threat in the Virgin Islands as it may be in heavily trafficked ports such as San Juan.

Continued monitoring efforts are needed to establish population sizes and management plans for both these species. Colonies should be censused several times annually in order to determine colony sizes and nesting success. A minimum of weekly monitoring visits to nesting sites would help to prevent egging and reduce intrusion by boaters. Nesting islands should be posted against trespassing. Only authorized individuals should be allowed access. Authorized individuals could be scientists and researchers, or wardens managing the colony for predation control, weed control, boating disturbance, etc.

The genetic relationships of Sandwich and Cayenne Terns should be examined throughout their range to determine if they are one species (with two subspecies) or if they are two species. As the potential for pollution increases in the marine environment, tissue samples should be collected periodically to identify potential trends of increasing pollutants in the birds. Oceanographic data should be collected to determine whether sea-level rise is occurring and at what rate, in order to predict the short- and long-term effects on seabird ecology and populations.

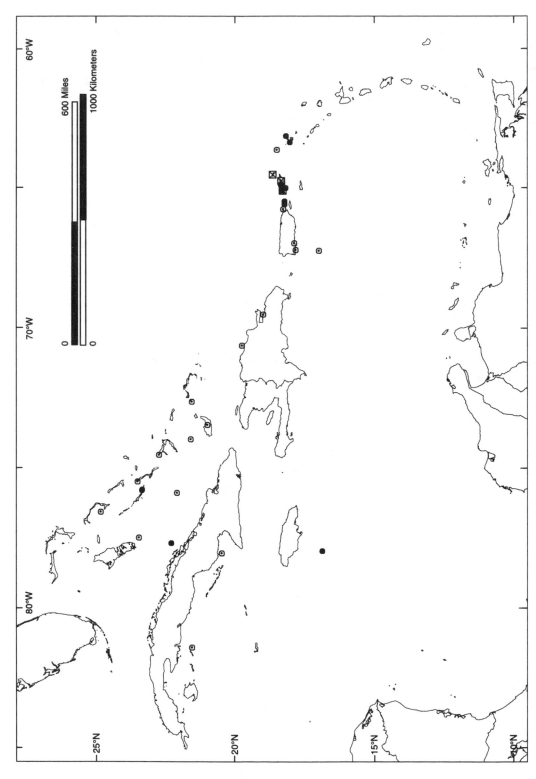

Figure 1: The status of known Sandwich Tern breeding sites in the West Indies. ● = confirmed breeding location that has been surveyed recently. ⊡ = historic breeding location with no report that the colony has been extirpated. ⊠ = historic breeding location that is extirpated or thought to be extirpated.

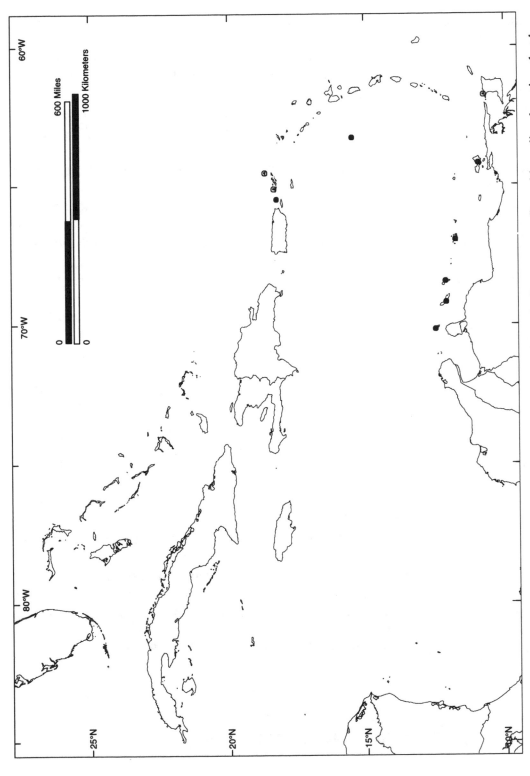

Figure 2: The status of known Cayenne Tern breeding sites in the West Indies. ● = confirmed breeding location that has been surveyed recently. ☉ = historic breeding location with no report that the colony has been extirpated. ⊠ = historic breeding location that is extirpated or thought to be extirpated.

Literature Cited

Buckley. P. A. and F. G. Buckley. 1984. Cayenne Tern new to North America, with comments on its relationship to Sandwich Terns. Auk 101: 396-398.

Clapp, R.B., D. Morgan-Jacobs, and R. C. Banks. 1983. Marine birds of the Southeastern United States and Gulf of Mexico. Part III. Charadriiformes. U.S. Fish and Wildlife Service, Division of Biological Services, Washington, D.C.

Gochfeld, M., J. Burger, A. Haynes-Sutton, R. van Halewyn, and J. Saliva. 1994. Successful approaches to seabird protection in the West Indies. BirdLife Conservation Series 1: 186-209.

Junge, G. C. A., and A. K. Voous. 1955. The distribution and relationship of *Sterna eurygnatha* Saunders. Ardea 43: 226-247.

Kepler, C. B. and A. K. Kepler. 1978. The sea birds of Culebra and adjacent islands., Puerto Rico. Living Bird 16: 21-50.

LeCroy, M. 1976. Bird observations in Los Roques, Venezuela. American Museum Novitates. No. 2599. 30 pp.

Murphy, R. C. 1936. Oceanic birds of South America. MacMillam Co., Am. Mus. Nat Hist. New York

Norton, R. L. 1984. Cayenne x Sandwich terns nesting in the Virgin Islands, Greater Antilles. J. Field Ornithol. 55: 243-246.

Schaffner, F. C., R. L. Norton and J. Taylor. 1986. Range extension of Cayenne terns on the Puerto Rico Bank. Wilson Bull. 98(2): 317-318.

Shealer, D. 1999. Sandwich Tern (Sterna sandvicensis). No. 405 in A. Poole, and F. Gill, eds., *The Birds of North America*, The Birds of North America, Inc. Philadelphia, PA.

Sprunt, A. IV. 1984. The status and conservation of seabirds of the Bahama Islands. Pp 157- 168, in J. P. Croxall, P. G. H. Evans, and R. W. Schreiber, eds. *Status and Conservation of the World's Seabirds*, Cambridge, U.K.: International Council for Bird Preservation (Tech. Publ.) 2.

Tostain, O., J.-L. Dujardin, C. Erard, and J.-M. Thiollay. 1992. Oiseaux de Guyane. Société d'Études Ornithologiques, Brunoy, France.

van Halewyn, R. 1985. Marine birds of Aruba. Report on 1985 and conservation campaign. Res. Inst. Nat. Manag. Arnhem, Netherlands.

van Halewyn, R., and R. L. Norton. 1984. The status and conservation of seabirds in the Caribbean. Pp. 169-222 in J. P. Croxall, P. G. H. Evans, and R. W. Schreiber, eds. *Status and Conservation of the World's Seabirds*, Cambridge, U.K.: International Council for Bird Preservation (Tech. Publ.) 2.

Voous, K. H. 1983. Birds of the Netherlands Antilles. De Walberg Press. Zutphen, The Netherlands. 327 pp.

Conservation Priorities for Roseate Terns in the West Indies

ᏣᏣᏣᏣ   ᏋᏋᏋᏋ

JORGE E. SALIVA

U.S. Fish and Wildlife Service, P. O. Box 491, Boqueron, Puerto Rico 00622, U.S.A., Email
jorge_saliva@fws.gov

Introduction

The West Indian population of the Roseate Tern (*Sterna dougallii*) breeds from Florida through the West Indies to islands off Central America and northern South America. Roseate Terns also breed in North America, the Palearctic, Indian Ocean, southern Africa, and Australasia. In addition to the North American population, the European and southern African populations are endangered (Nisbet 1980, Randall and Randall 1980, Gochfeld 1983). The history and status of the Caribbean colonies are little known. Much of our knowledge of the status and distribution of birds in the West Indies was compiled by Bond (1958), who originally misidentified Caribbean Roseate Terns as Common Terns (*Sterna hirundo*) because of the similarity in their bill coloration (Furniss 1983). Failure to distinguish between the two species makes it difficult to reconstruct the history of Roseate Terns in the Caribbean. Reliable information on the distribution of these two species in the Caribbean first became available in 1984 (van Halewyn and Norton 1984). This report updates that account.

The Roseate Tern has a black crown, pale grey upper surface and immaculate white underparts. Both the upper and under surfaces are paler than in the very similar Common Tern. The long tail streamers are pure white and extend past the folded wing tips; whereas those of Common Terns are grayish with a black outer margin and do not extend past the wing tips. Male and female Roseate Terns are essentially identical in size and color. In non-breeding plumage, both Common and Roseate Terns have a dark carpal bar over the bend of the wing, although it is slightly lighter in Roseate Terns. During the breeding season only the tip of the bill of the Caribbean birds is black; the basal three-quarters is reddish orange, unlike the northeastern Roseate Terns (Shealer and Saliva 1992).

When Roseate Terns arrive at their colonies in the Caribbean their bills are mostly black, with the basal quarter reddish orange. By the time egg-laying begins, the basal three-fourths of the bill is reddish-orange, and this condition remains until after the chicks fledge and adults leave their breeding colonies (Saliva, pers. obs.). At this time, the red on the bill starts fading and the forehead begins to lose its black color. After the breeding season, most adults lose the tail streamers and the forehead becomes whitish.

In the Caribbean, Roseate Terns breed primarily on small offshore islands, or marine rocks, cays, and islets (Burger and Gochfeld 1988, Norton 1988, Shealer 1995: Table 1, Fig. 1). Rarely do they breed on large islands (e.g., Punta Soldado, Culebra in 1989 and 1991, Saliva, pers. obs.). On Culebra and the Virgin Islands the birds constantly shift locations from year to year moving from one small islet to another, possibly as a result of human disturbance. Nisbet (1980, 1989) reviewed accounts of Roseate Tern habitat use in the northeast United States where they typically nest under vegetation or other shelter (Spendelow 1982). This is not characteristic of the Caribbean birds where they nest near vegetation or jagged limestone rock (Robertson 1976, Voous 1983, Burger and Gochfeld 1988), on open sandy beaches (Robertson 1976), close to the water line on narrow ledges of emerging rocks (R. Norton and J. Pierce, pers. comm.), or among coral rubble (Saliva, pers. obs.). Although they may nest on slopes up to 70 degree angle, they generally seek flat or even back-sloping ledges for their nests. Most of them add little or no material to the nest but lay their eggs directly on the ground, rock, or vegetation.

Roseate Terns in the Caribbean usually begin egg laying in mid May, and hatching occurs from mid-June through early July. However, they may abandon a nesting area, re-lay on the same island, or move to up to three different islands in one breeding period. Sometimes laying may be reinitiated as late as mid-July, after the terns have attempted to nest on several islands (Saliva, pers. obs.). Reasons for failing on one island and moving to another are not always known since colonies are not monitored, but most likely are related to human disturbance.

Population Status

In the West Indies, there are very few published data on Roseate Tern colony sizes so that historical and current estimates of the population for the area are speculative (Table 1, Fig. 1). The only long documented history is that of the Dry Tortugas population (Robertson 1964). The history of the northeastern U. S. population has been summarized (Nisbet 1980, 1989; Gochfeld 1983; Kirkham and Nettleship 1987) and these accounts document the dramatic reduction of all species of terns in the late 19th century owing to market hunting, egging and, particularly, the millinery trade. In the U. S., nearly universal bird protection was instituted in 1913 with the passage of the Migratory Bird Treaty Act, significantly curtailing the exploitation of the past century. Following protection, Roseate Tern populations slowly recovered until the 1950's and 1960's when, somewhat erratically, they began to decline again. In the 1970's the decline became alarming, particularly in the face of a general increase in the population of Common Terns with which the Roseate Terns nest in the northeast (Buckley and Buckley 1981).

Potential predators on Roseate Tern in the West Indies include Magnificent Frigatebirds (*Fregata magnificens*), Laughing Gulls (*Larus atricilla*), Red-tailed Hawks (*Buteo jamaicensis*), Peregrine Falcons (*Falco peregrinus*), American Kestrels (*Falco sparverius*), Short-eared Owls (*Asio flammeus*), Cattle Egrets (*Bubulcus ibis*), Night Herons (*Nycticorax nycticorax*), Ruddy Turnstones (*Arenaria interpres*), American Oystercatchers (*Haematopus palliatus*), mockingbirds (*Mimus gilvus*), hermit crabs (*Coenobita clypeatus*), land crabs (*Gecarcinus ruricola*), marine or sally lightfoot crabs (*Grapsus grapsus*), feral cats, and rats (Saliva and Burger 1989). Mostly eggs and small chicks are taken by these predators.

Nisbet (1989) reported that Roseate Terns tend to shift colonies quickly in response to predation or reproductive failure. The number of potential predators found in or near some of the Caribbean Roseate Tern colonies (Saliva and Burger 1989, Shealer and Burger 1992) may be an important factor explaining the poor colony-site fidelity, aggressive behavior, and lower reproductive success of this species in some of those areas.

In the Caribbean, humans take eggs for food or linger on nesting islands causing fatal disturbance (J. Pierce and D. Shealer, pers. comm.). Egging is perhaps the major factor threatening many of the Caribbean colonies (van Halewyn and Norton 1984, J. Pierce pers. comm.). Human residential, commercial, and recreational activities in proximity to Roseate Tern colonies is a significant source of disturbance to breeding terns. Although terns can habituate to some human disturbance, it does nonetheless cause chicks to run from nesting ledges or may keep adults off their nests, allowing predators to steal eggs.

According to Nisbet (1980), the Virgin Islands population ranged from 750 to 1,500 pairs, Culebra Island held 325, Florida up to 200, the Exumas up to 200 pairs, and Antigua 50 pairs. Formerly, Roseate Tern colonies were reported in the Grenadines in 1902, Grenada in 1935, Dominica from 1941 to 1951, and Islas Las Aves in 1956 (Table 1). Many potential breeding sites have rarely been visited. Nisbet (1980) estimated the West Indian population to be 1,500 to 2,000 pairs. Van Halewyn and Norton (1984) argued that there was no evidence of a decreasing population and estimated the Puerto Rico-Virgin Islands population at 2,500 pairs. They concluded that the regional West Indian population was greater than 2,500 pairs and put the maximum at about 4,000 pairs but many areas were not surveyed at that point. Based on monitoring of Roseate Tern colonies in Puerto Rico and the Virgin Islands since 1990 and reports from biologists in other Caribbean countries, the estimated number of breeding pairs in the West Indies today is between 4,000 and 6,000 pairs (Table 1, Fig. 1).

Conservation Needs
The greatest challenge in the conservation of the Roseate Tern in the West Indies is the monitoring of colonies to determine population size and breeding success to assess the stability of the Caribbean metapopulation. Most countries in the West Indies have limited manpower and economic resources to study, manage, and protect the Roseate Tern. The fact that the Caribbean has large areas of potential Roseate Tern breeding habitat (e.g., the Bahamas), and Roseate Terns have low philopatry, monitoring of all potential sites becomes impractical for many countries. The protection of currently known Roseate Tern breeding areas, therefore, should be given the highest priority.
Conservation programs that promote the protection of Roseate Tern colonies should be developed. Posting of breeding areas, regular patrolling of these areas during the breeding season, limiting recreational use, and developing techniques for predator control are examples of programs necessary to achieve protection of breeding terns. The recovery of this species will depend on the development of these programs and on coordinating efforts with all the different countries involved (USFWS 1993).

Ownership of sites used by Roseate Terns should be determined to effect protective measures. Landowners in these areas should be appraised of the importance of their land for breeding terns, and appropriate guidance should be provided to them as to how to avoid disturbance to nesting terns. Government agencies and entities with jurisdiction over Roseate Tern colonies should become involved in the education of the public on general conservation values, as well as on the importance of protecting this species and adhering to government regulations. One step could be the preparation of an illustrated brochure to be distributed to local groups, schools, and organizations.

Management of breeding habitat may be necessary to increase Roseate Tern reproductive success, particularly when coupled with predator control programs. Based on the available information on Roseate Tern habitat selection in Caribbean colonies, it appears as if the preferred nesting areas have little or no vegetation cover. However, the terns seem to like some type of shelter near the nests. Therefore, a vegetation control program should be developed with guidance from knowledgeable biologists to prevent vegetation encroachment into nesting areas.

In otherwise suitable areas where Roseate Terns breed, sometimes nearby shelters such as rocks, boulders, or logs are not available. This situation renders eggs and younger chicks vulnerable to predators. Artificial shelters (e.g., nest boxes, tires, logs, coral crevices) should be provided were natural shelters are scarce. Roseate Terns usually select areas where a depression can be excavated in soft terrain to receive the eggs, or where a natural cavity or shelter exists. In cases where these are not available, artificial shelters may be provided.

The presence of predators at Roseate Tern colonies may result in nest abandonment or direct predation on eggs, young, or adult terns (Shealer and Burger 1992). Therefore, the effect of potential predators on breeding Roseate Terns should be evaluated and appropriate management techniques to prevent or deter predators should be implemented. Individual avian predators may specialize in preying on terns, and may regularly visit tern nesting areas to feed. Whenever possible, these nuisance birds should be scared off or trapped and relocated away from Roseate Tern colonies. Hermit and land crabs prey upon hatchlings and very young terns. However, it seems as if chicks are vulnerable to these predators only when adult terns are disturbed off the nests by people. Otherwise, adult terns usually prevent crabs from getting close to the nests. Some species of ants (e.g., *Solenopsis invicta*) may kill young terns when eggs are pipping or soon after hatching. The use of ant poisons or traps in areas of high incidence of these insects may be necessary.

Poaching of eggs is an important human factor affecting Roseate Terns. In some areas egging is legal, but there is no control on the number of eggs collected. For endangered or threatened species, such as the Roseate Tern, egging should be illegal. In areas where egging is illegal, governments may not have the facilities or manpower to patrol tern colonies to prevent it. Patrolling colonies during incubation, coupled with education of nearby communities may be the best tools to prevent poaching.

Although studies on the biology of the Roseate Tern in some parts of the Caribbean have been conducted (Burger and Gochfeld 1988, Shealer and Burger 1992, Shealer and Saliva 1992, Shealer 1995), these have been limited to very few colonies. Additional research is needed on the genetics of the West Indies metapopulation, as well as colony-site fidelity, to determine the degree of intermixing between sub colonies. Preliminary information from banded birds suggests that some populations may not intermix, whereas others do (Saliva, unpub. data). Banded Roseate Terns from Culebra and the Virgin Islands, for example, have been recorded breeding at either location, whereas no exchange has been observed between Roseate Terns from these two areas and western Puerto Rico (Saliva, unpub. data).

The implementation of conservation measures to maintain, protect, and enhance populations of the Roseate Tern, with the contribution and coordination of all Caribbean countries where this species breeds and winters, will ensure a self-sustaining Roseate Tern metapopulation in the West Indies.

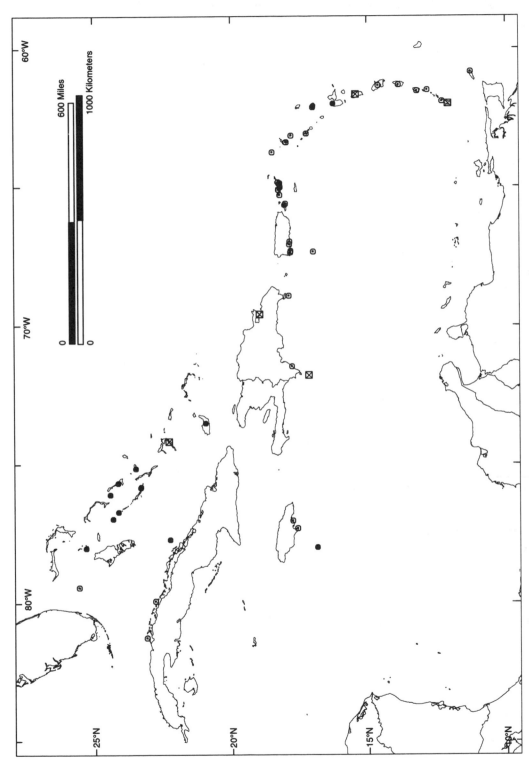

Figure 1: The status of known Roseate Tern breeding sites in the West Indies. ● = confirmed breeding location that has been surveyed recently. ☉ = historic breeding location with no report that the colony has been extirpated. ⊠ = historic breeding location that is extirpated or thought to be extirpated.

Table 1. Known breeding sites and estimated number of breeding pairs of Roseate Terns in the West Indies (Netherlands Antilles and South American colonies are not considered part of the West Indies).

Location	Historical Colony Size	Current Colony Size
Bahamas	100-200	?
Cuba	A	C
Jamaica, Pedro Cays	B	3-5
Portland Bight	A	?
Haiti	B	?
Dominican Republic, Beata Island	12-20	C
Puerto Rico, Culebra cays	5-325	5-30
La Parguera	A	300-650
Guayanilla	A	2-350
Barceloneta/Manatí	A	75-200
U. S. Virgin Islands, Booby Rock	A	E
Carval Rock	A	E
Dog Island	A	E
Flanagan Island	A	200-1000 sporadically
Flat Cays	A	20-200
Kalkun Cay	A	50-350 sporadically
Le Duck Island	A	500-800
Pelican Cay	A	100-400 sporadically
Saba Island	A	20-400
Shark Island	A	100-800
British Virgin Islands, Carrot Rock	A	0-20
Cockroach	A	0-600
Dog Islands	A	C
Fallen Jerusalem	A	0-20
Green Cay	A	C
Guana Island	A	E
Indian Rocks	A	C
Round Rock	A	C
Anguilla, Sombrero Island	A	30-40
Antigua	50	50 ?
Dominica	A	C
St. Kitts	A	100-200
St. Martin	24+	?
St. Lucia	A	?
Grenada	A	?
Grenadines	A	?
Guadeloupe	A	C

continued -

Table 1 continued –

Location	Historical Colony Size	Current Colony Size
Martinique	B	C
Nevis	B	?
Tobago	500-1,000	?
Aruba	A	C
Bonaire	A	?
Curaçao	20-40	?
Venezuela	A	?
Honduras	A	?
TOTAL	**5,000-10,000**	**4,000-6,000**

A= Breeding reported before 1984, but number of pairs not known.
B= Breeding suspected, but not confirmed.
C= Breeding reported after 1984, but number of pairs not known.
?= Used to breed but no recent reports.
E – extirpated.

Cory 1891a, Cory 1891b, Noble 1916, Wetmore 1927, Wetmore and Swales 1931, Danforth 1936, Bond 1941, Devas 1942, Bond 1950, Phelps and Phelps 1955, Voous 1957, Bond 1958, Van der Werf et al. 1958, Pinchon 1963, Montaña and Garrido 1965, Pelzl 1969, Bond 1970, Dinsmore 1972, Garrido and Montaña 1975, LeCroy 1976, Robertson 1976, Holland and Williams 1978, Buckley and Buckley 1981, Prys-Jones 1982, Spendelow 1982, Gochfeld 1983, Voous 1983, van Halewyn and Norton 1984, Sprunt 1984, Ogden et al.1985, van Halewyn 1987, Norton 1987, Nisbet 1989, Saliva and Burger 1989, Shealer and Burger 1992, Shealer and Saliva 1992, Shealer 1995.

Literature Cited

Bond, J. 1941. Nidification of the birds of Dominica, British West Indies. Auk 58:364-375.
Bond, J. 1950. Check-list of the birds of the West Indies. Philadelphia, Acad. Nat. Sci., 163.
Bond, J. 1958. Third supplement to the Check-list of birds of the West Indies (1956). Acad. Nat. Sci. Phila., Philadelphia. 11 pp.
Bond, J. 1970. Native and winter resident birds of Tobago. Philadelphia, Acad. Nat. Sci., 89 pp.
Buckley, P. A. and F. G. Buckley. 1981. The endangered status of North American roseate terns. Colonial Waterbirds 4:166-173.
Burger, J. and M. Gochfeld. 1988. Nest-site selection by roseate terns in two tropical colonies on Culebra, Puerto Rico. Condor 90:843-851.

Cory, C. B. 1891a. A collection of birds taken by Cyrus S. Winch in the islands of Anguilla, Antigua, and St. Eustatius, West Indies during April, May, June, and part of July 1890. Auk.8:46-47.

Cory, C. B. 1891b. List of birds collected on the island of Inagua, Bahama Islands from May 1 to July 10, 1891. Auk 8:5.

Danforth, S. T. 1936. The Birds of St. Kitts and Nevis. Tropical Agric. 13:213-217.

Devas, R. P. 1942. Birds of Grenada, St.Vincent and the Grenadines, 92 pp. (Published privately).

Dinsmore, J.J. 1972. Birds of Little Tobago. Quart. J. Florida Acad. Sci. 355:55-71.

Garrido, O. H. and F. G. Montaña. 1975. Catálogo de las aves de Cuba. Habana, Acad. Cienc. Cuba, 208 pp.

Gochfeld, M. 1983. World status and distribution of the roseate tern, a threatened species. Biol. Conserv. 25:103-125.

Furniss, S. 1983. Status of the seabirds of the Culebra Archipelago, Puerto Rico. Colonial Waterbirds 6:121-125.

Holland, C. S. and J. M. Williams. 1978. Observations on the Birds of Antigua. Amer. Birds 32: 1095-1105.

Kirkham, I. R. and D. N. Nettleship. 1987. Status of the roseate tern in Canada. J. Field Ornithol. 58:505-515.

LeCroy, M.1976.Bird observations in Los Roques, Venezuela. Amer. Mus. Novitates 2599: 1-30.

Montaña, F. G. and Garrido, O. H. 1965. Nuevos registros de nidificación de aves en Cuba. Poeyana 9:1-3.

Nisbet, I. C. T. 1980. Status and trends of the roseate tern (*Sterna dougallii*) in North America and the Caribbean. U.S. Fish & Wildlife Service, Contract Report 50181-084-9, Newton Corner, Massachusetts, 52 pp.

Nisbet, I. C. T. 1989. Status and biology of the northeastern population of the roseate tern Sterna dougallii: a literature survey and update 1981-1989. Report prepared for U.S. Fish and Wildlife Service, Massachusetts, 68 pp.

Noble, G. K. 1916. The resident birds of Guadeloupe. Bull. Mus.Comp. Zool. Harvard Coll. 60 (10), 18 pp.

Norton, R. L. 1987. West Indies Region. American Birds 41:1491-1492.

Norton, R. L. 1988. Extra-egg clutches and interspecific egg-dumping of the roseate tern (*Sterna dougallii*) in the West Indies. Florida Field Naturalist 16:67-70.

Ogden, N. B., W. G. Gladfelter, J. C. Ogden and E. H. Gladfelter. 1985. Marine and terrestrial flora an fauna notes on Sombrero Island in the Caribbean. Atoll Research Bull. 292:61-74.

Pelzl, H. W. 1969. Preliminary Report: Birds of the British Honduras Keys. Unpublished Manuscript in American Museum of Natural History, 11 pp.

Phelps, W. H. and W. H. Phelps, Jr. 1955. Seven new birds from Cerro de la Neblina, Territorio Amazonas, Venezuela. Proc. Biol. Soc. Wash. 68: 113-124.

Pinchon, P. R. 1963. Fauna des Antilles Francaises. Les Oiseaux. Fort-de-France, Martinique, 211 pp.

Prys-Jones, R. P 1982. A synopsis of the status and ecology of the birds of Dominica. Percy Fitzpatrick Institute, Rondebosch, South Africa, 43 pp.

Randall, R. M. and B. M. Randall. 1980. Status and distribution of the roseate tern in South Africa. Ostrich 51:14-20.

Robertson, W.B., Jr. 1964. The terns of the Dry Tortugas. Bull. Fl. State Mus. Biol. Sci. 8:1-95.

Robertson, W. B., Jr. 1976. Birds in Rare and Endangered Biota of Florida. H. W. Kale and P.S. Pritchard, eds., Florida Univ. Press, Gainesville, 332 pp.

Saliva, J. E. and J. Burger. 1989. Effect of experimental manipulation of vegetation density on nest-site selection in sooty terns. Condor 91:689-698.

Shealer, D. A. 1995. Comparative feeding ecology of roseate and sandwich terns in Puerto Rico and its relation to breeding performance. Ph.D. diss., Rutgers University, New Brunswick , New Jersey. 228 pp.

Shealer, D. A. and J. Burger. 1992. Differential responses of tropical roseate terns to aerial intruders throughout the nesting cycle. Condor 94:712-719.

Shealer, D. A. and J. E. Saliva. 1992. Northeastern Roseate Terns seen at Puerto Rican colony during breeding season. Col. Waterbirds 15: 152-154.

Spendelow, J. A. 1982. An analysis of temporal variation in, and the effects of habitat modification on, the reproductive success of roseate terns. Col. Waterbirds 5:19-31.

Sprunt, A. IV. 1984. The Status and conservation of seabirds of the Bahamas,. Pp. 157-168 in J. P. Croxall, P. G. H. Evans and R. W. Schreiber, eds. *Status and Conservation of the World's Seabirds*, Intl. Council of Bird Preservation, Techn. Publ. No. 2.

U.S. Fish and Wildlife Service. 1993. Caribbean Roseate Tern Recovery Plan. U.S. Fish and Wildlife Service, Atlanta, Georgia. 40 pp.

Van der Werf, P.A., J. S. Zaneveld, and K. H. Voous. 1958. Field observations on the birds of the Isla Las Aves in the southern Caribbean Sea. Ardea 46: 37-58.

van Halewyn, R. 1987. History of the seabird populations of San Nicolas Bay Keys, Aruba. Pp. 33-59 in Studies in Honour of Dr. Pieter Wagenaar Hummelkinck. Found. Scient. Res. in Surinam and the Netherlands Antilles, No. 123, Amsterdam.

van Halewyn, R., and R. Norton. 1984. The status and conservation of seabirds in the Caribbean. Pp. 169-222, in J. P. Croxall, P. G. H. Evans and R. W. Schreiber, eds. *Status and Conservation of the World's Seabirds*, Intl. Council of Bird Pres. Techn. Publ. No. 2.

Voous, K. H. 1957. The Birds of Aruba, Curacao and Bonaire. Studies Fauna Curacao and Other Caribbean Islands No. 29:1-260.

Voous, K. H. 1983.Birds of the Netherlands Antilles. De Walburg Pers, Utrecht, 79 pp.

Wetmore, A. 1927. The Birds of Puerto Rico and the Virgin Islands: Colymbiformes to Columbiformes. Scien. Survey of Puerto Rico and the Virgin Islands Vol. IX, Part 3: 248-406.

Wetmore, A. and B. H. Swales. 1931. The Birds of Haiti and the Dominican Republic. U.S. Natl. Mus. 155:1-481.

Breeding Common Terns in the Greater West Indies:
status and conservation priorities.

ငဒ ငဒ ငဒ ငဒ   ဘဝ ဘဝ ဘဝ ဘဝ

P. A. BUCKLEY[1] and FRANCINE G. BUCKLEY[2]

[1]*US Geological Survey-Patuxent Wildlife Research Center, Box 8 @ Graduate School of Oceanography, University of Rhode Island, Narragansett RI 02882, USA, Email pabuckley@gsosun1.gso.uri.edu*
[2]*Deparment of Natural Resource Sciences, University of Rhode Island, Kingston, Rhode Island 0288,1 USA*

Introduction

The presence of Common Terns (*Sterna hirundo*) in the Greater West Indies has been argued for decades owing to confusion with the very similar Roseate Tern (*Sterna dougallii*). It has only been very recently that the widespread distribution of Roseates and Common Terns has been appreciated. North American and European field guides typically depict temperate Roseate Terns with all black bills, usually neglecting to mention that tropical Roseate Terns have two-toned bills very similar to that of the Common Tern. Moreover, few temperate workers were familiar with the local West Indian Roseate (especially its immediately diagnostic call notes). These all combined to set the stage for routine misidentifications of both these species. There are few data on the population size in the West Indies as a result.

Breeding distribution

The A.O.U. Checklist (1998) lists Common Terns as breeding in "Bermuda, the Greater Antilles (islets off Hispaniola east to the Virgin Islands), Dominica and the Netherlands Antilles," 'Dominica' being the only change form the 6th edition in 1983. Van Halewyn and Norton (1984) reported that "Very small numbers breed on Bermuda...; between 350-600 pairs regularly breed at six or more islands off Venezuela [this includes both Venezuelan islets and Aruba-Curaçao-Bonaire]"; that "a few additional nesting sites may exist on the nearby coast of eastern Colombia and western Venezuela"; and that it might also breed in northern Cuba and the Bahamas. Gochfeld et al. (1994) believed West Indian (sensu latissimo) breeding population to comprise fewer than 750 pairs nesting at least 10 sites, but gave no further details.

Amos (1991) reported it as "locally common...all 25 or so pairs..at their scattered islet nest sites" in eight locations on Bermuda. Buden (1987) described its southern Bahamas status as "Uncertain, though the few records suggest transient [sic]"; he then augments this with several 1930s 'breeding records,' but cautions that 'none of the Bahamian breeding records is verified.' For the West Indies as a whole, Raffaele et al. (1998) lists it as "a rare breeding resident in small numbers in the Bahamas and Cuba. Earlier reports of breeding from Puerto Rico, the Virgin Islands, St. Martin and Saba likely pertain to the Roseate Tern". Raffaele et al. (1998) excluded the Venezuelan coast islands from their ambit. Keith (1997: 89) noted that on St. Lucia it "may breed occasionally on the Maria Islands" and that "clarification of its status is badly needed."

DeSchauensee and Phelps (1978) noted breeding colonies, without any details, at two islands in the Caribbean: Los Roques and Las Aves de Barlavento (usually just called 'Las Aves'); these would include islands discussed by van Halewyn and Norton (1984) and Gochfeld et al. (1994).

    Apart from a marginal breeding population (normally fewer than 30 pairs) at a few locations on the U.S. Gulf coast (notably on the Chandeleur Islands east of the delta of the Mississippi River), and "lone pairs" every now and then along the Florida Gulf Coast (Roberston and Woolfenden 1992), breeding Common Terns are unknown from the Gulf/Caribbean coasts of: Mexico (Howell and Webb 1995); Honduras (Monroe 1968); Costa Rica (Stiles and Skutch 1989); Panama (Ridgely and Gwynne 1989); Colombia (Hilty and Brown 1986), although recent data are lacking from Providenciales and San Andres, Colombian islands that are possible breeding sites in the western Caribbean east of Costa Rica; Suriname (Haverschmidt and Mees 1994): French Guiana; Trinidad and Tobago (ffrench1991); Cayman Islands (Bradley and Rey-Millet 1985); Jamaica (Downer and Sutton 1990); and Barbados (Hutt et al. in press). More than a few of these authors have commented on confusion with Roseate Tern.

Nonbreeding status

    The Common Tern occurs regularly throughout the West Indies as a migrant and winter resident. Perhaps even more important biologically, the West Indies is a maturation area where prebreeding subadults remain for several years until ready to return north to breed for the first time in the boreal summer, usually at 3 years of age. Nonbreeders also account for most of the West Indian Common Tern records in the summer months, birds which are frequently not described as to age class and plumage. Owing again to confusion with Roseates, they have surely been overlooked in the West Indies (e.g., the very first report for Jamaica came only in 1998: Leo Douglas, pers. comm.). Because nonbreeders often frequent colonies of other terns in the West Indies, such individuals are sometimes erroneously assumed to be breeding.

History in the West Indies

    Van Halewyn and Norton (1984) list Common Tern as having been suspected of breeding in the West Indies in the following locations: Bahamas, Turks and Caicos, cays off the n. coast of Cuba, unnamed cays plus Saona and Catalinita (off the Dominican Republic), and cays off the Venezuelan coast west of the Guira peninsula. To this list may be added sites listed in other sources: Dominica, St. Martin, Saba and St. Lucia.

    Nonetheless, breeding has been confirmed only on Bermuda, Gudeloupe and Marie Galante, La Orchila, the Los Roques archipelago, Las Aves, and the lower Netherlands Antilles (Aruba, Bonaire, and Curaçao, the so-called A-B-C islands; Table 1). The only published data on Bermudian Common Terns have already been given above. The Venezuelan islands have apparently not been visited in many years; the last known counts were of 4+ pairs on La Orchila, 75+ pairs on Los Roques, and 10+ pairs on Las Aves (LeCroy 1976).

    The only detailed information on Common Tern colony size and site use is from the Netherlands Antilles, the most recent summary being Voous's (1983). At that time, Common Terns bred on all 3 A-B-C islands, but nests had not yet been found at two major ternery sites, Klein Curaçao and Klein Bonaire. The total Common Tern breeding population (described without further qualification as "recently decreasing") was unknown but estimated at 200-300 pairs, the majority on Aruba. The species first bred in 1892, and since 1952 had been found at ten or more [unnamed] sites on Aruba, 4 on Curaçao and 4 on Bonaire; typically all sites were not occupied each year. It often nested solitarily even though Least, Royal, Sandwich/Cayenne,

Bridled, Sooty also breed in the area. Occasionally Roseates nested at the edge of A-B-C Common Tern colonies, but ironically for the West Indies, Voous commented that Roseates might have been overlooked because of confusion with the more numerous Commons!

Van Halewyn (in Gochfeld at al. 1994) added some information to Voous's account, reporting that on the Lago Reef colony off San Nicolas Bay, Aruba, Common Terns (no counts given) arrived some time after a large Cayenne Tern colony established there in 1970, but had disappeared by 1980. Yet Table 7 in the same paper shows 16-36 nests found there each year from 1984-90, so perhaps the earlier reference to the colony's disappearance should have read 1990, not 1980. On the Pardenbaai keys opposite Oranjestad, "small numbers" nested annually. Details of colony sizes and sites on Aruba during the 80s have been published in van Halewyn (1985, 1987)

Gochfeld et al. (1994) estimated that fewer than 750 pairs nested at over 10 sites in the entire West Indies (including the Netherlands Antilles and islands off Venezuela). We believe today those numbers should read 290-490 pairs at 6 sites. The above are the only known Common Tern colony-site and breeding-population data for the entire Greater West Indies that we know of.

Taxonomic Note

Van Halewyn and Norton (1984) state that the breeding population of Common Tern in the West Indies "[might] even constitute a separate subspecies," citing Voous (1957). We have examined Voous (1957) closely, and can find no such statement. To the contrary, Voous (1957: 138) stated that he had "not succeeded in discovering any constant differences in colour, wing pattern, proportions or measurements between individuals from the South Caribbean, North America, and western and northern Europe. South Caribbean birds [do] show a tendency towards smaller size." This is affirmed in Voous 1983. Exchange of European and American birds is confirmed by at least one recovery on Trinidad/Tobago of a bird ringed in Finland (ffrench 1991).

Notwithstanding the above, we report a series of puzzling Common Terns photographed by David Shealer on the south coast of Puerto Rico in late May in several years in the early 1990s. His excellent slides depict apparently breeding-plumaged adult Common Terns (confirmed by voice), but whose extremely dark ventral coloration and all dark bills accompanied by full black caps most closely approximate the east Siberian longipennis. This is a taxon so far unreported from the entire Atlantic Ocean but is hardly impossible in a species well-known as a long-distance migrant. Whether the Puerto Rican birds are longipennis or just very dark hirundo, or represent an undescribed taxon, or are merely in an undescribed or unappreciated plumage worn by nonbreeders towards the end of their maturation period, remains to be determined.

West Indian Breeding Biology

The only published data we know of on the breeding biology of West Indian Common Terns are those of Voous (1957, 1983) from Aruba- Curaçao -Bonaire; we excerpt here from Voous (1983):

> "With regard to nesting habitat and breeding distribution...there is close similarity between Common and Least Terns, but the two species rarely nest side by side. Common Tern often [associates]

with [breeding Black-necked] Stilts...Eggs found from about the middle of April onward...Egg-laying may continue until July or early August. Eggs are deposited on bare rock or in shallow depressions in white coral sand or on dry mud. Most nests are lined with plant stems or adorned with shells and coral debris. Some are placed in the shade of low salt plants...Eggs generally paler than in North America and Europe. Average measurements... 40.5 x 29.3mm. Clutch size recorded 1-3, mostly 2-3...Chick remains in the nest for a few days to be...fed by parents... [Fledging occurs] from the middle of June onwards."

Threats and Pressures

Occasional, sometimes locally severe, egging of seabirds occurs throughout the West Indies, and so there is no reason to assume that the Common Tern is exempt from such pressures. In addition, killing of wintering birds for food may be more widespread than generally believed, and West Indies breeder may be among those killed. Globally, the Common Tern is not a threatened species, and its English name is well-deserved. Still, West Indian populations are marginal, small, isolated, and thus far more vulnerable than most others. The problems facing Common Terns are similar to those facing other West Indian seabirds (human disturbance, development, pollution, pathological predation by specialist predators (land crabs, night-herons), exotic species (goats, cats, mongooses, monkeys, vegetation), are of especial concern for West Indian Common Terns. Van Halewyn and Norton (1984) describe the pressures-plus problems associated with oil refineries (direct toxicity, air, noise, and food-chain pollution, night-time illumination) and tourism-on breeding terns in Aruba, of which Common Tern is one. Throughout the entire West Indies signing and active wardening of known colonies constitute the single most obvious management action that would produce immediately beneficial results. Enforcement and prosecution must go hand-in-glove with them, and widespread and aggressive publicity glues them together.

Data Gaps

The largest and most obvious gap in our knowledge is the precise breeding range of Common Terns in the West Indies. Data are also lacking on the relationship of Common Terns to Roseates, what its West Indian metapopulation status is (its need for alternate sites, its turnover rates, its population trends), what (if any) gene exchange occurs between North American (and even European) and West Indian breeders, and if West Indian birds are genetically unusual or even unique. The identity of the dark Puerto Rican birds forms an intriguing sidebar.

Acknowledgements

For various kinds of information on West Indian Common Terns we thank Karel H. Voous, Allan R. Keith, Philippe Feldmann, and Leo Douglas, and for inviting our participation in the West Indian seabird symposium held on Aruba in August 1997, David Lee and Betty Anne Schreiber.

Table 1. Number of pairs of Common Terns at colonies in the West Indies (Bermuda, Netherlands Antilles and Venezuela not included in West Indies).

Location	Number of Pairs	Reference
Bermuda (at 8 sites)	25	Amos 1991
Bahamas	a few	Raffaele et al. 1998
Cuba (cays off north coast)	?	Raffaele et al. 1998
Anguilla, Scrub Island	50±	ICF Kaiser 1999
St. Lucia (cays offshore)	a few, occasionally	Keith 1997
Guadeloupe/Marie-Galante	a few, occasionally	Feldmann et al. 1999
Aruba-Bonaire-Curaçao	200-300	Voous 1983
Venezuela, isles off coast		
La Orchila	4+	LeCroy 1976
Los Roques	75+	LeCroy 1976
Las Aves	10+	LeCroy 1976
WEST INDIES TOTAL	**50-100**	

Literature Cited

American Ornithologists' Union. 1998. A.O.U Check-list of North American Birds, 7th ed. Washington, D.C., American Ornithologists' Union. 829 pp.

Amos, A. 1991. A guide to the birds of Bermuda. Warwick, Bermuda, privately published. 206 pp.

Bradley, P. and Y-J. Rey-Millet. 1985. Birds of the Cayman Islands. George Town, C.I., privately published. 245 pp.

Buden, D. 1987. The birds of the southern Bahamas. B.O.U. Check-list No. 8. London, British Ornithologists' Union. 119 pp.

DeSchauensee, R., and W. Phelps. 1978. The birds of Venezuela. Princeton, Princeton University Press. 425 pp.

Downer, A. and R. Sutton. 1990. Birds of Jamaica: a photographic field guide. Cambridge, Cambridge University Press. 152 pp.

Feldmann, P., E. Benito-Espinal, and A. Keith. 1999. New bird records from Guadeloupe and Martinique, West Indies. Journal of Field Ornithology 70: 80-94

ffrench, R. 1991. A guide to the birds of Trinidad and Tobago, 2nd ed. Ithaca, Cornell University Press. 426 pp.

Gochfeld, M., J. Burger, A. Haynes-Sutton, and R. van Halewyn. 1994. Successful approaches to seabird conservation in the West Indies. Pp. 186-209 in Nettleship, D., J. Burger, and M. Gochfeld, eds. *Seabirds on island: threats, case studies and action plans*. Cambridge, BirdLife International.

Haverschmidt, F. and G. Mees. 1994. Birds of Suriname. Paramaribo, Vaco. 580 pp.

Hilty, S., and W. Brown. 1986. A guide to the birds of Colombia. Princeton, Princeton University Press. 836 pp.

Howell, S. and S. Webb. 1995. A guide to the birds of Mexico and northern Central America. Oxford, Oxford University Press. 855 pp.

Hutt, M.B., H.F. Hutt, P.A. Buckley, F.G. Buckley, E.B. Massiah, and M.D. Frost. In press. The Birds of Barbados, West Indies. B.O.U Check-list No. 20. Tring, British Ornithologists' Union. 195 pp.

Keith, A. 1997. The birds of St. Lucia, West Indies. B.O.U. Check-list No. 15. Tring, British Ornithologists' Union. 176 pp.

LeCroy, M. 1976. Bird observations from Los Roques, Venezuela. American Museum of Natural History Novitates 2599: 1-30.

Monroe, B. 1968. A distributional survey of the birds of Honduras. Ornithological Monographs No. 7. Lawrence, American Ornithologists' Union. 459 pp.

Raffaele, H., J. Wiley, O. Garrido, A. Keith, and J. Raffaele. 1998. A guide to the birds of the West Indies. Princeton, Princeton University Press. 511 pp.

Robertson, W., and G. Woolfenden. 1992. Florida bird species: an annotated list. Florida Ornithological Society Special Publication No. 6. Gainesville, FOS.

Ridgely, R. and J. Gwynne. 1989. A guide to the birds of Panama, 2nd ed. Princeton, Princeton University Press. 535 pp.

Stiles, F., and A. Skutch. 1989. A guide to the birds of Costa Rica. Ithaca, Cornell University Press. 511 pp.

van Halewyn, R. 1985. Report on 1984 survey of marine birds of Aruba, Netherlands Antilles. Utrecht: Foundation for Scientific Research in Suriname and the Netherlands Antilles.

van Halewyn, R. 1987. Marine birds of Aruba. Report on 1995 survey and conservation campaign. Arnhem: Research Institute for Nature Management.

van Halewyn, R. and R. Norton. 1984. The status and conservation of seabirds in the Caribbean. Pp. 169-222 in Croxall, J., P. Evans, and R. Schreiber, eds. *Status and conservation of the world's seabirds*. ICBP Tech. Publ. No. 2. Cambridge, ICBP.

Voous, K. 1957. The birds of Aruba, Curaçao and Bonaire. Studies on the fauna of Curaçao and other Caribbean Islands 6: No. 25. 216 pp.

Voous, K. 1983. Birds of the Netherlands Antilles, 2nd ed. Curaçao, De Walburg Pers. 327 pp.

Conservation Priorities for Sooty Terns in the West Indies

_____ ‌ぱ ぱ ぱ ぱ   ぞ ぞ ぞ ぞ _____

JORGE E. SALIVA

U. S. Fish and Wildlife Service, P. O. box 491, Boqueron, Puerto Rico 00621 USA, Email jorge_saliva@fws.gov

Introduction

The highly pelagic Sooty Tern (*Sterna fuscata*) has a cosmopolitan distribution, primarily nesting on small offshore islands in all tropical and subtropical oceans. They generally lay one egg per breeding season, but they commonly relay if an egg or small chick is lost (Ridley and Percy 1958). During poor food years birds may abandon eggs and relay several times, greatly extending the nesting season. Like other pelagic seabirds, their chicks have an extended nestling period and fledge at about 8 weeks.

Sooty Terns in the Caribbean area arrive at their nesting areas as early as February, but most commonly in late April or early May, with most individuals departing the area by late August. It is not unknown where Caribbean Sooty Terns spend their time between breeding cycles because there are no records of wintering birds. Robertson's study (1964), showing the migrating pattern of juvenile Sooty Terns from Florida to the western coast of Africa, suggests that perhaps the Caribbean population may follow a similar migration pattern. Since Sooty Terns cannot land on water because of their poorly-developed oil gland (Johnston 1979), it is generally believed that they may remain on the wing for most or all of the time between breeding cycles (Harrington 1974). Their long wingspan related to body size suggests that they may be adapted for long periods of soaring and low-cost, energy-saving flight.

In most locations where they breed, Sooty Terns nest in exposed areas with little or no vegetation cover over the nest (Sprunt 1948, Ashmole 1963, Schreiber and Ashmole 1970). This is typical of birds nesting on the Dry Tortugas (Florida) and Jamaica (W. Robertson and A. Haynes-Sutton, pers. comm.), although the birds do nest under cover if no open areas are available. In Puerto Rico and the Virgin Islands, however, Sooty Terns nest exclusively under or at the edge of vegetation (Saliva and Burger 1989). Such differences in nest-site selection may be related to the amount and types of predators found in colonies on exposed areas compared to vegetated sites (Saliva and Burger 1989). Similar to many other pelagic seabirds, nest-site fidelity in Sooty Terns is very strong, and birds nest in the same area every year (Saliva, unpub.).

Nesting areas in the Caribbean

The reported number of breeding pairs of Sooty Terns in the Caribbean before the mid-eighties was based, in many cases, on visual estimates of colony size and not on actual counts (van Halewyn and Norton 1984), and most of these estimates were done before the 1970's. Except for colonies at Culebra Island (Puerto Rico), the U.S. Virgin Islands and some in the British Virgin Islands, systematic yearly surveys of breeding Sooty Terns are not currently conducted at other Caribbean locations, primarily due to the lack of monitoring programs for seabirds in most countries. The most recent information on the distribution and number of breeding Sooty Terns in the Caribbean, prior to this publication, is that reported by van Halewyn and Norton (1984). They reported 73 breeding sites totaling some 500,000 breeding pairs in the Caribbean. Although recently biologists from different Caribbean countries have reported no major changes regarding the presence of nesting Sooty Terns in historical nesting areas, or significant colony shifts in the last decade, they recognize that not all colonies are monitored regularly and not all colonies are visited during their surveys. The most recent data available on colony locations and number of nesting pairs are presented in Table 1 and Figure 1. The actual nesting island may shift from year to year, at least in part owing to human disturbance of colonies.

The estimated number of breeding pairs at Culebra, Puerto Rico has been increasing in recent years as traditional areas that had been abandoned for over 10 years are being slowly repopulated. However, the current population is just now similar to what it was 50 years ago. It is not clear whether or not this recent increase in area use and number of birds may be due to recruitment of birds from abandoned colonies at other sites since there are few banded birds from which movements can be tracked. Some previously-used nesting areas in Puerto Rico have been abandoned, however (e.g., Cordillera Keys and Monito Island).

In the U.S. Virgin Islands there were no good data on historical colony size. Today an estimated 30,000 – 40,000 pairs breed there. The British Virgin Islands have about 100 pairs each year. The largest concentrations of nesting Sooties in the West Indies are on the keys off northern Cuba, Morant Cays (Jamaica) Culebra Cays (Puerto Rico: Table 1). Other large concentrations could exist but there are no recent counts of many areas (Table 1). At least two sites in Jamaica on the Pedro Cays have lost nesting Sooty Terns, probably to egging (A. Haynes-Sutton pers. comm.; Fig. 1). Other colonies are no doubt extirpated, also.

Conservation Needs

Although Sooty Terns are one of the most abundant breeding seabirds in the Caribbean (Robertson 1964, Burger and Gochfeld 1986) and their populations do not appear to be immediately threatened, standardized, consistent monitoring of Caribbean colonies is needed to prevent major declines or local colony extinctions. Censuses conducted at least every two years would allow detection of population changes in a timely manner. Resources needed by each country to monitor Sooty Tern populations and the actions needed to obtain these resource should be identified. Caribbean countries that regularly monitor their Sooty Tern colonies may be able to provide guidance and assistance.

The most important factor affecting Sooty Terns in the eastern Caribbean is predation; where up to 14 different predators may prey upon eggs, chicks, and adult Sooty Terns. Raptors (Peregrine Falcon, *Falco perergrinus*; Red-tailed Hawk, *Buteo jamaicensis*, Short-eared Owl, *Asio flammeus*; and American kestrel, *Falco sparverius*), feral dogs (*Canis familiaris*), and feral cats (*Felis cattus*) cause the greatest amount of disturbance at the Sooty Tern colonies, attacking adult and juvenile Sooties and promoting egg and downy chick predation by Laughing Gulls

(*Larus atricilla*) and crabs (*Gecarcinus ruricola* and *Coenobita clypeatus*) by keeping adult Sooty Terns off their nests (Saliva and Burger 1989). Laughing Gulls, Yellow-crowned Night Herons (*Nyctanassa violacea*), Cattle Egrets (*Egretta thula*), Norwegian rats (*Rattus norvegicus*), black rats (*Rattus rattus*), and fire ants prey upon eggs and downy chicks (Saliva and Burger 1989).

     Cats and feral dogs have caused the largest mortality of adult and young Sooty Terns at one of the Culebra colonies. Both these predators actually kill more terns than they consume (Saliva, unpub. data). Dogs usually appear in packs that may kill many eggs, young, and adult Sooty Terns. An eradication program to eliminate feral cats and dogs is important in Sooty Tern colonies. Raptors take some terns but not nearly as many as do cats and dogs, partly because the covering vegetation makes it more difficult for raptors to capture the terns. Raptors generally prey upon terns that are exposed outside or at the edge of vegetation (Saliva, unpub. data), and they may not represent a major threat to Sooty Terns.

Table 1. Historical (from van Halewyn and Norton 1984 and previous publications) and current information on the number of breeding pairs of Sooty Terns in the Caribbean.

Location	Historical Size	Current Size
Anguilla, Dog Island	B	2000±
Sombrero Island	B	300-400
Antigua	1,000+	?
Bahamas, 20 + cays	10,000+	4,000-8,000
Turks & Caicos	B	?
British Virgin Islands, total	?	100±
Carval Rock		
Fallen Jerusalem		
Round Rock		
Cuba, north cays	3,000+	40-60,000
south cays	B	?
Dominica	1,000+	?
Dominican Rep., north islands	B	1,000+
Beata Island	100,000+	50,000?
Grenada	B	?
Grenadines	B	?
Guadeloupe	B	4,000-6,000
Jamaica, Pedro Cays, 2 sites	B	E
Pedro Cays, Southwest Cay	B	1,000-2,000
Morant Cays	1,000	70,000-90,000

continued -

Table 1 continued -

Location	Historical Size	Current Size
Martinique	B	?
Puerto Rico, Culebra cays	25-30,000	25-35,000
Mona and Monito	3,000	300-400
Monito Island	B	E
Cordillera Cays	250	E
St. Kitts	B	50-100
St. Martin	C	?
St. Bartholomew's	B	?
St. Eustatius	B	?
St. Lucia	B	?
Tobago	2,000+	?
Trinidad	2,500	?
US Virgin Islands, Saba Island	B	30,000-40,000
Flat Cay	B	50-200
Frenchcap Cay	-	50-200
Turtledove Cay	-	50-200
Aruba	400	?
Colombia, Roncador Cay	B	?
Serrana and Serranilla Bank	B	?
Venezuela, Aves Island	10-20,000	?
Las Aves Isles	1,000+	?
Los Hermanos Island	B	?
Los Roques Archipelago	B	?
French Guyana	B	?
Honduras	B	?
Mexico, Caribbean coast cays	100	?
Gulf coast cays	B	?
TOTAL WEST INDIES	**170,000-400,000**	**200,000-300,000**
GREATER CARIBBEAN	200,000-500,000	230,000-400,000

B = Reported breeding before 1950, but number of pairs not known.
C = Breeding suspected but not confirmed.
? = No recent data.
E = extirpated

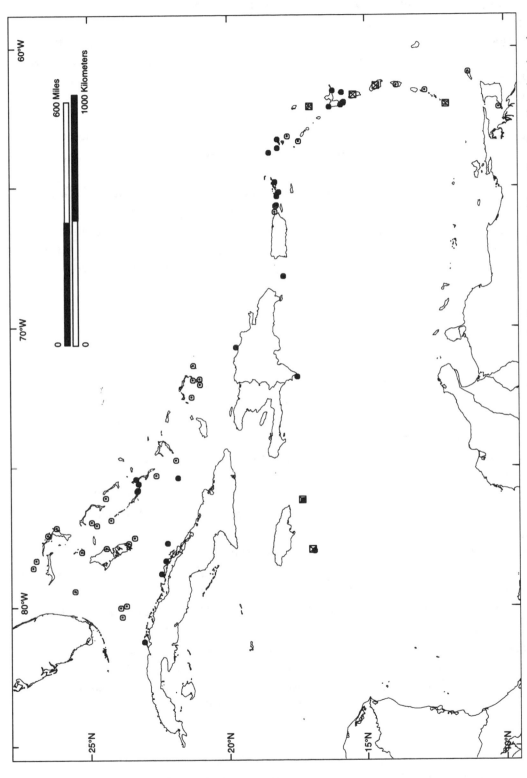

Figure 1: The status of known Sooty Tern breeding sites in the West Indies. ● = confirmed breeding location that has been surveyed recently. ⊙ = historic breeding location with no report that the colony has been extirpated. ⊠ = historic breeding location that is extirpated or thought to be extirpated.

There is some Laughing Gull (*Larus atricilla*) predation on Sooty Terns which can generally be controlled by removal of the few individual Laughing Gulls that specialize on Sooty Tern eggs and chicks. Such individuals constantly patrol tern colonies throughout the entire egg-laying and hatching period, and can eliminate large numbers of exposed eggs (particularly when the terns are disturbed from their nests). These specialists may also learn to prey upon other seabird eggs and young, potentially affecting sensitive species like the Roseate Tern (*Sterna dougallii*).

Crabs take some very young Sooty Terns, mainly when adult terns are disturbed off their nests (Saliva, unpub. data). Humans have harvested Sooty Tern eggs for many decades and egg collection, although illegal on most Caribbean countries, continues to occur. Enforcement of laws protecting seabird islands is difficult because of the remoteness of the islands and the lack of sufficient enforcement officers to cover large areas regularly during the breeding season. Education programs could help change attitudes about seabirds and create an environmental ethic that would help halt poaching. Countries should post islands with signs declaring that poaching is illegal and should attempt to increase colony patrolling, particularly during the first two weeks after egg-laying when egg collection takes place.

Literature Cited

Ashmole, N. P. 1963. The biology of the Wideawake or Sooty Tern (*Sterna fuscata*) on Ascencion Island. Ibis 103b: 297-364.

Burger, J. and M. Gochfeld. 1986. Nest-site selection in Sooty Terns (*Sterna fuscata*) in Puerto Rico and Hawaii. Col. Waterbirds 9: 31-45.

Harrington, B. A. 1974. Colony visitation behavior and breeding ages of Sooty Terns *Sterna fuscata*. Bird Banding 45: 115-144.

Johnston, D. W. 1979. The uropygial gland of the Sooty Tern. The Condor 81: 430-432.

Ridley, M. W. And R. Percy. 1958. The exploitation of seabirds in Seychelles. Colonial Research Studies 25: 1-78.

Robertson, W. B., Jr.1964.The terns of the Dry Tortugas. Bull. Fl. State. Mus. Biol. Sci. 8: 1-95.

Saliva, J. E. and J. Burger. 1989. Effect of experimental manipulation of vegetation density on nest-site selection in Sooty Terns. The Condor 91: 689-698.

Schreiber, R. W. and N. P. Ashmole. 1970. Sea-bird breeding seasons on Christmas Island, Pacific Ocean. Ibis 112: 363-394.

Sprunt, A., Jr. 1948. The tern colonies of the Dry Tortugas Keys. The Auk 65: 1-19.

van Halewyn, R. and R. L. 1984. The status and conservation of seabirds in the Caribbean. Pp. 169- 222 in Croxall, J. P., P. G. H. Evans and R. W. Schreiber, eds. *Status and Conservation of the World's Seabirds*. Intl. Council of Bird Preservation, Techn. Publication No. 2. 1984.

Distribution, Population Changes and Threats to Least Terns in the Caribbean and Adjacent Waters of the Atlantic and Gulf of Mexico.

CB CB CB CB   BO BO BO BO

JEROME A. JACKSON

Whitaker Center for Science, Mathematics, and Technology Education, Florida Gulf Coast University, 10501 FGCU Blvd. South Ft. Myers, FL 33965, Emailjjackson@fgcu.edu .

Introduction

The Least Tern (*Sterna antillarum*) is still considered a common breeding species around the Gulf of Mexico, through the Bahamas, the Greater Antilles, and some of the Lesser Antilles. It has also been reported to nest on the coast of Venezuela (van Halewyn and Norton 1984). This review is intended to supplement and update the information on this species included in van Halewyn and Norton (1984) and Sprunt (1984). Sources include a review of the literature, personal communications with researchers in West Indian countries, and personal observations. The review is not exhaustive, but is intended to provide an overview of the current status and populations of the species in the region.

Habitat Needs, Population Changes, and the State of Our Knowledge of Least Terns

Least Terns are opportunistic nesters, using early successional, open habitat such as beaches, bare rock, sand bars, salt flats, and manmade habitats such as dredge spoil, parking lots, airports, agricultural fields, flat rooftops, and construction sites (Thompson et al. 1997). They need good feeding areas nearby, which can be shallow estuarine bays, salt ponds, freshwater rivers and ponds, or aquaculture facilities.

Our knowledge of Least Terns in the Caribbean is quite imperfect and the result more of casual observation than of detailed study. Many observations of the species in the Bahamas are a result of those islands being a frequent destination for North American birders and of the availability of guides such as Brudenell-Bruce (1975) and White (1998). Less frequent tourist destinations have correspondingly less information available. New field guides for the West Indies (e.g., Raffaele et al. 1998) and for individual island nations (e.g., Bradley 1995) and an increase in ecotourism in the region provide hope for increased knowledge of birds of the region. There is an increased awareness of the need for nesting records thanks to such efforts as see Appendix A in White (1998) which provides information on approaches to estimating colony sizes for ground-nesting seabirds). Certainly a key need for identifying and understanding changes in populations requires consistency of effort in monitoring for comparability of the resulting data.

Based on the current biased record, it appears that Least Terns have declined in some areas of their U.S. and Caribbean nesting range (owing to habitat destruction, increased disturbance from growing human populations) and have expanded in a few places (owing to development of aquaculture habitats, clearing of land that then becomes suitable for nesting, some protective measures). Certainly the nature of Least Tern nesting sites is changing. In northwest Florida, for example, of 42 colonies supporting about 2364 nests, only nine were on sand beaches (Gore 1991). Another nine were on altered substrates such as dredge spoil, and 24 were on the flat roofs of buildings. As human populations continue to grow throughout the region, we need to look closely at how the birds are adapting to their new habitats. Some evidence suggests serious thermal problems on roofs (Jackson 1994), but due to reduced disturbance from humans, safety from storm surges, and possibly reduced predation, a higher hatching rate has been found at roof colonies (Gore 1991).

Two populations of the Least Tern are listed as endangered under the U.S. Endangered Species Act of 1973: the California Least Tern (*Sterna antillarum browni*), and the Interior Least Tern (*S. a. athalassos*). The nominate subspecies (*S. a. antillarum*) is the form recognized from eastern coastal U.S. and Caribbean breeding areas. While there is evidence to suggest that taxonomic distinction among these populations may not be warranted (see review in Thompson et al. 1997), there is clear evidence that numbers of birds in both endangered populations have plummeted since the 1930s. These losses, as well as losses elsewhere, have been primarily a result of habitat destruction and human disturbance. Breeding Least Terns in the Caribbean are not officially designated as endangered or threatened, although local populations are often tenuous. Migration and wintering distributions of birds from the endangered populations are not known, but likely include the Caribbean and coastal areas of northeastern South America.

Most Least Terns arrive at breeding grounds (Fig. 1) in the Caribbean and adjacent areas in early April and nesting begins by late April to late May. Re-nesting efforts in North America have usually been completed by mid-August; some Caribbean nesting has been reported to continue into October.

Breeding Populations Noted for Specific Bahamian and Caribbean Islands
The following summary of recent nesting information for Least Terns is divided into three geographic sub-regions: the Bahamas, Greater Antilles, and Lesser Antilles (see Table 1). Within each sub-region, the data are arranged alphabetically by major islands or island groups.

Bahamas
The Least Tern is considered a common, but local, breeding bird throughout the Bahamas. Buden (1987a) notes that it is most common as a breeder at salt flats and broad sandy beaches on the windward side of islands, on rocky ridges, and on flat areas of dog-tooth limestone.

Acklins Island. Reported nesting (Buden 1987a).

Cat Island. Nesting reported at salt ponds north of Smokey Point (6 nests, 1986, Buden 1987a), northern end of Gambier Lake (2 nests, 1986, Buden 1987a), McKinney's Pond and at the ponds west of Port Howe (White 1998).

Eleuthera. Least Terns can be found over much of Eleuthera nesting on pebbly surfaces near ponds (Connor and Loftin 1985).

Exumas. Reports include nesting on Little Bell Island (2-5 pairs), Marion Cay (15-20 pairs), Cistern Cay (20 pairs), Warderick Wells (5-40: Sprunt 1984, Lee and Clark 1995); Warderick Wells Cay, two nests at an islet off Hall's Pond Cay, 20-30 adults and many eggs on Elbow Cay, all in May-June 1991 (Buden 1992a); a colony on the west side of Moriah Harbour Cay (White 1998); a colony at Grog Pond, Great Exuma (Norton 1997); and a colony at Staniel Cay (9 birds, Norton 1997).

Ft. George Cay. Reported nesting (Buden 1987a).

    <u>Grand Turk.</u> Reported nesting (Buden 1987a).

    <u>Great Inagua, Little Inagua</u>. Least Terns nest on Great Inagua and Little Inagua. While most reported colonies are small (5-20 pairs), as many as 300 pairs have been reported nesting on Great Inagua (Buden 1987a).

    <u>Long Island</u>. Found nesting in 1990 (Buden 1992b): 2 nests with eggs, coastal pond ne. of O'Neils, 12 May; 2 nests with eggs, Deep Lake, 25 July.

    <u>New Providence.</u> Least Terns have nested for many years at Lyford Cay near the west end and at Coral Harbor to the south, but also in scattered colonies and "not necessarily by the coast" (Brudenell-Bruce 1975).

    <u>Pine Cay.</u> Reported nesting (Buden 1987b).

<u>Providenciales</u>. Reported nesting (Buden 1987b).

    <u>Rum Cay.</u> In 1989, on 31 May, 22 nests with eggs were found on the north shore of Carmichael Pond; on 5 June, 19 nests with eggs (one chick) were found on the northwest shore of Lake George; on 16 June, 6 nests with eggs were found on a small island at the west end of Carmichael Pond (Buden 1990).

    <u>Salt Cay.</u> Reported nesting (Buden 1987b).

    <u>San Salvador</u>. Least Terns apparently nest on flats at interior ponds (Norton 1990). White (1991) notes that they nest on "sandy backshore areas of beaches, in fore-dunes, and along the shores of some inland lakes. He suggests that they are more abundant as nesting birds on the southern part of the island.

Greater Antilles
Cuba

    In Cuba, the Least Tern is common in summer and nests along the beaches of the mainland and on the many small adjacent islands, especially along the northern coast (Garrido and Montana 1975).

Hispaniola

    No recent reports are available.

Jamaica

    Least Terns have disappeared from many nesting sites: St. Catherine, Port Henderson Swamps, Hunt's Bay causeway, St. Elizabeth, Parttee Pond, Pedro Pond, St. James, Montego Freeport, Port Royal Cays. The species appears to change colony sites frequently. Recent breeding sites include (but may not be limited to): Yallahs Salt Pond, Long Pond sewage ponds, Portland Bight, and Jackson's Bay (pers. comm., A. Hayes-Sutton 1997). Each site has from 10-50 pairs.

Puerto Rico

    Least Terns nest in sand or on coral rubble at remote flats on off-shore islands east of Puerto Rico (Evans 1990). Johnson (1988) mentions "Little Tern" [=Least Tern?] breeding on Vieques. Although searches were made for nesting Least Terns on Culebra in mid-June 1985, and other species were found nesting, Least Terns were not found (Norton 1985).

Lesser Antilles

Antigua and Barbuda

On Antigua Least Terns nest 1 April-17 October (Bond 1956, 1980). On Barbuda they probably nest at northern salt flats (Norton 1990). Nesting Least Terns can be found south to St. Christopher (Raffaele et al. 1998).

Aruba

In 1985, 141 pairs of Least Terns were found nesting on Aruba (Norton 1985), and in early August 1997, I found over 100 pairs nesting on salt flats very near resort hotels.

Barbados

Recorded at Barbados in spring, in July, and from September into November (Keith 1997), but apparently as a transient or vagrant.

Cayman Islands

Little Cayman. Least Terns may still nest on the east end. The site moves from year to year and included 50-60 pairs in the 1990s (P. Bradley, pers. comm.)

Cayman Brac. Through the 1990s 30-50 pairs nested annually split among two westerly lagoons and Salt Water Pond (P. Bradley, pers. comm.).

Grand Cayman. Up to 120 pairs annually nested at various ponds and flats from 1995-1997 (P. Bradley, pers. comm.).

St. Christopher

Nests (Bond 1956).

St. Lucia

Keith (1997) notes that the Least Tern is a vagrant in fall to St. Lucia, citing only 4 records: one in the "fall" of 1970, 1-4 adults at Vieux Fort between 3 and 22 Sep. 1992.

St. Martin

Nests along the coast of St. Martin (Bond 1980, Evans 1990).

U.S. Virgin Islands

Buck Island. Least Terns were confirmed nesting on Buck Island, St. Croix, Virgin Islands National Park in July 1985 (Norton 1985).

St. Croix. In June 1985, 195 pairs of Least Terns were found nesting on St. Croix (Norton 1985). By 1989, only 60 nests could be found, most at Southgate Pond (Norton 1989).

St. Thomas. Although searches were made for nesting terns on St. Thomas in early June 1985 and other species were found, nesting Least Terns were not found (Norton 1985).

British Virgin Islands

Anegada. In June 1985, 44 pairs of Least Terns nested on Anegada. In 1988, only 2 pairs were found in an area where more had been seen in other years (Norton 1988). This species was also reported nesting on the island at interior ponds in 1990 (Norton 1990). They have apparently been extirpated from Beef Island (J. Pierce, pers. comm. 1997)

Great Thatch Island. Thirty pairs nested (J. Pierce, pers comm. 1997)

Table 1. Extant and extirpated colonies of Least Terns in the Greater Caribbean Area. The total is listed only for the West Indies.

Location	Estimated No. of Pairs
Bahamas (considered common breeder)	
Acklins Island	B
Cat Island	8-20±
Eleuthera	B
Exumas (on many islets in small numbers)	B
Ft. George Cay	B
Grand Turk	B
Great Inagua, Little Inagua	250-350±
Long Island	4-10±
New Providence(small numbers in scattered areas)	B
Pine Cay	B
Providenciales	B
Rum Cay	40-50±
Salt Cay	B
San Salvador (several small colonies)	B
Greater Antilles	
Cuba (on mainland and scattered islets)	B
Hispaniola	?
Jamaica (several small colonies, scattered)	B
Puerto Rico (on scattered islets off east coast)	B
Lesser Antilles	
Antigua (scattered small colonies)	?
Barbuda (on northern Salt Flats)	?
Aruba	100-200
Cayman Islands, Little Cayman	50-60
Cayman Brac	30-50
Grand Cayman	80-120
St. Christopher	?
St. Martin (along coasts)	B
U. S. Virgin Islands, Buck Island	B
St. Croix	60-195
British Virgin Islands, Anegada	a few
Beef Island	E
Great Thatch Island	30±
St. Thomas	E
Estimated Total for West Indies	**1500-3000±**

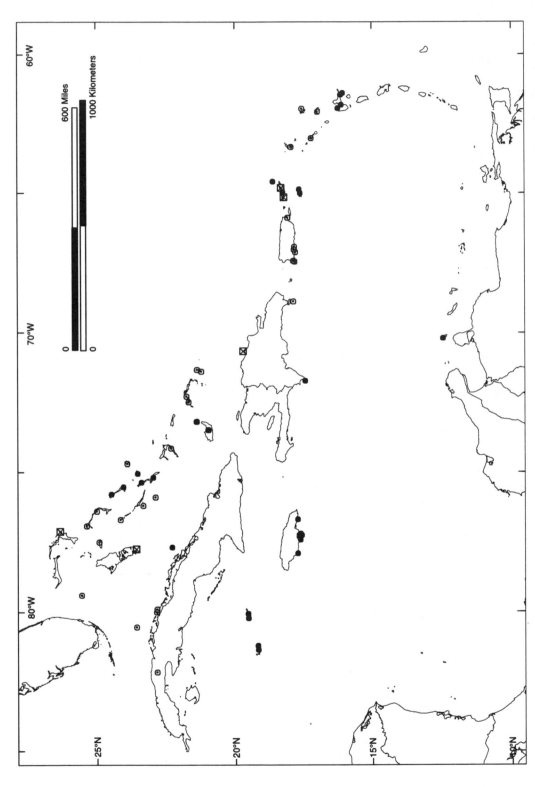

Figure 1: The status of known Least Tern breeding sites in the West Indies. ● = confirmed breeding location that has been surveyed recently. ◉ = historic breeding location with no report that the colony has been extirpated. ⊠ = historic breeding location that is extirpated or thought to be extirpated.

<u>Other</u>
Dry Tortugas
Robertson (1964) presents a particularly detailed review of the history of decline of Least Terns in the Dry Tortugas, a result of collection of their eggs for human consumption. The birds were reported nesting at both ends of Loggerhead Key, and a colony on Bush Key was estimated to have included 1000 birds early in the century. Although small groups resumed nesting on Loggerhead Key beginning in 1932, the birds ultimately disappeared, probably in part to destruction and disturbance caused by dogs and cats brought to the island by lighthouse personnel. In July 1963, 5 adults were seen around Garden and Long keys. Robertson suggests that the rapid disappearance of the Tortuga Least Terns might be linked to an increase in the number of Least Tern colonies in coastal Florida and/or to the great increase in Sooty Tern numbers in the Tortugas.

Problems Faced by Nesting Least Terns

Problems faced by nesting Least Terns range from the historic natural exigencies of weather and a diversity of predators to problems caused or enhanced by growing human populations: habitat destruction, exotic predators, increases in native predator populations, chemical pollutants, killing of birds for various reasons, destruction of eggs, and disturbances in colony areas. Here I will focus on some of those problems related to human activities.

<u>Jet skis</u>. They are not as ubiquitous in the Caribbean as in U.S. coastal areas, but their numbers are increasing. Problems posed by jet skis for Least Terns include: (1) disturbance of nesting colonies, making eggs and chicks more vulnerable to predators and heat, (2) disturbance of feeding birds, forcing them to travel farther in search of food, and (3) disturbance of bottom substrates, creating more turbid water that reduces potential for primary productivity, otherwise alters prey species habitat, and reduces visibility of potential prey. Quantitative studies of the nature and magnitude of impacts of jet skis are needed.

<u>Increased human uses of coastal habitats.</u> The human presence in coastal habitats has grown dramatically in recent years, in part a result of growing human populations, and in part a result of affluence that fosters use of coastal environments for leisure activities. Problems for the birds include (1) increased disturbance as a result of increased numbers of humans using beaches and near-shore waters, and (2) increased pollution of near-shore waters as a result of oil and gas residues, pesticides used on lawns and golf courses, and other chemicals and debris associated with the increased human presence.

<u>Killing of birds and collection of eggs.</u> Although Least Terns are now protected by state and national laws and international treaties in the United States, other areas often lack such formal protection. Even where they are protected, however, killing of Least Terns and destruction of their eggs continues.

<u>Other human problems</u>. People bring dogs to the beaches to "exercise" them and the dogs chase and kill chicks and flush adults from nests.

<u>Maintenance of protected nesting areas.</u> Although designating Least Tern colony sites as protected areas seems a step in the right direction, such designation can create problems for the birds. Land managers and planners tend to want permanent sanctuary boundaries and, through management, prevent natural succession so they can maintain habitat in the condition preferred by Least Terns. They also want to protect the largest colonies. Smaller colonies, which are typical of the species, are generally unprotected and sometimes deliberately destroyed, with perpetrators noting that "the birds have their area." The concentration of birds in a few large

colonies rather than having many smaller, naturally dispersed colonies puts all of their "eggs in a few baskets." The birds are more vulnerable to disasters such as storm tides, chemical pollution, disease, or parasites. They are also putting greater pressure on local prey resources and creating a greater potential reservoir for human pathogens such as encephalitis.

Literature Cited

Bond, J. 1956. Check-list of birds of the West Indies. Academy of Natural Sciences, Philadelphia, Pennsylvania.

Bond, J. 1980. Twenty-third supplement to the Check-list of Birds of the West Indies (1956). Academy of Natural Sciences, Philadelphia, Pennsylvania.

Bradley, P.E. 1995. Birds of the Cayman Islands. Caerulea Press, Italy.

Brudenell-Bruce, P.G.C. 1975. The Collins guide to the birds of New Providence and the Bahama Islands. Stephen Greene Press, Lexington, Massachusetts.

Buden, D.W. 1987a. The birds of Cat Island, Bahamas. Wilson Bull. 99:579-600.

Buden, D.W. 1987b. The birds of the southern Bahamas. British Ornithologists' Union, B.O.U. Check-list No. 8.

Buden, D.W. 1990. The birds of Rum Cay, Bahama Islands. Wilson Bull. 102:451-468.

Buden, D.W. 1992a. The birds of the Exumas, Bahama Islands. Wilson Bull. 104:674-698.

Buden, D.W. 1992b. The birds of Long Island, Bahamas. Wilson Bull. 104:220-243.

Connor, H.A., and R.W. Loftin. 1985. The birds of Eleuthera Island, Bahamas. Florida Field Nat. 14:77-93.

Evans, P. 1990. Birds of the eastern Caribbean. Macmillan Education Ltd., London.

Garrido, O.H., and F. Garcia Montana. 1975. Catalogo de las aves de Cuba. Academia de Ciencias de Cuba, La Habana.

Gore, J.A. 1991. Hatching success in roof and ground colonies of Least Terns. Condor 93:759-762.

Jackson, J.A. 1994. Terns on tar beach. Natural History 103(7):46-53.

Johnson, T.H. 1988. Biodiversity and conservation in the Caribbean: profiles of selected islands. International Council for Bird Preservation, Monogr. No. 1. Cambridge, England.

Keith, A.R. 1997. The birds of St. Lucia. B.O.U. Check-list No. 15. British Ornithologists' Union.

Lee, D.S., and M.K. Clark. 1995. Seabirds of the Bahamas Land and Sea Park, Part 2. Bahamas J. Sci. 2(2):15-21.

Norton, R.L. 1985. West Indies Region. Am. Birds 39:965-966.

Norton, R.L. 1988. West Indies Region. Am. Birds 42:1343-1344.

Norton, R.L. 1989. West Indies Region. Am. Birds 43:1372-1373.

Norton, R.L. 1990. West Indies Region. Am. Birds 44:1191-1192

Norton, R.L. 1997. West Indies Region. Field Notes 51:1058-1059.

Raffaele, H., J. Wiley, O. Garrido, A. Keith, and J. Raffaele. 1998. A guide to the birds of the West Indies. Princeton Univ. Press, Princeton, New Jersey.

Robertson, W.B. 1964. The terns of the Dry Tortugas. Bull. Fla. State Mus. 8:1-94.

Sprunt, A. 1984. The status and conservation of seabirds at the Bahama Islands. Pp. 157-168, in J.P. Croxall, P.G.H. Evans, and R.W. Schreiber, eds. *Status and Conservation of the World's Seabirds*. International Council for Bird Preservation Tech. Publ. No. 2.

Thompson, B.C., J.A. Jackson, J. Burger, L.A. Hill, E.M. Kirsch, and J. Atwood. 1997. Least Tern Sterna antillarum. No. 290 in A. Poole and F. Gill, eds., *The Birds of North America*,. The Academy of Natural Sciences, Philadelphia, Pennsylvania, and The American Ornithologists' Union, Washington, D.C.

Van Halewyn, R., and R.L. Norton. 1984. The status and conservation of seabirds in the Caribbean. Pp. 169-222 in J.P. Croxall, P.G.H. Evans, and R.W. Schreiber, eds., *Status and Conservation of the World's Seabirds*. International Council for Bird Preservation, Tech. Publ. No. 2. Cambridge, England.

White, A.W. 1998. A birder's guide to the Bahama Islands (including Turks and Caicos). American Birding Association, Inc., Colorado Springs, Colorado.

White, B. 1991. Common birds of San Salvador Island, Bahamas. Bahamian Field Station, Ltd., San Salvador, Bahamas.

Status and Conservation Needs of
Brown Noddies and Black Noddies in the West Indies

CR CR CR CR   RO RO RO RO

JOHN W. CHARDINE[1], RALPH D. MORRIS[2] and ROBERT L. NORTON[3]

[1] Canadian Wildlife Service, P.O. Box 6227, Sackville, New Brunswick, E4L 1G6, Canada, Email john.chardine@ec.gc.ca, [2] Department of Biological Sciences, Brock University, St. Catharines, Ontario, L2S 3A1, Canada, Email rmorris@spartan.ac.brocku.ca, [3] Alachua County Environmental Protection Dept., Gainesville, FL 32601 USA, Email rnorton@co.alachua.fl.us

Introduction

There are three or four noddies worldwide, the Brown Noddy (*Anous stolidus*) the Black Noddy (*A. minutus*), the Lesser Noddy (*A. tenuirostris*; sometimes considered conspecific with *A. minutus*), and the Blue-grey Noddy (*Procelsterna cerulea*). Brown Noddies typically breed in relatively small colonies (20 to 200 pairs) on islands in warm seas around the globe. They number in the thousands in the Caribbean. Black Noddies are scarce in the Caribbean and they often nest in colonies with Brown Noddies. Owing to the similarity in appearance of these two species they can easily be confused and nesting Black Noddies are probably often overlooked in Brown Noddy colonies. Little is known about Black Noddies in the Caribbean and while we have some counts of the numbers of Brown Noddies over the years, we have little to no information on Black Noddies. The Black Noddy is smaller and darker brown than the Brown Noddy and has a proportionately longer thinner bill and a whiter head. The voices are distinctive.

They generally arrive in their breeding grounds in April (may arrive in some areas by March) and have departed by the first of September. Black Noddies are only known to nest in bushes and trees while Brown Noddies will nest in bushes and trees as well as on the ground and on rocky cliff faces. When nesting in trees, bushes and the like, both species build a nest of twigs. grass, leafy vegetation or seaweed. Brown Noddies often add bits of shell, coral or small stones to the nest, with some individuals showing a preference gathering more of a particular item. Cliff-nesting Brown Noddies usually dispense with building a nest at all and instead scatter a few pieces of shell, coral or other small item on the ledge. Both species lay one egg.

Brown Noddy, *Anous stolidus stolidus*

The monogamous Brown Noddy lays a single, large (ca. 19% of female body mass) egg usually in late spring-early summer. The egg is incubated for about 35 days and chicks fledge at about 46 days. They first breed at 3-7 years old and have high adult survival rates (90% +; Morris and Chardine 1992, Chardine and Morris 1996, Chardine and Morris in prep.). Breeding success is highly variable across the range of the species, and appears to be related to levels of egg or chick predation experienced at the colony. Male Brown Noddies are larger than females in all body measurements and can be sexed using discriminant function analysis (Chardine and Morris 1989).

Table 1. Number of nesting pairs of Brown Noddies in the West Indies.

Location	Number of Pairs
Bahamas	600-800
Cuba	?
Jamaica, Morant Cays, Northeast Cay	E
Rest of Morant Cays	5,000±
Pedro Cays, 3-4 sites	E
Pedro Cay, Southwest Cay	1,500±
Portland Bight Cays	500±
Puerto Rico, Mona	100s
Culebra, Cayo Molinos	70-110
Cayo Noroeste	120-140
Cayo del Agua	B
Cayo Yerba	50-60
Cayo Raton	B
Cayo Geniqui	100±
Cayo Alcarraza	250±
U. S. Virgin Islands (600-800 pairs)	
Carval Rock	B
Cockroach Cay	25-50
Congo Cay	20-40
Cricket Cay	15-25
Dutchcap	B
Flanagan	B
Flat Cay	25-50
Frenchcap	150-350
Kalkun Cay	10-20
Round Rock	B
Saba Cay	200-400
Sail Cay	B
Sula Cay	B
Turtledove Cay	25-50
British Virgin Islands (100-300 pairs)	
Carval Rock	B
Ginger Island	B
Round Rock	B
Saba	B
Redonda	B
Guadeloupe, Pointe des Chateaux	20
Marie Galante	140
Desirade	80

continued -

Table 1 continued -

Location	Number of Pairs
The Saints	10-90
Basse-Terre	50
Dominica	1,000
Martinique	500
St. Lucia	B
St. Vincent	E
Grenada	B
Tobago	1,200
WEST INDIES TOTAL	**12,000-18,00**

E – extirpated

B – breeds in unknown numbers,

? - bred in the past, no recent numbers, may be extirpated

Four subspecies of Brown Noddies are recognized worldwide, the nominate race *A. s. stolidus* breeding in the tropical Atlantic and Caribbean region. The Brown Noddy is a fairly common seabird breeding in the West Indies but is apparently in decline. The population exceeded 24,000 pairs at about 60 sites in 1984 (Sprunt 1984, van Halewyn and Norton 1984) and we estimate it to be between 12,000-18,000 today owing to continuing loss of nesting habitat and predation (Table , Fig. 1). Brown Noddies are distributed widely throughout the West Indies and breed almost everywhere suitable habitat is found. Small islands where there is the option of elevating the nest above ground on a cliff or in a bush or tree are to be preferred. Relatively few nest in the western Caribbean.

The sizes of most Brown Noddy colonies in the West Indies are poorly known. The population on Bush Key, Dry Tortugas, Florida has probably increased since 1977 (Robertson 1996). The small colonies around Culebra, Puerto Rico have remained relatively stable at about 300-400 pairs (Table 1). Over the past 14 years one small colony at Cayo Noroeste, Culebra has had about 125 pairs each year (Chardine and Morris unpubl.). The total population of the U. S. Virgin Islands is estimated at 600-800 pairs today (J. Pierce pers. comm.) and was estimated at 2,000-4,000 in 1984 (van Halewyn and Norton 1984). The British Virgin Islands is estimated to have 100-300 pairs today and we can find no historic record of the number prior to 1990. Numbers are considered to be declining in this area (J. Pierce pers. comm.). Islets around Guadeloupe have about 350-400 pairs. Jamaica may have the largest West Indian population with about 7,000 pairs. They undoubtedly occur on more islands in the West Indies today as the historic record records them breeding in other places but we have no data on actual population sizes.

Timing of breeding varies considerably among locations in the Caribbean. Eggs are laid in May at Culebra (Chardine and Morris 1996), Aruba (van Halewyn pers. comm.) and the Bahamas (A. Sprunt IV pers. comm.), but two months earlier at Tobago (Morris 1984) and the Dry Tortugas (Robertson 1996). At Culebra, first eggs are usually laid in the first week of May

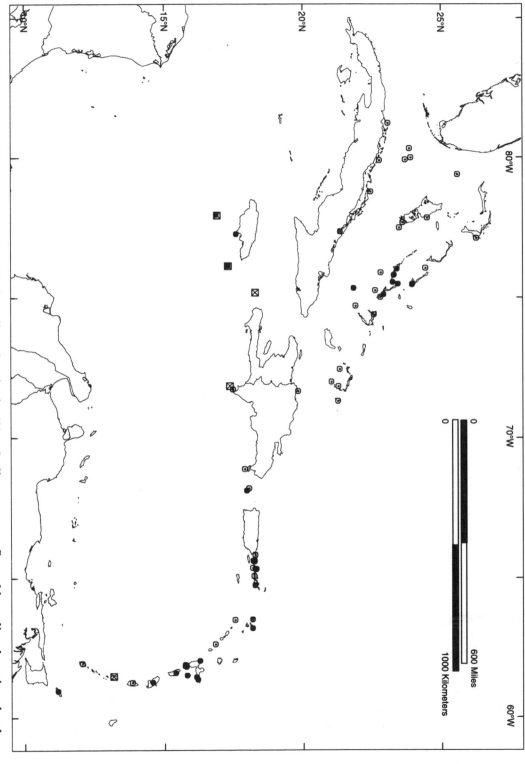

Figure 1: The status of known Brown Noddy breeding sites in the West Indies. ● = confirmed breeding location that has been surveyed recently. ⊙ = historic breeding location with no report that the colony has been extirpated. ⊠ = historic breeding location that is extirpated or thought to be extirpated.

and peak laying occurs in the second or third week of May. The nesting season lasts approximately 3.5 months from first eggs to chick fledging.

Black Noddy, *Anous minutus americanus*

Formerly, the Black Noddy was common at a single location off Belize in the 1800s (Salvin 1864), where thousands of pairs nested in a little archipelago. By the 1950s, this population was greatly reduced and later extirpated as a breeding species there prior to 1970 (Russell 1970). Today it is probably represented in the whole Caribbean by only a few hundred pairs primarily on Los Roques off Venezuela (Le Croy 1979, van Halewyn and Norton 1984), which is outside the region described in this text.

A few pairs may breed with the Brown Noddies on Sombrero Island off Anguilla (Norton 1989a) but they were not seen there during a brief June 1999 survey (J. Pierce pers. comm.). Black Noddies are seen regularly at a Brown Noddy colony on Cayo Noroeste, Culebra, Puerto Rico (J.W. Chardine and R.D. Morris, pers. comm.), and are seen in moderate numbers in June at Aruba, where an average of 17 breeding pairs was observed between 1992 and 1994 (fide van Halewyn in Norton 1994). Their frequent sightings around the West Indies during the breeding season must lead one to speculate that up 100 pairs may possibly breed in the area. In sum, since the decline of the Honduran colony in the 1950s, Black Noddies have suffered a population decline as a result of habitat lost, but they appear to be emigrating around the Caribbean to other islands with Brown Noddy populations. Because they often nest in colonies with Brown Noddies, nesting birds are difficult to locate unless observers are present who are familiar with the vocalizations and color differences are present. We estimate the total West Indian nesting population at between 10 and 100 pairs (Table 2, Fig. 2).

Table 2. Number of nesting pairs of Black Noddies in the West Indies. Other sites undoubtedly exist.

Location	No. of Pairs	Reference
Anguilla, Sombrero	1-6	Norton 1989
Puerto Rico, Culebra, Noroeste Cay	a few	J. & R. Morris pers. comm.
Aruba	a few	Norton 1994
WEST INDIES TOTAL	**10 - 100**	

Research needs and Conservation Priorities

The literature on Brown Noddies is large (see Chardine and Morris 1996). However, the species has been studied in detail at only two locations in the Caribbean area: Culebra, Puerto Rico (Morris and Chardine 1992), and at the Dry Tortugas (Robertson 1964); the former is the only long-term demographic study of individually marked birds. Significant inter-colony variation may exist in patterns of breeding biology, feeding ecology, and demography. There is even less information available about Black Noddy breeding biology and demographics. We recommend that other long-term studies of both of these species be established in the West

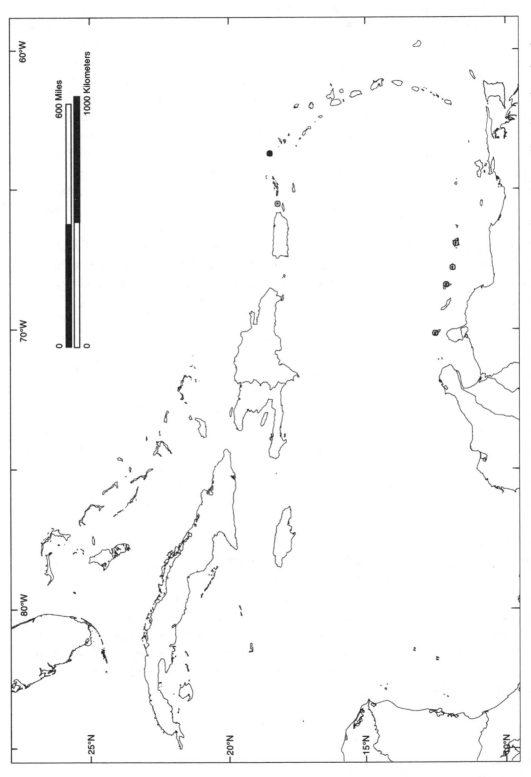

Figure 2: The status of known Black Noddy breeding sites in the West Indies. ● = confirmed breeding location that has been surveyed recently. ◉ = historic breeding location with no report that the colony has been extirpated. ⊠ = historic breeding location that is extirpated or thought to be extirpated.

Indies. In addition, a concerted effort to census both species in the West Indies is badly needed. Populations are declining but we do not have a good idea how fast or how much.

Research done at Culebra (Morris and Chardine 1992, 1995) suggests the potential value of the Brown Noddy as a monitor of the marine environment in the Caribbean. We recommend the establishment of a number of coordinated seabird monitoring sites in the West Indies where breeding biology, feeding ecology, demographics, and toxic chemical/contaminant loads of Brown Noddies and other suitable seabird species are monitored routinely. Banding of chick and adult noddies at these locations will uncover patterns of natal philopatry and breeding dispersal. Blood samples should be routinely taken from captured birds so that intra- and inter-population genetic structure can be determined. On the issue of egging, little information is available on the current prevalence of this activity in the West Indies and the impacts of controlled egging on noddy breeding success. In order to determine if controlled egging is sustainable we need to understand factors that influence re-laying, the ultimate success of re-laid eggs, and the effects of re-laying on adult survival.

Van Halewyn and Norton (1984) make the important point that present-day Caribbean seabird populations are only remnants of former, much larger populations, and further that humans were likely responsible for the declines. Therefore an overriding conservation goal for Caribbean/West Indian seabirds should be to restore their abundance to former levels. However, given the intense level of human development in the region this goal in unlikely to be achieved. A major hindrance to effective seabird conservation in the West Indies is lack of information and a major research initiative to (1) survey colonies and establish population status, and (2) determine values of demographic parameters and the factors that affect them, should be undertaken.

These species are vulnerable to a variety of potential threats shared by many tropical seabirds at this and other locations (see Gochfeld et al. 1994). Introduced rats (*Rattus rattus* and *R. norvegicus*) and other predators can render colony sites completely unproductive for resident seabirds. Rats continue to be problem in many locations throughout the Caribbean region. Since methods of rat eradication at seabird colonies are now well developed and tested, priority locations in the West Indies should be identified and treated. Egging remains a major conservation concern for Caribbean seabirds.

Human disturbance by tourists and fishermen is probably a frequent event at some colonies and can cause abandonment by adults and consequent overheating of eggs and small young or predation of eggs or chicks. Public education and wardening of disturbed colonies at sensitive times of the breeding season would likely be effective solutions. Climate cycles may be the cause of the more frequent hurricanes experienced in the Caribbean region over the past few years. Hurricanes can destroy trees or shrubs used by nesting Brown Noddies (Robertson 1978) and can significantly reduce survival rates of birds (Morris and Chardine 1995). We need to monitor adult survival rates so that impacts of hurricanes can be assessed and considered in overall management plans for West Indian seabirds.

Literature Cited

Chardine, J. W. and R. D. Morris. 1989. Sexual size dimorphism and assortative mating in the Brown Noddy. Condor 91: 868-874.

Chardine, J.W. and R.D. Morris. 1996. Brown Noddy (Anous stolidus). In A. Poole and F. Gill, eds. The Birds of North America, No. 220 The Academy of Natural Sciences, Philadelphia, PA, and The American Ornithologists' Union, Washington, D.C.

Gochfeld, M., J. Burger, A. Haynes-Sutton, R. van Halewyn, and J.E. Saliva. 1994. Successful approaches to seabird protection in the West Indies. Pp. 186-209 in D. N. Nettleship and J. Burger eds., *Seabirds on islands: Threats, case studies and action plans*. Birdlife Conserv. Ser. No. 1. Cambridge.

LeCroy, M. 1979. Bird observation in Los Roques, Venezuela. American Museum Novitates. No. 2599. 30 pp.

Morris, R. D. 1984. Breeding chronology and reproductive success of seabirds on Little Tobago, Trinidad, 1975-1976. Colon. Waterbirds 7: 1-9.

Morris, R. D., and J. W. Chardine. 1992. The breeding biology and aspects of the feeding ecology of Brown noddies nesting near Culebra, Puerto Rico, 1985-1989. J. Zool., London 226: 65-79.

Morris, R.D. and J.W. Chardine. 1995. Brown Noddies on Cayo Noroeste, Culebra, Puerto Rico: What happened in 1990? Auk 112: 326-334.

Norton, R.L. 1989a. First West Indian report of the Black Noddy and nesting of Masked Booby at Sombrero Island, Lesser Antilles. Colonial Waterbirds 12: 120-122.

Norton, R. L. 1989b. West Indies region – Winter report. American Birds 43:1372-1373.

Robertson, W. B., Jr. 1964. The terns of the Dry Tortugas. Bull. Fl. State Mus. 8: 1-94.

Robertson, W. B., Jr. 1978. Species of special concern. Noddy Tern. Pp. 95-96, in H. W. Kale II, ed., *Rare and Endangered Biota of Florida*. Univ. Presses of Florida. Gainesville, FL.

Robertson, W. B., Jr. 1996. Species of special concern. Brown Noddy. Pp. 559-570 in J. A. Rodgers Jr., H. W. Kale II, and H. T. Smith, eds., Rare and endangered biota of Florida. Vol. 5: Birds. Univ. Presses of Florida, Gainesville, FL.

Russell, S.M. 1964. A distributional study of the birds of British Honduras. Ornithological Monographs No. 1, A.O.U. 195 pp.

Salvin, O. 1864. A fortnight amongst the sea-birds of British Honduras. Ibis 6: 372-387.

Sprunt, A. IV. 1984. The status and conservation of seabirds of the Bahama Islands. Pp. 157-168 in J. P. Croxall, P. G. H. Evans, and R. W. Schreiber, eds., *Status and conservation of the world's seabird*. ICBP Tech. Publ. No. 2, Cambridge.

van Halewyn, R., and R. L. Norton. 1984. The status and conservation of seabirds in the Caribbean. Pp.169-222 in J. P. Croxall, P. G. H. Evans, and R. W. Schreiber, eds., *Status and conservation of the world's seabird*. ICBP Tech. Publ. No. 2 . Cambridge.

The Vital Role of Research and Museum Collections
in the Conservation of Seabirds

_____   ᨅ ᨅ ᨅ ᨅ   ᨀ ᨀ ᨀ ᨀ   _____

E. A. SCHREIBER

*National Museum of Natural History, Smithsonian Inst., MRC 116, Washington D. C. 20560
USA, Email SchreiberE@aol.com.*

Introduction

A thorough knowledge of the breeding biology and ecology of a species is necessary in order to develop conservation plans. All too often attempts to save species have been made with little knowledge about the species habits, needs or even a knowledge of what is causing its demise. Without research wrong assumptions are made and when acted upon may, in fact, harm the species in spite of good intentions. We must have good, scientific information on birds in order to preserve them.

Until recently, ornithology in the West Indies has focused on land bird studies, particularly on zoogeography and conservation. Unfortunately, research on seabirds has been neglected over the years. This may be because seabirds often nest in remote areas where it is difficult or expensive to conduct research. In many cases, the birds have been driven to nest in inaccessible areas because their original colony sites have been developed. What this means in the Caribbean is that we have little knowledge about the current status of most seabirds, and even less knowledge about their local natural history. This makes developing conservation criteria for them very difficult. If we are to preserve seabirds in the Caribbean, we must develop and implement some basic research and monitoring plans in a consistent, long-term format.

We know that many seabird species suffered egg shell thinning from the use of DDT before it and other pesticides were banned from use in the United States (Hickey and Anderson 1968, Risebrough et al.1968, Anderson and Hickey 1976). Since that time there has been a heightened awareness of the problems caused to birds by various sources of pollution: pesticides, heavy metals, PCBs, and oil (Ohlendorf et al.1978, Batty 1989, Koskimies 1989, Root 1990). We have essentially no data from the Caribbean area on various pollutant levels in fish or birds and yet we know that many substances are dumped into the water. There is a great need for a basin wide assessment of current pollutant levels in birds.

Specimens exist for so few areas in the Caribbean that no detailed historic record of population ranges and sizes can be reconstructed, and no record of geographic variation exists. Museum collections are an integral part of our knowledge about species and often play a significant role in understanding the conservation needs of species. Having collections is imperative for research on species identification, species diversity (biodiversity), species distributions, documenting changes in species distribution, and documenting effects of anthropogenic changes in our environment that affect bird species (such as historic levels of heavy metals in bird feathers and changes in this over time).

Perhaps more than any other organism, seabirds are symbolic of the land-water interface of Caribbean Islands. They can serve as indicators of the health of the land based environment as well as the sea because they depend on both. Setting up well designed research and monitoring programs for seabirds will enable us to use them as a means of monitoring the environment, as well as enabling us to preserve them. Seabirds can also provide a source of income to countries that do preserve them as eco-tours become more and more popular.

The Need for Research In The West Indies

Basic research on the breeding biology and ecology of birds is necessary in order to make well-informed decisions about conservation of those birds. The Caribbean is a unique ecosystem and the fact that a petrel or tern has been well-studied on a Pacific Ocean island does not necessarily mean that those data will be particularly relevant to the same species in the Caribbean. While the needs of each country may vary somewhat, there are some basic research needs that apply to all seabird colonies in the Caribbean. There are few historic data on colonies and in most cases we do not even know the size of colonies historically or today (Croxall et al. 1984 and papers therein, this publication). The current populations of seabirds present in the Caribbean probably represent about 10% of levels before human exploitation (Steadman et al. 1984, Kirch et al. 1992, Pregill et al.1994). Since the first humans arrived (about 7,000 BP), seabirds have been exploited as a food source and still are today on some Caribbean Islands (van Halewyn and Norton 1984). In addition to the fact that there are few historic data on seabirds, the little data we have are often inadequate. People frequently reported only the number of seabirds present in an area. Did this represent total birds or number of nests or just the number of birds seen? Were the birds even nesting? Because seabirds often travel hundreds of miles from colonies when they are not breeding, the presence of birds in an area does not mean that they nest there.

For many Caribbean countries there are no good data on what seabird species nest there currently, partly because nesting sites are often on uninhabited islands. Yet, the successful conservation of biodiversity depends greatly on an accurate assessment of the status of the animals to be preserved (Winker 1996). This basic research (quantitative listing) needs to be carried out on a Caribbean wide basis in order to determine the current status of seabirds in the Caribbean. Then current data need to be compared to any existing historic counts and to any available data from museum collections to examine trends in population levels and loss of former nesting colonies. The lack of this source of information (collections) for the Caribbean makes it more difficult to determine and defend populations goals for species.

The number of nests is probably the single most important piece of data that can be collected. The next step in monitoring is to make an estimate of nest success: proportion of nests that fledge a chick. These data are not always easy to collect. If a nesting season is extended, with adults laying eggs over 2-4 months, it is more difficult and labor intensive to determine the total number of nests for the colony since a census cannot be conducted in a single visit. Added to this difficulty is that getting to specific colonies may be difficult and expensive. Bad weather can prevent scheduled boat trips to colonies and boats are expensive to maintain and run. Many colonies are in sites that are dangerous to access: on steep cliffs where landing must be made on rocks with surging surf. It is easy to see why we do not know more about the status of many colonies. Yet, this inaccessibility is exactly what has protected these colonies. Once surveys of seabird colonies are completed, action plans can be formulated for preservation of important colony sites. Top priority sites for preservation are listed in individual chapters on each species.

the last chapter by Schreiber and Lee lists criteria for determining important sites. Each site should have legal protection and fines for trespassers.

Another problem that needs to be addressed is that the taxonomic status of seabirds in the Caribbean is poorly determined in many cases. In general, the decision to describe the complete population of a species in the Caribbean as a subspecies was based merely on the fact that the Caribbean was considered to be one continuous region. It was assumed that seabirds from one island move freely between islands, interbreeding with other island populations. The decision was not based on actual data about the birds. A recent analysis of Magnificent Frigatebird (*Fregata magnificens*) sizes in the Caribbean determined that there are significant size and mass differences of adults between colonies on Barbuda, the British Virgin Islands and the Cayman Islands (E. A. Schreiber, unpubl.). This indicates that even among the northern Caribbean islands there is little to no movement of birds between colonies, as found in the central Pacific with Great Frigatebirds (*Fregata minor*; Schreiber and Schreiber 1988). Further analyses may, in fact, determine that northern and southern Caribbean colonies of frigatebirds are different subspecies. Pitman and Jehl (1998) suggest that size and soft-part color differences in Masked Boobies (*Sula dactylatra*) nesting in separate areas on one island in the Pacific indicate that they should be considered separate species. Analyses such as this, combined with DNA analyses are needed for all Caribbean seabird species to determine accurate taxonomy. If some species have two or more subspecies in the Caribbean basin this has tremendous ramifications for conservation, by reducing, even further, the size of subspecific populations.

Ideally, a collection should be made of each seabird species from 3-4 areas in its range through the Caribbean. These specimens should be archived in a museum where they would be available to scientists to study. Specimens not only document colony locations today and current phenotypic variation in the species, they also will be available to scientists in the future as we develop other study needs (such as documentation of heavy metal levels in birds at that time) and techniques. If some seabird species are divided into new subspecies as a result of this study these collections will represent type specimens and be a necessary part of the documentation for taxonomic description (Banks et al. 1993).

The research recommended below may be difficult for some Caribbean countries to carry out since not every country has trained ornithologists on their staff. However, there are organizations available to assist in such studies (see last chapter). Another method for getting assistance with the needed research is to encourage researchers to come from elsewhere to study seabirds. These scientists can then provide a report on their findings and recommendations for conservation. Visiting researchers often provide important collaborative opportunities or training for local staff. The expertise and knowledge provided by visiting researchers can be very helpful and provide the information needed for management and conservation of seabird colonies.

Recommended Research

1) Locate and map nesting colonies of seabirds within each country. Surveys of all potential nesting sites should be undertaken and colony sites mapped. Timing of surveys will have to be determined for each species as the length and timing of the nesting season varies for different species. Seabirds in the Caribbean have two basic nesting seasons so that surveys of potential colony areas may need to take place monthly to determine a baseline for what species are nesting and where. Unfortunately the exact nesting phenology of most Caribbean seabirds is poorly known and, annual and regional variation in this has not been determined. Most tern species lay eggs in the Spring; April to June. Most boobies, frigatebirds and petrels lay in the late fall to

winter: October through January. Burrow and hole nesting birds such as petrels and tropicbirds will be more difficult to locate and often birds flying around a cliff side is the first indication of nesting activity in the area.

2) <u>Determine the status of birds present and set up a monitoring program</u>. Part of determining if a species is in trouble is knowing the number of nesting birds each year and monitoring for annual variation in this. A drastic decline in the nesting population in one year or a slow decline over several years can both be indications of a problem occurring to the birds.

Colonies should be surveyed (meaning that the number of nests is counted and their contents noted) at least three times during a breeding season: 1) near the end of the egg laying period, 2) during the small chick stage and 3) during the stage when larger chicks are present. The first survey records an approximate number of nests with eggs. The second survey records approximate hatching success. The third survey indicates an approximate number of young that will fledge from that colony in that year (reproductive success). The ideal survey plan would be to survey colonies monthly during the active nesting season. Colony sites that only had terns nesting from May through August only need to be surveyed each month through that time period. However, if Fall and Spring nesting species are present, the colony really needs to be surveyed monthly year-round.

3) <u>Determine what if any perturbations are occurring to seabirds and their habitat</u>. Each seabird colony should be specifically surveyed for any potential problems. Do boaters visit the island? Are there predators present on the island? Are goats present on the island, destroying nesting vegetation and causing erosion? Is the area protected by law so that it will not be developed?

If boaters visiting an island are a problem the island should probably be posted with signs. Legal protection for colonies is the most preferable situation but in lieu of this, people will often respect signs that ask them to stay away and explain that nesting seabirds need to be left undisturbed. Goats, sheep, rats, cats and other introduced mammals on nesting colonies should be removed. Cats and rats will eat seabird eggs and cats will take young chicks. Goats and sheep grazing an island trample ground nests and cause erosion that causes nests to be washed away in rains. They also destroy vegetation that is used for nesting habitat by many species.

During monitoring surveys, when nests are counted, observations should be made and recorded on other aspects of nesting and vegetation. Recorded observations often turn out to be very important in interpreting data. Any changes to vegetation should be noted. Any dead birds found should be recorded, along with age of bird (adult or chick) and reason for death (if this can be determined: broken wing, eaten by mammal, etc.). Annual changes can be monitored when notes are taken throughout the year and can be helpful in determining if anything is happening to the birds. For instance, an increase in the number of dead young found during surveys would be cause for concern and further investigation.

4) <u>Determine and protect important roosting and feeding sites</u>. Roosting and feeding sites are almost as important to seabirds as nesting sites and these areas should also be protected when possible. Roost sites are places where birds sit, rest and preen when they are not feeding.

Birds need to be able to rest, preen, sleep and feed safely to survive. If they are disturbed every time they sit down to roost on a sandbar, beach or rocky outcropping, they will not remain in an area. Protected wetlands serve as feeding areas for many birds, and as nursery grounds of the fish that many seabird species need for food. Protecting wetlands is vital not only to seabirds, but to the fishing industry. Sites such as these are often ignored when areas are considered for protection for seabirds, yet they are vital to the birds.

5) <u>Band representative samples of nesting adult and young seabirds each year</u>. We currently have almost no knowledge of the movements of seabirds in the Caribbean (except for a couple studies being carried out in Puerto Rico and the U.S. Virgin Islands). Banded birds are needed in order to determine movements of birds and to study demographics. The proposal to build a rocket launching facility on Sombrero Island will destroy the nesting area for Brown (*Sula leucogaster*) and Masked Boobies (*Sula dactylatra*); species considered "Threatened" and "Endangered" (respectively) in the Caribbean (see final chapter). It has been proposed that other islands could be set aside and protected for these birds to use. Data from banded birds of these species in the Pacific indicate that they do not readily change nesting islands (Schreiber et al. 1993, 1996), thus expecting them to move is probably untenable. Without banded birds, we have no way of knowing this type of information for Caribbean seabirds and it has severe ramifications for conservation efforts.

6) <u>Encourage research projects on seabirds</u>. Research by qualified scientists can often provide an inexpensive way for governments to obtain valuable information about their birds. Most researchers have funding to pay for their research and are not asking the local government to support their work. Full advantage should be taken of the findings of these studies. Most scientists are willing to advise on conservation issues that will help preserve the birds they want to study and they should be asked to do so.

7) <u>Establish a series of museum specimens for research and reference</u>. See below.

The Need For Specimens

A series of specimens of local seabirds can be very important to conservation efforts. Part of the reason for the lack of recent specimens in collections has been the reluctance of governments to give permits to collect birds. This is in some part owing to the environmental movement which works to protect species and habitat. Yet, one of the most important aspects of any conservation program is to ensure that voucher specimens exist for that area in that time. Vouchers are vital to documenting basic life history information, morphology, genetics, geographic variation, zoogeography, heavy metal levels and other pollutants, and the presence of genetic aberrations. For instance, if it were suspected that the deposition of heavy metals were increasing in Caribbean seabirds for some reason a set of samples could be taken to test for heavy metal levels but that would tell us little without historic data for comparison. Some heavy metals are naturally occurring in the environment and all seabirds will have them in their tissues naturally. To determine if levels are increasing we need a data set from a previous time-period for comparison. Currently this does not exist. A 14 year study, designed to analyze seabird diets and study molt by collecting specimens, has produced the only available evidence for increased consumption of plastic debris by seabirds (Moser and Lee 1992). This study also provided data on the importance of a specific ocean area to feeding seabirds and helped stop oil-drilling in the area (Lee and Socci 1989).

Today there are few specimens of seabirds from the Caribbean in any collection in the world. For instance, the National Museum of Natural History in Washington, D.C. (one of the largest collections in the world) has 13 round skin specimens of Red-billed Tropicbirds (*Phaethon aetherus*) from 5 islands, and has no skeletons or tissues. They have 19 round skin specimens and 2 unsexed skeletons of Magnificent Frigatebirds from 7 islands. Given the already documented variability in frigatebirds on the northern Caribbean islands (above), we would need 20 skeletons (10 of each sex) from each of four sites through the Caribbean (80 total skeletons) in order to examine the differences in their morphology throughout their Caribbean range and to determine their taxonomic status. Remsen (1995) suggests it is likely that many island populations of birds of widespread species should be classified as separate biological species. But these studies require specimens and genetic material. Collections also have many other uses which involve conservation and documentation of the effects on birds of anthropogenic changes in our environment.

Uses of museum specimens which aid in conservation.

1) <u>Documentation of the distribution of species in time and space</u>. In many cases we only know if a species range has changed over time because of the existence of historic museum specimens with accurate data. Specimens of skins can also document changes in species over time within an area. Egg specimens validate nesting seasons and presence of nesting in an area, as well as providing documentation of eggshell thinning.

2) <u>Understanding species diversity</u>. The only way to document diversity of a species throughout an area is by comparison of museum specimens. Collections are used to study species-level taxonomy and such research often affects our interpretations of local biodiversity and endemism (Stiles 1995).

3) <u>Discovery of new species and subspecies</u>. To know that a new species or subspecies has been found, and to describe it, depends on having collections of similar species for side-by-side comparison. Watson et al. (1991) made extensive use of museum collections in order to describe a new subspecies of Double-crested Cormorant (*Phalacrocorax auritus heuretus*) from the Bahamas.

4) <u>Teaching and training aides</u>. Collections form a vital educational tool for training people in the sciences, environmental studies and conservation. Museums use their collections as teaching aides for training people in conservation of natural resources. This training opportunity can only be provided because these institutions have actively collected specimens and maintained them. While a country may not have the funding to support a full training program itself, it can still assist in these programs by supplying permits for the needed specimens and then benefit from the training available to all people.

5) <u>Solving environmental problems</u>. Collections that have been actively maintained and added to over time play a significant role in the problem solving process when determining the presence of and reasons for perturbations occurring to birds. Frozen tissue collections can be particularly important in documenting environmental perturbations (Remsen 1995) yet none exist for Caribbean seabirds.

6) <u>Use of specimens by researchers</u>. Most large museum collections contain specimens from around the world and they are also used by researchers from around the world. A significant part of the cost of maintaining a collection is making it available for researchers by having museum staff members who correspond with potential visiting researchers and process loans of specimens to institutions for research. Thus a country or a state, which may not have the money to maintain a large scientific collection, can have a series of bird specimens from their country in existence in an institution with the funding to care for it simply by approving collecting permit requests from Institutions.

7) <u>Conservation</u>. Sound conservation decisions must be based on the biology of the bird and a tremendous volume of information can be obtained from museum collections. "Species" and "subspecies" are the taxonomic categories most used in determining conservation priorities and evaluating these categories depends on having specimens in collections (Remsen 1995).

8) <u>Writing of Field Guides</u>. As ecotourism has increased around the Caribbean, there is a greater demand for field guides to the birds, and for more detail in these guides. Virtually all field

guides are written and illustrated by making extensive use of museum collections since authors and artists cannot generally afford to visit and do research in each site in order to write the guides.

Conclusion

The successful conservation of West Indian seabirds depends upon having an accurate knowledge of the species, and their biological diversity and needs. This research should be a priority for any conservation action plans for Caribbean seabirds. As human population size increases and development and pollution increase, it has never been more important to know how this is affecting our natural resources and to monitor them closely. Birds, particularly birds such as seabirds which are top-level predators, provide a sensitive indicator to our environmental health.

There are means to assist in ensuring that the research is done. Many conservation and government organizations offer aid and assistance for environmental studies (such as BirdLife, American Bird Conservancy, U.S. Fish and Wildlife Service, Organization of Eastern Caribbean States and World Wildlife Fund). These sources can help in multiple ways from advising, to providing literature, to arranging for a scientist to come and carry out a study with local resource managers. Full advantage should be taken of this assistance.

Literature Cited

Anderson, D. W., and J. J. Hickey. 1976. Dynamics of organochlorine pollutants in herring gulls. Envrion. Pollut. 10: 183-200.

Banks, R. C., S. M. Goodman, S. M. Lanyon and T. S. Schulenberg. 1993. Type specimens and basic principles of avian taxonomy. Auk 110: 413-414.

Batty, L. 1989. Birds as monitors of marine environments. Biologist 36: 151-154.

Croxall, J. P., P. G. H. Evans and R. W. Schreiber. 1984. Status and conservation of the world's seabirds. Internatl. Council for Bird Preservation, Tech. Publication No. 2.

Hickey, J. J., and D. W. Anderson. 1968. Chlorinated hydrocarbons and eggshell changes in raptorial and fish-eating birds. Science 162: 271-273.

Kirch, P. V., J. R. Flenley, D. W. Steadman, F. Lamont and S. Dawson. 1992. Ancient environmental degradation. Natl. Geographic Research & Exploration 8: 166-179.

Koskimies, P. 1989. Birds as a tool in environmental monitoring. Ann. Zool. Fennici 26: 153-166.

Lee, D. S. and M. C. Socci. 1989. Potential effects of oil-spills on seabirds and selected other oceanic vertebrates off the North Carolina coast. Occas. Papers North Carolina Biological Survey 1989-1: 1-64.

Moser, M. L., and D. S. Lee. 1992. A fourteen-year survey of plastic ingestion by western North Atlantic seabirds. Colonial Waterbirds 15: 83-94.

Ohlendorf, H. M., r. W. Risebrough and K. Vermeer. 1978. Exposure of marine birds to environmental pollutants. Wildlife Research Rept. 9. U.S. Dept. of Interior, Washington, D.C.

Pitman, R. L., and J. R. Jehl, Jr. 1998. Geographic variation and reassessment f species limits in the "Masked" Boobies of the eastern Pacific Ocean. Wilson Bull.110: 155-170.

Pregill, G. K., D. W. Steadman and D. R. Watters. 1994. Late quaternary and vertebrate faunas of the Lesser Antilles: historical components of Caribbean biogeography. Bull. Carnegie Museum of Natl. History, No 30. Pittsburgh.

Remsen, J. V., Jr. 1995. The importance of continued collecting of bird specimens to ornithology and bird conservation. Bird Conservation International 5: 177-212.

Risebrough, R. W., P. Reiche, D. B. Peakall, S. G. Herman and M. N. Kirven. 1968. Polychlorinated biphenyls in the global ecosystem. Nature 220: 1098-1102.

Root, M. 1990. Biological monitors of pollution. Bioscience 40: 83-86.

Schreiber, E. A., and R. W. Schreiber. 1988. Great frigatebird size dimorphism on two central Pacific atolls. Condor 90: 90-99.

Schreiber, E. A., and R. W. Schreiber. 1993. Red-tailed Tropicbird (*Phaethon rubricauda*). No. 43 in A. Poole and F. Gill eds. *The Birds of North America*, Philadelphia, The Academy of Natural Sciences; Washington, D.C., The American Ornithologists' Union. No. 241

Schreiber, E. A., R. W. Schreiber and G. A. Schenk. 1996. Red-footed Booby (*Sula sula*). No. 241 in A. Poole and F. Gill eds. *The Birds of North America*, Philadelphia, The Academy of Natural Sciences; Washington, D.C., The American Ornithologists' Union.

Steadman, D. W., G K. Pregill and S. L. Olson. 1984. Fossil vertebrates from Antigua, Lesser Antilles: evidence for late Halocene human-caused extinctions in the West Indies. Proc. Natl. Academy of Sciences 81: 4448-4451.

Stiles, G. F. 1995. Museums and Bird Conservation. World Birdwatch 17: 24.

van Halewyn, R., and R. L. Norton. 1984. The status and conservation of Caribbean seabirds. Pp. 169-222 in J. P. Croxall, P. G. H. Evans, and R. W. Schreiber, eds. *Status and Conservation of the World's Seabirds*, Cambridge, U.K.: Intl. Council for Bird Preservation, Tech. Publ. No. 2.

Watson, G. E., S. L. Olson and J. R. Miller. 1991. A new subspecies of Double-crested Cormorant, Phalacrocorax auritus, from San Salvador, Bahamas. Proc. Biological Society of Washington 104: 356.369.

Winker, K. 1996. The crumbling infrastructure of biodiversity: the avian example. Conservation Biology 10: 703-707.

The Role of Helicopters in Seabird Censusing

ᘓ ᘓ ᘓ ᘓ   ᘔ ᘔ ᘔ ᘔ

P. A. BUCKLEY[1] AND FRANCINE G. BUCKLEY[2]

[1] USGS, Patuxent Wildlife Research Center, Box 8, Graduate School of Oceanography, University of Rhode Island, Narragansett RI 02882 USA, Email pabuckley@gsosun1.gso.uri.edu. [2] Dept. of Natural Resource Sciences, College of the Environment and Life Sciences, University of Rhode Island, Kingston RI 02881 USA, Email fgb@uri.edu

Introduction

The literature on techniques for surveying and censusing seabirds is widely scattered, and recent books treating wildlife census methods in general (Giles 1969) or birds in particular (Ralph and Scott 1981) have ignored colonially nesting waterbirds and seabirds. If reviews did consider seabirds, they concentrated nearly exclusively on methods used on the ground (Bibby et al. 1992, Gibbons et al. 1996). We address the pros and cons of commonly used methods of counting seabirds, from the air and on the ground, evaluate each, and recommend one in particular for use in the survey-census of all seabirds of the West Indies. Owing to the paucity of published seabird studies from the West Indies, virtually all examples come from far afield.

Terminology and Concepts

Surveying - the process of locating *sites* where seabirds are breeding (*colonies*).

Censusing - the enumeration of the population of each species at each site.

Monitoring - periodic surveying to detect the presence or absence of any (likely breeding) birds at each site.

Evaluation - detailed, onsite study in a particular colony to determine its health in terms of productivity, recruitment, predation, disturbance, loss of habitat, etc.

A major question is whether there can ever be any *one* number to represent colony 'size.' Is it the total number of breeding pairs in a breeding season; total number of successful breeding pairs across a single season; either of the foregoing but excluding renesters from that colony or only from other colonies; number of attended/occupied nests or burrows? We argue that there is no single value for *any* of these metrics because colonies are in a constant state of flux across a breeding season. Indeed, some authors (Drury 1980) have argued that order-of-magnitude ranges of numbers (10-100, 100-1000, etc.) are sufficient, but greater levels of accuracy can be attained and are much more useful: all possible attempts should be made to be more accurate.

To facilitate comparisons and detect changes, the global standard has now become reporting breeding seabird populations (and other colonial nesters) as *numbers of breeding pairs at each site* as has been done in this publication. Pairs are better than birds or nests: the former might contain non-breeders, and the latter might misrepresent the colony's size if birds that are about to breed have not yet done so. Numbers of breeding pairs are normally obtained by actual nest (or burrow) counts (one per pair), or by estimating or counting the number of breeding adults present in a colony and then applying conversion factors to translate these to breeding pairs.

In mixed-species colonies, aerial surveying and censusing is optimally done once, during that window when the greatest number of species are simultaneously breeding. This is much easier in temperate and polar areas, where breeding times are narrow. In the tropics, the duration of site occupancy may extend over many months, and it may not be uncommon for wholly different populations (genetically or even specifically distinct) to occupy the same site (Ainley 1980). Thus, more traditional, temperate-derived notions of survey and census windows should not be used in tropical areas without detailed, site-specific tailoring. It is also possible for the same species to have significantly displaced breeding seasons on islands near each other. Therefore, we urge routine adoption of the *snapshot census*, whereby an intensive effort is made to survey and census an entire geographic area simultaneously, as close to the peak of maximum site occupation as possible.

Aerial census techniques obviously do not work for seabirds that reach and depart their colonies under cover of darkness. For such animals, surveying may best be done by boats looking for pre-arrival aggregations offshore of known or potential colony sites, or by sniffing known or suspected burrows for the characteristic (but not ubiquitous) odor of tubenoses, by physically checking burrows, by listening for calling birds, or by luring others in with recordings at or near colonies after dark. One method of great promise is tracking incoming seabirds on marine radar, once calibration and identification of appropriate radar wavelengths have been done. At this stage, radar discrimination of even major species groups (say, gadfly petrels from storm-petrels) is still primitive (Cooper et al. 1991, Day and Cooper 1995) but warrants close attention. Diurnal burrow- or crevice-nesters such as tropicbirds are normally susceptible to the techniques we discuss in this paper, although calibration of the number of adults in the air to the number of occupied nest sites remains to be determined empirically. It is also an open question just how extropolable any such conversion factors will be between islands.

Finally, many environmental variables (time of day; rain; cloud cover; sea state; wind; tide; El Niño-Southern Oscillation [ENSO] events) are likely to affect the number of adults present at a colony, and can lead to disparate counts (Vermeer et al. 1993, Ewins et al. 1995).

Comparing Surveying and Censusing Techniques

The commonly used techniques for locating and quantifying the numbers of birds in seabird colonies involve ground (or nest) counts, aerial photography, aerial videography, fixed-wing aircraft, and rotary-winged aircraft (helicopters).

<u>Ground counts</u> are most frequent, because anyone can do them, but therein lies a problem. Often involving volunteers with variable, limited, or no training, ground counts can be of low precision (Graham et al. 1996), so cost saving is often offset by greatly increased data unreliability. Moreover, colonial waterbirds may be severely disturbed by on-ground observers (especially untrained ones), and depending on species and stage in the breeding cycle, may desert the site entirely. However, all other things being equal, seabirds in general are least likely to desert immediately before hatching.

Ground counters also tend to visit only already-known colony sites, thus missing new colonies at unexpected sites. For logistic reasons, ground-counting is often spread across an entire breeding season at different sites in the same area, leading to the same birds being counted more than once when they move, as they frequently do, between colonies in the same year, to re-nest after disturbance, or washouts, etc. It is extremely difficult to coordinate ground counts so that they occur simultaneously, a procedure nonetheless essential for evaluation of true seabird/colonial waterbird population trends. It is also extremely difficult to prevent ground-counters from leaving scent trails that mammalian predators can use to locate seabirds, especially burrow-nesting, nocturnal seabird species. 'Scent-destroyers' are commercially available from hunting supply catalogues, but have never been evaluated with seabirds.

Controlled flushing (slowly and carefully flushing parts of a colony serially, so that reasonably segregated counts of adults in the air may be summed for the whole colony) can be exceedingly difficult on the ground, and it is not uncommon for only part of a colony to be erroneously reported as the whole. Still, if done carefully by experienced biologists, it can yield highly precise estimates of the number of breeding pairs at a site, but it is not the best way. Achieving wide-area simultaneity is also difficult with this method. Finally, even in a near-optimal situation (easily visible seabirds in colonies of a few hundred pairs), the range of variation in data obtained is thought-provoking. For example, Lloyd (1975) was unable to reduce error in estimating the number of breeding Razorbills any lower than ±10%, and this asymptote was reached only after 25 counts.

Aerial photography may seem the most objective and least subject-to-error method of censusing seabirds and colonial waterbirds. There have been a number of studies in the wildlife management literature on the problems with aerial photography, but the few dealing explicitly with seabirds or colonial waterbirds strongly caution against its blanket application. For example, ten observers made a total of 33 counts of the same photo of Northern Gannets (*Morus bassanus*) atop a flat island in the U.K. Counts ranged from 2823 to 3362 birds, this spread being no closer than -11% and +6% to the grand mean of all values (Harris and Lloyd 1977).

Prater (1979) also looked at within- and between-observer variation in abilities to estimate birds on aerial photographs. Flocks (not breeding birds) ranged in size from 20 to 3650 individuals (presumably counted without error). Eleven observers were allowed 30 seconds to estimate, and in some trials were shown the same photos days later, without having been given the true values. All observers underestimated larger flocks. Between-observer variation ranged from +20% to -75%; one person, across three trials over a two-year period, never did better than ±20%. When one considers that all of the subjects were birders with considerable previous field experience in estimating flock size, these are sobering findings for any studies purporting to compare seabird counts taken by different groups of volunteers, even with aerial photographs.

In addition, there is striking variation in nest-attendance among seabirds and colonial waterbirds at different stages in the breeding cycle within the same species. Kadlec and Drury (1968) found that the ratio of birds estimated during fixed-wing censuses of Herring Gulls (*Larus argentatus*) in New England (Table 1) varied, according to the stage of the breeding cycle, between 60% to 95%. During the egg-laying stage estimates between 60% and 95% in one year, and between 71% and 84% the following year, and all only in colonies no larger than 500 pairs.

Aerial vidoegraphy as a seabird censusing tool has only been recently evaluated. Dolbeer et al. (1997) compared fixed-wing, still photography with helicopter video censusing in a large (5000-pair) Laughing Gull (*Larus atricilla*) colony complex, augmented by in-colony, 30m x 30m study plots. They found that all three methods gave satisfactory results, and that videography by helicopter was about half the cost of the fixed-wing photography and one-quarter to one third that of on-ground nest counting.

Fixed-wing aircraft (airplanes) are often chosen for surveying and censusing large areas, usually because of availability and low per-hour costs. There are occasions when nothing else is convenient, but users should be aware of their limitations and possible defects in data resulting from their use. Savard (1982) contrasted airplane with ground-observer counts of wintering

---

Table 1. Variation in attendance of adult Herring Gulls at New England breeding colonies during two stages in the breeding cycle, and how these were perceived by census takers vs. counts on aerial photographs (Kadlec and Drury 1968). Column 3 is a ratio.

Stage in Breeding cycle	No. of Colonies	Birds estimated No. in photo
Eggs: year 1, group a	19	0.60
Eggs: year 1, group b	12	0.95
Eggs: year 2, group a	17	0.84
Eggs: year 2, group b	19	0.84
Chicks: year 3	20	0.94

---

waterbirds (loons, grebes, cormorants, and waterfowl), finding that more than twice as many *individuals* were detected by ground observers, who in turn were also able to discriminate on average four times as many *species* as the trained observers in planes. This study amply highlights the biggest drawbacks of fixed-wing aircraft: their relatively high stalling speeds and ceilings. Many more planes are low-wing than high-wing, yet the former are essentially useless for surveying and censusing, because downward visibility is exceedingly limited. Other difficulties with airplanes include: emergencies require adequate landing areas; aerial photography is difficult; landing at or near colonies for immediate ground-truthing is not possible, nor is counting birds by controlled flushing; they have large turning radii; they can't hover; and they can't be used at all with solitary nesters or dark species. They do have the apparent advantages of availability, economy, large fuel load, and ironically, because of altitude restrictions, relatively low noise levels and bird disturbance.

Few studies have examined the absolute efficiency of fixed-wing aircraft. In the New England USA area, counting birds on aerial photos taken from fixed-wing aircraft permitted regional estimates to only ±20-30% of the 'true' number of Herring Gulls present (Kadlec and Drury 1968). This in turn led the authors to conclude that this technique would not be useful in detecting regional changes of less than ±25%. We would further add that even this degree of accuracy is not to be expected of counts from single aerial photos taken at varying times during a breeding season.

Helicopters offer, we believe, the best compromise among currently available techniques for both surveying and censusing of seabirds and colonial waterbirds. They make the most efficient use of airtime because they generally have few ceiling or populated area restrictions (this can vary locally, however, and often is a function of air traffic controllers' familiarity with helicopters' flight characteristics and abilities). They can hover and fly very slowly sideways and backwards, thus offering unrivalled views of colonies, and these features can be used in controlled flushing to allow rapid, easy, and accurate counting as birds circle or exit colonies.

If asked, most companies will provide one free hour of ground time for each paid hour of airtime, put to good use in landing adjacent to colonies whenever in-colony data are required.

Visibility in helicopters is superb (Fig.1), and, coupled with their unique flying abilities, helicopters enable easy collection of simultaneous multiple-observer counts. Finally, and not trivially, disturbance to birds in colonies by helicopters is of exceptionally short duration, and leaves no trail for predators to follow. For these reasons, we are convinced that when trained observers are used, helicopters are optimal for obtaining wide-area coverage of all habitats, over a short-duration, and with the highest precision readily available. We believe that only such simultaneous data allow long-term comparisons, trend detection, and population modeling to be done with confidence over wide geographic areas.

However, helicopters are not without drawbacks. Nearly all require jet-A fuel, not always available at small airports, per-hour cost is expensive (but see below), airtime per fuel load is relatively short (2-3 hours), they are noisy, and can cause unexpected and occasionally severe within-colony panic leading to egg loss and even colony desertion. However, even birds' panic and lack of exposure to helicopters can be put to good use in surveying and censusing seabirds and colonial waterbirds (see below). One cannot expect to become successful at helicopter censusing on first try, and finding pilots who can learn to fly 'low and slow' and then 'work' a colony can take considerable effort. The manifold advantages of helicopter use outweigh their disadvantages and with some 500+ hours of airtime in surveying and censusing seabirds and colonial waterbirds we would, given our choice, use no other method.

Cost comparisons between fixed-wing aircraft and helicopters are frequently mentioned as unfavorable to helicopters, although personnel costs are rarely included in comparisons. Recent U.S. costs for the commonest four-door, five-seat jet helicopter, the Bell Jet Ranger (206-B or – C), average about US$600/hour, while comparable costs for a four-seat, two-door, high-wing, single-engine plane run about US$100/hour. In the West Indies, where helicopters are less common, rental on Barbados in 1996 was US$600/hour, but US$1200/hour by 1997; we are unsure if it was negotiable. On Aruba in 1997, the latter rate was quoted, although we were advised that for scientific purposes it was negotiable, perhaps down to US$1000/hour or even lower. On Barbados, the free hour of ground time was moot because helicopters there are allowed to land only at approved heliports, and we also had to maintain a 300m altitude over populated areas—an unfortunate example of controllers' unfamiliarity with helicopters' capabilities. Fixed-wing aircraft (high-wings are scarce) on both Barbados (in 1996 and 1997), and on Aruba (in 1997), rented for US$120/per hour, virtually identical to U.S. rates.

Relative efficiency of fixed-wing craft and helicopters. What raw rental costs omit is value for money. For example, we were able to survey the entire coastline (and a few inland sites) on Barbados in a little over one hour, in the process locating and examining one and perhaps two previously unknown, suitable breeding sites for Audubon's Shearwaters (*Puffinus lherminieri*) that are being investigated on-ground. This was possible only by our approach to within a few meters of sites, and hovering close while they were slowly and carefully inspected— impossible in fixed-wing aircraft irrespective of cost. In our work in the U.S. (Buckley and Buckley 1980a, 1984, 1999), we were able to perform the first complete survey-census of the complete 1600 km coastline of Long Island, N.Y., with hundreds of square km of salt marshes and 18+ species of colonially breeding waterbirds distributed at 231 sites, in only 30-40 hours of airtime each year. While the helicopter cost today would be US$18,000-24,000, the amount of high-precision population and habitat data obtainable would be enormous.

Prior to our helicopter work, no one had suspected that nearly one-quarter of the entire Long Island Common Tern population (up to 8027 pairs) were breeding and thriving in tidal salt-marshes. We also discovered three new breeding species on well-studied Long Island (Double-

Figure 1. Visibility from the co-pilot's seat of a Bell Jet Ranger helicopter (Photo by P.A. Buckley).

crested Cormorant [*Phalacrocorax auritus*], Laughing Gull, and Gull-billed Tern [*Sterna nilotica*]), documented the increase and unexpected decline of breeding Herring Gulls, and detected the catastrophic decrease in regional Roseate Tern numbers that led directly to its U.S. listing as an Endangered Species. On Long Island, NY in 1977, we detected, in less than one day, 7700 pairs of Common Terns at 26 sites, while another worker, coordinating dozens of on-ground volunteers across the same breeding season, was able to locate only 6000 pairs at 20 sites (1980a). Assuming it were possible to send counters to each of our 231 colonial waterbird sites simultaneously, consider what a logistical nightmare it would be, and what the costs would be, if trained observers had to be paid while censusing. In a word, our data could not have been obtained in any other way, regardless of cost. It is no wonder that complete on-ground surveying of all the 1000 islands in the Bahamas has never been done. Yet, helicopters are uniquely suited to that task.

At the time we were aerially censusing Long Island, N.Y. intensively (1974-83), others were collecting data on the ground there in a number of locations. Comparison of results of the two methods gives an indication of the validity of the snapshot method to both detect and preclude the same birds being counted in multiple locations when all counting was not simultaneous, as well as the accuracy of our helicopter censuses. Table 2 compares helicopter counts at the peak of colony occupancy with earlier or later ground counts the same years and confirms that in two different mixed heronries, numbers counted by both methods were remarkably close.

Table 2. Comparison of on-ground and helicopter censuses of two Long Island heronries: Seganus Thatch counted both ways at the same time in the nesting cycle (but not at the same time day); Pearsall's Hassock ground-counted a month before helicopter censusing

	Seganus Thatch		Pearsall's Hassock	
Species	**15 June (ground)**	**10 June (helo)**	**18 May (ground)**	**11 June (helo)**
Great Egret	15-20	33	10	40
Snowy Egret	80-90	85	200	250
Cattle Egret	0	0	2	2
Louisiana Heron	6-8	7	0	0
Little Blue Heron	10-12	11	4	4
Black-crowned Night-Heron	60+	60	30	20
Glossy Ibis	80	75	220	200

Simultaneous contrasts among the various techniques. Fixed-wing and helicopter efficiencies have been compared for counting waterfowl, eagles, turkeys, deer, large mammals, and other game species, and nearly all such studies have found helicopters strikingly superior (e.g., Shandruk and McCormick 1989; Lotter and Cornwell 1993). Very few studies have looked at non-game, colonially nesting waterbirds. Hutchinson (1980) has done the only simultaneous comparison of common seabird census techniques of which we are aware (aerial estimates and aerial photographs from fixed-wing aircraft; ground estimates from boats; and in-colony nest counts), working with Herring Gulls and Double-crested Cormorants in Maine. He determined that for both species, on-ground nest counts had the highest accuracy (±5%) and aerial estimates (gulls: ± 140%) and on-ground estimates (cormorants: ±82%) the lowest. As expected, aerial estimates were cheapest, and on-ground nest counts most expensive.

We are aware of only a single published comparison of the census-efficiency of helicopters and fixed-wing aircraft for colonial waterbirds, that of Kushlan (1979). This study is interesting because it is the only one contrasting numbers obtained simultaneously from airplane, helicopter, and ground counts of wading bird (storks, herons, and ibises) colonies in the Everglades, Florida. The helicopter (a small, piston-engine Bell 47G) disturbed the birds less than the plane, and while neither technique found all pairs present in each of the colonies, the airplane's census error rate by species varied between -32% and -100%, averaging -72%, while the helicopter's ranged between -93% and +11%, averaging -28% (Table 3).

Table 3. Results of a census of an Everglades National Park heronry by three methods. Ground counts are nests, others are birds; see text for discussion (Kushlan 1979).

Species	Ground census	Fixed-wing census	Helo census
Great Egret	155	100	130
Snowy Egret	720	250	650
White Ibis	27	0	30
Louisiana Heron	431	15	30
Little Blue Heron	22	15	0
Anhinga	3	0	3
Double-crstd. Corm.	5	0	5

Details of Helicopter Surveying and Censusing

Choice of aircraft is generally limited to what is available for rental. A variety of manufacturers make small, maneuverable, four-door, four- or five-passenger, jet-powered helicopters that work well in seabird surveying and censusing. Sometimes companies will donate airtime for scientific work. We recommend that anyone surveying birds by helicopter in the West Indies insist on a helicopter with floats (helicopter-skid pop-floats that open automatically when in contact with water). Some companies insist on two pilots for safety reasons. However, in our experience, the single most important seat in a survey-census helicopter is the co-pilot's. Visibility is excellent, identification of birds can be easily and quickly made at considerable distances, hand-signals can be instantly given to the pilot while the observer is still taking data, and the view approaches 360 degrees. Headsets for participants are essential for communication and to minimize hearing damage. All observers should have notebooks, and all data should be primarily taken in writing. If some are also to be taken by tape-recorder or laptop computer, written backup is essential; irreplaceable field data can be lost from equipment problems.

Larger machines (HUEYs, Sikorskys) are unsuitable for several reasons: noise, cost, inability to seat four persons with each looking out on a slightly different view, including one in the co-pilot's seat for course plotting, initial locating of colonies, and directions to the pilot. Some of the least effective machines are large military helicopters with only a single, sliding cargo-bay door for viewing, but if military helicopters are available, it is occasionally possible to ride along on training flights. In such cases, site access is more important than optimal viewing and large helicopters can be used with some success.

Timing of surveys is critical, and in the tropics most difficult of all. While there are general peaks of seabird breeding activity, tropical breeding seasons are often far longer than in temperate areas and there are winter and summer (or even spring and fall) breeding species. If local species' breeding times cannot be pinpointed beforehand or extrapolated from the literature, then multiple aerial surveys at different seasons of the year are mandated. For optimal efficiency, censusing should occur only after local species' colony locations and breeding times are reasonably well established.

Surveying can be done at whatever altitude and speed local breeding species and conditions dictate, and this will quickly become apparent on a trial-and-error basis. It often takes some time to get helicopter pilots comfortable flying low and slow, and hovering frequently. Should one find a pilot who seems nervous, or is unable to follow directions, avoid flying with such a person. We encountered only one pilot like that in all of our helicopter censusing, but after only three hours in the air, we cancelled the day's work, and requested another pilot. This serves as a reminder that one of the major duties of the observer in the co-pilot's seat is to watch out for air traffic (the pilot will be busy flying the craft and following your directions, while also on the radio) and especially for power lines and guy-wires.

We have found surveying at a speed of 100 km/h 100m above the ground to be very effective with most species, but surveying techniques will always be determined by local terrain, species, wind, and direction of sunlight. Obviously, light from behind is always best. Colonies are usually located by finding sitting or milling birds, sometimes by following flight lines. Working along miles of sea cliffs, over vast marshes, or among large island archipelagoes helicopters allow rapid access to areas out of reach to nearly all other techniques. Some species do not flush until the helicopter is very close, so their colonies can be missed more easily than others'. If birds are dark-colored they are also difficult to see. Other species leave the vicinity of the colony early in the morning to go offshore to fish. This kind of information must be known beforehand for all species likely to occur in the area. In general, do not visit only known colony sites, but rather inspect all areas that could even remotely harbor colonies; otherwise, new sites will be overlooked.

If large, rectilinear areas need to be covered, grid out the area, and then fly a 'horizontal' or 'vertical' search-pattern to ensure is the entire area fully covered. Topographic maps help greatly, and best of all are orthophotoquads showing exactly what the area looks like from the air. These can also be easily gridded beforehand on clear Mylar overlays. Hovering uses more fuel than level flight, works best the cooler (= heavier) the air is, and is easier to do when facing the wind, but when needed, there is no substitute; use it liberally.

Censusing is far more difficult and time-consuming than surveying; whenever conditions and the state of knowledge permit, they can be done simultaneously at considerable savings in time and money. Once a colony is located for censusing, make a high, wide circle to delimit it, identify the species present, and outline a plan of attack. Then divide the colony into several segments allowing easy aerial counting from any angle, and work it in a grid ensuring visual access by all counters. (Sea-cliff colonies are treated the same way, only segmented vertically.) At a minimum, use three observers plus the pilot: one in the co-pilot seat and one at each back seat window, and to try to obtain counts for each species in each colony from each observer. Make repeat counts in the reverse direction if possible, for slightly different viewing angles. If species and conditions permit, occupied nests can be counted in addition to breeding adults present, and later converted to pairs. In this way, and with data from intensive, in-colony evaluation, it is possible to define and refine the species-specific conversion factors used to derive "breeding pairs." Observers should try to obtain an estimate of sitting birds before they are flushed; circling or transiting of colonies in opposite directions gives everyone a look. When birds are flushing, most will be hidden from one of the backseat observers, so the helicopter should be maneuvered if possible so that the copilot and the person directly behind eventually get a simultaneous view.

Most species have reasonably consistent flush distances from an approaching helicopter; these have to be determined empirically at each site, as birds of the same species regularly exposed to helicopters frequently sit tighter than those that are not, and the same species in mixed colonies can behave differently when alone. It does not take long to learn when birds in a colony are going from aware to attentive to nervous to flighty to flying. For some species, it is sufficient to count them before they fly—once they are all visible. Other species are most easily counted only after they have been flushed, and it is often easiest to flush them in measured waves, counting each wave of birds as it leaves the colony. Occasionally the colony flushes en masse, but in all cases it is imperative to record numbers the very first time birds flush. Usually some fraction will not return immediately, going off to feed, drink, preen, or bathe, so that first pulse of birds must be counted as accurately as possible. With many birds in the air, most seasoned censusers section-count (or section-estimate). That is, a modest number (from 10 to 50 or even 100) is quickly counted, and then the number of such units is rapidly extrapolated to the entire flock. It sounds difficult, but with practice becomes surprisingly easy and can be quite precise.

If possible to do so without seriously disturbing the colony, land at or near it to verify species identification and numbers, stage of nesting cycle, to obtain repeat counts for the same colony, try to return in a day or two at the same time of day and repeat the census, which helps refine the original estimate. If one is more interested in duration of site occupancy, then returning quite some time later is indicated. However, the counts obtained earlier and later should be treated as separate, not combined, data sets, as one has no idea if the same individuals are involved, or whether they are re-nesters from another colony, late-breeding first-nesters, etc. numbers of non-breeders, habitat, etc., and to check for burrow- nesters. If it becomes desirable

Photography of sites from helicopters works well (Fig. 1), provided fast shutter speeds are used to dampen out the high-frequency vibrations. Never shoot through closed windows if you can avoid it. Polarizing filters work wonders in reducing reflections and glare from water, but cannot be used through Perspex windows. Through-the-lens exposure meters also work perfectly, provided you take a manual reading of the areas you want to photograph (colony, vegetation, water) and then manually set your f/stop and shutter speed. Using exposure meters on automatic yields slides far too dark for use. Published photographs should always give the date, compass direction of view, and the photographer's name.

The definition of what constitutes a colony predetermines the results of studies comparing colony size and persistence, importance, movements, turnover, elucidation of metapopulations, and can have profound political implications for Threatened and Endangered species' designation and protection. The recommended practice is to always describe very carefully the entire area being counted (define what you mean by colony) delineate each sub-area for which counts are taken, and then sketch or photograph the entire site enabling subsequent workers to compare or reanalyze your data, defining colonies as their needs dictate. People do not always agree on what constitutes a colony and thus describing what is being considered as a colony is important (1980b).

Data Treatment and Implications

One question that has received considerable attention is that of *conversion* or *correction factors* used to derive numbers of (breeding) pairs from counts of individual birds or (occupied) nests. In theory, the process is simple: count the number of adults attending a colony, *multiply* by a correction factor, and obtain the number of breeding pairs. There is little empirical research on this topic (Buckley et al. 1978, Erwin 1980) involving temperate-breeding species such as Common and Roseate Terns and herons, where linear regression coefficients provided the correction factor: aerial counts were regressed on known nest counts of birds from the same locations at the same time. Such datasets are very rare, and most correction figures have been intuited or empirically determined by calculating the 'average' number of adults attending a particular colony. For example, in the New York-New England area several studies have independently arrived at 0.9 for Common and Roseate Terns, and 0.5 for Black Skimmers. Practice among colonial waterbird biologists is now that, lacking data to the contrary, a conversion factor of 1.0 is the default standard for all species (i.e., one bird = one pair), and is so reported whenever data are published. Interestingly, Dolbeer et al. (1997) found that a conversion factor bracketing 1.0 for each of his three methods gave the best results for Laughing Gulls. In one sense it does not matter what conversion factors are used, so long as they are clearly indicated when reporting data. Then, should better conversion factors become available in the future, counts can always be reconverted.

Turnover rate is the most useful statistic for describing population movements (but not sizes) among sites in a clearly defined geographic area. In its most useful form (Erwin et al. 1981) it is:

$$T = \frac{(S_1 + S_2)}{(N_1 + N_2)\, t}$$

where S_1 = the number of sites used only in the first census year of the pair; S_2 = the number of sites used only in the second census year; N_1 = the total number of sites used the first year; N_2 = the total number of sites used the second year; t = census interval (always 1 in the present paper); and T = the turnover rate, which ranges from 0% (no newly occupied sites) to 100% (all sites are newly occupied), and which is often expressed as a percentage.

Turnover is a statistic for summed movement among *all* sites over a given period of time. There does not yet exist a tractable, comparable statistic enabling comparisons to be made between such patterns at individual sites. While high turnover rates do not necessarily indicate trouble (some species move between colony sites annually), they often pinpoint the need for protected, alternative colony sites. In such cases, protection of alternative (but not annually used) sites by means short of outright (fee-simple) purchase is often the preferred management strategy.

GPS (Global Positioning Systems) and GIS (Geographic Information Systems)

These systems are now the standards for precise location and graphical depiction, respectively, of sites of waterbird and seabird colonies. Handheld GPS instruments are now so inexpensive that all colonies should be given GPS coordinates to the highest level of accuracy available. All data should be entered into a GIS program (ARC-INFO™ and ARC-VIEW™ are among the most widely used) for display and analysis. In this manner, atlases can be easily prepared, rapidly updated, and readily disseminated.

In-colony biological productivity studies

A study of colony productivity is the complement to an aerial census, and both are needed if we are to understand not only *what* is happening on a landscape/geographic scale, but also *why* it is happening. Such studies often include detailed banding/ringing schemes, with individual color-marking, in efforts to confirm annual productivity, survival, and recruitment rates, and to quantify inter-colony movement of individual birds. Where appropriate, radio-telemetry can refine our knowledge of critical areas for feeding seabirds. Any mature plan for seabird management will incorporate such intensive, in-colony studies, and the choice of sites for them will often be indicated by trends detected during region wide censuses.

Recommendations

We are convinced that aerial surveying and censusing by helicopters is the most effective way of locating, censusing, and monitoring diurnal, non-burrowing, West Indian seabird colonies over wide geographic areas, augmented by ground censusing, and always complemented by in-colony studies of the species' biology, productivity, movements, and recruitment. Censusers should be carefully trained, follow standard protocols and procedures, and to the extent feasible, the same observers should be used year after year. Every effort should be made to do simultaneous, snapshot survey-censuses at the one (or the few) times when most species are at their peak of breeding activity. Because many tropical species have both extended breeding seasons, this might not be possible, and so surveys should be conducted during each of the four seasons to ascertain what are the breeding times for all seabirds at various locations in the West Indies.

We do not, at this point, know enough about West Indian seabird colonies to say how frequently they should be censused to be able to detect population declines or other biologically important phenomena. Judging from work in temperate colonies, which may or may not be extropolable to the West Indies, once the colonies in an area have been all located and accurately censused, then it might be possible to undertake region wide repeat censuses every five years or so, but we are nowhere near that point for any West Indian species yet. And where Endangered or Threatened taxa are involved, there may never be any alternative to annual censusing.

Seabird colonies are often attended by groups of non-breeding birds of varying ages. It is important that these individuals (which in many species have age-specific plumages) be noted, their numbers recorded, and that they be clearly distinguished from breeders. All primary census data should be presented as breeding pairs for each species; whenever conversion factors are used they should be stated. Clearly state exactly what techniques were used in the field and later for analysis. Colony sites should be located precisely with GPS and the data input into GIS programs if possible. Dated aerial and on-ground photographs of colonies should be taken whenever possible and archived. Data should be published whenever possible to ensure that it is part of the permanent record. Lastly, appropriate government officials and agencies, land managers and owners, and planners must be made aware of survey and census findings.

Acknowledgements

We have received support for our studies from many sources: the U.S. National Park Service, U.S. Fish and Wildlife Service, U.S. Geological Survey, and the various institutions where we have been based, especially Rutgers Univ. and the Univ. of Rhode Island. We have received the benefit of countless hours of discussions with colleagues. We particularly thank Michael Gochfeld for many hours in helicopters helping to develop our census techniques, and R. M. Erwin for ideas about conversion factors. We acknowledge the skills of our many helicopter pilots, and the Society of Caribbean Ornithology for the invitation to attend the SCO meeting and the West Indian seabird symposium in Aruba in 1997. We salute David Lee and Betty Anne Schreiber for convening the symposium. Finally, we thank the various reviewers whose care and experience greatly improved this paper's scope and clarity of presentation.

Literature Cited

Ainley, D. 1980. Geographic variation in Leach's Storm-petrel. Auk 97: 837-853.

Bertram, D.F., L. Cowen, and A.E. Burger. 1999. Use of radar for monitoring colonial burrow-nesting seabirds. Journal of Field Ornithology 70: 145-157.

Bibby, C.J., N.D. Burgess, and D.A. Hill. 1992. Bird census techniques. London: Academic Press. 257 pp.

Buckley, P.A. and F.G. Buckley. 1980a. Population and colony-site trends of Long Island waterbirds for five years in the mid 1970s. Trans. of the Lineman Soc. of N.Y. 9: 23-56.

Buckley, P.A. and F.G. Buckley.1980b. What constitutes a waterbird colony? Reflections from the northeastern U.S. Proceedings of the 1979 Conference of the Colonial Waterbird Group 3: 1-15.

Buckley, P.A. and R. Downer. 1992. Modeling metapopulation dynamics for single species of seabirds. Pp. 563-585 in McCullough, D.R. and R.H. Barrett, eds. *Wildlife 2001: Populations*. London: Elsevier. 1163 pp.

Buckley, P.A., M. Gochfeld, and F.G. Buckley. 1978. Efficacy and timing of aerial censuses of some colonial waterbirds on Long Island, N.Y.: a preliminary analysis. Proceedings of the 1977 Conference of the Colonial Waterbird Group 1: 48-61.

Cooper, B.A., R.H. Day, R.J. Ritchie, and C.L. Cranor. 1991. An improved marine radar system for studies of bird migration. Journal of Field Ornithology 62: 367-377.

Day, R.H. and B.A. Cooper. 1995. Patterns of movement of Dark-rumped Petrels and Newell's Shearwaters on Kauai. Condor 97:1011-1927.

Dolbeer, R., J. Balant, and G. Bernhardt. 1997. Aerial photography techniques to estimate populations of Laughing Gull nests in Jamaica Bay, New York, 1992-1995. Colonial Waterbirds 20: 8-13.

Drury, W. H. 1980. Coastal surveys—northeast and northwest. Transactions of the Linnaean Society of New York 9: 57-75.

Erwin, R.M. 1980. Censusing waterbird colonies: some sampling experiments. Transactions of the Linnaean Society of New York 9: 77-85.

Erwin, R.M., J. Galli, and J. Burger. 1981. Colony site dynamics and habitat use in Atlantic Coast seabirds. Auk 98: 550-561.

Ewins, P.J., D.E. Weseloh, and H. Blokpoel. 1995. Within-season variation in nest numbers of Double-crested Cormorants (*Phalacrocorax auritus*) nesting on the Great Lakes: implications for censusing. Colonial Waterbirds 18: 179-192.

Gibbons, D., D. Hill, and W. Sutherland. 1996. Birds. Pp. 227-259 in Sutherland, W., ed. Ecological census techniques. Cambridge, Cambridge University Press. 336 pp.

Giles, R.H., ed. 1969. Wildlife management techniques, 3rd ed. Washington, DC: The Wildlife

Society. 623 pp.

Graham, K., B. Collier, M. Bradstreet, and B. Collins. 1996. Great Blue Heron (*Ardea herodias*) populations from Ontario: data from and insights on the use of volunteers. Colonial Waterbirds 19: 39-44.

Harris, M.P. and C.S. Lloyd. 1977. Variations in counts of seabirds from photographs. British Birds 70: 200-205.

Hutchinson, A.E. 1980. Estimating numbers of colonially nesting seabirds: a comparison of techniques. Proc. 1979 Conference of the Colonial Waterbird Group 3: 234-244.

Kadlec, J.A. and W.H. Drury. 1968. Aerial estimates of the size of gull breeding colonies. Journal of Wildlife Management 32: 287-293.

Kushlan, J.A. 1979. Effects of helicopter censuses on wading bird colonies. Journal of Wildlife Management 43: 756-760.

Lloyd, C.S. 1975. Timing and frequency of census counts of cliff-nesting auks. *British Birds* 68: 507-513.

Lotter, C.F. and G.W. Cornwell. 1993. Comparison of airplane, air-boat, and helicopter for censusing Florida [= Mottled] Ducks, *Anas platyrhynchos fulvigula*. Proc. Ann. Conf. Southeast. Assoc. Game Fish Comm. 23: 97-101.

Prater, A.J. 1979. Trends in accuracy in counting birds. *Bird Study* 26: 198-200.

Ralph, C.J. and J.M. Scott, eds. 1981. Estimating numbers of terrestrial birds. *Studies in Avian Biology* No. 6. Lawrence: Cooper Ornithological Society. 630 pp.

Savard, J-P. L. 1982. Variability of waterfowl aerial surveys: observer and air-ground comparisons a preliminary report. Canadian Wildl. Service Progr. Notes, No. 127: 1-6.

Shandruk, L. J. and K. J. McCormick. 1989. The relative effectiveness of fixed-wing aircraft and helicopters for surveying Trumpeter Swans. Canadian Wildlife Service Progress Notes, No. 182: 1-3.

Vermeer, K., K. H. Morgan, and G. E. J. Smith. 1993. Colony attendance of Pigeon Guillemots as related to tide height and time of day. Colonial Waterbirds 16: 1-8.

Seabird Monitoring Techniques

_____   ೞ ೞ ೞ ೞ   ಟಿ ಟಿ ಟಿ ಟಿ   _____

Alan E. Burger[1] and Andrea D. Lawrence

BirdLife Seychelles, P. O. Box 1310, Mont Fleuri, Mahé, Seychelles. [1]Current address: Department of Biology, University of Victoria, Victoria, British Columbia, V8W 3N5, Canada, Email aburger@uvvm.uvic.ca

Introduction

The goals of this section are to provide researchers, government agencies, managers, island owners, and others with an interest in seabirds with a readily accessible compendium of tested methods for carrying out research and monitoring. It is recognised that many of the people who undertake censusing and monitoring are likely to have little or no formal training in field biology, and may need guidelines for conducting a monitoring program. Data need to be collected using statistically correct sampling methods so that the maximum benefit will come from the work. With some attention to sampling procedures, counts and other data can be much more valuable, for example by providing a measure of the variation about the mean (standard deviation or 95% confidence limits) as well as the average or mean count.

Most of the methods recommended in this handbook have been field tested. We have reviewed monitoring methods used on tropical birds (Schreiber and Schreiber 1986, Ratcliffe 1997). This handbook is modeled after the Seabird Monitoring Handbook for Britain and Ireland (Walsh et al. 1995). For the best use of this handbook and understanding of sampling methodology we recommend reading the General Methods in Walsh et al. (1995), the relevant sections on sampling in Bibby et al. (1992), as well as a recent book on ecological sampling (e.g., Sutherland 1996). Gilbert et al. (1998) provide useful summaries of monitoring methods, but their seabird section is taken from Walsh et al. (1995). We have provided extensive references to published literature and unpublished reports to assist people planning monitoring projects to obtain information on the species or family.

Essential background information

This section applies to all species, and should be read before monitoring populations and breeding performance.

Accuracy and precision in sampling

Accuracy and precision do not mean the same thing. **Accuracy** refers to the proximity of the sample estimate to the real situation, e.g., how close the estimated nest density approximates the actual density. This can be judged by how consistent the mean value is with varying sampling effort – once the sampling effort is sufficient the mean value should change little with additional samples. **Precision** refers to the degree of variation around the sample mean (how large is the standard deviation or 95% confidence limits) and is important for comparing changes over time or differences among colonies. To reveal significant trends the sampling methods should have high precision (i.e., low variance), even if the mean values are not as accurate as possible. Accuracy is the key goal for measuring the exact size and hence importance of an island's population. Precision is the key goal for long-term monitoring of change and so methods should have as little variance as possible, even if they do not give as accurate an estimate as possible. Ideally, sampling methods are both accurate and precise. In general large samples yield better accuracy and precision than smaller samples, but often require more time, people and money.

Efficiency

Personnel, time and money are often limiting. It is useful therefore for long-term monitoring to test the efficiency, as well as the accuracy and precision, of any sampling methods being considered. Is it more efficient, for example, to have a team of two people sampling plots rather than having each person attempt to sample plots alone. Considerable time can be wasted in trying to locate the exact random positions on a grid or map, thus it might be better to forgo some statistical rigour and use plots spaced systematically or randomly along transect lines, rather than spend the extra time to have plots completely randomly placed.

Censusing

The size and long-term trends (stable, declining, increasing) of the breeding population are usually the most important parameters for monitoring seabirds. Laying does not occur within a short time period and all breeders may not be present in the colony during any one survey. For these reasons a single census of a colony, while useful, is not sufficient to establish the size and trend of the population. Ideally repeated censuses using the same or comparable methods need to be done over many years. If time and resources are limited, a minimum of three census a year should be done in a colony: 1) during the height of laying, 2) during the early chick stage, and 3) during the late chick stage.

Units of censusing and reporting census data

Populations of seabirds are generally expressed as pairs of breeding birds. Usually it is impossible to determine the number of non-breeding birds (i.e., immature or non-breeding adults). Tropical species that breed all year round pose special problems because only a portion of the breeding population is active (with an egg or chick) at any one time and it is difficult to estimate that portion. For species in which the stage of breeding cannot easily be seen (e.g., nests high in trees or in burrows), the population measure is the number of **apparently occupied nests** (AONs) or **apparently occupied cavities** (AOCs). It is important to state the units of population estimates in all reports or databases.

In some cases census figures are adjusted to take into account nests that failed before the census was made. It is very important to state clearly what the census numbers refer to. Ideally give both the unadjusted counts for the time of the census as well as the adjusted seasonal totals and explain how both figures were derived.

For year-round breeders (e.g., Brown Boobies, White-tailed Tropicbirds and Audubon's Shearwaters) only a portion of the total population is breeding at the time of any census. Such species need to be censused at least 2-3 times a year to determine the spread of breeding. There are no easy ways to extrapolate from "snap-shot" census figures to a year-round total population. If some attempt is made to estimate the year-round breeding population, it is still essential to report the results of each census separately, because comparisons among islands and across time are best made using unadjusted raw data.

Sample plots and randomization

At small colonies it might be possible to count all the nests. For larger and more dispersed colonies some sampling is needed. Generally this involves using plots or transects of known area to count the number of nests and then multiplying the average nest density (e.g., nests per hectare) by the estimated area of the colony or habitat in which the birds are nesting to get the total population of breeding pairs.

There is some debate over whether systematic plots (e.g., regularly placed along a transect line or in a grid) provide statistically valid measures of variance (Sutherland 1996, Walsh et al. 1995). For a large number of well dispersed samples this is unlikely to be a problem in a pragmatic field design (Milne 1959, Hurlbert 1984). Savard and Smith (1985) found that systematically placed plots were more precise (i.e., had lower variance) than random plots when sampling burrowing seabirds. Systematic plots are generally easier to lay out in the field than random plots, and are more useful for mapping habitat and the extent of colonies (Sutherland 1996, Walsh et al. 1995).

Some general rules for laying out sampling areas:
- plots or quadrats are generally better than transects;
- circular plots are generally more efficient to sample and give fewer edge-effects (errors of inclusion or exclusion at boundaries) than square plots;
- if transects are used they should be laid out across habitat boundaries, not along habitat boundaries, unless the sampling is stratified (each habitat type sampled separately);
- dividing transects into adjacent sections does not give independent sampling (the habitat in each section is not independent of the habitat in neighbouring sections) and this is not a statistically valid method of independent sampling (Hurlbert 1984);
- randomly placed plots are generally better than systematically placed plots but systematic plots are acceptable if they do not coincide with habitat changes, are sufficiently numerous, help the mapping of nests or are more efficient;
- use a computer or calculator to generate random numbers for randomly locating plots if you are using this method, do not attempt to randomly select plots yourself while in the colony (humans are incapable of truly random selections).

Calculating colony area

The extent of the colony is mapped on a topographic map, aerial photograph or sketch map of the island. The colony map is overlaid with a transparent grid of known dimensions with the same scale as the map. The area is then estimated by counting the number of grid squares (or portions of squares) occupied by the colony. Computer programs also exist for calculating areas by tracing the outline with a pointer.

Number and size of sample plots

The size and number of plots or transects used for censusing seabirds is usually selected arbitrarily, or set by the time and personnel available. If regular censusing is planned for an island or a colony it is worth doing some tests to determine the optimal size and number of plots needed to obtain accurate (a stable mean value) and precise (a low standard deviation) population estimates with the least effort. Burger and Lawrence (1999a) tested the effects of the size (circular plots of 50, 100, 200 and 300 m^2) and number of plots (10 through 150) on estimates of nest density in tree-nesting Noddies and ground-nesting White-tailed Tropicbirds in Seychelles. For Lesser Noddies with high nest densities (653-2919 nests ha^{-1}), there was no difference in accuracy and precision among the four plot sizes, and 50 or more plots were required. For White-tailed Tropicbirds, which had lower nest densities (30-44 nests ha^{-1}), plots of 300 m^2 yielded more accurate and precise results, and 70 plots were needed. Overall, for sampling the two species simultaneously, 70 or more plots of 200 m^2 was the best compromise and yielded the most efficient sampling. When sampling these species where densities were lower, plots of 300 m^2 worked well (Burger and Lawrence 1999b).

The radii needed to get circular plots of 10-400 m^2 are given here.

Table 1. Radii of circular plots.

Plot area (m^2)	Radius (m)
10	1.78
25	2.82
50	3.99
100	5.64
200	7.98
300	9.77
400	11.28

The optimum size of the plot will depend upon the density of the nests. If nests are sparse, then small plots will give many zeroes, or low numbers, which makes statistical treatment difficult. On the other hand if plots are too large then counting the nests in each plot becomes a problem, because there is a higher risk of double-counting, or missing nests, and also because the longer time spent in the plot prolongs the disturbance to the birds.

Table 2, using nest densities of Sooty Terns (Feare et al. 1997) illustrates the problem of selecting an appropriate plot size with widely varying nest densities. In these examples, a plot size of 1 m^2, while possibly adequate for very high density areas is clearly inadequate for low densities, since only one in fifty plots would have a nest! Conversely, while plots of 300 m^2 would be ideal for these low density nesting, they would each include 1500 nests in the high

Table 2. Number of nests of Sooty Terns that will occur within sample plots with varying plot size and nest density.

Plot size (m^2)	Nest density (nests per m^2)		
	0.02 Low density areas	2.0 Medium density areas	5.0 High density areas
1	0.02	2	5
10	0.2	20	50
25	0.5	50	125
50	1	100	250
100	2	200	500
300	6	600	1500

density sites, which would be arduous to count. It is not advisable to use too many different plot sizes in a single colony, but the use of two or three in complex colonies stratified for areas of different nest density can enhance the accuracy and efficiency of sampling. In general a larger sample of small plots is better than a small sample of large plots (Walsh et al. 1995).

Stratification of habitat

For very large colonies with variable nest densities, it might be necessary to stratify or sub-divide the habitat and sample each layer or subdivision separately. If nests are very dense in one habitat you might consider using smaller plots there, or if nests are sparse or clumped in another part of the colony larger plots might be necessary there. Aerial photographs or vegetation maps are useful for stratifying a colony. Some preliminary exploration and mapping are needed too. Stratification creates problems when re-combining the data to get the mean and variance for the entire colony, but formulae exist for estimating the variance of the total mean from stratified sub-samples (Sutherland 1996).

Mapping of colonies and use of aerial photographs

Mapping a colony is an essential step in planning censusing and long-term monitoring of a population, as well as providing a permanent record of the breeding distribution and size of colony for that season. Orthophotos, combining aerial photography with Geographic Information System (GIS) digital imaging of contour lines and other topographic features, will provide the best medium on which to map colonies. With increasing use of GIS, the size and distribution of the colonies will be accurately monitored.

Using a compass and GPS for mapping and locating plots

It is best to lay out grid or transect lines using true north as a reference. Hand-held Global Positioning Systems (GPS) are becoming increasingly affordable and accurate and can be used to locate predetermined grid points or randomly selected points in a colony. Some practice is required before using a GPS and they should always be calibrated or tested at points with known co-ordinates. GPS do not work under dense forest canopy so you might need to get fixes in nearby clearings and measure the distances to the plot locations. A major advantage of a GPS is that it provides co-ordinates that can then be used in GIS mapping of plots or colony borders.

Codes for field data sheets and computer databases

To reduce confusion use the same codes for recording data in notebooks or field sheets as in the computer spreadsheet or database, and use the same codes for both censusing and monitoring breeding performance.
    Suggested codes are:
        a – adult bird in nest;
        2a – pair of adults in nest;
        e – egg present;
        c – chick present;
        dc – dead chick;
        n – nest present (e.g., for species like noddies which build an obvious nest);
        i – incomplete nest or under construction (for noddies)
        x – nest has fallen off the branch or broken apart;
        0 – no egg or chick in the nest;

u – contents of nest unknown.

These codes can be used in combinations, e.g.:

ae – adult with an egg;

ac – adult with a chick;

ai – adult in an incomplete nest; note difference between under construction
       and an older nest falling apart from which a chick probably fledged;

a0 – adult with no egg or chick at nest site.

Use the codes carefully to reduce uncertainty. For example, if a tropicbird has lost an egg but the adult is still in the nest, it is better to use the code "a0" rather than just "a" to make it clear there is no egg or chick and you haven't just forgotten to add the e or c. If there is any uncertainty about the presence of an egg or chick (not clearly seen), report them as e? or c?, respectively.

It is often useful to record the approximate age of the chick, and the following is the simplest system for aging chicks:

c1 – chick recently hatched and entirely downy, contour feathers not obvious or
       still hidden under the down(growing first down or 100% downy);

c2 – chick is covered by a mixture of down and contour feathers (between 90%
       downy and about 15% downy with the rest being first flight plumage);

c3 – chick has little or no external down, is covered with contour feathers or has up
       to about 10-15% down remaining.

Collecting and archiving data

Information that is not readily accessible is generally a waste of time and money. All data should be collected in a set format or on data sheets. Simple computer spreadsheets can be set up for any data format, and are probably the most efficient way to store seabird census and monitoring data. Spreadsheets have limitations for accessing and archiving data and so databases which run on MS Access should be constructed and all data entered into these.

General census methods for tree- and ground-nesting seabirds

Following is a general outline of censusing methods applicable to most tree- and ground-nesting seabirds. Further details for some species are given in the species accounts. Monitoring for species which are not discussed can use the plan outlined for a similar species below.

Complete colony counts

In many cases every nest in the entire colony can be counted. By subdividing the colony and using a team of people even a relatively large colony can be counted. By repeatedly searching the entire colony and marking nests at each visit, a large proportion of the nests can be located, and the likely total calculated. Laying chronology can be documented at the same time. During searches, one or more observers (keep the number constant for each visit) walks through potential nesting areas, noting the positions of adults and searching for evidence of nesting. Nests are generally clumped in distribution and so more search time can be spent in areas where nests were found, but limit search time in each nest aggregation to 15 minutes to reduce disturbance. Embryos in eggs exposed to direct sun will die in 15-20 minutes, so try to conduct nest searches in the early morning, late evening or during overcast weather. Mark nests with numbered flagging tape or with a spot of spray paint on the ground next to it to avoid re-counting the same nests.

Map the locations of nests with reference to local topography and any useful reference points, such as grid markers.

On the second and subsequent visits the observers note the number of marked nests re-discovered as well as the number of new unmarked nests. A "re-visit coefficient" can be calculated as the total number of nests from both visits divided by the number found on the first visit, and used to adjust the numbers of nests found when some areas are visited only once.

A simple mark-recapture analysis can be used to determine the total number of nests, including those not found. The total number of nests likely in an area (N_t) is estimated from the number of nests marked on the 1st visit ($M1$), number of marked nests rediscovered on the 2nd visit ($M2$), and the total number of nests found on the second visit ($N2$), using the formula:

$$Nt = N2(M1/M2)$$

Sampling using plots

For larger or more dispersed colonies the best approach is to use random or systematically placed plots to sample a representative area of the colony and then multiply the density of nests in the plots by the total area of the colony, obtained from a map or field measurements. The method outlined below is for circular plots, but it can be modified for square plots if desired.

Personnel

Ideally two people. One records the data (recorder), the other counts the nests and measures the boundaries of the plot (counter). Additional counters might be useful in large plots but each counter should count a separate species to avoid confusion and double-counting of nests. For consistency it is best for these people to keep the same jobs throughout the sampling, but they should check among themselves to ensure they are doing things correctly and efficiently. Where nests are sparse both people could search for nests but the counter is responsible for laying out the boundary of the plot and ensuring that the nests fall within the boundary.

Equipment

- map or aerial photograph of the island;
- compass;
- GPS (optional);
- 30-100 m tape measure or pre-measured non-stretchable cord for measuring distances between plots;
- non-stretchable cord marked out with the correct radii for the circular plots (the same cord could be used for several plot sizes by tying a different coloured flag at each radius);
- flagging tape;
- waterproof felt-tip marker or spray paint;
- rods or stakes to mark plots, if permanent plot centres are desired;
- binoculars (if censusing birds nesting high in trees);
- notebook or field data sheets.

Preliminary mapping and stratification

Before doing any plots or sampling it is necessary to map out the extent of the colony. This can be done by walking about on the island or colony, mapping the distribution of nests on the map or aerial photograph. Consult residents or others familiar with the island to ensure that you include habitat which is important, even if it is not currently occupied by many nests. For large or complex colonies stratification into two or three sub-divisions might be needed.

Positioning and laying out sample plots

Use the map or aerial photograph to lay out an array of sample plots. Ideally these should be randomly placed. In the colony, use the map, compass and measuring tape to locate each sampling point. If you are returning to the plot for additional sampling, mark the sampling point with flagging tape or stake (birds will sometimes pull flagging tape off), using the waterproof marker to record the plot number. For more permanent monitoring use a metal or plastic marker with engraved number or a plastic pipe as a marker driven into the ground. A permanent sampling and mapping grid can be maintained in Sooty Tern colonies using flexible fibreglass rods or other staking material, and should be installed before laying starts (Feare 1976a).

Counting nests

For circular plots fix one end of the radius rope to a stake in the center of the plot and put a temporary marker (pile of stones or piece of tape) on the bearing where you start sampling. The counter moves slowly about the plot in one direction, clockwise or anticlockwise, calling out the count and contents of nests for the scribe to record, until he/she returns to the marked starting point. In Sooty Tern colonies with no tall vegetation, Feare (1976a) used a pre-measured cord with a ring at each end. At each sample station the one ring was slipped over the rod marking the plot, while the other ring was placed over a finger so that the cord could freely rotate around the rod as the observer moved around the perimeter.

At the circumference of the plot the counter has to check carefully whether a nest is in or out of the plot. For nests high in trees this can be difficult and the best method is for the counter to stand on the boundary facing at a tangent to the boundary curve and use a plumb line, vertical stick or hand to help judge whether a nest is in or out.

For ground and cavity nesting birds check carefully beneath boulders and logs for nests (see more detailed methods for sampling shearwaters).

For tree-nesting birds scan each tree several times from different vantage points. Nests are often hidden by branches or leaves, and sunlight can either hide or highlight birds or nests. It is often necessary to move outside the plot circle in order to see some of the nests. The counter does not have to remain inside the circle while searching for nests but must ensure that all the nests do fall within the plot circle. If part of a tree is completely obscured by lower foliage estimate the number of obscured nests based on the density of nearby visible branches.

Estimating the total population

The density of nests can be calculated for each plot from the number of nests and size of the plot. The mean and standard deviation of density can then be calculated for the entire sample of plots. This can then be multiplied by the area of the entire colony being sampled to give the mean and standard deviation of the entire colony population.

Sampling using transects

The procedures are generally similar to plot sampling. Transects should be laid out across habitat gradients (e.g., at right angles to slopes and not along a contour line, or across beach fringe vegetation, not along it). Ideally, the location of transects should be randomly located. This can be done by selecting randomly distributed points along a baseline set up along the coast and running the transects from the selected starting points across the colony or island, parallel to each other at fixed compass bearings. Since each transect represents a single sample, it is better to have many narrow transects than a few wide ones.

When censusing boobies in hazardous habitat it may be impossible to walk straight strip transects. Instead nests can be counted that fall within two markers 10 or 15 m apart, on a cord, stretched between two 2 m poles, held by each observer. A third marker can be tied in the middle of the cord and each observer counts the nests on his/her side of the middle marker. This arrangement allows observers to move along the strip transect without having to actually step along the boundaries (the poles could be moved one way or the other as needed).

Flush counts

For ground-nesting terns, a rough estimate of the number of breeding pairs can be obtained by briefly flushing the incubating adults off their nests and then counting the number of adults flying over the colony. This might be less disruptive than walking through a colony to do plot sampling, but yields only a crude estimate. Accuracy can be improved if you can determine the ratio of nests to adults by intensively searching a section of the colony for nests after having flushed and counted the adults. The ratio can then be applied to the rest of the colony.

General methods for monitoring breeding performance
Survival of eggs and chicks

The breeding success (survival of eggs and chicks to fledging) is a very useful indicator of prevailing conditions at sea and in the colony (Cairns 1987, Furness and Greenwood 1993). The methods for each species vary somewhat but certain general principles apply to all species. Foremost is the need to minimise loss of eggs or chicks as a result of the monitoring itself. If the monitoring process is itself a significant cause of nest failure then the study should not have been undertaken. For most sensitive species, such as Roseate Terns, frigatebirds or boobies, breeding success can be monitored without visiting nests, by observing the nests from a hide or from a distance with binoculars or telescope.

The following is a checklist of information that should be reported from studies of breeding performance. Accurate figures are difficult to obtain and depend on the number of visits made to the colony. If visits to the colony are over 10-14 days apart, eggs can be laid and lost, or lost and re-laid between observer visits.

- Monitoring sample
  - Total number of nests selected
  - Number of eggs or chicks lost to observer disturbance during nest check (be honest!)
  - Total number of nests monitored (excluding nests lost to observer disturbance)
- Laying success after nest built
  - Number of nests lost before egg recorded
  - Number of nests with no egg ever found
  - Number of nests with eggs laid
- Egg survival
  - Number of eggs lost
  - Number of eggs hatched
  - Number of eggs found broken, pecked open or eaten
- Chick survival
  - Number of chicks lost

- Number of chicks found dead
- Number of chicks fledged
• Overall breeding success
    - Proportion of chicks fledged per nests built
    - Proportion of chicks fledged per eggs laid
• Re-laying (replacement) of lost eggs
    - Number of lost eggs which were replaced
    - Hatching success of replacement eggs
    - Survival of chicks from replacement eggs

It is best to treat replacement eggs separately, and report breeding success for each breeding attempt and not per pair. This is particularly relevant to species which routinely lay replacement eggs (e.g., White-tailed Tropicbirds).

Chick growth and fledging size
Chick growth
The growth, maximum mass and fledging mass of chicks are often sensitive indicators of food availability in seabirds and therefore worth monitoring (Ricklefs et al. 1984, Cairns 1987, Montevecchi 1993, Schreiber and Schreiber 1993, Schreiber 1994, Schreiber et al. 1996). Growth is usually measured by repeated regular measurements of the body mass and a standardised body dimension (wing length). Wing and culmen measurements, which change throughout the nestling period, are better indicators of chick growth than tarsus, which reaches near-adult size fairly early in chicks of most seabirds.

Getting these measurements requires handling the birds and disturbing chicks and adults, and should therefore only be undertaken by trained and experienced field personnel. Measuring growth is not recommended for very timid or sensitive species, or when it is likely to cause considerable disturbance and loss of eggs or small chicks (e.g., noddies nesting on cliff edges). Comments on chick growth and tips on the correct way to catch and handle chicks are given in the species accounts.

An ornithological textbook or banding manual should be consulted for the correct methods for measuring bird body dimensions. Spring balances can be obtained from:

The Association of Field Ornithologists'
AFO Mist Nets, Manomet, Inc., P. O. Box 1770, Manomet MA 02345, USA
Phone 508 224-6521
Internet: http://www.afonet.org

or

SAFRING, University of Cape Town, Rondebosch 7700, South Africa
Fax: (021) 650-3434
e-mail: dieter@maths.uct.ac.za).

Vernier or dial callipers for measuring culmen and tarsus can be obtained from engineering or biological supply companies. A meter stick can be used to measure wing lengths. All measurements should be taken in the metric system.

Mass and condition of fledglings

The mass and body condition (ratio of mass divided by body dimensions such as wing, culmen or a combination of measures) of fledglings is a useful indicator of local feeding conditions, and the likely survival of the fledglings. Body condition (as defined above), reported along with body mass, is more useful for indicating body condition than mass alone. Weimerskirch and Cherel (1998) give an example of the use of multivariate body measures to determine body condition in a shearwater. Feare (1976a) analysed fledgling condition in Sooty Terns and later found some evidence that heavier fledglings were more likely to survive to breeding than light ones (Feare 1998).

Specific Monitoring Directions for Different Groups and Species

The following directions for groups of birds (such as petrels and shearwaters that nest in burrows or cavities) and for specific species will assist the researcher by providing tested methodologies that can be applied to these and other similar species. Not all Caribbean nesting species are discussed but the field methods described can be used for other similar species.

Shearwaters and Petrels

General accounts of shearwaters and petrels can be found in Warham (1990, 1996), and Carboneras (1992a). Shearwaters and petrels generally come and go from their nests at night, and are often censused at night. Burger and Lawrence (1999c) found that censuses could be done during daylight, which minimizes risk of injury to the personnel, reduces disturbance to the birds and increases the chances of finding cavities. They found, however, that call playback responses were higher at night than by day, and so applied the night-time response values when estimating the occupancy of cavities where birds could not be seen or felt during the daytime visit. Other species of burrowing procellariiform seabirds have also been successfully censused in daylight using call-playback (James and Robertson 1985, Ratcliffe et al. 1998).

Estimating burrow density: The procedure is similar to that outlined for tree and ground-nesting seabirds:
- Map the extent of the colony;
- Lay out sample plots, stratifying the habitat if necessary;
- Determine the optimal plot size (100 m^2 circular plots are recommended for high densities, larger plots up to 300 m^2 for lower densities)
- Determine the density of potential cavities within each plot.

The last step requires some special procedures if the birds are nesting under large boulders or in poorly defined cavities. Here the number of active pairs can best be determined directly by sight, feel (using a stick to feel under boulders) or with the call playback method. If parts of the plot are completely obscured (deep below very large boulders) then estimate the number of obscured nests based on call playback responses or the density of similar areas elsewhere in the plot.

Determining occupancy: For most nests of shearwaters and petrels, occupancy can be determined by looking or probing into the cavity (use a short stick to carefully feel for adults or chicks). It may be advisable to wear a glove on the hand that is used to reach into a cavity to prevent damage from bites. A small bright flashlight is needed, even in daylight, to check cavities.

Where cavities are too deep or complex for this method, or if the species of shearwater is uncertain, use the call playback method (below). Optical "burrow-scopes" can also be used to check deep or contorted cavities (Dyer and Aldworth 1998). If a cavity is empty but shows signs of previous occupancy (broken or discarded egg, droppings, obvious digging or trampling) this should also be recorded. Cavities should thus be recorded in three categories:

- N_{OK} – number of cavities with occupancy known (adult or chick seen or felt);
- N_U – number of cavities with occupancy unknown (contents not visible or felt);
- N_{PRE} – number of predated or abandoned eggs;
- N_{EMP} – number of empty potential cavity (empty but signs of previous occupancy).

Call playback method for testing occupancy: Call playback has become a standard method for censusing cavity-nesting seabirds (James and Robertson 1985, Warham 1996, Gibbons and Vaughan 1998, Ratcliffe et al. 1998). Taped calls of the birds are played at the entrance to potential nest cavities and adults, and sometimes chicks, respond by calling back. In some species birds only respond to calls from the same sex. It is best to include some duets in taped calls so that calls of both sexes are being played back.

   Tests need to be made at night (at least 1 hour after sunset) at samples of cavities known to be occupied, as well as those with unknown contents (30 or more of each type). The proportion of cavities with responses is recorded:

R_O – proportion of cavities known to be occupied with a response;

R_U – proportion of cavities with contents unknown that give a response.

   Calculating density of occupied cavities – From the daytime censuses at plots and the night-time call-playback tests the density of occupied cavities can be calculated at each plot using the following steps.

- $N_U(R_U/R_O)$ – the number of cavities of unknown occupancy assumed to be occupied;
- N_{ACT} – the number of occupied cavities active at the time of the census, calculated as:
$$N_{OK} + N_U(R_U/R_O)$$
- N_{OCC} – the number of cavities likely occupied in the season, calculated as:
$$N_{OK} + N_U(R_U/R_O) + N_{PRE};$$
- N_{POT} – the number of all potential cavities calculated as:
$$N_{OK} + N_U + N_{EMP}$$

N_{ACT} and N_{OCC} are the recommended measures for population size, but the other measures should also be reported to allow comparisons with studies that used different measures.

Calculating the total population - The total breeding population is calculated by multiplying the density of apparently occupied cavities by the area of habitat in which nests were found.

Monitoring breeding performance – A sample of nests should be marked at the time when pairs are returning to nest, but before laying. These should be checked every 7 to 14 days during the day through incubation. Once hatching begins, for more accurate data on nest success, nests should be checked every 5-7 days if possible especially if chicks are being measured.

White-tailed (*Phaethon lepturus*) and Red-billed Tropicbirds (*P. aethereus*)
Tropicbirds are conspicuous, have accessible nests, and are tolerant of frequent checks and handling if the proper precautions are taken to reduce disturbance. Breeding biology is discussed

in Diamond (1975a), Prys-Jones and Peet (1980), and Stonehouse (1962). Useful reviews and bibliographies of tropicbirds are by Orta (1992) and Schreiber and Schreiber (1993).

These birds are offshore foragers, wandering over large tracts of ocean. Unlike most local seabirds, they seldom join foraging flocks or feed in association with large predatory fish. Tropicbirds are thus useful for monitoring prey availability over offshore regions. They nest year-round, usually on the ground, but may nest in large trees or on cliffs where rats or cats are present. Nests can be difficult to find.

Censusing – Follow the general instructions for ground- and tree-nesting species. Tropicbirds often nest quite deep in cavities and might be difficult to see. They also may nest under a mat of grass or other vegetation. Small chicks are particularly difficult to see in such nests. Search all cavities within sample plots carefully. Record the contents of each nest (eggs or chicks), the age classes of the chicks, and the number of adults in nests without eggs or chicks in order to report the proportions of the population at each stage of breeding (breeding chronology).

Monitoring breeding performance - Methods generally follow those of Phillips (1987). Mark nests with long-lasting tags or paint and map them. A minimum sample of 80-100 nests is recommended for monitoring.

The accuracy of data on breeding success will depend on the frequency of nest checks. For the most accurate data nests should be checked at 1-3 day intervals. This level of effort is frequently not possible and with weekly, or even monthly nest checks, some information on nesting numbers and success can be obtained. Eggs which fail soon after laying will be missed if the checking interval is too long. Record the presence of adults in empty nests to increase the chance of finding newly laid eggs. Record the day eggs or chicks first appear or disappear. The hatching date can be more accurately estimated based on the condition of the chick (body mass, down dried, eyes opened etc.) and egg membranes.

Minimise handling and disturbance of breeding birds. The nest contents can be checked by carefully raising the adult with a stick about 1 m in length held at arm's length. Keep your body low and as far from the bird as possible to reduce the threat you pose. This rarely causes desertion. Do not make sudden movements or loud noises near nests. Never assume that a bird has an egg or a chick. Adults have been observed sitting on broken eggs, dead chicks or an empty nest for several days after the failure, before they abandon the nest. Always make sure the bird is sitting on an intact egg or a live chick.

Record the apparent cause of egg or chick loss if it can be determined. Check the nest vicinity for missing eggs or chicks. Predated eggs or chicks may be pulled from nests by crabs. Chicks close to fledging might wander up to 10 m from the nest or hide under logs and vegetation.

For monitoring nest fidelity and re-laying intervals adults should be banded. To reduce the risk of desertion, do this toward the end of incubation. Newly banded adults can be temporarily marked on the head with a black waterproof felt-tip marker, tattoo ink or small dab of paint so that you don't have to check the legs to see if it is banded. The mark fades in a few weeks.

Report breeding success as:
- proportion of eggs laid which hatch (hatching success);
- proportion of chicks hatched which fledge (fledging success);
- proportion of eggs laid which fledge (overall breeding success).

Always give the sample sizes for each category. A pair might re-lay within a few weeks of losing an egg or chick, or might remain at sea to go through a moult. Report breeding success per breeding attempt but note which pairs re-lay immediately and which moult before re-laying.

Measuring growth of chicks – With due care and experience, trained observers can readily measure the growth of tropicbird chicks, ideally under the supervision of a qualified bander or trained ornithologist. Growth of chicks provides a valuable measure of the prevailing availability of prey and ocean conditions (Cairns 1987, Schreiber and Schreiber 1993). Measuring mass (weight) with a spring balance and measuring wing chord with a meter stick are the recommended measures. Other standard measures, such as tarsus length (tibiotarsus length), culmen length (beak) can also be taken but require more time and vary more among personnel doing the measuring. Mass and wing length should be measured at hatching and then at 5-6 day intervals until fledging. Comparative growth data are found in Diamond (1975a), Phillips (1987), Schaffner (1990), Sheridan (1998) and Lawrence and Burger (1999).

Chicks which are beginning to grow their flight feathers can be banded and all attempts should be made to do this. Data are badly needed on survival of birds, age of first breeding, colony fidelity, and movements, which can only be obtained from banded birds.

Tips on handling tropicbird chicks and adults – Tropicbird adults become agitated when handled and may attack their own chick as it is returned to the nest (Sheridan 1998, Lawrence and Burger 1999). Care should be taken to be sure this does not happen. Most adults feed their chicks between 9:00 a.m. and 2:00 p.m.. By checking nests as early as possible in the morning, you will greatly lessen the chance of having an adult present, interrupting chick-feeding or causing regurgitation by the chicks or adults. In some situations disturbing nests with eggs or small chicks should be avoided after 4:00 p.m. If adults abandon the nest overnight, it increases the risk that the egg or chick will be eaten by crabs. When possible, approach the nest from the side and below: adults are most threatened when approached from above. This particularly applies in rock crevice nest sites. Adults and chicks remain calmer if they are placed head first in a thin cloth bag while being banded or measured, and held firmly but not tightly to reduce struggling.

Tips for removing a small chick from under the adult for weighing and measuring:
- reduce the amount of time standing in view of the adult;
- use a stick or gloved hand to hold back the adult while quickly removing the chick;
- move your hand along the ground to reach the chick, not above the adult;
- move out of view of the adult while handling the chick;
- replace the chick carefully, right-side-up, beside the adult while holding the adult back;
- move away quickly.

Tips for returning an adult after banding to a nest with a small chick:
- replace the adult facing outwards or away from the chick and to one side of the chick, not on top of it. In their confusion, adults can injure chicks by pecking them if replaced head-first into the nest or on top of the chick.
- move away from the nest or out of sight as quickly as possible

Banding tropicbirds – All banding must be done by a qualified person. Chicks can be banded when they have begun to grow their first flight feathers (about 70% downy and 30% contour feathers). To reduce disturbance and possibility of abandonment of the nest, adults may need to be banded late in incubation or after the chick hatches when they are more committed to the nest site. This varies in different colonies. Incubating adults, in some areas, are more likely to desert an egg than a chick and are most likely to desert eggs early in incubation. Mark each ringed adult with a black felt pen (or tattoo ink or small spot of paint) on the top of the head to avoid repeat checking for bands during that season. These marks last about a month.

Ground-nesting Boobies
Masked Booby (*Sula dactylatra*), Brown Booby (*Sula leucogaster*)

These two species are treated together because they nest in similar habitats and can be censused and monitored using similar methods. The tree-nesting Red-footed Booby is treated separately (although, when trees are lacking, red-foots will nest on the ground). Populations of both Masked and Brown booby are today a small fraction of what they were a century or more ago, due to the effects of guano harvesting, human consumption and widespread disturbance at colonies (Feare 1978, Carboneras 1992b, Anderson 1993, Pregill et al. 1994). Regular censusing of known colonies and searches for new colonies are urgently needed, despite the logistical difficulties of working on the outer islands.

General accounts of the biology of boobies are found in Nelson (1978), Carboneras (1992b), Anderson (1993), and Schreiber et al. (1996). Other studies include Dorward (1962), Simmons (1967), Kepler (1969) and Anderson and Ricklefs (1992).

Censusing – Small colonies can be counted completely. Larger colonies require sampling, using plots or transects. Follow the methods for ground-nesting seabirds. Sampling can be difficult and hazardous when boobies are nesting on cliffs and in other difficult to access locations.

Monitoring breeding performance – For the most accurate determination of nest success (survival of eggs and chicks) a sample of nests should be visited at regular intervals of between 4 and 8 days. This frequency of visits to a colony is often not possible and a schedule of visits every 10-30 will still provide data on nest success. To reduce disturbance and loss of chicks select nest sites that can be viewed from a distance (or from a blind if nests are close together – see Sooty Tern methods) using binoculars, without disturbing the adults and chicks. Minimise time within a sub-colony area to 20 minutes or less when possible and avoid disturbing adults off nests exposing eggs or chicks to direct sun in the heat of the day. A crude measure of breeding success could be made by comparing the number of near-fledging chicks counted late in the season with an earlier count of the number of nests with eggs in a section of the colony.

Chick growth – Growth can be measured as described above, taking precautions to minimise time in the colony and avoiding exposing chicks to intense mind-day sun.

Red-footed Booby (*Sula sula*)

In common with the other two booby species, the tree-nesting Red-footed Booby has suffered the same massive decline in populations over the past century as a result of guano harvesting, poaching and other human disturbances (Feare 1978, Carboneras 1992b, Schreiber et al. 1996). Accounts of the biology of this species are found in Diamond (1974), Nelson (1969, 1978), Carboneras (1992b) and Schreiber et al. (1996).

Censusing – Small colonies and those on small islets can usually be counted completely. For large, extended colonies Diamond (1971, 1974) used the same methods that are described below for frigatebirds; i.e., counting randomly chosen strips of mangrove 200 m long, using a boat and binoculars. It is often impossible to count the nests deep in the trees without disturbing the birds by approaching too closely. In such cases the number of nests can be estimated by first counting all the adults visible on the trees, and then determining the ratio of those that are obviously on a nest to those obviously not on a nest, and applying the necessary correction (Diamond 1971).

Monitoring breeding performance – Use the same methods as for frigatebirds and the other booby species. The success of a cohort laid at a peak of laying could be checked by counting near-fledging chicks four months later.

Chick growth – Growth can be measured for the first 80 days, longer if delayed by food shortages, by which time the chicks will have reached an asymptote (Schreiber et al. 1996).

Magnificent Frigatebird (*Fregata magnificens*)

Frigatebirds nest in dense colonies as a rule (where they can touch their neighbour while sitting on the nest) and because of this, there are difficult to work with without causing severe disruption to the birds and resultant decreased nest success. Researchers need to exercise caution when attempting to work in a colony and should carefully observe any disturbance they are causing. If eggs and small chicks are getting knocked out of nests by adults flapping to get away, it may be that no work can be done in the colony and observations should take place from a distance. Accounts of the biology of this species can be found in Diamond (1972, 1973), Trivelpiece and Ferraris (1987), Carboneras (1992c), and Diamond and Schreiber (in press).

Censusing – Frigatebirds nest predominantly in mangrove trees and are susceptible to disturbance from humans (Diamond 1975b). This makes censusing difficult and the standard methods for seabirds cannot always be applied. Those nesting on small islets in the lagoon can be counted directly, but the larger colonies require sampling. Following Diamond (1975b):

Equipment and personnel needed:
- boat;
- at least two people – one to count and the other to navigate the boat;
- map or aerial photograph to record the locations of the colonies and sample areas;
- hand-held global positioning system (GPS), calibrated to a known reference point (if available);
- binoculars;
- hand-held tally counter;
- notebook and pencil;
- tide-chart (optional);
- camera (to photograph birds flying overhead for later counting).

For monitoring long-term changes, the following should be counted:

- numbers of displaying males with inflated pouches (peak time September-December);
- nests (optimal time is November-January);
- large chicks near fledging (optimal time is March to mid-April).

These counts can be made in sections of the colony, selected as follows:

1. Map the extent of the colony on a topographic map or aerial photograph.
2. Divide the colony into 1 x 1 km squares, each further subdivided into 5 strips 200 m wide.
3. Select two of the strips per 1 km section for counting (one if time is limiting).
4. Count the number of adults and nests along the 200 m wide strip, using binoculars and a tally-counter, from a boat anchored 35-40 m from the edge of the mangroves. The optimal time is at high spring tides at dawn. A GPS will help locate sampling strips.
5. First count the number of frigatebirds in the trees, then identify as many as possible to species, sex and age (if immatures present);
6. Then count the birds flying over the trees, taking photographs for later counting if there are large numbers.
7. Calculate the mean and standard deviation (SD) of the count of each strip.
8. To calculate the mean and SD of the entire colony, multiply the mean and SD per strip by the number of strips sampled and by 2.5 (multiply by 5 if every fifth strip is counted).
9. Report the time, dates, mean and SD of the counts per strip, number of strips counted, and total population estimate. Include a map of the colony and sample strips with all reports or publications.
10. If necessary, adjust the count if it occurred later than the peak of nesting activity (see Diamond 1975b for details).
11. The total breeding population can be estimated as 1.33 x active breeders, assuming that the active breeders represent 75% of the total breeding population.

Regular monitoring of the same section of colony (sub-colony) from year-to-year is likely to give a biased measure of the numbers breeding, because the nesting birds are likely to abandon the sub-colony if regularly disturbed (Diamond 1975b). It is better to randomly select a new sample of new sub-colonies to estimate nest densities each season.

Monitoring breeding performance – Two methods are suggested. First, details of egg and chick survival are best obtained by monitoring one or more sub-colonies at regular intervals throughout the season (ideally every 4-7 days) with observations done from a blind. Longer intervals between checks will result in an underestimate of egg survival because eggs can be will be laid and lost between checks. However, knowing this, nest checks can be carried out every 10 days to one month and data on nest success can still be obtained. Another method, with only two visits, gives a less accurate measure of breeding performance but will supply some data. The number of large chicks counted in the study sub-colonies (optimal time March-April) can be compared with the number of nests counted at the end of laying (November-December) to give an estimate of overall breeding success.

Chick growth – Reliable measures of chick growth can be obtained during the first 120 days after hatching, by which time the mass and bill length should have reached an asymptote (Diamond 1975b). Larger chicks are difficult to catch and may scramble a long way from the nest if care is not taken by the researcher.

Monitoring non-breeding birds: roost counts – Year-round counts at roost sites provide a means of monitoring frigatebirds using local seas. Over many years this should provide a measure of local feeding conditions. Regular counts can be done from a boat travelling around the edges of the roost. when roosts are counted, data should be taken on the age classes and sexes of the birds present. Changes in the proportion of juveniles in the roosting population can indicate changes in the reproductive success of colonies in previous years. A lack of juveniles in the roosting population means that no successful reproduction is occurring and this should be investigated in local colonies.

Sooty Tern (*Sterna fuscata*) and other densely nesting gulls and terns

This is the most abundant seabird breeding in the area, yet numbers are declining. Eggs are commonly taken for food and human disturbance in colonies frequently causes nest desertion. There have been several detailed studies of the breeding biology, diets and movements of Sooty Terns (Ashmole 1963, Feare 1976a, Feare et al. 1997, Harrington 1974). In the Seychelles there is a commercial harvest of Sooty Tern eggs. Before this can be attempted, detailed studies need to be done on the demographics and reproductive success of a local population. Harvesting should not be done without adequate monitoring or an entire population can be lost. Management options and the effects of the egg harvest in Seychelles have been investigated (Ridley and Percy 1958, Feare 1976a,b) and are part of an ongoing research project (Feare 1998, 1999, Feare and Gill 1997). These publications should be consulted and a study designed and carried out locally before any harvesting is done.

The techniques used for monitoring Sooty Tern colonies can be used with other densely nesting, ground nesting species.

Censusing : background information – Two methods have been successfully used for censusing Sooty Terns. In the large colonies, circular or square plots spread across a systematic 50 x 50 m grid were used, with the grid points marked with bamboo, wood or fibreglass poles (Feare 1976a, Feare et al. 1997). Plots can vary in size from 1 m^2 to 25 m^2. On some islands Sooty Terns nest beneath bushes or forest canopy as well as in the open. These nest densities are recorded in strip transects 12.5 m wide running transversely across the island (Feare et al. 1997, Betts 1998). Each transect is divided into sequential sections 12.5 x 25 m in size to provide some measure of variance for the mean.

In general randomly placed plots would be the most accurate and least biased census method, but methods need to be adapted to suit the terrain, the historical database and the goals of the censusing. The optimum size of the plot will depend upon the density of the nests, which varies a lot in Sooty Terns (see above) and is strongly affected by vegetation, especially the type and percentage of ground cover (Feare et al. 1997). To avoid bias caused by vegetation, there should either be sufficient sample plots to cover the basic vegetation types roughly in proportion to their occurrence, or the colony should be sub-divided into 2-4 sections based on the dominant vegetation and/or differing nest densities (i.e., stratified sampling). Post-sampling analysis of the effects of vegetation can also be done (Feare et al. 1997) to improve future censusing.

Censusing: recommended methods – In general follow the general census methods for ground-nesting seabirds. Censusing is best done during the incubation period (most likely during late June or early July in the Caribbean), but laying might differ in some years and among colonies. If possible, monitor the colony to determine when most nests have eggs. Prior to visiting the colony try to obtain previous maps of the colony (see e.g., Feare et al. 1997) or aerial photographs showing the vegetation types. Map out the likely extent of the colony. If possible determine the optimal size and number of plots to be sampled, given the likely density of nests, number of people and time available.

On arrival at the colony confirm the extent of nest distribution, modifying the map to cover the areas actually being used. If grid markers are not available, overlay the map with a grid running along the principal compass bearings (i.e., N-S and E-W). Make a note whether you are using bearings that are corrected for the local magnetic declination (see the discussion above on using a compass or GPS), or just using the magnetic bearings unadjusted, but be sure to report the method in your database and reports. Select a prominent, permanent landmark as your starting point and use the compass to locate the various transect lines along which you will place your sample points. Alternatively, use a line along one edge of the colony as a starting point, mark off fixed or random distances along this line and then run the transect lines at right angles to this line. The sample points are then placed at random distances along each transect line. Centre the circular plot on the sample point, count the birds using the radius cord to determine whether the birds are in the plot or outside. In forest, it is not possible to carry the cord unobstructed around the plot perimeter. Here you have to move it in and out of the trees to reach the perimeter, but this is only necessary where there are nests close to the perimeter that need to be checked, so it is usually not necessary to measure out the entire circumference of the plot.

Record the contents of each nest (empty nest, egg or chick) and the age class of the chick if required (see Feare 1976a for detailed age classes, or use the three stage classes given above).

Monitoring breeding performance – This is best done from a blind or other hidden vantage point, perhaps using a spotting scope to remain at a distance. One visit to the colony is all that is necessary to put markers at each nest. Thereafter use the scope or binoculars to check the contents of each nest. Since the chicks begin to move from the nest when a few days old, tracking chick success might be difficult.

In the absence of a detailed study, Feare (1998) suggests that breeding success at a colony can be roughly assessed, and that even a simple assessment helped explain annual variations. The following is a modified version of his colony output categories:
- **good**: more than 50% of pairs rear chicks to fledging;
- **moderate**: 25-50% rear chicks to fledging;
- **poor**: 1-25% rear chicks to fledging;
- **zero**: total breeding failure, no chicks fledged.

Growth of chicks – Monitoring growth is not recommended for Sooty Terns. Feare (1976a) found that regular capturing of chicks for a growth study caused the chick mortality to double compared to undisturbed areas in the same colony. If growth data are needed, follow the methods outlined in Feare (1976a). Chicks should be measured early in the morning to reduce the chances of regurgitation. Some studies of terns have used fencing around the study area to prevent the chicks running too far but this can cause mortality of chicks if they cannot escape aggressive neighbours and is not recommended.

Recording size of fledglings – Although growth studies are discouraged, it is useful and less disruptful to measure the mass and body dimensions (e.g., wing chord, culmen and tarsus) of chicks at fledging (Feare 1976a, 1998). Criteria for assessing whether a chick is at the fledging stage are outlined in Feare (1976a). A ratio of mass divided by some measure of body size (wing, culmen or a combination of measures), reported along with body mass, is more useful for indicating body condition than mass alone.

Bridled Tern (Sterna anaethetus)

Although superficially similar to the larger Sooty Tern, the Bridled Tern has a very different lifestyle, breeding patterns and foraging behaviour. It is predominantly an inshore feeder, generally remaining year-round near land and often roosting on the same islands as its breeding colonies. Unlike the dense Sooty Tern colonies, those of Bridled Terns have nests scattered over a wide area and often well hidden beneath boulders or ground vegetation. The size and trends of the population, and the distribution of nests in the Caribbean is poorly documented.

Censusing – Mapping the distribution of nests is an essential first step to censusing. Regular checks of breeding sites are needed to determine the onset of laying, so that the census can cover the peak of laying and incubation. The optimal time to census Bridled Terns is when most pairs have eggs and before chicks have hatched. Nests with chicks are extremely difficult to find as even small chicks hide in small crevices when disturbed (Diamond 1976). Two census techniques are suggested: repeated nest searches covering the entire colony and the use of sample plots (see above). Flush counts of adults will also provide a rough indication of the number of breeding pairs, although the ratio of nests to adults is not known but could be calculated for a section of the colony. This ratio will vary with time of day and more adults are found in the colony towards late afternoon. For dispersed large colonies counts of adults from boats can give an approximation of the breeding population, and should also be done repeatedly at the same time of day.

Monitoring breeding performance – Repeated checking of nests to record egg and chick survival is not recommended. Chicks are easily disturbed and hide or run from the intruder making it difficult to get an accurate estimate of their survival (Diamond 1976). A crude index of breeding success can be obtained by counting the numbers of fledged chicks (more easily counted) seen at the colony relative to the number of eggs known to be laid.

Chick growth – For the reasons outlined above, measuring chick growth in Bridled Terns is not recommended and may cause mortality among the sample chicks (Diamond 1976).

Roseate Tern (*Sterna dougallii*)

This cosmopolitan tern is declining in most parts of its range and requires careful monitoring (Gochfeld 1983, Gochfeld and Burger 1996). Useful studies of Roseate Terns are by Nisbet (1978), Nisbet et al. (1990), Randall and Randall (1981), Ramos (1998a,b, in press), Ramos et al. (1998), Shealer (1998), Nisbet and Spendelow (1999).

Censusing – Nests should be counted 2 weeks after the first eggs are seen and ideally the colony is censused every 5-10 days to cover the spread of laying. On small colonies of fewer than 100 pairs, all the nests can usually be counted. At larger colonies plot sampling might be necessary (as described above). Ramos (1998a) used plots 25-64 m^2. Nests should be marked with a numbered wooden stake (e.g., tongue depressor) when found to avoid double counting on repeated visits. Visits to each area in the colony should be restricted to 20-25 minutes. Plot sampling will cause considerable disturbance and so mapping and repeated counts of nests, using binoculars or a spotting scope, from a hide or other hidden vantage point is recommended as an alternative method (Ramos 1998a,b). On Aride Island in the Seychelles nest densities ranged from 0.63 nests m^{-2} at the edge of the colony to 1.23 nests m^{-2} in the centre (Ramos 1998b).

Monitoring breeding performance – Egg and chick survival are best monitored visually from a blind using binoculars or a spotting scope to check the contents of marked nests. The observation sub-colony need only be disturbed occasionally during laying to place numbered markers at nest sites. Ramos (1998b) made daily observations from a hide raised 1 m above ground at the edge of the colony. Given the difficulty of locating mobile chicks, estimating fledging success is difficult. Nisbet et al. (1990) give several methods for recording fledging success and productivity in Roseate Terns. Of these, survival to 20 days (in general most all birds over 20 days will fledge), and low disturbance monitoring (i.e., from a blind) are recommended.

Chick growth – Like other ground-nesting terns, chicks of Roseate Terns run and hide when the colony is disturbed making it difficult to locate individual chicks. Growth studies should only be done by an experienced professional biologist. Ramos (1998b) found that undisturbed chicks remained for 15 days at the nest site whereas those caught for measurements remained only 2-7 days. He constructed small shelters near nests to encourage chicks to hide there during his visits and not run. Wandering chicks are often severely pecked or killed by neighbouring adults.

Brown Noddy (*Anous stolidus*) and Black Noddy (*A. minutus*)

The biology of these two species is discussed in a previous chapter (Chardine et al.). See also Ashmole (1962), Chardine and Morris (1987, 1989, 1996), Morris and Chardine (1992, 1995) The Black Noddy is quite rare in the Caribbean, and generally nests in colonies with the Brown. Brown Noddies will nest either in bushes and trees (census methods below) or on the ground (see census methods for Roseate Terns) while Black Noddies nest only in bushes or trees.

The ability to color band adults and monitor accessible nests with ease make Brown Noddies one of the most suitable species for long-term monitoring of adult survival, age of first breeding, site fidelity, inter-island movements, population changes and breeding performance. Useful studies of their breeding have been done by Dorward and Ashmole (1963), Brown (1976), Diamond and Prys-Jones (1986), Chardine and Morris (1987), and Morris and Chardine (1992, 1995). Chardine and Morris (1996) and Gochfeld and Burger (1996) provide more general reviews and bibliographies.

Extra care must be taken to differentiate the two species (see species account chapter). Also, chicks and adults of each are similar in plumage and an observer must be able to tell them apart for censusing. Chicks begin to leave the nest about 6-8 weeks after hatching and might be recorded as missing one week and then recorded at the nest a week later. It is best to regard 8 weeks as the time of fledging, even though many chicks remain at or near the nest until their 15th week, and might die before actually becoming independent. When chicks are close to fledging, they closely resemble adults, but can still be separated from adults on the following criteria:

- voice – chicks give high wheezy calls, while adults give harsher, deeper calls;
- posture and behaviour – adults fly about more freely than large chicks and tend to scold the intruder, whereas chicks tend to keep their heads lower and stay immobile;
- head plumage – large chicks have dark flecks in the light grey forehead whereas adults have more uniform colouring;

- chicks often have slightly shorter beaks;
- the white edging around the eye is dull and indistinct in chicks;
- large chicks tend to have a slightly different color plumage than adults.

Censusing – Follow the methods for ground and tree-nesting seabirds. Censusing is best done during incubation (generally June or July) because the chicks run or hide when disturbed and can easily be missed or fall off cliffs. Nests in trees may be hard to see from the ground. Their number can be estimated by counting the nests in a sample of easily trees and multiplying the mean nest count per tree by the number of trees in the colony.

The unit for censusing is apparently occupied nests (AON) but since the contents of most nests high in trees cannot be determined, all the apparently completed nests are counted. Count the incomplete nests (under construction), but report these data separately. It is useful for documenting the breeding chronology to check the contents of a sub-sample of nests at the time of the census and report the proportions that are complete but empty (not yet laid or lost egg), or that have an egg or a chick. Spot checks are necessary to determine when laying is taking place, since it varies among years.

Monitoring breeding performance – The survival of eggs and chicks can be monitored by visiting a sample of nests (ideally 100-200) at regular intervals (ideally every 5-7 days). To reduce disturbance and loss of chicks select nest sites that can be viewed from a distance (or from a blind) without disturbing the adults and chicks. Minimise time within a sub-colony area to 20 minutes and avoid exposing eggs or chicks to direct sun.

Chick growth – Growth can be measured in the usual way (see above).

Acknowledgements

This chapter on seabird monitoring is based on and has been adapted from the Seabird Monitoring Handbook for Seychelles (2000) by BirdLife Seychelles. Funding for this project came from the Second Dutch Trust Fund and BirdLife Seychelles. Many people contributed to the project and to developing and testing the methods described here, and we are indebted to them all: N. J. Shah, K. Henri, S. Parr, D. Currie, M. Hill, J. Pillay, F. Payet, J. Bowler, G. Wright, J. Millett, N. Ratcliffe, E. A. Schreiber, J. A. Ramos, A. Skerrett, G. Rocamora, M. Betts, A. W. Diamond, M. de L. Brooke, L. Ballance, J. Sears, C. P. Burger, L. F. Burger, C. J. Feare, S. Remie, and K. Blomerley.

Literature Cited

Anderson, D. J. 1993. Masked Booby (*Sula dactylatra*). No. 73 in A. Poole and F. Gill eds. *The Birds of North America*, Philadelphia, The Academy of Natural Sciences; Washington, D.C., The American Ornithologists' Union.

Anderson, D. J. and R. E. Ricklefs. 1992. Brood size and food provisioning in masked and blue-footed boobies. Ecology 73:1363-1374.

Ashmole, N. P. 1962. The Black Noddy *Anous tenuirostris* on Ascension Island. Ibis 103b:235-273.

Ashmole, N. P. 1963. The biology of the Wideawake or Sooty Tern *Sterna fuscata* on Ascension Island. Ibis 103b:297-364.

Bibby, C. J., N. D. Burgess and D. A. Hill 1992. Bird census techniques. Academic Press, London and San Diego.

Brown, W. Y. 1976. Growth and fledging age of the Brown Noddy in Hawaii. Condor 78:263-264.

Burger, A. E. and A. D. Lawrence. 1999a. Effects of the size and number of sample plots in censuses of nesting tropical seabirds. Unpublished report to BirdLife Seychelles, Victoria, Mahé, Seychelles.

Burger, A. E. and A. D. Lawrence. 1999b. A census of seabirds on Frégate Island, Seychelles, in August 1999. Unpublished report to BirdLife Seychelles, Victoria, Mahé, Seychelles.

Burger, A. E. and A. D. Lawrence. 1999c. Census of Wedge-tailed Shearwaters and tests of the call playback census method on Cousin Island, Seychelles. Unpublished report to BirdLife Seychelles, Victoria, Mahé, Seychelles.

Cairns, D. K. 1987. Seabirds as indicators of marine food supplies. Biological Oceanography 5:261-271.

Carboneras, C. 1992a. Procellariidae (Petrels and Shearwaters). Pp. 216-257, in *The handbook of birds of the world*, Vol. 1 (J. del Hoyo, A. Elliott and J, Sargatal, eds.). Lynx Edicions, Barcelona.

Carboneras, C. 1992b. Sulidae (Gannets and Boobies). Pp. 312-325, in *The handbook of birds of the world*, Vol. 1 (J. del Hoyo, A. Elliott and J, Sargatal, eds.). Lynx Edicions, Barcelona.

Carboneras, C. 1992c. Fregatidae (Frigatebirds). Pp. 362-374, in J. del Hoyo, A. Elliott and J, Sargatal, eds. *The handbook of birds of the world*, Vol. 1, Lynx Edicions, Barcelona.

Chardine, J. W. and R. D. Morris. 1987. Trapping and color banding Brown Noddy and Bridled Tern adults at the breeding colony. Colonial Waterbirds 10:100-102.

Chardine, J. W. and R. D. Morris. 1989. Sexual size dimorphism and assortative mating in the Brown Noddy. Condor 91: 868-874.

Chardine, J. W. and R. D. Morris. 1996. Brown Noddy (*Anous stolidus*). In A. Poole and F. Gill eds. *The Birds of North America*, Philadelphia, The Academy of Natural Sciences; Washington, D.C., The American Ornithologists' Union. No. 220.

Diamond, A. W. 1971. The ecology of the sea birds of Aldabra. Philosophical Transactions Royal Society London B 260:561-571.

Diamond, A. W. 1972. Sexual dimorphism in breeding cycles and unequal sex ratio in Magnificent Frigatebirds. Ibis 114: 395-398.

Diamond, A. W. 1973. Notes on the breeding biology and behaviour of the Magnificent Frigatebird. Condor 75: 200-209.

Diamond, A. W. 1974. The Red-footed Booby on Aldabra Atoll, Indian Ocean. Ardea 62:196-218.

Diamond, A. W. 1975a. The biology of tropicbirds at Aldabra Atoll, Indian Ocean. Auk 92:16-39.

Diamond, A. W. 1975b. Biology and behaviour of Frigatebirds *Fregata* spp. on Aldabra Atoll. Ibis 117:302-323.

Diamond, A. W. 1976. Subannual breeding and moult cycles in the Bridled Tern *Sterna anaethetus* in the Seychelles. Ibis 118:414-419.

Diamond, A. W., and R. P. Prys-Jones. 1986. The biology of terns nesting at Aldabra Atoll, Indian Ocean, with particular reference to breeding seasonality. Journal of Zoology, London A210:527-549.

Diamond, A. W., and E. A. Schreiber. In press. The Magnificent Frigatebird, *Fregata magnificens*. In A. Poole and F. Gill eds. *The Birds of North America*, Philadelphia, The Academy of Natural Sciences; Washington, D.C., The Am. Ornithologists' Union.

Dorward, D. F. 1962. Comparative biology of the White and the Brown Booby *Sula* spp. at Ascension. Ibis 103b:174-220.

Dorward, D. F. and N. P. Ashmole. 1963. Notes on the biology of the Brown Noddy *Anous stolidus* on Ascension Island. Ibis 103b:447-457.

Dyer, P.K. and K. Aldworth. 1998. The 'Burrowscope': modifications to burrow viewing equipment. Emu 98:143-146.

Feare, C. J. 1976a. The Breeding of the Sooty Tern *Sterna fuscata* in the Seychelles and the effects of experimental removal of its eggs. Jour. of Zoology London 179:317-360.

Feare, C. J. 1976b. The exploitation of Sooty Tern eggs in the Seychelles. Biological Conservation 10:169-181.

Feare, C. J. 1978. The decline of Booby (Sulidae) populations in the western Indian Ocean. Biological Conservation 14:295-305.

Feare, C. J. 1998. The sustainable exploitation of Sooty Tern eggs in the Seychelles. Sixth annual report. Report Wildwings Bird Management, Haslemere, Surrey, UK.

Feare, C. J. 1999. The sustainable exploitation of Sooty Tern eggs in the Seychelles. Seventh annual report. WildWings Bird Management, Haslemere, Surrey, U.K.

Feare, C. J. and E. L. Gill. 1997. The sustainable exploitation of Sooty Tern eggs in the Seychelles. Fifth annual report. Report to Seychelles Division of Environment and Bird Island Lodge.

Feare, C. J., E. L. Gill, P. Carty, H.E. Carty, and V.J. Ayrton. 1997. Habitat use by Seychelles Sooty Terns *Sterna fuscata* and implications for colony management. Biological Conservation 81:69-76.

Furness, R. W. and J. J. D. Greenwood. 1993. Birds as monitors of environmental change. Chapman and Hall, London.

Gibbons, D.W. and D. Vaughan. 1998. The population size of Manx Shearwater *Puffinus puffinus* on 'The Neck' of Skomer Island: a comparison of methods. Seabird 20:3-11.

Gilbert, G., D. W. Gibbons, and J. Evans. 1998. Bird monitoring methods. RSPB in association with BTO, Wildfowl and Wetlands Trust, Joint Nature Conservation Committee, Institute for Terrestrial Ecology and the Seabird Group. RSPB, The Lodge, Sandy, Bedfordshire, U.K.

Gochfeld, M. 1983. The Roseate Tern: world distribution and status of a threatened species. Biological Conservation 25:103-125.

Gochfeld, M. and J. Burger. 1996. Family Sternidae (Terns). Pp. 624-667, in The handbook of birds of the world, Vol. 3 (J. del Hoyo, A. Elliott and J, Saragtal, eds.). Lynx Edicions, Barcelona.

Harrington, B. A. 1974. Colony visitation behaviour and breeding ages of Sooty Terns (*Sterna fuscata*). Bird-Banding 45:115-144.

Hurlbert, S. H. 1984. Pseudoreplication and the design of ecological field experiments. Ecological Monographs 54:187-211.

James, P. C. and H. A. Robertson. 1985. The use of playback recordings to detect and census burrowing seabirds. Seabird 8:18-20.

Kepler, C. 1969. The breeding biology of the Blue-faced Booby (*Sula dactylatra personata*) on Green Island, Kure. Publication Nuttall Ornithological Club 8.

Lawrence, A. D. and A. E. Burger. 1999. Breeding success and chick growth in White-tailed Tropicbirds on Cousin Island: an interim report for 1999. Unpublished report to BirdLife Seychelles, Victoria, Mahé, Seychelles.

Milne, A. 1959. The centric systematic area sample treated as a random sample. Biometrics 15:270-297.

Montevecchi, W. A. 1993. Birds as indicators of change in marine prey stocks. Pp. 217-266, in Birds as monitors of environmental change (R. W. Furness and J. J. D. Greenwood, eds.). Chapman and Hall, London.

Morris, R. D. and J. W. Chardine. 1992. The breeding biology and aspects of the foraging ecology of Brown Noddies nesting near Culebra, Puerto Rico 1985-1989. Journal of Zoology, London 226:65-79.

Morris, R. D. and J. W. Chardine. 1995. Brown Noddies on Cayo Noraeste, Culebra, Puerto Rico: what happened in 1990? Auk 112:326-334.

Nelson, J. B. 1969. The breeding ecology of the Red-footed Booby in the Galapagos. Journal of Animal Ecology 38:181-198.

Nelson, J. B. 1978. The Sulidae: gannets and boobies. Oxford Univ. Press, Oxford, UK.

Nisbet, I. C. T. 1978. Dependence of fledging success on egg size, parental performance and egg-composition among Common and Roseate Terns, *Sterna hirundo* and *S. dougallii*. Ibis 120:207-215.

Nisbet, I. C. T., and J. A. Spendelow. 1999. Contribution of research to management and recovery of the Roseate Tern: review of a twelve-year project. Waterbirds 22:239-252.

Nisbet, I. C. T., J. Burger, C. Safina and M. Gochfeld. 1990. Estimating fledging success and productivity in Roseate Terns (*Sterna dougallii*). Colonial Waterbirds 13:85-91.

Orta, J. 1992. Family Phaethontidae (Tropicbirds). Pp. 280-289, in J. del Hoyo, A. Elliott and J. Sargatal, eds., *Handbook of the birds of the world*, Vol. . Lynx Editions, Barcelona.

Phillips, N. J. 1987. The breeding biology of White-tailed Tropicbirds *Phaethon lepturus* at Cousin Island, Seychelles. Ibis 129:10-24.

Pregill, G. K., D.W. Steadman, and D. R. Watters. 1994. Late quaternary vertebrate faunas of the Lesser Antilles; historical components of Caribbean biogeography. Bull. of Carnegie Museum of Natural History No. 30.

Prys-Jones, R. P. and C. Peet. 1980. Breeding periodicity, nesting success and nest site selection among Red-tailed Tropicbirds *Phaethon rubricauda* and White-tailed Tropicbirds *P. lepturus* on Aldabra Atoll. Ibis 122:76-81.

Ramos, J. A. 1998a. The 1997 breeding season of Roseate Tern and Lesser Noddy on Aride Island. Pp. 329-355, in M. Betts (ed.) Aride Island Nature Reserve, Seychelles. Annual report 1997. Royal Society for Nature Conservation, The Green, Witham Park, Waterside South, Lincoln, UK.

Ramos, J. A. 1998b. Nest-site selection by Roseate Terns breeding on Aride Island, Seychelles. Colonial Waterbirds 21:438-443.

Ramos, J. A. In press. Seasonal variation in reproductive measures of tropical Roseate Terns: previously undescribed breeding patterns in a seabird. Ibis.

Ramos, J. A., E. Solá, L. R. Monteiro and N. Ratcliffe. 1998. Prey delivered to Roseate Tern chicks in the Azores. Journal of Field Ornithology 69:419-429.

Randall, R. M. and B. M. Randall. 1981. Roseate Tern breeding biology and factors responsible for low chick production in Algoa Bay, South Africa. Ostrich 52:17-24.

Ratcliffe, N. 1997. Monitoring methods for seabirds on Ascension Island. Unpubl. MS, Royal Society for Protection of Birds, U.K.

Ratcliffe, N., D. Vaughan, C. Whyte and M. Shepherd. 1998. The status of Storm Petrels on Mousa, Shetland. Scottish Birds 19:154-159.

Ricklefs, R. E., D. Duffy and M. Coulter. 1984. Weight gain of Blue-footed Booby chicks: an indicator of marine resources. Ornis Scandinavica 15:162-166.

Savard, J.-P. L. and G. E. J. Smith. 1985. Comparison of survey techniques for burrow-nesting seabirds. Canadian Wildlife Service Progress Notes 151:1-7.

Schaffner, F. C. 1990. Food provisioning by White-tailed Tropicbirds: effects on the developmental pattern of chicks. Ecology 71:375-390.

Schreiber, E. A. 1994. El Niño-Southern Oscillation effects on provisioning and growth in Red-tailed Tropicbirds. Colonial Waterbirds 17:105-215.

Schreiber, E. A., and R. W. Schreiber. 1986. Seabird census and study techniques. NATO ASI Series, Vol. G12:207-218. Springer-Verlag, Berlin.

Schreiber, E. A., and R. W. Schreiber. 1993. Red-tailed Tropicbird (*Phaethon rubricauda*). In The birds of North America, No. 43 (A. Poole and F. Gill, eds.). Academy of Natr. Sciences, Philadelphia, PA, and Am. Ornithologists' Union, Washington, DC. 24 p.

Schreiber, E. A., R. W. Schreiber, and G. A. Schenk. 1996. Red-footed Booby (*Sula sula*). No. 241 in A. Poole and F. Gill, eds., *The birds of North America,*. Academy of Natr. Sciences, Philadelphia, PA, and Am.Ornithologists' Union, Washington, DC. 24 p.

Shealer, D.A. 1998. Size-selective predation by a specialist forager, the Roseate Tern. Auk 115:519-525.

Sheridan, L. 1998. White-tailed Tropicbirds on Aride, 1987-1997. Pp. 291-310, in Betts, M. (ed.). Aride Island Nature Reserve, Seychelles. Annual report 1997. Royal Society for Nature Conservation, The Green, Witham Park, Waterside South, Lincoln, UK.

Simmons, K. E. L. 1967. Ecological adaptations in the life history of the Brown Booby at Ascension Island. Living Bird 6:187-212.

Stonehouse, B. 1962. The tropicbirds (genus *Phaethon*) of Ascension Island. Ibis 103b:123-161.

Sutherland, W. J. 1996. Ecological census techniques: a handbook. Cambridge University Press, Cambridge, UK.

Trivelpiece, W. Z., and J. D. Ferraris. 1987. Notes on the behavioural ecology of the Magnificent Frigatebird *Fregata magnificens*. Ibis 129: 168-174.

Walsh, P. M., D. J. Halley, M. P. Harris, A. del Nevo, I. M. W. Sim and M. L. Tasker. 1995. Seabird monitoring handbook for Britain and Ireland. JNCC / RSPB / ITE / Seabird Group, Peterborough, U.K.

Warham, J. 1990. The petrels: their ecology and breeding systems. Academic Press, London.

Warham, J. 1996. The behaviour, population biology and physiology of the petrels. Academic Press, London.

Weimerskirch, H. and Y. Cherel. 1998. Feeding ecology of short-tailed shearwaters: breeding in Tasmania and foraging in the Antarctic? Marine Ecology Progress Series 167:261-274.

A Geographic Information System for Seabird Breeding Sites in the West Indies.

ᙏ ᙏ ᙏ ᙏ   ᙐ ᙐ ᙐ ᙐ

W. A. MACKIN

Biology Department, UNC-CH; CB#3280, Coker Hall; Chapel Hill, NC USA 27599-3280, Email mackin@email.unc.edu

Introduction

All the maps in this volume were produced from the West Indies Seabird Geographic Information System (GIS), which was developed using the literature available on seabirds in the West Indies and information from recent visits to colonies by researchers. This system provides a geographic atlas for the conservation and management of seabird populations and is designed to incorporate data from future censuses. As information accumulates, the GIS can make increasing contributions to research on the phenology, ecology, and conservation of West Indian seabirds. This chapter first describes the design and potential uses of the GIS and how the maps for this volume were produced. Finally, I discuss two challenges to the effectiveness of the system and describe how information about seabird breeding sites in the West Indies can be submitted for inclusion in the GIS.

Design of the West Indies Seabird GIS

Geographic Information Systems combine the analysis capabilities of databases with software that can analyze the geographic distribution of the data and produce maps. The most important part of a GIS is the quality of its database. In the database for this GIS, some included surveys note only the presence or absence of a species from a particular location while others provide estimates and census methodology. The system stacks surveys from different years to allow for historical comparisons and provide cumulative information, and it includes references so that the original source of the data can be identified. Breeding sites in the West Indies and the Caribbean coasts of Central and South America are included, because these areas include parts of the populations of most seabirds in the West Indies.

The database includes (1) the reports from each survey, (2) contact information for contributors, (3) references for sources from the literature, (4) the physical and vegetative characteristics of the breeding sites, and (5) threats to the sites. For each survey, the database stores the location, date, species, survey method, high and low estimates, egg-laying dates, fledging dates, the surveyor's name, and comments about the survey. Current threats to the breeding sites are not yet known for most colonies, because it is difficult to survey breeding sites for rats, cats, and other potential threats to populations of seabirds. In the future, the reported threats may play an important role in conservation.

The latitude and longitude coordinates of each site identify its location. If contributors provided only the common name of the breeding island, latitude and longitude coordinates have been acquired from online gazetteers. The United States Geological Survey (USGS)'s

Geographic Names Information System (GNIS) provided the coordinates for sites in Puerto Rico and the U.S. Virgin Islands, and the National Imagery and Mapping Agency (NIMA)'s GEOnet names server provided coordinates for sites in the other island groups. Unfortunately, common names of islands are ambiguous because the same name is often used for many different islands or cays in the same country (for instance, NIMA's GEOnet provides coordinates for four sites under "White Cay, Bahamas." When contributors grouped many surveys to provide a total estimate for large islands, a point within that island was chosen to represent the site until more accurate locations can be found. In future submissions, the locations of breeding sites should be specified by latitude and longitude coordinates to avoid ambiguity.

Microsoft Access is used to enter and review the data before it is transferred into Environmental Systems Research Institute (ESRI)'s ArcView 3.2 GIS software. At this time, the database includes 521 breeding locations, 1317 surveys, 23 breeding species, 45 contributors, and 81 threats to the breeding sites. The Digital Map of the World (a 1:100,000 scale Robinson spherical projection) is the current base map for the GIS. This small-scale map does not have the resolution to include most of the small islets on which seabirds nest in the West Indies. High-resolution digital maps can be integrated into the system as they become desirable. With large-scale maps, the finer details of each colony can eventually be included in the database, so that the portions of each island used for nesting can be mapped as shapes rather than points. Eventually, the sites could be mapped within 1 meter of their true locations.

Geographic Information Systems in Biological Research

In addition to managing and analyzing a database, GIS technology can produce maps and analyze the geographic distribution of the mapped locations. Images from remote sensing and aerial photography can be analyzed to study the vegetational and geological characteristics of the landscape and quantify changes in such characteristics over time. Large-scale digital maps of the West Indies are not yet widely available, but the level of accuracy of available digital maps is now being increased in many island groups. More detailed base-maps and imagery should become available as the database of West Indies seabird breeding sites continues to grow.

Eventually, the West Indies Seabird GIS can be used to analyze the spatial distribution of species. For example, GIS has been used to estimate the abundance of species in large areas based on mapped geological and ecological factors that were associated with the species' abundance in more localized surveys (Jarvis and Robertson, 1999). Galatowitsch and Tester (1998) used GIS to relate the composition of plant and animal communities to various levels of anthropogenic disturbance. Long et al. (1996) used a GIS covering the world's restricted-range species to identify endemic bird areas, areas supporting two or more species with ranges of less than 50,000 km2. GIS can also serve to examine landscape changes over time. Murkin et al. (1997) used aerial photographs and GIS to characterize a prairie wetland habitat in North America. Then, they analyzed the responses of different avian species to systematic manipulations in the habitat. Finally, a recent study of a Red-footed Booby (*Sula sula*) colony in the Cayman Islands analyzed a series of aerial photographs with GIS to describe changes in the nesting habitat over time (Burton et al., 1999).

Uses of the West Indies Seabird GIS

The maps accompanying the other chapters in this volume demonstrate the ability of the GIS to unify information from the entire region. The GIS can display and analyze subsets of data other than the distribution of species throughout the West Indies. The figures in this chapter illustrate three alternative types of information that can be analyzed with the GIS. Figure 1 displays the number of species breeding at each site in the western Virgin Islands. Figure 2 displays the threats to seabirds in the same area, the only area for which the threats to the colonies are well documented in the database. Figure 3 displays the same view with the highest estimate for the number of breeding pairs of White-tailed (*Phaethon lepturus*) and Red-billed Tropicbirds (*P. aethereus*) labeled on each colony. These images also demonstrate the limits of resolution on the 1:100,000-scale maps. Most islands where breeding occurs are too small to appear on this map.

Other than mapping the distribution of breeding sites, the most immediate application of the GIS is to highlight places where more fieldwork is needed. Most breeding sites of seabirds in the West Indies have never been censused. As results from future censuses are incorporated, estimates of the populations should become more accurate. In addition, as repeat surveys for many breeding sites are included, the GIS can track changes in the populations over time and compare populations to historical reports.

Spatial analysis and remote sensing imagery could be used to test hypotheses or evaluate experimental habitat manipulations. High-resolution satellite images could be compared to the breeding distributions to identify appropriate sites for conservation initiatives, such as providing nest boxes or improving habitat by clearing vegetation. Such imagery might also identify potential breeding sites for difficult-to-census species such as Audubon's Shearwater (*Puffinus lherminieri*).

Populations of most West Indian seabirds nest at sites controlled by different nations where different languages are spoken (van Halewyn and Norton, 1984). One purpose of summarizing the status of seabirds in the West Indies is to unify seabird conservation within the region. The GIS provides a permanent forum for collaboration. This cooperation could involve collecting data on species other than the investigator's focal species or teaming up to visit uncensused colonies when it is not possible for a single individual to perform an effective survey. In fact, contributors from different island groups have already joined to obtain information for this publication.

A simple way to obtain more data on breeding sites throughout the West Indies is to encourage individuals who live near the breeding sites to collect the data themselves. These individuals are also in the best position to help protect the breeding sites in the future. The GIS provides a means for local individuals or groups who are interested in seabirds to contribute data, and it also encourages grassroots participation, which is essential for conservation efforts to succeed.

Notes on the Maps in this Volume
    On the distribution maps in this book, each symbol appears over the exact coordinates to which it refers. The resulting detail creates a few problems that need to be explained. First, the tables within the chapters do not correspond exactly to the maps. For example, if the text gives an estimate for the population of a species in the Exumas, the map might show many breeding sites in the Exumas that have been summed to produce the estimate in the text. Some island groups have been more intensively studied and more precisely mapped than others. These areas are often completely obscured by symbols on the maps. However, because these distribution maps contain no information about the number of pairs breeding at the site, the areas with the most reports are not always the most important nesting areas for a species. To make the maps more visually literate, some symbols were removed from densely-covered areas. Care was taken

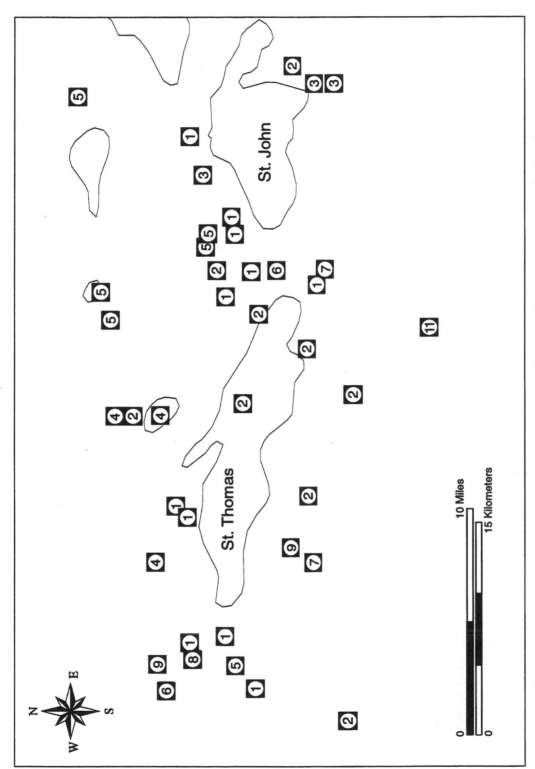

Figure 1: The number of species breeding at each known site in the western Virgin Islands.

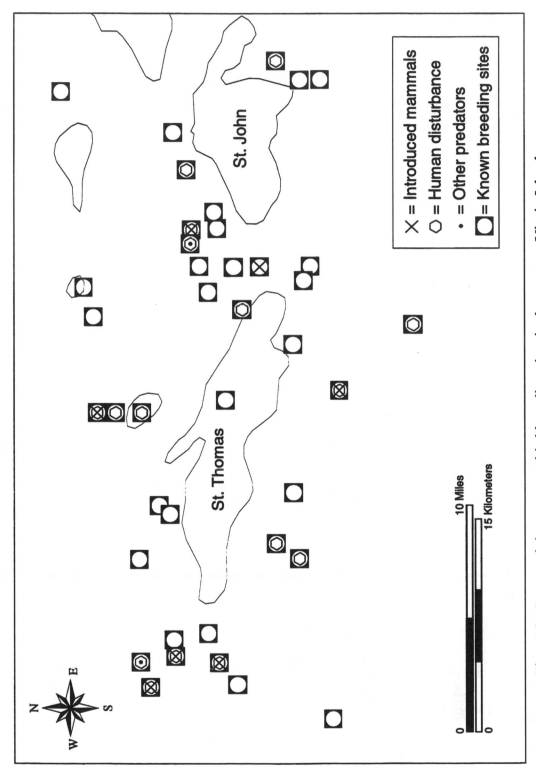

Figure 2: Reported threats to seabird breeding sites in the western Virgin Islands.

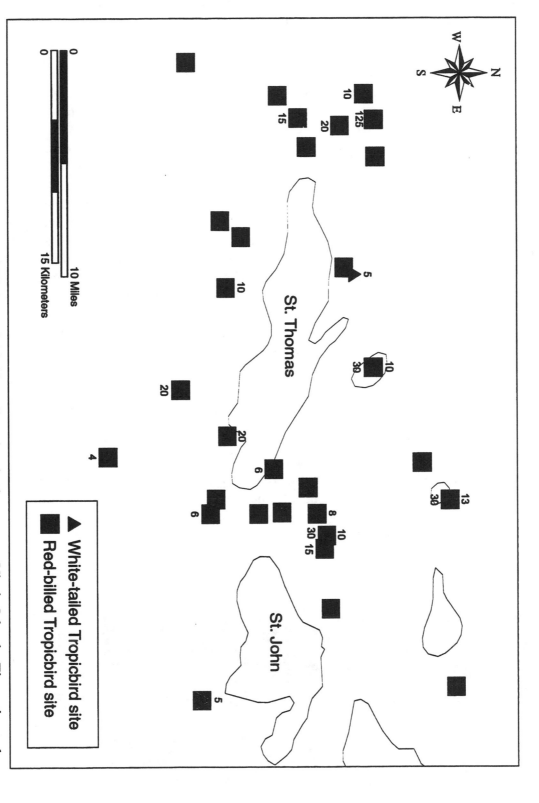

Figure 3: The White-tailed and Red-billed Tropicbird breeding sites in the western Virgin Islands. The estimated number of breeding pairs is placed above each White-tailed Tropicbird site and below each Red-billed Tropicbird site. Sites without estimates are thought to have only a few pairs.

so that only colonies of similar status were removed from the maps. Thus, one point on any of the distribution maps could indicate one breeding site or several close together sites.

Making the GIS Work

Because the information included in the GIS was collected by many different researchers, several logistical difficulties were encountered during the creation of this GIS. Differences in the precision to which breeding sites are mapped have been the greatest challenge. These differences result from the lack of a standardized definition for the term "breeding site" for all seabirds. For this GIS, one breeding site is defined as any contiguous area within which one or several species of seabirds nest. Thus, if White-tailed Tropicbirds breed at several points on one island, each point is considered a separate breeding site. Problems arose because many sources applied less specific definitions of "breeding site," possibly because the investigators were not able to survey all the individual locations. In order to obtain accurate estimates for the entire region, care must be taken to insure that the same definition of "breeding site" is applied within each geographical unit so that sites are not counted twice. Spatial analysis using the GIS will not be completely satisfactory until all breeding sites in the database are mapped to exact locations.

Another problem is that contributors sometimes omit the methodology used to estimate the number of breeding pairs. Without knowing these methods, the GIS cannot produce meaningful estimates of population sizes or compare the number of pairs at particular sites in different seasons. The methods for estimating each species should be standardized. Standardization on a reasonably accurate measure will enable fluctuations in populations to be monitored in conservation efforts and provide a method of detecting declines.

Submitting Data and Obtaining the GIS

To submit data for the database, first contact the local wildlife conservation authorities to be referred to the appropriate contact person. As a second resort, contact the leader of the Seabird Working Group of the Society of Caribbean Ornithology (SCO) or look up the SCO home page on the World Wide Web (below). The information for submitting data or obtaining a copy of the database will soon be available on that website. In the future, it will be possible to accomplish these tasks over the internet at a specific site for the West Indies Seabird GIS.

Acknowledgements

The number of collaborators for this project is extensive, and this list is certainly not exhaustive. Without many of these collaborators, the project would not have been possible. I thank the following groups and individuals; The authors of the chapters, the other members of the Seabird Working Group of the SCO, researchers provided the data from their own fieldwork and knowledge of the literature, P. Bradley (Cayman Islands), A. Haynes-Sutton (Jamaica), and J. Pierce (U.S. Virgin Islands) provided detailed accounts that allowed me to expand the coverage of the GIS. J. Weyl suggested correctly that GIS software would be appropriate for the project. S. Whitfield helped with the production of the maps for publication. E.A. Schreiber collaborated in the design of the maps for this text and provided comments on the manuscript of the chapter. J. Hyman, A. Skypala, J. Vondrasek, C. Hogan, H. Mueller, and the behavior group at UNC assisted with the design of the database and comments on the manuscript. My wife, A. Mackin, provided insightful help with writing and support during compilation of the database. My advisor, R.H. Wiley, helped in choosing the project, designing the GIS, producing the maps, and reviewing the text. D. Lee conceived of an atlas of seabird breeding sites in the West Indies, recruited me to implement it, helped with the design, and provided comments on the text.

Literature Cited

Burton, F.J., P.E. Bradley, E.A. Schreiber, G.A. Schenk, and R.W. Burton. 1999. Status of Red-footed Boobies (*Sula sula*) on Little Cayman, British West Indies. Bird Conservation International 9(3): 227-34.

Murkin, H.R., E.J. Murkin, and J.P. Ball. 1997. Avian habitat selection and prairie wetland dynamics: a 10-year experiment. Ecological Applications 7(4): 1144-59.

Long, A.J., M.J. Crosby, A.J. Stattersfield, and D.C. Wege. 1996. Towards a global map of biodiversity: patterns in the distribution of restricted-range birds. Global Ecology & Biogeography Letters 5(4-5): 281-304.

Mensing, D.M., S.M. Galatowitsch, and J.R. Tester. 1998. Anthropogenic effects on the biodiversity of riparian wetlands of a northern temperate landscape. Journal of Environmental Management 53(4): 349-77.

Van Halewyn, R. and R.L. Norton. 1984. The Status and Conservation of Seabirds in the Caribbean. Pp. 169-222 in J.P. Croxall, P.G.H. Evans, and R.W. Schreiber, Eds., *Status and Conservation of the World's Seabirds*. ICBP Technical Publication No. 2, Cambridge, UK.

Web Resources:
NIMA's GEOnet: http://164.214.2.59/gns/html/index.html
USGS's GNIS: http://mapping.usgs.gov/www/gnis/gnisform.html
The SCO Web Page: http://www.nmnh.si.edu/BIRDNET/SCO/index.html

Action Plan for Conservation of West Indian Seabirds

_____ ∾ ∾ ∾ ∾   ∾ ∾ ∾ ∾ _____

E. A. SCHREIBER

National Museum of Natural History, Smithsonian Institution, MRC 116 Washington D.C. 20560
SchreiberE@aol.com.

Introduction

This chapter is designed to serve as a practical guide to preserving seabirds in the West Indies. It is the result of consultations with many people from the Caribbean nations and the United States, including dedicated researchers, natural resource units, and non-governmental organizations. By following these guidelines the beginning steps will be taken toward the preservation of seabirds in the West Indies. Seabird conservation has lagged far behind conservation of land bird species and this has allowed many seabird species to decline to very low levels. If we do not soon begin to acknowledge the value of preserving our seabirds and take some action many species will be lost.

There are four international Conventions instituted over the past 25 years, each having significant implications for conservation of natural resources. All four are applicable to seabird conservation: CITES, Bonn, Ramsar and World Heritage. These Conventions provide assistance to countries to protect natural resources and, very significantly, they provide a means of international cooperation to accomplish this (Oldfield 1987). Most West Indian nations are signatory to the Conventions and can take advantage of the resources they offer for assistance. Other Conventions which relate to protection of the environment and provide assistance to accomplish this include the Cartagena Convention and the Western Hemisphere Convention. Within the Caribbean, the Caribbean Conservation Association and the Organization of Eastern Caribbean States are both play an important role in conservation by providing various forms of assistance: training in wildlife and environmental protection, research, environmental education programs, establishing legislation, and an opportunity to share resources across nations.

It is often difficult for small countries to have the trained personnel and monetary resources available to undertake conservation programs. This makes conservation a more difficult task, where funding and expertise must both be found. The above conventions and organizations can provide valuable assistance. Information and help also are available from other groups such as BirdLife International, the World Wildlife Fund, RARE, U.S. Fish and Wildlife Service International Division, local natural history groups or birding societies. Full advantage should be taken of all these resources in our efforts to conserve seabirds in the West Indies. All of these groups can be reached through the internet (world wide web). Information on the four international conventions which help protect birds and their habitat can be found there also.

Some of the nations in the Caribbean do not have laws to protect seabirds and their habitat or do not enforce laws if they do exist. If seabirds are to continue to be an important part of the marine ecosystem or even continue to survive in the Caribbean region, the birds and their habitat must be actively protected. It is not only for seabirds that it is important to preserve habitat: this same habitat supports plants, other animals and us. When feral goats destroy an island for birds they are also destroying the surrounding reef as the overgrazed land washes into the sea and kills the reef. Then the fish populations that feed and live on the reef then die, also. All parts of the environment are connected and the loss of one resource can affect many other resources.

Tourism is a very important reason for preserving seabirds and their habitat because of the economic benefit (jobs) gained by maintaining an appealing natural world in the Caribbean islands. People have always come to this area to enjoy the natural beauty and with the growth of eco-tourism, this is happening even more so. A significant portion of many Caribbean nations' income is from tourists. If the natural beauty, birds and reefs of these islands are lost, many millions of dollars will be lost to local economies. Nature preserves such as the Baths on Virgin Gorda, the Booby Pond Nature Reserve on Little Cayman Island, and the Frigatebird colony on Barbuda, bring thousands of tourists to the islands, encourage young people to get training in the natural sciences to serve as tour guides, and encourage locals to support conservation of natural resources. There is a great need to establish more preserves in the West Indies and to protect those that do exist. There is also a great need for training in the wildlife sciences. The wildlife and natural resources of the West Indies can continue to provide income and a healthy environment as long as we learn to properly protect these resources.

On the following pages I provide descriptions of:
1) the primary threats to the survival of West Indian seabirds,
2) categories used to rank declining species,
3) criteria used to place species in specific categories,
4) a list of species falling under each threatened category, and
5) a plan of needed action to preserve seabirds and their habitat.

Primary Threats to Seabirds in the West Indies
In order of estimated severity:
1) Continued loss of nesting habitat owing to development. Thousands of acres of seabird habitat have been irrevocably lost to development and more are destroyed every day.

2) Human disturbance in colonies. Disturbing birds off their nests at a minimum can cause eggs and small chicks to be cooked in the hot sun. It also can cause adults to abandon nests and desert nesting islands when it occurs too frequently. Increasing uncontrolled tourist visits to islands have put increased pressure on seabird colonies. When adult birds are disturbed off nests eggs and chicks are easy prey for predators such as frigatebirds, Laughing Gulls, hawks, dogs, and others. Often people have no idea what harm they are causing when they enter a seabird colony.

3) Introduced predators, feral animals in colonies, uncontrolled livestock grazing. Predators are a tremendous problem for nesting seabirds. Animals such as goats, sheep, donkey, pigs, cats, and mongeese are present on many seabird nesting islands. They eat eggs and/or young, trample nests, and eat the vegetation that prevents erosion and provides nesting habitat. Livestock grazing has destroyed many colonies of burrow nesting seabirds such as petrels, as well as causing erosion. Grazing mammals not only kill birds by trampling on them, but also the surrounding reef can be destroyed by the erosion caused by loss of vegetation.

4) Limited data on natural resources and limited expertise on management of these. Conservation efforts are hampered by the lack of knowledge about the status of seabirds, their annual reproductive success, and the health of their environment. Added to this lack of data is the need for professional expertise in both gathering and interpreting data.

5) Human predation on eggs and birds. This was a much more severe problem 50-100 years ago, but still does occur in some areas.

6) Pollution of the waters in which seabirds feed can cause the decline or loss of their food source. Pollution can also cause insidious effects on the birds that are not easily seen. For instance ingestion of petrochemicals by seabirds can alter the immune system response of birds and increase mortality (Briggs et al. 1997). Considerable amounts of pesticides and herbicides are imported into the Caribbean but we do not have good data on the effects of their use. It is known that water pollution (including the use of pesticides and herbicides) has been responsible for fish-kills in the past (Towle 1991). There are many sources of water pollution around the Caribbean basin:
   a) Agricultural runoff, including fertilizers, pesticides, herbicides and waste.
   b) Soil runoff from denuded islands that have lost their natural vegetation from overgrazing, and farming.
   c) Ocean dumping of industrial waste which includes heavy metals. These metals get into the food chain and eventually end up in the food that seabirds eat, fish. Heavy metals are known to cause hormonal disruptions and development of deformities in embryos.
   d) Ocean dumping of untreated human waste.
   e) Ocean dumping of untreated garbage.

7) Over fishing by humans. We do not have good data in the West Indian region on the commercial fish resource but the number of people fishing and the amount of fish taken has increased greatly over the past 50 years.

8) Hurricanes which are a natural occurrence were not a problem when seabird populations were large. Today, with a few small remaining populations, a hurricane could easily destroy a major nesting site of a species. With the reduced bird populations present today the loss of a colony site is a severe problem. Since we believe many of these species are philopatric, they will not readily move to another island to nest and the loss of their nesting colony represents the end of their breeding.

Status of Species of Special Concern and Criteria for Listing
Population levels of some Caribbean seabird species are low enough to warrant special designation. There are some problems with trying to rank species status owing to the lack of information about the species in the Caribbean. We have used the basics of the International Union for the Conservation of Nature (IUCN) criteria (Collar et al. 1994) for putting species on the "Red List" as a guideline to categorize seabird populations in the West Indies. The Guidelines were designed to be applied to any taxonomic unit at or below the species level and to either the global population or a regional sub-population (Gärdenfors et al. 1999), which for our purposes is the West Indies. The IUCN criteria can be applied to regional sub-populations

which are geographically distinct with little demographic or genetic exchange with other populations (IUCN/SSC Criteria Review Working Group 1999). Data are beginning to be gathered which show that individual seabirds do not readily move between regions for nesting (see Schreiber chapter on boobies in this publication) and West Indian populations may, in fact, represent separate breeding populations of these species from those in Central and South America. While definitive taxonomic studies on the status of West Indian populations are lacking, what little data exist on morphometrics of some species indicate that there is some separation of populations within the Caribbean basin.

The categories of designation for birds in trouble, beginning with the most critical are "Critically Endangered", "Endangered", "Vulnerable" and "Near Threatened". These categories reflect the extinction risk of a taxon. The data used in this assessment and assignment of species to the specific categories is the regional population size (number of nesting pairs) as described for Red List criteria, and thus indicates status within the West Indies. The IUCN uses the number of mature individuals in the population, not the number of nesting pairs. To obtain this figure for the species herein, simply multiply the number of pairs in the tables by two. The criteria for each category provide a means to quantify population status according to adult population size, trends in adult population size, and range size as reflected in the number of colonies.

The IUCN criteria work well for land birds but there are some difficulties applying them to seabirds. Some of the criteria were changed to make them more appropriate for seabird nesting habits. For instance, the IUCN categories have a criteria based on the area (100 – 20,000 sq. km.) in which the species occurs. Since seabirds are colonial, a highly concentrated portion of a species population can occur in only one or two small nesting areas (nesting areas of 0.1 – 0.2 sq. km). Much of the area in which they occur during the breeding season is open sea, not actually inhabited by the birds but used for feeding. We have changed the IUCN area criteria to specify a number of nesting locations with a viable population (30 or more pairs), rather than the size of the area used by the birds. The population size criteria we set for seabirds reflect the fact that they nest in colonies and a whole colony can easily be lost (to human destruction, hurricane, etc) representing an immediate massive loss of individuals. Because we have so few data on changes in population size over time, we were basically unable to use this criteria in categorizing species. Specifying a probability of extinction within a certain number of years also requires more data than we have for any seabird species in the West Indies, and thus this criteria is not used here.

Critically Endangered
1. a decline of greater than 80% of the population in 40 years or 2 generation (1 generation is considered 20 years for seabirds).
2. nesting either at two or fewer locations or experiencing continuing decline (locations with fewer than 30 pairs are not considered viable populations for this category).
3. fewer than 1,000 mature individuals or 500 nesting pairs remaining.

Endangered
1. a decline between 50% and 79% in 40 years or 2 generations.
2. nesting at four or fewer locations (with a minimum of 30 pairs each) and experiencing continuing decline.
3. fewer than 3,000 mature individuals or 1,500 nesting pairs remaining.

Vulnerable
1. a decline between 20% and 49% in 40 years or 2 generations.
2. nesting at eight or fewer locations (with a minimum of 30 pairs each) and experiencing continuing decline.
3. fewer than 6,000 mature individuals or 3,000 nesting pairs remaining.

Near Threatened
1. a decline between 10% and 19% in 40 years or 2 generations (40 years).
2. nesting at fewer than 10 locations (with a minimum of 30 pairs each) and experiencing continuing decline.
3. fewer than 10,000 mature individuals or 5,000 nesting pairs remaining and under continuing decline.
4. taxon is the focus of a continuing taxon-specific conservation program, the cessation of which would result in the taxon qualifying for one of the above categories.

Table 1. Species designations and estimated number of nesting pairs remaining.

Species and Designation	Number of Pairs
A. Critically Endangered	
Black-capped Petrel (*P. hasitata*)*	1000-2000
Jamaica Petrel (*P. caribbaca*)*	0-15
Gull-billed Tern (*Sterna nilotica*)	100-500
Cayenne Tern (*Sterna sandvicensis eurygnatha*)*	10-100
Common Tern (*Sterna hirundo*)	50-100
Black Noddy (*Anous minutus*)	fewer than 100
B Endangered	
Masked Booby (*Sula dactylatra*)	550-650
Brown Pelican (*Pelecanus occidentalis*)*	1500±
Royal Tern (Sterna maxima)	450-800
C. Vulnerable	
White-tailed Tropicbird (*Phaethon lepturus*)	2500-3500
Red-billed Tropicbird (*Phaethon aetherus*)	1800-2500
Sandwich Tern (*Sterna sandvicensis acuflavida*)	2100-3000
Least Tern - (*Sterna antillarum*)	1500-3000
D. Near Threatened	
Magnificent Frigatebird (*Fregata magnificens*)	4300-5300
Audubon's Shearwater (*Puffinus lherminieri*)*	3000-5000

---

* indicates an endemic subspecies

Recommended Action for Seabird Preservation

A combination of actions is needed for the preservation of West Indian seabirds. Although number one below, surveys of existing colonies, is the most important thing to do immediately, the other actions following that are not listed in order of importance. Each country is a unique situation and the order of priorities will vary. The order will also vary by species. I do strongly recommend that natural resource managers not hesitate to ask for assistance if they are unsure about what needs to be done. As mentioned in the introduction, they are many avenues available to obtaining assistance. In most cases these recommendations will be better carried out with some outside assistance. No one of us could attempt to save a species alone. We all need expertise in addition to that we have ourselves, and we can be most effective in concert with others trying to accomplish the same goals.

In the past controlled egging (harvesting some eggs for human consumption) of some seabird colonies (particularly of sooty terns) has been attempted (Gochfeld et al 1994). While it is an added incentive to conserve a species if some harvesting can be done, this activity must be closely monitored by trained wildlife people and maximum harvest levels set. It is recommended that no more than 20% of the total eggs laid be taken and that they be taken in only one part of the colony (Feare 1976a, Feare pers. comm.). Monitoring and banding of the birds is needed to ensure continued survival of the colony under this added pressure (Feare 1976a, 1976b).

1) Survey existing seabird colonies. Since we know little about current population sizes and even current nesting areas for some species, surveys are very important and have been a major recommendation in the past (Croxall et al. 1984, King 1985). We cannot determine what areas to protect for some species because we do not know for sure where they nest. Data are also needed on population sizes and perturbations occurring to the birds in order to make decisions about conservation. Surveys should collect data on location of nesting (including location on a specific island and type of habitat used), number of nests present, and potential threats to the birds (such as the presence of predators). It may not be possible to do the survey in one visit since not all species lay at the same time of year, and some species lay over an extended period. If trained people are not locally available to conduct surveys, help should be sought from the outside. Human disturbance in seabird colonies can cause severe damage. The use of appropriate techniques when working in seabird colonies is very important.

2) Develop monitoring and management plans for seabirds. Monitor known nesting colonies to determine nest success. If birds are not successfully reproducing, determine the reasons why. Outside experts may need to be called in to help set up a monitoring program. Barbuda, with the assistance of the Organization of Eastern Caribbean States and World Wildlife Fund, has developed a monitoring plan for their frigatebird colony and carried out training programs for colony wardens and tour guides (Schreiber 1998a, 1998b). This program could serve as a model for other Nations. A monitoring network could be set up with neighboring countries to share data and methodologies. A central data base of Caribbean seabird colonies should be established. A group of birds does not necessarily nest in just one country. There is movement between countries and to truly monitor the size of Caribbean seabird populations it must be done across islands. A web-based database would make data accessible to all.

Set appropriate species goals and habitat preservation goals. Establish a timeline for action. Carryout a consistent monitoring plan to collect data that can be compared from year to year in order to determine if changes in populations are occurring.

3) Legally protect seabirds and their habitat once important sites are determined. Pass laws that protect seabirds, their eggs, their young and their habitat. These laws should state penalties for possession of birds or parts of birds, for disturbance of colonies and any harassment of birds. Specific islands should be listed as protected for the use of seabirds and human access should be monitored. The physical stress to birds of being constantly disturbed in breeding and roost sites decreases nesting success (Highsmith 1997) and tourists should not be allowed in colonies during the breeding season, unless on specific, conducted tours.

4) Post existing colonies with signs. Signage can be an effective deterrent to disturbance. Visitors to an island have no way of knowing if areas or birds are protected unless signs tell them so. In areas that are protected by law signs can tell people that, but even in legally unprotected areas, signs are effective to ask people to please respect the birds and stay away.

5) Training in wildlife management and monitoring techniques. Each West Indian country should have qualified personnel who have been professionally trained in monitoring and management techniques. Untrained people working in colonies can easily cause more damage than good. All West Indian Universities should offer courses in wildlife monitoring and management, and there should be regional coordination of training for policy-makers involved with wildlife (Walker 1998).

A multispecies, ecosystem based approach to conservation of seabirds would well in the Caribbean, where the same habitat is used by several species.

6) Remove introduced predators and grazing animals from nesting colonies. No introduced mammal or reptile species should be present on nesting islands. They do tremendous damage to nesting populations of seabirds. Predation is the cause of extinction for 42% of lost island bird species and is a major factor in the listing of 40% of the endangered island species (King 1985).

7) Patrol colony sites and roosting sites. Enforce laws that protect wildlife. Patrols and some monitoring could be carried by local conservation groups in conjunction with the government employees as a means of extending government resources. Working with local groups also helps to educate more people about seabirds.

8) Protect existing undisturbed coastal habitat, mangroves, wetlands, and other areas that are used by birds for feeding or roosting. Nesting sites are not the only important places for seabirds. If birds are to be preserved as a valuable resource, then they must have healthy feeding areas, and safe roost sites. Roost sites are needed for birds to have a safe place to sit and preen and rest. Without these protected sites in an area, birds will leave.

9) Develop a public education program. The cultural context plays an important role in wildlife conservation programs (Blanchard 1994) and education plays an important role in changing attitudes about wildlife so that people are concerned about preservation of their natural history. No country can afford the cost of constant policing and patrolling to save species from human persecution. Once people learn about birds they begin to care about them and

want to preserve them as an important part of their culture. This is accomplished through education programs and non-government groups can be enlisted to help with these. A workshop was held at the Society of Caribbean Ornithology meeting in Guadeloupe (July 1998) at which representatives from 18 Caribbean countries determined that their top conservation priority was education (Walker 1998). These education programs will need to be developed as they do not currently exist in a relevant form for the West Indies. Needed are:

a) School instruction programs. These educational materials need to be developed at all school levels.

b) Development of adult instruction and educational pamphlets for local inhabitants and tourists. Educational programs and materials for hunters are needed, also, since seabirds are still shot in some countries. These education programs can help stop the taking of eggs and birds for food.

c) Development of appropriate material for decision makers.

d) Training of colony wardens and monitors, including training in data collection and information management.

e) Dissemination of information through posters, magazine articles, radio announcements and programs.

10) Encourage research on seabirds. This will help promote further understanding of the resource and provide valuable management data to better protect the resource (see chapter on "The Role of Research and Museum Collections in Conservation of Seabirds".

11) Additional conservation priorities.

a) Create economic incentives or alternative sources of income generation that preserve seabird habitat and the birds themselves. The people of Barbuda have begun using their Magnificent Frigatebird colony as an eco-tourist site. Before beginning a large scale program of doing this they sought help from the Organization for Eastern Caribbean States and had a training program for colony wardens and guides (Schreiber 1998). Better and more extensive marketing of nature based tourism is needed, in conjunction with development of eco-tourist sites and programs.

b) Manage tourism, recreational activities and coastal development that will affect seabirds and their habitat. Develop comprehensive coastal zone management plans that include seabirds by integrating economic and land use planning.

c) Evaluate fisheries and the consequences of over fishing to seabirds and humans.

d) Determine if seabird bycatch is a problem for fisheries.

e) Work with existing local conservation groups to draw attention to seabird needs and to enlist their help with monitoring and protection activities.

f) Introduced plants may need to be removed (such as Australian Pines [*Casurina*] so that appropriate habitat is available for the birds to use.

g) Start a natural history museum. This will provide an opportunity not only for educational experiences but to involve the whole community in the effort.

Conclusions

The above listings of Critically Endangered (6 species), Endangered (3 species), Vulnerable (4 species), and Near Vulnerable (2 species) West Indian seabirds illustrates the severity of the problems seabirds have in this area: 14 species and one subspecies of 21 total nesting species are listed as being in trouble. If even one of these species goes extinct it represents a loss of 6.6% of the seabird biodiversity of the region. Jamaican Petrels may already be extinct. More species have probably become extinct but the archaeological evidence has not yet been extracted from digs (Steadman 1997). Other areas surrounding the Caribbean have similar problems with the loss of bird biodiversity: Brazil, Colombia, Venezuela and Mexico (Steadman 1997). Immediate action is needed in the West Indies to preserve seabirds.

Obviously funding for conservation programs is badly needed. The organizations discussed at the beginning of this chapter can help with this. But funding conservation can be accomplished in innovative ways, also. There could, for instance, be a tax on tourist visits to the country that goes directly to conservation programs. Sales of some wildlife-related items could carry a special conservation tax that also goes directly to conservation programs. To help get such taxes implemented, it may be necessary to collect data on the extent of eco-tourism in the country to present to policy makers.

An integral part of preserving seabirds is the protection and management of the whole ecosystem or landscape. Birds cannot survive without nest sites and food sources so that just protecting the birds is not enough. The end results of successful management for seabirds and their habitat are beneficial to all of us in several ways:
   1)   jobs and income are gained from tourists who come to enjoy the wildlife,
   2)   healthy reefs are maintained that serve as nurseries for the fish we eat,
   3)   watersheds maintain the local water supply, and
   4)   a healthy environment is preserved that supports all of us.

It frequently takes an active involved public writing to and putting pressure on government officials to get action on issues. Public attention may have to be drawn to a problem to get any action. This is where communicating is important. People have to know there is a problem in order to do anything about it. Local conservation groups can be very helpful and can often provide extra manpower for monitoring, education programs and getting publicity. Cooperative efforts between governmental organizations and non-governmental organizations are very effective and useful.

Literature Cited

Blanchard, K. A. 1994. Culture and seabird conservation: the north shore of the Gulf of St. Lawrence, Canada. *BirdLife Conservation Series* 1: 294-310.

Briggs, K. T., Gershwin, M. E., and Anderson, D. W. 1997. Consequences of petrochemical ingestion and stress on the immune system f seabirds. *ICES Journ of Marine Sciences* 5 4: 718-725.

Collar, N. J., Crosby, M. J., and Stattersfield, A. J. 1994. Birds to watch 2: the world list of threatened birds. BirdLife Internl., Cambridge.

Feare, C. J. 1976a. The exploitation of sooty tern eggs in the Seychelles (1976) Biol. Conserv. 10: 169-181.

Feare, C. J. 1976b. The breeding status of the sooty tern *Sterna fuscata* in the Seychelles and the effects of experimental removal of its eggs. J. Zool. London 179: 317-360.

Ferratti, S. and Thrace, J. 1998. La petit sterne (*Sterna antillarum*) et la Sterne pierregarin (*S. hirundo*), enjeux de la biodiversite de la reserve naturelle du Grand cul-de-sac, Marin

(Guadeloupe, F.W.I.). El Pitierre 11: 48-49.

Gärdenfors, U., J. P. Rodriguez, C. Hilton-Taylor, C. Hyslop, G. Mace, S. Molur, and S. Poss. Draft guidelines for the application of IUCN Red List Criteria at national and regional levels. Species 31: 58-70.

Gochfeld, M., Burger, J., Haynes-Sutton, A., van Halewyn, R., and Saliva, J. E. 1994. Successful approaches to seabird protection in the West Indies. Pp. 186-209 in D. N. Nettleship, J. Burger, and M. Gochfeld, eds. *Seabirds on islands: threats, case studies and action plans*, BirdLife Conservation series No. 1, Cambridge.

Highsmith, R. T. 1997. No rest for the weary? vying for the best spots on the beach costs shorebirds both sleep and calories. Conservation Sciences Summer 1997: 18-20.

IUCN/SSC Criteria Review Working Group. 1999. IUCN Red List criteria review provisional report: draft of the proposed changes and recommendations. Species 31: 43-57.

King, W. B. 1985. Island birds: will the future repeat the past? Pp. 3-16 in P. J. Moors, ed. *Conservation of island birds*, ICBP Technical Publ. No. 3, Cambridge.

Kirch, P. V., Flenley, J. R., Steadman, D. W., Lamont, F. and Dawson, S. 1992. Ancient environmental degradation. Natl. Geographic Research & Exploration 8: 166-179.

Oldfield, S. 1987. Fragments of paradise: a guide for conservation action in the U. K. dependent territories. Pisces Publ. Oxford. 191pp.

Schreiber, E. A. 1996. Barbuda Frigatebird Colony Status Report – Preserving Birds as an Economic Resource. Report to the Organization of Eastern Caribbean States, Natural Resources Management Unit. 21 pp.

_____ 1998a. Barbuda Magnificent Frigatebird Colony Management and Monitoring Plan. Organization of Eastern Caribbean States and Brit. Dept. for Development in the Caribbean. 19pp.

_____ 1998b. Barbuda Magnificent Frigatebird Colony Tour Guide Training Manual. Organization of Eastern Caribbean States and Brit. Dept. for Development in the Caribbean. 13pp.

Steadman, D. W. 1997. Human caused extinction of birds. Pp 139-161 in M. L. Reaka-Kudla, D. E. Wilson, and E. O. Wilson, eds. *Biodiversity II: understanding and protecting our biological resources*, Joseph Henry Press, Washington, D.C.

Steadman, D. W., Pregill, G. K. and Olson, S. L. 1984. Fossil vertebrates from Antigua, Lesser Antilles: evidence for late Halocene human-caused extinctions in the West Indies. Proc. *Natl. Academy of Sciences* 81: 4448-4451.

Towle, J. A. 1991. Environmental agenda for the 1990's: a synthesis of the eastern Caribbean country environmental profile series. Caribbean Consv. Assoc. and Isl. Resources Foundation.

van Halewyn, R., and Norton, R. L. 1984. The status and conservation of Caribbean seabirds. Pp. 169-222 in J. P. Croxall, P. G. H. Evans, and R. W. Schreiber, eds. *Status and Conservation of the World's Seabirds*, Cambridge, U.K.: International Council for Bird Preservation (Tech. Publ.) 2.

Walker, M. 1998. Avian conservation priorities for the Caribbean region and priorities for the Society of Caribbean Ornithology. El Pitirre 11: 76-79.

A BIBLIOGRAPHY OF SEABIRDS IN THE WEST INDIES

——————— ෆ ෆ ෆ ෆ   ဢ ဢ ဢ ဢ ———————

JAMES W. WILEY[1]

Biological Resources Division, U. S. Geological Survey, Reston, Virginia 22092, USA. [1] Mailing address: Grambling Cooperative Wildlife Project, P. O. Box 841, Grambling State Univ., Grambling, LA 71245, Ph: 313 274-2499, wileyjw@alpha0.gram.edu

Introduction

This bibliography contains most, but by no means all, of the literature on seabirds in the West Indies. The area covered by the bibliography is the Greater West Indies, as delimited by Bond (1980, Birds of the West Indies, Fourth American ed., Boston: Houghton Mifflin Co.), and includes the Bahama Islands; the Greater and Lesser Antilles, south to Barbados and Grenada; and several extralimital islands (Isla San Andrés [St. Andrew Island], Isla Providencia [Old Providence Island], and Swan Islands). It does not include the Dutch islands of Aruba, Bonaire, or Curaçao, nor does it include Trinidad, Tobago, and the several islands off Venezuela. The bibliography includes references from 1526 to 1997, but concentrates on the period through 1995. The bibliography excludes James Bond's Check-lists and Supplements; Regional Reports that appear in *American Birds, Audubon Field Notes,* and *National Audubon Society Field Notes*; and many general references for the region. The search for titles was made through the computer version of *A bibliography of ornithology in the West Indies* (in prep.), using specific key words for species or groups of seabirds (Table 1). A total of 1056 references are included in the bibliography.

Acknowledgments.

Many people and institutions have helped in the production of the bibliography and deserve special recognition for their contributions: L. Garrett, W. Manning (Patuxent Wildlife Research Center), J. A. Feheley (U. S. Dept. Agriculture); V. Fuentes (Puerto Rican Agriculture Experiment Station); E. Cardona (Puerto Rico Dept. Natural Resources); R. Vera, E. Aguado Figueiras (Mus. Nacl. de Historia Natural, La Habana); N. M. Lorenzo and C. Z. Quirantes Hernández (Biblioteca Nacional "José Martí," La Habana); S. Achuthan (Grambling State Univ.); D. Amadon, M. LeCroy, R. Gnam (Am. Museum of Natl. History); F. Gill, C. Bush (Acad. Natl. Sciences); Kathy Donahue (Univ. California at Los Angeles); K. Garrett, E. A. Schreiber (Los Angeles County Mus. Natl. History); L. Kiff, J. Jennings, E. Harrison, J. Fisher (Westr. Fndt. Vert. Zool.); E. Smyth, E. Robinson, L. Wells, C. Riquelmy (Louisiana State Univ.); J. Buys, J. Langston (Southern Science Center, Natl. Biol. Service); J. Hinshaw, R. Payne (Univ. Michigan); C. Levy (Gosse Bird Club); and the late Oscar T. Owre (University of Miami), who insisted that I compile a bibliography on West Indian birds. I thank the many authors who generously provided copies of their publications and who generousely reviewed their sections of the bibliography.

TABLE 1. Key words used in search for references on seabirds in the West Indies.

Brown Noddy *Anous stolidus*	Parasitic Jaeger *Stercorarius parasiticus*
Brown Pelican *Pelecanus Occidentalis*	Pink–footed Shearwater *Puffinus creatopus*
Caspian Tern *Sterna caspia*	Pomarine Jaeger *Stercorarius pomarinus*
Cayenne Tern *Sterna eurygnatha*	*Puffinus* Cf. *P. puffinus*
Common Tern *Sterna hirundo*	Red–billed Tropicbird *Phaethon aethereus*
Cory's Shearwater *Calonectris diomedea*	Red–footed Booby *Sula sula*
Dovekie *Alle alle*	Ring–billed Gull *Larus delawarensis*
Forster's Tern *Sterna forsteri*	Roseate Tern *Sterna dougallii*
Franklin's Gull *Larus pipixcan*	Royal Tern *Sterna maxima*
Glaucous Gull *Larus hyperboreus*	Sabine's Gull *Xema sabini*
Black–legged Kittiwake *Rissa tridactyla*	Sandwich Tern *Sterna sandvicensis*
Black Noddy *Anous minutus*	Seabird
Band–rumped Storm–Petrel *Oceanodroma castro*	Shearwater
Bermuda Petrel *Pterodroma cahow*	Slender–billed Gull *Larus genei*
Black–browed Albatross *Diomedea melanophris*	Sooty Shearwater *Puffinus griseus*
Black–capped Petrel *Pterodroma hasitata*	Sooty Tern *Sterna fuscata*
Black–headed Gull *Larus ridibundus*	South Polar Skua *Catharacta maccormicki*
Black Skimmer *Rynchops niger*	*Sterna* sp.
Black Tern *Chlidonias niger*	*Sterna plumbea*
Bonaparte's Gull *Larus philadelphia*	Storm–Petrel *Thalassidroma*(?)
Brown Booby *Sula leucogaster*	*Sula* sp.
Bridled Tern *Sterna anaethetus*	*Thalasseus* sp.
British Storm–Petrel *Hydrobates pelagicus*	Tropicbird *Phaeton* sp.
Glaucous Gull *Larus hyperboreus*	Trudeau's Tern *Sterna trudeaui*
Great Black–backed Gull *Larus marinus*	Whiskered Tern *Chlidonias hybridus*
Great Skua *Catharacta skua*	White–tailed Tropicbird *Phaethon lepturus*
Greater Shearwater *Puffinus gravis*	White–winged Tern *Chlidonias leucopterus*
Gull	Wilson's Storm–Petrel *Oceanites oceanicus*
Gull–billed Tern *Sterna nilotica*	
Herald Petrel *Pterodroma arminjoniana*	
Herring Gull *Larus argentatus*	
Jamaican Petrel *Pterodroma caribbaea*	
Laridae	
Large–billed Tern *Phaetusa simplex*	
Laughing Gull *Larus atricilla*	
Leach's Storm–Petrel *Oceanodroma leucorhoa*	
Least Tern *Sterna antillarum*	
Lesser Black–backed Gull *Larus fuscus*	
Long–tailed Jaeger *Stercorarius longicaudus*	
Magnificent Frigatebird *Fregata magnificens*	
Manx Shearwater *Puffinus puffinus*	
Masked Booby *Sula dactylatra*	
Northern Fulmar *Fulmarus glacialis*	
Northern Gannet *Sula bassanus*	

[1] Bahama Islands, Greater and Lesser Antilles, and several extralimital islands (Isla San Andrés, Isla Providencia, and Swan Islands).

A Bibliography of Seabirds in the West Indies

A., J. A. 1909. Chapman on the life–histories of the booby and man–o'–war bird. Auk 26(2):205.

ABBAD Y LASIERRA, F. I. 1788. Historia geográfica, civil y natural de la isla de San Juan Bautista de Puerto Rico. Madrid, Spain.

ABBOTT, G. A. 1922. In Cuba. Oölogist 39:173.

ACOSTA, M., AND L. MUGICA. 1994. Notas sobre la comunidad de aves del embalse Leonero, provincia Granma. Cienc. Biol. Acad. Cienc. Cuba No. 27:169–171.

ACOSTA, M., L. MUGICA, AND S. VALDES. 1994. Estructura trófica de una comunidad de aves acuáticas. Cienc. Biol. Acad. Cienc. Cuba No. 27:24–44.

ACOSTA CRUZ, M., AND V. BEROVIDES ALVAREZ. 1984. Ornitocenosis de los cayos Coco y Romano, Archipiélago de Sabana–Camagüey, Cuba. Poeyana No. 274:1–10.

ACOSTA CRUZ, M., M. E. IBARRA, AND E. FERNANDEZ. 1988. Aspectos ecológicos de la avifauna de Cayo Matías (Grupo Insular de los Canarreos, Cuba). Poeyana No. 360:1–11.

ACOSTA CRUZ, M., J. A. MORALES, M. GONZALEZ, AND L. MUGICA VALDÉS. 1992. Dinámica de la comunidad de aves de la playa La Tinaja, Ciego de Avila, Cuba. Cienc. Biol. Acad. Cienc. Cuba No. 24:44–58.

ACOSTA CRUZ, M., L. MUGICA VALDÉS, AND G. ALVAREZ. 1991. Ecología trófica de la principales especies de aves que afectan el cultivo del camaron blanco en Tunas de Zaza. Pitirre 4(2):7.

AGARDY, T. 1982. A preliminary report on the status of the Brown Pelican in the U. S. Virgin Islands, 1980–81. Unpublished administrative report, Division of Fish and Wildlife, U. S. Virgin Islands.

AGUAYO CASTRO, C. G. 1937. Sobre algunas aves halladas en Cuba. Mem. Soc. Cubana Hist. Nat. "Felipe Poey" 11:57–60.

AGUERO COBIELLAS, R., AND F. HERNANDEZ DRIGGS. 1988. Lista preliminar de las aves observadas en las playas de Estero y Pesquero Nuevo de la provincia de Hoguín. Garciana 9:4.

AIKEN, K. A. 1986. Observations on bird roosting changes at the Mona reservoir. Nat. Hist. Notes Nat. Hist. Soc. Jamaica, new ser. 2:3–4.

ALDRIDGE, B. M. 1987. Sampling migratory birds and other observations on Providenciales Islands B. W. I. N. Am. Bird Bander 12:13–18.

ALEXANDER, W. B. 1927. Kittiwake gull in the Caribbean Sea. Auk 44(2):241–242.

ALLEN, J. A. 1880. List of the birds of the island of Santa Lucia, West Indies. Bull. Nuttall Ornith. Club 5:163–169.

ALLEN, J. A. 1881. Supplementary list of birds of the island of Santa Lucia, W. I. Bull. Nuttall Ornith. Club 6:128.

ALLEN, G. M. 1905. Summer birds in the Bahamas. Auk 22(2):113–133.

ALLENG, G. 1990. Recovery of nesting sites in the Port Royal mangroves, south coast, Jamaica, following Hurricane "Gilbert." Gosse Bird Club Broads. No. 55:5–9.

ALLENG, G. P., AND C. A. ALLENG. 1993. Survey of Least Tern nesting sites along the south coast of Jamaica. Pitirre 6(1):4.

ALLENG, P., AND C. A. M. WHYTE–ALLENG. 1993. Survey of Least Tern nesting sites on the south coast of Jamaica. Colon. Waterbirds 16:190–193.

ALVAREZ CONDE, J. 1945. La Laguna del Tesora. Dos excursiones cientificas a la Ciénaga de Zapata, costa sur de la provincia de Las Villas. Impresa Monte e Indio, La Habana.

ANONYMOUS. 1891. Feilden on the domicile of the Diablotin. Ibis 3:131.

ANONYMOUS. 1963. More birds listed for Grand Bahama. Fl. Nat. 36:78.

ANONYMOUS. 1972. Breeding of the Least Tern in Jamaica. Gosse Bird Club Broads. No. 18:18.

APPLEBY, R. H., AND C. R. CLARK. 1974. September birdwatching in Jamaica. Gosse Bird Club Broads. No. 22:10–14.

APPLEBY, R. H., AND C. R. CLARK. 1974. Black Tern. Gosse Bird Club Broads. No. 23:23.

APPLEBY, R. H., AND C. R. CLARK. 1974. Ring–billed Gull. Gosse Bird Club Broads. No. 23:23.

ARENDT, W. J. 1995. Assessment of avian relative abundance on Guana Island, British Virgin Islands, with emphasis on the Pearly–eyed Thrasher (*Margarops fuscatus*). Unpublished report, Project No. IITFW–WJA59140264, to The Conservation Agency and the Guana Island Club, International Institute of Tropical Forestry, Río Piedras, Puerto Rico.

ARENDT, W. J., AND A. I. ARENDT. 1985. Wildlife assessment of the southeastern peninsula, St. Kitts, West Indies, unpaginated *in* Environmental assessment report on the proposed southeast peninsula access road, St. Kitts, West Indies (E. Towle et al., Eds.). Report to U.S. Agency for International Development/USDA Forest Service, and Island Research Foundation, .

ASHCROFT, M. T. 1965. A visit to St. Kitts, Nevis and Anguilla. Gosse Bird Club Broads. No. 4:10–12.

ASHMOLE, N. P. 1963. Molt and breeding in populations of the Sooty Tern *Sterna fuscata*. Postilla No. 76:1–18.

ATTRILL, R. 1979. Little San Salvador. Bahamas Natur. 4:2–8.

ATWOOD, T. 1791. The history of the island of Dominica: Containing a description of its situation, extent, climate, mountains, rivers, natural productions & c. & c. together with an account of the civil government, trade, laws, customs, and manners of the different inhabitants of that island, its conquest by the French, and restoration to the British dominions. Privately printed for J. Johnson, No. 72, St. Paul's Church–yard, London.

AUSTIN, O. L. 1951. Group adherence in the Common Tern. Bird–Banding 22:1–15.

AUSTIN, O. L. 1953. The migration of the Common Tern (*Sterna hirundo*) in the western hemisphere. Bird–Banding 24:39–55.

BAHAMAS NATIONAL TRUST. 1986. Bahamas. Pages 433–446 *in* A directory of neotropical wetlands (D. A. Scott and M. Carbonell, Eds.). International Union for Conservation of Nature and Natural Resources, Cambridge, and International Waterfowl Research Bureau, Slimbridge, United Kingdom.

BALAT, F. 1986. Contribución al conocimiento de comunidades de aves de la Ciudad de La Habana. Zpr. Geogr. ust. Csav. 23:11–23.

BANNERMAN, D. A. 1904. Ornithological notes made on a trip to the West Indies. Zoologist 4 8:228–230.

BARBOUR, T. 1923. The birds of Cuba. Memoirs of the Nuttall Ornithological Club No. 6, Cambridge, Massachusets.

BARBOUR, T. 1943. Cuban Ornithology. Mem. Nuttall Ornithol. Club No. 9:144 pp.

BANGS, O. 1900. Notes on a collection of Bahama birds. Auk 17(3):283–293.

BANGS, O., AND F. H. KENNARD. 1920. A list of the birds of Jamaica. Pages 684–701 *in* Handbook of Jamaica (F. Cundall, Ed.). Govt. Printing Office, Kingston.

BANGS, O., AND T. E. PENARD. 1919. Some critical notes on birds. Bull. Mus. Comp. Zool. 63:21–40.

BANGS, O., AND W. R. ZAPPEY. 1905. Birds of the Isle of Pines. Am. Nat. 39:179–215.

BARLOW, J. C. 1978. Records of migrants from Grand Cayman Island. Bull. Br. Ornithol. Club 98:144–146.

BARNÉS, V., Jr. 1946. The birds of Mona Island, Puerto Rico. Auk 63(3):318–327.

BARRIGA–BONILLA, E., J. HERNANDEZ–CAMACHO, I. JARAMILLO T., R. JARAMILLO MEJIA, L. E. MORA OSEJO, P. PINTO ESCOBAR, AND P. M. RUIZ CARRANZA. 1969. La Isla San Andrés. Contribución al conocimiento de su ecología, flora, fauna y pesca. Vol. 2. Instituto de Ciencias Naturales, Universidad Nacional de Colombia, Bogotá.

BARTSCH, P. 1918. Biological explorations in Cuba and Haiti. Smithson. Misc. Coll. 68:40–48.

BAUTISTA M., E. A., T. A. VARGAS MORA, G. M. SANTANA Z., AND G. GROSS. 1986. Informe sobre estudio basico de la fauna y consideraciones ecologicas del "Parque Nacional Los Haitises." Propuesta para la elaboracion plan de manejo. Departamento de Vida Silvestre, Secretaria de Estado de Agricultura, Santo Domingo.

BEATTY, H. A. 1930. Birds of St. Croix. J. Dept. Agric. P. R. 14:135–150.

BEATTY, H. A. 1936. New bird records for St. Croix, V. I. Auk 53(4):456–457.

BEATTY, H. A. 1938. Notes from St. Thomas and cays, Virgin Islands. Auk 55(3):552–553.

BEATTY, H. A. 1941. New bird records and some notes for the Virgin Islands. J. Agric. Univ. P. R. 25:32–36.

BEATTY, H. A. 1944. The insects of St. Croix, V. I. J. Agric. Univ. P. R. 28:114–172.

BECK, R. H. 1921. Bird collecting in the highlands of Santo Domingo. Nat. Hist. 21:37–49.

BEEBE, W. 1927. List of Haitian birds observed. Appendix D. Pages 216–224 *in* Beneath tropic seas. A record of diving among the coral reefs of Haiti. G. P. Putnam's Sons, New York.

BEEBE, W. 1927. Notes on the birds of Haiti. Bull. N. Y. Zool. Soc. 30:136–141.

BELANT, J. L., AND R. A. DOLBEER. 1993. Migration and dispersal of Laughing Gulls in the United States. J. Field Ornithol. 64:557–565.

BELLINGHAM, P. 1991. Leach's Petrel. Gosse Bird Club Broads. No. 57:18.

BENITO–ESPINAL, E. 1982. Shooting in Guadeloupe. Architecture and Environmental Regional Survey. Regional Delegate's Office, Guadeloupe.

BENT, A. C. 1921. Roseate Tern *Sterna dougalli* Montagu. Pages 256–264 *in* Life histories of North American gulls and terns. Order Longipennes. Bulletin 113 (A. C. Bent, Ed.). U. S. National Museum, Washington, D. C.

BENT, A. C. 1922. Black–capped Petrel *Pterodroma hasitata* (Kuhl). Pages 106–121 *in* Life histories of North American petrels and pelicans and their allies. Order Tubinares and Order Steganopodes. Bulletin 121 (A. C. Bent, Ed.). U. S. National Museum, Washington, D. C.

BENT, A. C. 1922. Yellow–billed Tropic–bird *Leptophaethon lepturus catesbyi* (Brandt). Pages 181–187 *in* Life histories of North American petrels and pelicans and their allies. Order Tubinares and Order Steganopodes. Bulletin 121 (A. C. Bent, Ed.). U. S. National Museum, Washington, D. C.

BENT, A. C. 1922. Booby *Sula leucogastris*. Pages 200–208 *in* Life histories of North American petrels and pelicans and their allies. Order Tubinares and Order Steganopodes. Bulletin 121 (A. C. Bent, Ed.). U. S. National Museum, Washington, D. C.

BENT, A. C. 1922. Red–footed Booby *Sula piscator*. Pages 211–216 *in* Life histories of North American petrels and pelicans and their allies. Order Tubinares and Order Steganopodes. Bulletin 121 (A. C. Bent, Ed.). U. S. National Museum, Washington, D. C.

BENT, A. C. 1922. Brown Pelican *Pelecanus occidentalis occidentalis* Linnaeus. Pages 294–301 *in* Life histories of North American petrels and pelicans and their allies. Order Tubinares and Order Steganopodes. Bulletin 121 (A. C. Bent, Ed.). U. S. National Museum, Washington, D. C.

BENT, A. C. 1922. Man–o'–War–Bird *Fregata magnificens* Mathews. Pages 306–315 *in* Life histories of North American petrels and pelicans and their allies. Order Tubinares and Order Steganopodes. Bulletin 121 (A. C. Bent, Ed.). U. S. National Museum, Washington, D. C.

BENT, A. C. 1947. Cabot's Tern *Sterna sandvicensis acuflavida* Cabot. Pages 221–227 *in* Life histories of North American gulls and terns. Order Longipennes (A. C. Bent, Ed.). Dodd, Mead & Company, New York.

BENT, A. C. 1947. Sooty Tern *Sterna fuscata* Linnaeus. Pages 279–287 *in* Life histories of North American gulls and terns. Order Longipennes (A. C. Bent, Ed.). Dodd, Mead & Company, New York.

BENT, A. C. 1947. Bridled Tern *Sterna anaetheta* Scopoli. Pages 287–287 *in* Life histories of North American gulls and terns. Order Longipennes (A. C. Bent, Ed.). Dodd, Mead & Company, New York.

BENT, A. C. 1947. Noddy *Anous stolidus* (Linnaeus). Pages 301–310 *in* Life histories of North American gulls and terns. Order Longipennes (A. C. Bent, Ed.). Dodd, Mead & Company, New York.

BEN–TUVIA, A., AND C. E. RIOS. 1970. Report on a R/V Chocó cruise to Providence Island and adjacent banks of Quitasueño and Serrana near the Caribbean Islands of Colombia. Proyecto para el desarrollo de la pesca marítima en Colombia (PNUD). Fondo Esp. – FA) – INDERENA, Com. 1:9–45.

BEROVIDES ALVAREZ, V., AND R. SMITH CANET. 1983. Aspectos ecológicos de la nidificación de *Sterna hirundo* y *S. albifrons*. Cienc. Biol. Acad. Cienc. Cuba No. 9:128–131.

BLACK, A. 1969. Magnificent Frigatebird. Gosse Bird Club Broads. No. 13:18.

BLACK, A. 1972. Black Tern. Gosse Bird Club Broads. No. 18:20.

BLACK, A. 1972. Magnificent Frigatebird. Gosse Bird Club Broads. No. 19:22.

BLACK, A. 1973. Brown Pelican. Gosse Bird Club Broads. No. 20:20.

BLACK, A. 1982. Brown Pelican. Gosse Bird Club Broads. No. 39:14.

BLACK, A. 1983. Brown Pelican. Gosse Bird Club Broads. No. 40:16.

BLACK, A. 1989. Pelican. Gosse Bird Club Broads. No. 52:12.

BLACK, A., AND C. BLACK. 1981. Black Tern. Gosse Bird Club Broads. No. 37:12.

BLACK, A., C. BLACK, A. DOWNER, I. KERR–JARRETT, K. MCMURRAY, S. SPENCE, AND B. PEARSON. 1973. Migrant dates. Gosse Bird Club Broads. No. 21:11–12.

BLACK, C. 1966. Brown Pelican. Gosse Bird Club Broads. No. 6:14.

BLACK, C. 1966. Magnificent Frigate Bird. Gosse Bird Club Broads. No. 6:15.

BLACK, C. 1980. Magnificent Frigatebird. Gosse Bird Club Broads. No. 34:15–16.

BLANCO, P., AND H. GONZALEZ. 1995. Nuevos registros de *Rynchops niger* Linneo, 1758 (Aves: Laridae) para Cuba. Poeyana No. 448:1–8.

BLANCO, E. T. 1969. Apuntes para la historia de la fauna ornitológica de Puerto Rico. Editorial Coqui, San Juan.

BLAKE, C. H. 1956. Some bird weights from Jamaica. Bird–Banding 27:174–178.

BOND, J. 1928. The distribution and habits of the birds of the Republic of Haiti. Proc. Acad. Nat. Sci. Philadelphia 80:483–521.

BOND, J. 1928. On the birds of Dominica, St. Lucia, St. Vincent, and Barbados, B. W. I. Proc. Acad. Nat. Sci. Philadelphia 80:523–545.

BOND, J. 1939. Notes on birds from the West Indies and other Caribbean islands. Notulae Naturae, Acad. Nat. Sci. Philadelphia 13:1–6.

BOND, J. 1941. Nidification of the birds of Dominica, B. W. I. Auk 58(3):364–375.

BOND, J. 1942. Additional notes on West Indian birds. Proc. Acad. Nat. Sci. Philadelphia 94:89–106.

BOND, J. 1945. Identity of Catesby's Tropic–bird. Auk 62(4):660.

BOND, J. 1946. The birds of Mona. Notulae Naturae, Acad. Nat. Sci. Philadelphia 176:1–10.

BOND, J. 1950. Results of the Catherwood–Chaplin West Indies Expedition, 1948. Part II. Birds of Cayo Largo (Cuba), San Andrés and Providencia. Proc. Acad. Nat. Sci. Philadelphia 102:43–68.

BOND, J. 1963. Derivation of the Antillean avifauna. Proc. Acad. Nat. Sci. Philadelphia 115:79–98.

BOND, J. 1965. A few problems concerning the bird life of Jamaica, which the amateur ornithologist may be able to clarify. Gosse Bird Club Broads. No. 4:1–3.

BOND, J. 1967. Jamaican Black Capped Petrel. Gosse Bird Club Broads. No. 8:15.

BOND, J., AND R. M. DE SCHAUENSEE. 1944. The birds. Pages 7–56 in Results of the Fifth George Vanderbilt
    Expedition (1941) (Bahamas, Caribbean Sea, Panama, Galápagos Archipelago and Mexican Pacific waters).
    Academy of Natural Sciences of Philadelphia, Monographs No. 6, Philadelphia.
BOND, J., AND A. MORENO BONILLA. 1947. Notas ornitologicas (No. 5). Mem. Soc. Cubana Hist. Nat. "Felipe
    Poey" 19:109–110.
BONHOTE, J. L. 1899. A list of birds collected on the island of New Providence, Bahamas. Ibis 5:506–520.
BONHOTE, J. L. 1901. On a collection of birds made by Mr. T. R. Thompson at the Cay Lobos Lighthouse, Bahamas.
    Auk 18(2):145–149.
BONHOTE, J. L. 1903. Bird migration at some of the Bahama lighthouses. Auk 20(2):169–179.
BONHOTE, J. L. 1903. Field notes on some Bahama birds. Part IV. Avicult. Mag., new ser. 1:87–95.
BON SAINT COME, M. 1989. Rapport de Mission du Comité Scientifique du Parc Régional Naturel de la Caravelle
    effectuée en Guadeloupe du 20 au 23 Octobre 1989 après le passage de l'Ouragan Hugo. Pages 30–48 in
    Mission d'Étude en Guadeloupe après l'Ouragan "Hugo" effectuée par le Comité Scientifique du PNRM. Parc
    Naturel Régional de la Martinique, Fort–de–France.
BOULON, R. H., R. L. NORTON, AND T. A. AGARDY. 1982. Status of the Brown Pelican (Pelecanus o.
    occidentalis) in the Virgin Islands. Department of Conservation & Cultural Affairs, Government of the Virgin
    Islands, St. Thomas.
BOURLIERE, F. 1949. The Ornithographia Americana of Father Plumier, 1689–1696. Wilson Bull. 61:103–105.
BOWDISH, B. S. 1900. Some winter birds on the island of Vieques. Oölogist 17:71–74.
BOWDISH, B. S. 1900. A day on De Cicheo Island. Oölogist 17:117–120.
BOWDISH, B. S. 1902. Birds of Porto Rico. Auk 19(4):356–366.
BOWDISH, B. S. 1918. [Letter]. Oölogist 35:119.
BRADLEY, P. E. 1984. A bird's eye view. Gosse Bird Club Broads. No. 44:2–4.
BRADLEY, P. E. 1984. Masked Booby (Blue–faced Booby) – Sula dactylatra. Gosse Bird Club Broads. No. 42:11.
BRADLEY, P. E. 1986. Unusual sighting from Cayman. Gosse Bird Club Broads. No. 46:5.
BRADLEY, P. 1990. Notes on conservation in the Turks and Caicos Islands and in the Cayman Islands. Pitirre 3(3):2.
BRADLEY, P. E. 1994. The avifauna of the Cayman Islands: an overview. Pages 377–406 in The Cayman Islands:
    natural history and biogeography. Monographiae biologicae, v. 71 (M. A. Brunt and J. E. Davies, Eds.).
    Kluwer Academic Publishers, Dordrecht, The Netherlands.
BRADLEY, P. [1995]. The birds of the Turks & Caicos Islands. The official checklist. National Trust of the Turks &
    Caicos Islands, Grand Turk.
BRADLEY, P. E. 1996. Cayman Islands report. Pitirre 9(3):17–18.
BRAY, D. 1972. Mona Reservoir 1972. Gosse Bird Club Broads. No. 18:9–10.
BRAY, D. 1972. Least Tern. Gosse Bird Club Broads. No. 18:20.
BRINSLEY, G. G. 1971. White–tailed Tropicbird. Gosse Bird Club Broads. No. 16:22.
BRISSON, M. J. 1760. Ornithologie ou méthode contenant la division des oiseaux en ordres, sections, genres, espèces
    & leurs variétés. A laquelle on a joint une description exacte de chaque espèce, avec les citations des auteurs
    qui en ont traité, les noms qu'ils leur ont donnés, ceux que leur ont donnés les différentes nations, & les noms
    vulgaires. Par M. Brisson ... Ouvrage enrichi de figures en taille–douce. Cl. Jean–Baptiste Bauche, Paris.
BRISSON, M. J. 1763. Ornithologica sive synopsis methodica sistens avium divisionem in ordines, sectiones, genera,
    species, ipsarumque varietates. Cum accurata cujusque speciei descriptione, citationibus auctorum de iis
    tractantium, nominibus eis ab ipsis & nationibusimpositis, nomi–nimbusque vulgaribus. Theodorum Haak,
    Paris.
BRODKORB, P. 1963. Catalogue of fossil birds: Part 1 (Archaeopterygiformes through Ardeiformes). Bull. Fl. State
    Mus., Biol. Sci. 7:179–293.
BRODKORB, P. 1967. Catalogue of fossil birds: Part 3 (Ralliformes, Ichthyornithiformes, Charadriiformes). Bull. Fl.
    State Mus., Biol. Sci. 11:99–220.
BRODKORB, P. 1974. Bird remains from Pre–Columbian middens in the Virgin Islands. Q. J. Florida Acad. Sci. [for
    1972] 35:239–240.
BROWN, G. J., C. DEGIA, R. WILLIAMS, AND D. WILLIAMS. 1992. The cays – Bushy & Maiden. Gosse Bird
    Club Broads. No. 59:14.
BROWNE, P. 1756. The civil and natural history of Jamaica. Containing I. An accurate description of that island, its
    situation, and soil; with a brief account of its former and present state, government, revenues, produce, and
    trade. II. An history of the natural productions, including the various sorts of native fossils; perfect and
    imprefect vegetables; quadrupeds, birds, fishes, reptiles, and insects; with their properties and uses in
    mechanics, diet, and physic. Illustrated with forty–nine copper plates; in which the most curious productions
    are represented of their natural sizes, and delineated immediately from the objects, by George Dionysius Ehret.

There are now added complete Linnæn indexes, and a large and accurate map of the island. B. White and Son, Jamaica and London.

BRUNER, S. C. 1925. The Man–o'–War Birds. Nature Mag. 6:283–286.

BRUNER, S. C. 1934. El "Dovekie" en Cuba, un nuevo record para nuestra avifauna. Mem. Soc. Cubana Hist. Nat. "Felipe Poey" 8:51–52.

BRUNER, S. C. 1938. Datos sobre la migracion de aves en Cuba. Parte I. Mem. Soc. Cubana Hist. Nat. "Felipe Poey" 12:167–179.

BRUNER, S. C. 1939. Aves del bosque de la Havana. Mem. Soc. Cubana Hist. Nat. "Felipe Poey" 13:331–344.

BRUNER, S. C. 1943. Notas ornitologicas: miscelanea. Mem. Soc. Cubana Hist. Nat. "Felipe Poey" 17:19–21.

BRUNER, S. C. 1943. Adiciones a las aves del bosque de la Habana. Mem. Soc. Cubana Hist. Nat. "Felipe Poey" 17:135–138.

BRYANT, H. 1859. A list of birds seen at the Bahamas, from Jan. 20th to May 14th, 1859, with descriptions of new or little known species. Proc. Boston Soc. Nat. Hist. 7:102–134.

BRYANT, H. 1868. A list of the birds of St. Domingo, with descriptions of some new species or varieties. Proc. Boston Soc. Nat. Hist. 11:89–99.

BUCKLEY, P. A., AND F. G. BUCKLEY. 1970. Notes of the distribution of some Puerto Rican birds and on the courtship behavior of White–tailed Tropicbirds. Condor 72:483–486.

BUCKLEY, P. A., AND F. G. BUCKLEY. 1974. Ecology.

BUCKLEY, P. A., AND F. G. BUCKLEY. 1984. Cayenne Tern new to North America, with comments on its relationship to Sandwich Tern. Auk 101(2):396–398.

BUDEN, D. W. 1987. Birds of the Cay Sal Bank and Ragged Islands, Bahamas. Fl. Sci. 50:21–33.

BUDEN, D. W. 1987. The birds of Cat Island, Bahamas. Wilson Bull. 99:579–600.

BUDEN, D. W. 1990. Report on the birds collected during the Armour–*Utowana* West Indian Expeditions. Bull. Br. Ornithol. Club 110:14–20.

BUDEN, D. W. 1990. The birds of Rum Cay, Bahama Islands. Wilson Bull. 102:451–468.

BUDEN, D. W. 1991. Bird band recoveries in the Bahama Islands. Caribb. J. Sci. 27:63–70.

BUDEN, D. W. 1992. The birds of the Exumas, Bahama Islands. Wilson Bull. 104:674–698.

BUDEN, D. W. 1992. The birds of Long Island, Bahamas. Wilson Bull. 104:220–243.

BUDEN, D. W. 1993. Bird band recoveries from Haiti and the Dominican Republic. Caribb. J. Sci. 29:179–185.

BUDEN, D. W. 1993. Summer recoveries of banded neotropical migrants in the West Indies. Fl. Field Nat. 21:11–15.

BUDEN, D. W., AND S. L. OLSON. 1989. The avifauna of the cayerias of southern Cuba, with the ornithological results of the Paul Bartsch Expedition of 1930. Smithsonian Contributions to Zoology Number 477, Smithsonian Institution Press, Washington, D. C.

BUDEN, D. W., AND A. SCHWARTZ. 1968. Reptiles and birds of the Cay Sal Bank, Bahama Islands. Q. J. Florida Acad. Sci. 31:290–320.

BUDEN, D. W., AND A. SPRUNT IV. 1993. Additional observations on the birds of the Exumas, Bahama Islands. Wilson Bull. 105:514–518.

BUDEN, D. W., AND R. L. WETENKAMP. 1993. North American bird band recoveries from the Lesser Antilles. Ornitol. Neotrop. 4:83–90.

BUFFON, G. L. L., comte de. 1770–1786. Histoire naturelle des oiseaux, avec la description du Cabinet du Roi. Imprimerie Royale, Paris.

BUIDE GONZALEZ, M. S., J. FERNANDEZ MILERA, O. GARCIA MONTAÑA, O. H. GARRIDO, H. DE LOS SANTOS IZQUIERDO, G. SILVA TABOADA, AND L. S. VARONA CALVO. 1974. Las especies amenazadas de vertebrados cubanos. Academia de Ciencias de Cuba, Instituto de Zoología, La Habana.

BUREAU, L. 1907. Monographie de la Sterne de Dougall (*Sterna dougalli*). Pages 289–346 in Proceedings of the Fourth International Ornithological Congress (1905) (E. J. O. Hartert and J. L. Bonhote, Eds.). Dulan & Co., London.

BURGER, J., AND M. GOCHFELD. 1984. Comparative nest site selection in Caribbean and Hawaiian Sooty Terns. Colon. Waterbirds Group Newsl. 8:37.

BURGER, J., AND M. GOCHFELD. 1985. Nest site selection by Laughing Gulls: comparison of tropical colonies (Culebra, Puerto Rico) with temperate colonies (New Jersey). Condor 87:364–373.

BURGER, J., AND M. GOCHFELD. 1986. Nest site selection in Sooty Terns (*Sterna fuscata*) in Puerto Rico and Hawaii. Colon. Waterbirds 9:31–45.

BURGER, J., AND M. GOCHFELD. 1988. Defensive aggression in terns: effect of species, density, and isolation. Aggressive Behav. 14:169–178.

BURGER, J., AND M. GOCHFELD. 1988. Nest–site selection by Roseate Terns in two tropical colonies on Culebra, Puerto Rico. Condor 90:843–851.

BURGER, J., AND M. GOCHFELD. 1989. Response of young terns to human handling. Pitirre 2(2):6–7.

BURGER, J., AND M. GOCHFELD. 1990. Heavy metal levels in Culebra terns. Pitirre 3(3):6.

BURGER, J., AND M. GOCHFELD. 1991. Lead, mercury, and cadmium in feathers of tropical terns in Puerto Rico and Australia. Arch. Environ. Contam. Toxicol. 21:311–315.

BURGER, J., M. GOCHFELD, D. J. GOCHFELD, AND J. E. SALIVA. 1989. Nest site selection in Zenaida Doves (*Zenaida aurita*) in Puerto Rico. Biotropica 21:244–249.

BURGER, J., M. GOCHFELD, J. E. SALIVA, D. GOCHFELD, D. GOCHFELD, AND H. MORALES. 1989. Antipredator behaviour in nesting Zenaida Doves (*Zenaida aurita*): parental investment or offspring vulnerability. Behav. 111:129–143.

BURGER, J., M. GOCHFELD, J. E. SALIVA, D. J. GOCHFELD, D. A. GOCHFELD, AND H. MORALES. 1991. Habitat use by nesting Zenaida Doves *Zenaida aurita* in Puerto Rico: avoidance of islands without nesting seabirds. Ornis Scand. 22:367–374.

BURKE, W. 1992. Second winter sighting of the Common Black–headed Gull (*Larus ridibundus*) in St. Lucia, Lesser Antilles. Pitirre 5(2):4.

BUTCHER, R. D. 1956. A visit to the Virgin Islands National Park. Nat. Parks Mag. 30:164–168.

BUTLER, P. J., R. E. LEWIS, R. E. TURLEY, AND I. CAFFOOR. 1978. North East London Polytechnic Saint Lucia research report. Unpublished report, North East London Polytechnic, London.

CABRALES, M. 1977. "El pajaro de la bruja": principio y fin de una leyenda. Bohemia (Habana) 69:88–89.

CAMPBELL, E. W. 1991. The effect of introduced roof rats on bird diversity of Antillean cays. J. Field Ornithol. 62:343–348.

CAPSTICK, E. 1971. Red–footed Boobies? Gosse Bird Club Broads. No. 16:22.

CAPSTICK, E. 1972. Water birds. Gosse Bird Club Broads. No. 18:20.

CARTE, A. 1866. On an undescribed species of petrel from the Blue Mountains of Jamaica. Proc. Zool. Soc. London 1866:93–95.

CASEMENT, M. B. 1979. Sea report sheets. Sea Swallow 28:23–42.

CASSIN, J. 1860. Catalogue of birds from the island of St. Thomas, West Indies, collected and presented to the Academy of Natural Sciences by Mr. Robert Swift. With notes. Proc. Acad. Nat. Sci. Philadelphia 13:374–379.

CATESBY, M. 1731–1743. The natural history of Carolina, Florida, and the Bahama Islands: containing the figures of birds, beasts, fishes, serpents, insects, and plants; particularly the forest–trees, shrubs, and other plants, not hitherto described, or very incorrectly figured by authors. Together with their descriptions in English and French. To which, are added observations on the air, soil, and waters; with remarks upon agriculture, grain, pulse, roots, etc. To the whole is prefixed a new and correct map of the countries treated of. Histoire naturelle de la Caroline, la Floride, & les Isles Bahama; contenant les desseins des oiseaux, animaux, poissons, serpents, insectes, & plantes. Et en particulier des arbres des forets, arbrisseaux, & autres plantes, qui n'ont point ete decrits, jusques a present par les uuteurs, ou peu exactement dessines. W. Innys and R. Manby, London.

CHAPMAN, F. M. 1907. A season's field work. Bird–Lore 9:256–263.

CHAPMAN, F. M. 1908. Camps and Cruises of an Ornithologist. D. Appleton and Co., New York.

CHAPMAN, F. M. 1908. A contribution to the life–histories of the Booby (*Sula leucogastra*) and Man–of–War Bird (*Fregata aquila*). Papers from the Tortugas Laboratory of the Carnegie Institution of Washington. Vol. II. Carnegie Inst. Washington Publ. No. 103:139–151.

CHAPMAN, F. M. 1918. Notes from a traveler in the tropics. I. Down the coastline to Cuba. Bird–Lore 20:393–397.

CHAPMAN, S. E. 1981. Notes on seabird reports received 1979–1980. Sea Swallow 30:45–67.

CHAPMAN, S. E. 1982. Notes on seabird reports received 1980–81. Sea Swallow 31:5–24.

CHARDINE, J. W. 1987. Brown Noddy vocal behavior. Auk 104(4):790.

CHARDINE, J. W., AND R. D. MORRIS. 1987. Trapping and color banding Brown Noddy and Bridled Tern adults at the breeding colony. Colon. Waterbirds 10:100–102.

CHARDINE, J. W., AND R. D. MORRIS. 1989. Morphometric analysis of external body measurements of Brown Noddies. Population biology and conservation of marine birds. Canadian Wildlife Service/Memorial University joint workshop, St. John's, NF.

CHARDINE, J. W., AND R. D. MORRIS. 1989. Sexual size dimorphism and assortative mating in the Brown Noddy. Condor 91:868–874.

CHARDINE, J. W., AND R. D. MORRIS. 1997. Hurricanes and Brown Noddies. Colon. Waterbird Soc. Bull. 20:65.

CHARDINE, J. W., R. D. MORRIS, AND F. C. SCHAFFNER 1985. Sexual dimorphism, reproductive success and chick growth of Brown Noddies nesting on Culebra, Puerto Rico. Colon. Waterbirds Group Newsl. 9:22.

CHARLEVOIX, P. F. X. de. 1730. Histoire de l'isle Espagnole ou de S. Domingue. Ecrite particulièrement sur des mémoires manuscrits du P. Jean–Baptiste Le Pers, Jesuite, missionaire à Saint Domingue, & sur les pièces originales, qui se conservent au depôt de la marine. F. Barois, Paris.

CHERRIE, G. K. 1896. Contribution to the ornithology of San Domingo. Field Columbian Mus., Publ. 10, Ornith. Ser., 1:1–26.

CHESHIRE, N. G. 1993. Notes on seabird reports received in 1992. Sea Swallow 42:5–15.

CHILMAN, P. W. G. 1979. A voyage in the Caribbean and Gulf of Mexico, April, 1977. Sea Swallow 28:11–14.

CHILMAN, P. W. G. 1984. Migrants in the Western Atlantic—Spring 1982. Sea Swallow 33:61–64.

CHIRIVI GALLEGO, H. 1988. Fauna tetrapoda y algunos aspectos ecologicos de los cayos del archipielago de San Andrés y Providencia, Colombia. (Acta Cient. Tecn. INDERENA) 2:277–337.

CHRISTY, C. 1897. Field–notes on the birds of the island of San Domingo. Ibis 3:317–343.

CLAPP, R. B. 1986. A resurvey of the Red–footed Booby colony on Little Cayman Island. Unpubl. Rep. U. S. Fish Wildlife Serv., Natl. Mus. Nat. Hist., Washington, D. C.

CLAPP, R. B. 1987. Status of the Red–footed Booby colony on Little Cayman Island. Atoll Res. Bull. No. 304:1–15.

CLAPP, R. B., M. K. KLIMKIEWICZ, AND J. H. KENNARD. 1982. Longevity records of North American birds: Gaviidae through Alcidae. J. Field Ornithol. 53:81–124.

CLARK, A. H. 1905. The migration of certain shore birds. Auk 22(2):134–140.

CLARK, A. H. 1905. Birds of the southern Lesser Antilles. Proc. Boston Soc. Nat. Hist. 32:203–312.

[CLARK, A. H.] 1905. The birds of St. Vincent. West Ind. Bull. 5:75–95.

CLARK, A. H. 1911. A list of the birds of the island of St. Lucia. West Ind. Bull. 11:182–193.

CLOUGH, G. C., AND G. FULK. 1971. The vertebrate fauna and the vegetation of East Plana Cay, Bahama Islands. Atoll Res. Bull. No. 138:1–15.

COBLENTZ, B. E. 1986. A possible reason for age–differential foraging success in Brown Pelicans. J. Field Ornithol. 57:63–64.

COLLAR, N. J., AND P. ANDREW. 1988. Birds to watch. The ICBP world checklist of threatened birds. ICBP Tech. Publ. No. 8. Smithsonian Institution Press, Washington, D. C.

COLLAZO, J. 1986. Status and ecology of the Brown Pelican in the Greater Puerto Rican Bank region. Ph.D. thesis, Iowa State University.

COLLAZO, J., AND T. AGARDY. 1982. Preliminary data on some aspects of the ecology of Brown Pelicans in Puerto Rico and the U. S. Virgin Islands. Pages 101–114 in Memorias del Tercer Simposio sobre la Fauna de Puerto Rico (L. O. Nievas Rivera and R. A. Pérez–Rivera, Eds.). Universidad de Puerto Rico, Departamento de Biologia, Humacao, Puerto Rico.

COLLAZO, J. , AND E. E. KLAAS. 1985. Status and ecology of the Brown Pelican in the Greater Puerto Rican Bank region. Final report to the Department of Natural Resources, San Juan, Puerto Rico. Iowa Cooperative Fish and Wildlife Research Unit, Ames, Iowa.

COLÓN, J. A. 1982. Notas sobre una colonia de Gaviota Chica, Sterna albifrons, en El Tuque, Ponce, Puerto Rico. Pages 115–122 in Memorias del Tercer Simposio sobre la Fauna de Puerto Rico (L. O. Nievas Rivera and R. A. Pérez–Rivera, Eds.). Universidad de Puerto Rico, Departamento de Biologia, Humacao.

CONNOR, H. A., AND R. W. LOFTIN. 1985. The birds of Eleuthera Island, Bahamas. Fl. Field Nat. 14:77–93.

COOKE, M. T. 1938. Some interesting recoveries of banded birds. Bird–Banding 9:184–190.

COOKE, M. T. 1942. Returns from banded birds: some longevity records of wild birds. Bird–Banding 13:70–74.

COOKE, M. T. 1943. Returns from banded birds: some miscellaneous recoveries of interest. Bird–Banding 14:67–74.

COOKE, M. T. 1945. Returns from banded birds: some interesting recoveries. Bird–Banding 16:15–21.

COOKE, M. T. 1945. Transoceanic recoveries of banded birds. Bird–Banding 16:123–129.

COOKE, M. T. 1946. Returns of banded birds: some recent records of interest. Bird–Banding 17:63–71.

CORY, C. B. 1880. Birds of the Bahama Islands; containing many birds new to the islands, and a number of undescribed winter plumages of North American species. Privately published by the author, Boston.

CORY, C. B. 1881. List of the birds of Haiti, taken in different parts of the island between January 1 and March 12, 1881. Bull. Nuttall Ornith. Club 6:151–155.

CORY, C. B. 1885. A list of birds of the West Indies, including the Bahama Islands and the Greater and Lesser Antilles, excepting the islands of Tobago and Trinidad. Estes & Lauriat, Boston

CORY, C. B. 1886. A list of the birds of the West Indies, including the Bahama Islands and the Greater and Lesser Antilles, excepting the islands of Tobago and Trinidad, Revised ed. Estes & Lauriat, Boston.

CORY, C. B. 1887. A list of the birds collected by Mr. W. B. Richardson, in the island of Martinique, West Indies. Auk 4(2):95–96.

CORY, C. B. 1887. A list of the birds taken by Mr. Robert Henderson, in the islands of Old Providence and St. Andrews, Caribbean Sea, during the winter of 1886–87. Auk 4(3):180–181.

CORY, C. B. 1888. The birds of the West Indies, including the Bahama Islands, the Greater and the Lesser Antilles, excepting the islands of Tobago and Trinidad. Auk 4(1):48–92.

CORY, C. B. 1889. The birds of the West Indies, including all species known to occur in the Bahama Islands, the Greater Antilles, the Caymans, and the Lesser Antilles, excepting the islands of Tobago and Trinidad. Estes & Lauriat, Boston.

CORY, C. B. 1889. A list of the birds collected by Mr. C. J. Maynard in the islands of Little Cayman and Cayman Brack, West Indies. Auk 6(1):30–32.

CORY, C. B. 1890. On a collection of birds made during the winter of 1889–90, by Cyrus S. Winch, in the islands of St. Thomas, Tortola, Anegada, and Virgin Gorda, West Indies. Auk 7(4):373–375.

CORY, C. B. 1890. Birds of the Bahama Islands containing many birds new to the islands, and a number of undescribed winter plumages to North American birds, Revised (2nd) ed. Estes & Lauriat, Boston.

CORY, C. B. 1891. A collection of birds taken by Cyrus S. Winch in the islands of Anguilla, Antigua, and St. Eustatius, West Indies, during April, May, June, and a part of July, 1890. Auk 8(1):46–47.

CORY, C. B. 1891. A list of the birds collected in the islands of St. Croix and St. Kitts, West Indies, during March and April, and in Guadeloupe during August, September, and October, 1890. Auk 8(1):47–49.

CORY, C. B. 1891. A list of birds taken and observed in Cuba and the Bahama Islands, during March and April, 1891. Auk 8(3):292–294.

CORY, C. B. 1891. List of birds collected on the island of Inagua, Bahama Islands, from May 1 to July 10, 1891. Auk 8(4):351.

CORY, C. B. 1891. On a collection of birds made on the islands of Anguilla and Cay Sal or Salt Cay, Bahama Islands, by Mr. Cyrus S. Winch, during May, 1891. Auk 8(4):352.

CORY, C. B. 1892. A list of birds taken on Maraguana, Watling's Island, and Inagua, Bahamas, during July, August, September, and October, 1891. Auk 9(1):48–49.

CORY, C. B. 1892. Remarks on a collection of birds made by Wilmot W. Brown, Jr., on Mona and Porto Rico during February and a part of March, 1892. Auk 9(3):228–229.

CORY, C. B. 1892. Catalogue of West Indian birds, containing a list of all species known to occur in the Bahama Islands, the Greater Antilles, the Caymans, and the Lesser Antilles, excepting the islands of Tobago and Trinidad. Privately publ. by the author, Alfred Mudge & Son, Printer, Boston, Massachusetts.

CROMBIE, R. I., D. W. STEADMAN, AND J. C. BARBER. 1984. A preliminary survey of the vertebrates of Cabarita Island, St. Mary Parish, Jamaica. Atoll Res. Bull. No. 280:1–15.

CRUZ, A. 1977. The use of mangroves by birds in Jamaica. Gosse Bird Club Broads. No. 29:4–5.

CRUZ, A., AND P. FAIRBAIRN. 1980. Conservation of natural resources in the Caribbean: the avifauna of Jamaica. Pages 438–444 in Transactions of the Forty–fifth North American Wildlife and Natural Resources Conference (K. Sabol, Ed.). Miami, Florida.

CRUZ LORENZO, J. de la, AND R. ALAYO SOTO. 1984. Primeros datos sobre la nidificación del Vencejo de Collar, Streptoprocne zonaris pallidifrons y del Contramaestre, Phaethon lepturus catesbyi (Aves: Apodidae y Phaethontidae) de Cuba. Page 456 in IV Conferencia Cientifica sobre Educacion Superior, 1984. Universidad de La Habana, Cuba.

CRUZ LORENZO, J. de la, AND O. H. GARRIDO. 1973. Lista de los anfibios, reptiles, aves y mamiferos colectados en el Plan Jibacoa–Cayojabos. Pages 16–25 in Informe del trabajo faunístico realizado en el plan Jibacoa–Cayojabos (I. Garcia, R. Alyayo, N. Novoa, A. Nicholas, R. Gonzalez, L. de Armas, D. Dominguez, C. Somoza, A. de la Osa, J. de la Cruz, O. H. Garrido, J. Ramon Cuevas, and J. Fontaines, Eds.). Academia de Ciencias de Cuba, Serie Biologica No. 43, La Habana.

CUBILLAS HERNANDEZ, S. O., A. KIRKCONNELL, R. M. POSADA RODRIGUEZ, AND A. LLANES SOSA. 1988. Aves observadas en los cayos Rosario y Cantiles, Archipiélago de los Canarreos, Cuba. Misc. Zool., Inst. Zool. Acad. Cienc. Cuba 38:1–2.

CUELLO, J. P. 1988. Lista de las aves fósiles de la región neotropical y de las islas antillanas. Paula–Coutiana, Porto Alegre 2:3–79.

CUBILLAS HERNANDEZ, S. O., A. KIRKCONNELL, R. M. POSADA RODRIGUEZ, AND A. LLANES SOSA. 1988. Aves observadas en los cayos Rosario y Cantiles, Archipiélago de los Canarreos, Cuba. Misc. Zool., Inst. Zool. Acad. Cienc. Cuba 38:1–2.

CURRIE, H., AND R. B. H. SMITH. 1992. Least Tern. Gosse Bird Club Broads. No. 59:18.

CUSTER, T. W., I. C. T. NISBET, AND A. J. KRYNITSKY. 1983. Organochlorine residues and shell characteristics of Roseate Tern eggs, 1981. J. Field Ornithol. 54:394–400.

DAMMANN, A. E., AND D. W. NELLIS. 1992. A natural history atlas to the cays of the U. S. Virgin Islands. Pineapple Press, Inc., Sarasota, Florida.

DANFORTH, S. T. 1922. Some impressions of Porto Rican bird life. Oölogist 39:10–11.

DANFORTH, S. T. 1925. New birds for Porto Rico. Auk 42(4):558–563.

DANFORTH, S. T. 1925. Birds seen between Porto Rico and New York. Wilson Bull. 37:76–77.

DANFORTH, S. T. 1926. The Least Tern (*Sternula antillarum antillarum*), in Grenada, Lesser Antilles. Auk 43(3):363.

DANFORTH, S. T. 1926. An ecological study of Cartagena Lagoon, Porto Rico, with special reference to the birds. J. Agric. Univ. P. R. 10:1–136.

DANFORTH, S. T. 1928. Birds observed in Jamaica during the summer of 1926. Auk 45(3):480–491.

DANFORTH, S. T. 1928. Birds observed in the vicinity of Santiago de Cuba. Wilson Bull. 40:178–182.

DANFORTH, S. T. 1929. Notes on the birds of Hispaniola. Auk 46(3):358–375.

DANFORTH, S. T. 1930. Bird records from the Virgin Islands. J. Dept. Agric. P. R. 14:107–134.

DANFORTH, S. T. 1930. Notes on the birds of St. Martin and St. Eustatius. Auk 47(1):44–47.

DANFORTH, S. T. 1930. Bird records from the Virgin Islands. J. Dept. Agric. P. R. 14:107–134.

DANFORTH, S. T. 1931. Puerto Rican ornithological records. J. Dept. Agric. P. R. 15:33–106.

DANFORTH, S. T. 1933. A list of the birds known from Antigua, B. W. I. Suppl. Leeward Islands Gazette, 16th Nov.:1–4.

DANFORTH, S. T. 1934. Some West Indian records of Charadriiformes. Auk 51(1):103.

DANFORTH, S. T. 1934. The birds of Antigua. Auk 51(3):350–364.

DANFORTH, S. T. 1935. Leach's Petrel in the West Indies. Auk 52(1):74.

DANFORTH, S. T. 1935. Investigations concerning Cuban birds, with special reference to their economic status, and consideration of those which might be desirable for introduction into Puerto Rico. J. Agric. Univ. P. R. 19:421–437.

DANFORTH, S. T. 1935. Supplementary account of the birds of the Virgin Islands, including Culebra and adjacent islets pertaining to Puerto Rico, with notes on their food habits. J. Agric. Univ. P. R. 19:439–472.

DANFORTH, S. T. 1935. The birds of Barbuda, with notes on their economic importance, and relationship to the Puerto Rican avifauna. J. Agric. Univ. P. R. 19:473–482.

DANFORTH, S. T. 1935. The birds of Saint Lucia. Monogr. Univ. P. R., Phys. Biolog. Sci. B, No. 3:129.

DANFORTH, S. T. 1936. A bird new to the West Indian avifauna. Auk 53(1):82.

DANFORTH, S. T. 1936. New records for Mona Island, West Indies. Auk 53(1):100.

DANFORTH, S. T. 1936. The birds of St. Kitts and Nevis. Trop. Agric. [Trinidad] 13:213–217.

DANFORTH, S. T. 1937. Ornithological investigations in Vieques Island, Puerto Rico, during December 1935. J. Agric. Univ. P. R. 21:539–550.

DANFORTH, S. T. 1938. The birds of Saba. J. Agric. Univ. P. R. 22:503–512.

DANFORTH, S. T. 1939. The birds of Montserrat. J. Agric. Univ. P. R. 23:47–66.

DANFORTH, S. T. 1939. The birds of Guadeloupe and adjacent islands. J. Agric. Univ. P. R. 23:9–46.

DANFORTH, S. T. 1939. The birds of Montserrat. J. Agric. Univ. P. R. 23:47–66.

DAUBENTON, Edmé–L. 1765–1781. Planches enluminées pour servir a l'histoire naturelle de M. Le compte de Buffon.

DAVIS, D. E. 1941. Notes on Cuban birds. Wilson Bull. 53:37–40.

DAVIES, J. E. 1994. Rare and endemic plants, animals and habitats in the Cayman Islands, and related legislation. Pages 527–541 in The Cayman Islands: natural history and biogeography. Monographiae Biologicae volume 7 (M. A. Brunt and J. E. Davies, Eds.). Kluwer Academic Publishers, Dordrecht, The Netherlands.

DAVIS, S., AND A. SMITH. 1995. Birds at Fort Clarence Beach Park, beside the Great Salt Pond, St. Catherine. Gosse Bird Club Broads. No. 65:15.

DATHE, H., AND W. FISCHER. 1969. Bemerkenswerte beobachtungen auf Kuba im frühjahr 1968. J. Ornithol. 110(1):111–112.

DATHE, H., AND W. FISCHER. 1979. Beiträge zur ornithologie Kubas. Beitr. Vogelkd. 25:171–203.

DELACOUR, J. 1938. Journal de Croisière (Yacht *Rosaura*, octobre 1937–janvier 1938). Oiseau Rev. Fr. Ornithol. 8:541–557.

DEPARTAMENTO DE RECURSOS NATURALES. 1985. Evaluacion ambiental y determinacion de impacto ambiental no significativo. Reglamento propuesto para regir el manejo de las especies vulnerables o en peligro de extincion en el estado libre asociado de Puerto Rico. Departamento de Recursos Naturales, San Juan, Puerto Rico.

DESCOURTILZ, M. É. 1809. Voyages d'un naturaliste, et ses observations faites sur les trois règnes de la nature, dans plusieurs ports de mer français, en Espagne, au continent de l'Amérique septentrionale, à Saint–Yago de Cuba, et à Saint–Domingue, ou l'auteur devenu le prisonnier de 10,000 noirs révoltés, et par suite mis en liberté par un colonne del'armée française, donne des détails circonstanciés sur l'expédition du général LeClerc. Père Dufart, Libraire–Éditeur, Paris.

DESCOURTILZ, M. É. 1935. Voyages d'un naturaliste et ses observations Abridged ed. Plon, Paris.

DEWEY, R. A., AND D. W. NELLIS. 1980. Seabird research in the U. S. Virgin Islands. Pages 445–452 *in* Transactions of the Forty–fifth North American Wildlife and Natural Resources Conference (K. Sabol, Ed.). Miami, Florida.

DEAN, T., AND D. OSBORNE. No date (1992 or later). Checklist of the birds of North Andros Island, Bahamas. Privately published.

DIAMOND, A. W. 1972. Sexual dimorphism in breeding cycles and unequal sex ratio in Magnificent Frigatebirds. Ibis 114:395–398.

DIAMOND, A. W. 1973. Notes on the breeding biology and behavior of the Magnificent Frigatebird. Condor 75:200–209.

DIAMOND, A. W. 1975. Biology and behaviour of frigatebirds *Fregata* spp. on Aldabra Atoll. Ibis 117:302–323.

DIAMOND, A. W. 1980. The Red–footed Booby colony on Little Cayman: size, structure and significance. Atoll Res. Bull. No. 241:165–170.

DIAMOND, T. 1971. Least Tern. Gosse Bird Club Broads. No. 17:27.

DOD, A. S. de. 1972. Aves de nuestra pais: la Tijereta, gran volandora. El Caribe 2:11–A.

DOD, A. S. de. 1973. Aves de nuestra pais: la Gaviota Dominicana. El Caribe 6:11–A.

DOD, A. S. de. 1973. Aves de nuestra pais: las gaviotas son gregarias. El Caribe 8:11–A.

DOD, A. S. de. 1973. Aves de nuestra pais: el majestuoso Pelicano. El Caribe 1:11–A.

DOD, A. S. de. 1976. Loma Jamao: en Busca del Diabliotín. El Caribe:9.

DOD, A. S. de. 1979. Llegan nuevos miembros familia de gaviotas. El Caribe:9.

DOD, A. S. de. 1979. Aparecen piedras volcánicas desplazadas en Jaiquí Picado. El Caribe:9.

DOD, A. S. de. 1980. Colonia de *Pterodroma hasitata* en Republica Dominicana. 2/81 *in* Naturalista Postal 1980 (J. Cicero, Ed.). UASD, Departamento de Biologia Herbario, Santo Domingo.

DOD, A. S. de. 1981. Aparace la primera colonia de Diablotines. El Caribe:25.

DOD, A. S. de. 1982. Un paseso sin suerte por la Loma de Toro. El Caribe:19.

DOD, A. S. de. 1982. Sigue la mala suerte en Loma de Toro. El Caribe:19.

DOD, A. S. de. 1982. Ornitólogos frustrados en Loma de Toro. El Caribe:19.

DOD, A. S. de. 1982. ¡Adiós, Loma de Toro! El Caribe:19.

DOD, A. S. de. 1984. El Diablotín, un ave rara y una curiosidad. El Caribe:17.

DOD, A. S. de. 1985. Los Diablotines y los Lavapiés. El Caribe:18.

DOD, A. S. de. 1986. Jejenes y Tijeretas en un viaje feliz. El Caribe:18.

DOD, A. S. de. 1988. Los bubíes del Caribe. El Caribe:18.

DOD, A. S. de. 1988. Si no son bubíes ¿qué son? El Caribe:18.

DOD, A. S. de. 1992. Endangered and endemic birds of the Dominican Republic. Cypress House, Fort Bragg, California.

DOD, A. S. de, AND D. A. SIRI NUÑEZ. 1980. Aves migratorias accidentales observados este año en Republica Dominicana. 39/80 *in* Naturalista Postal 1980 UASD, Depto. Biol. Herbario (J. Cicero, Ed.). UASD, Santo Domingo.

DOMINGUEZ MONTANDON, T. G., AND D. SIRI. 1989. Estudio preliminar de la avifauna en las Lagunas Limón y Redonda, Miches. Pitirre 2(3):7–8.

DONALDSON, A. [N. R. C. A.]. 1996. Birds at Middle Cay, Morant, Cays (off the south east coast). Gosse Bird Club Broads. No. 66:29.

DOWNER, A. 1965. Magnificent Frigatebird. Gosse Bird Club Broads. No. 5:20.

DOWNER, A. 1967. Black Tern. Gosse Bird Club Broads. No. 8:16.

DOWNER, A. 1971. Herring Gull. Gosse Bird Club Broads. No. 16:18.

DOWNER, A. 1973. Caspian Tern. Gosse Bird Club Broads. No. 20:22.

DOWNER, A. 1974. White–tailed Tropicbirds. Gosse Bird Club Broads. No. 23:11–12.

DOWNER, A. 1975. White–tailed Tropicbird. Gosse Bird Club Broads. No. 25:19.

DOWNER, A. 1976. Brown Booby. Gosse Bird Club Broads. No. 26:16.

DOWNER, A. 1979. White–tailed Tropicbird. Gosse Bird Club Broads. No. 32:12.

DOWNER, A. 1981. Laughing Gull. Gosse Bird Club Broads. No. 37:12.

DOWNER, A. 1982. Sandwich Tern. Gosse Bird Club Broads. No. 38:13.

DOWNER, A. 1983. White–tailed Tropicbird. Gosse Bird Club Broads. No. 40:16.

DOWNER, A. 1983. Brown Pelican. Gosse Bird Club Broads. No. 40:16.

DOWNER, A. 1984. Least Tern. Gosse Bird Club Broads. No. 43:14.

DOWNER, A. 1985. Least Terns & Black Terns. Gosse Bird Club Broads. No. 44:12.

DOWNER, A. 1987. White–tailed Tropicbird. Gosse Bird Club Broads. No. 48:9.

DOWNER, A. 1988. Ibis nesting on Refuge Cay in Kingston Harbour, May 7, 1988. Gosse Bird Club Broads. No. 51:11.
DOWNER, A. 1988. Nesting colony at Parottee Pond, July 1988. Gosse Bird Club Broads. No. 51:11.
DOWNER, A. 1989. Brown Pelican. Gosse Bird Club Broads. No. 53:23.
DOWNER, A. 1989. Gull–billed Tern. Gosse Bird Club Broads. No. 53:25.
DOWNER, A. 1990. Trip to Pedro Cays. Gosse Bird Club Broads. No. 54:18.
DOWNER, A. 1990. Bridled Tern. Gosse Bird Club Broads. No. 54:20–21.
DOWNER, A. 1992. Brown Pelican. Gosse Bird Club Broads. No. 59:16.
DOWNER, A., AND A. BLACK [Editors]. 1972. Breeding of the Least Tern in Jamaica. Gosse Bird Club Broads. No. 18:18.
DOWNER, A., AND J. FLETCHER. 1980. Migrant dates. Gosse Bird Club Broads. No. 35:10.
DOWNER, A., J. FLETCHER, Y. BECKER, AND C. LEVY. 1989. Least Tern. Gosse Bird Club Broads. No. 53:25.
DOWNER, A., G. H. GALE, R. L. SUTTON, AND M. HODGSON. 1975. Herring Gull. Gosse Bird Club Broads. No. 24:19.
DOWNER, A., AND C. LEVY. 1989. Nesting terns & noddies. Gosse Bird Club Broads. No. 53:20–21.
DOWNER, A., AND D. VERLEY. 1976. Mullion Cove. Gosse Bird Club Broads. No. 27:12.
DUFFIELD, J. M., AND J. E. CARDONA. 1978. Estimated avian population density and diversity indices of Vieques Island. Department of Natural Resources, San Juan, Puerto Rico.
DUFFY, D. C., W. E. ARNTZ, H. T. SERPA, P. D. BOERSMA, AND R. L. NORTON. 1988. A comparison of the effects of El Niño and the Southern Oscillation on birds in Peru and the Atlantic Ocean. Pages 1740–1746 *in* Proceedings of the 19th International Ornithological Congress (1986), Ottawa.
DUGAND, A. 1947. Aves marinas de las costas e islas Colombianas. Caldasia 4:379–398.
DU MONT, Mrs K. 1964. Magnificent Frigatebird. Gosse Bird Club Broads. No. 3:14.
DUMONT, P. A. 1934. On the specimens of Fregata magnificens in the University of Iowa Museum. Wilson Bull. 46:120–122.
DUNHAM, J. B., K. BURNETT, AND G. WENZ [Editors]. 1990. The birds of Lee Stocking Island and Northern Great Exuma: records of observations from February 1987 to April 1989 by the staff of the Caribbean Marine Research Center. unpublished report.
DU TERTRE, J. B. 1654. Histoire générale des iles de S. Christophe, de la Guadeloupe, de la Martinique, et autres dans l'Amérique. Ou l'on verra l'establissement des colonies étrangères, & tout ce qui se passes dans les voyages & retours des Indes ... De plus, la description de tous les animaux de la mer, de l'air, & de la terre: & vn traite fort ample des moeurs des sauvages du pays. J. Langlois et E. Langlois, Paris.
DU TERTRE, L. R. P. J. 1667. Histoire générale des Antilles habitées par les Français. Divisée en deux tomes et enrichie de cartes & de figures. Thomas Iolly, Paris.
EATON, R. J. 1934. The migratory movements of certain colonies of Herring Gulls in eastern North America. Bird–Banding 5:1–19.
EKMAN, E. L. 1929. Plants of Navassa Island, West Indies. Ark. Bot. 22A:1–12.
EKMAN, E. L. 1941. Excursion botanique dans de nord–ouest de la République Dominicaine. Rev. Soc. d'Hist. Géogr. d'Haiti 12:37–50.
ENGLISH, T. M. S. 1916. Notes on some of the birds of Grand Cayman, West Indies. Ibis 4:17–35.
ERDMAN, D. S. 1960. Preliminary report on the sportfishery of Mona Island, with notes on the status of game birds and mammals. Unpublished report, Department of Natural Resources, San Juan, Puerto Rico.
ERDMAN, D. S. 1960. Mona Island fish and game investigational report, May 14–22, 1960. Unpublished report, Department of Natural Resources, San Juan, Puerto Rico.
ERDMAN, D. S. 1962. Mona Island sport fishery investigations, Oct. 11–17, 1962. Unpublished report, Commonwealth of Puerto Rico Department of Agriculture, San Juan, Puerto Rico.
ERDMAN, D. S. 1967. Sea birds in relation to game fish schools off Puerto Rico and the Virgin Islands. Caribb. J. Sci. 7:79–85.
ERSKINE, A. J. 1963. The Black–headed Gull (*Larus ridibundus*) in eastern North America. Audubon Field Notes 17:334–338.
ERWIN, R. M., J. A. KUSHLAN, C. LUTHIN, I. M. PRICE, AND A. SPRUNT IV. 1984. Conservation of colonial waterbirds in the Caribbean Basin: summary of a panel discussion. Colon. Waterbirds 7:139–142.
ESTRADA, A. R., AND J. NOVO RODRIGUEZ. 1984. Reptiles y aves de Cayo Inés de Soto, Archipiélago de los Colorados, Pinar del Río, Cuba. Misc. Zool., Inst. Zool. Acad. Cienc. Cuba 23:1.
ESTRADA, A. R., AND R. RODRIGUEZ. 1985. Lista de vertebrados terrestres de Cayo Campos, Archipiélago de los Canarreos, Cuba. Misc. Zool., Inst. Zool. Acad. Cienc. Cuba 27:2–3.

EVERMANN, B. W. 1902. General report on the investigations in Porto Rico of the United States Fish Commission Steamer Fish Hawk in 1899. Bull. U. S. Fish Comm. 20:3–302.

EWEN, B. 1982. White–tailed Tropicbird. Gosse Bird Club Broads. No. 38:11.

FAIRBAIRN, P. 1979. The Natural History Society of Jamaica outing to Treasure Beach, Great Pedro Pond, Parottee Pond, Black River and Luana Point 23–25 February, 1979. Nat. Hist. Notes Nat. Hist. Soc. Jamaica, new ser. 1:1–4.

FAIRBAIRN, P. W., AND A. M. HAYNES. 1982. Jamaican surveys of the West Indian manatee (*Trichechus manatus*), dolphin (*Tursiops truncatus*), sea turtles (families Cheloniidae and Dermochelydae) and booby terns (family Laridae). FAO Fish. Rep. No. 278 Supplement:289–295.

FARR, T. H. 1990. Recovery of banded bird. Gosse Bird Club Broads. No. 55:15.

FEILDEN, H. W. 1889. On the birds of Barbados. Ibis 1:477–503.

FEILDEN, H. W. 1902. Birds of Barbados. West Ind. Bull. 3:333–352.

FEILDEN, H. W. 1902. Birds of Barbados. West Ind. Bull. 3:333–352.

FEILDEN, H. W. 1888. Richardson's Skua in the island of Barbados. Zoologist 3 12:350.

FEILDEN, H. W. 1894. The deserted domicile of the Diablotin in Dominica. Trans. Norfolk and Norwich Naturalist Soc. 5:24–39.

FELDMANN, P., AND P. VILLARD. 1993. Oiseaux de Guadeloupe et de Martinique. Association pour l'Étude et la protection des Vertébrés des petites Antilles, Guadeloupe.

FELDMANN, P., A. LE DRU, C. PAVIS, AND P. VILLARD. 1995. Checklist of the birds of Guadeloupe, Martinique and their offshore islands. Association pour l'Étude et la protection des Vertébrés des petites Antilles, Petit Bourg, Guadeloupe.

FIELD, G. W. 1894. Notes on the birds of Port Henderson, Jamaica, West Indies. Auk 11(2):117–127.

FISCHER, W. 1969. Beobachtungen an Schlafplätzen des Kuhreihers auf Kuba. Falke 16:220–224.

FISHER, A. K., AND A. WETMORE. 1931. Report on birds recorded by the Pinchot Expedition of 1929 to the Caribbean and Pacific. Proc. U. S. Nat. Mus. 79:1–66.

FLETCHER, J. 1978. Common Stilts at the Yallahs Pond. Gosse Bird Club Broads. No. 31:3–6.

FLETCHER, J. 1978. Least Tern. Gosse Bird Club Broads. No. 31:11.

FLETCHER, J. 1979. Shorebirds – & others. Gosse Bird Club Broads. No. 32:7–8.

FLETCHER, J. 1979. A nesting site for Least Terns. Gosse Bird Club Broads. No. 33:9–10.

FLETCHER, J. 1980. Further notes on nesting Least Terns. Gosse Bird Club Broads. No. 35:2–3.

FLETCHER, J. 1981. Least Tern nesting. Gosse Bird Club Broads. No. 37:9.

FLETCHER, J. 1981. Laughing Gull. Gosse Bird Club Broads. No. 37:12.

FLETCHER, J. 1981. White–tailed Tropicbird. Gosse Bird Club Broads. No. 37:12.

FLETCHER, J. 1982. Brown Pelican. Gosse Bird Club Broads. No. 38:12.

FLETCHER, J. 1982. Brown Pelican. Gosse Bird Club Broads. No. 39:14.

FLETCHER, J. 1982. Least Terns. Gosse Bird Club Broads. No. 39:15.

FLETCHER, J. 1983. Black Tern. Gosse Bird Club Broads. No. 41:18.

FLETCHER, J. 1984. Laughing Gull. Gosse Bird Club Broads. No. 42:12.

FLETCHER, J. 1984. Sandwich Tern. Gosse Bird Club Broads. No. 43:14.

FLETCHER, J. 1986. Laughing Gull. Gosse Bird Club Broads. No. 46:9.

FLETCHER, J. 1987. Sandwich Tern. Gosse Bird Club Broads. No. 48:11.

FLETCHER, J. 1987. Gull–billed Tern. Gosse Bird Club Broads. No. 48:11.

FLETCHER, J. 1987. Sandwich Tern. Gosse Bird Club Broads. No. 48:11.

FLETCHER, J. 1988. Herring Gull. Gosse Bird Club Broads. No. 51:14.

FLETCHER, J. 1989. Refuge Cay visit. Gosse Bird Club Broads. No. 53:19–20.

FLETCHER, J. 1990. Field trips 1990. Gosse Bird Club Broads. No. 54:7.

FLETCHER, J. 1991. Terns. Gosse Bird Club Broads. No. 57:21.

FLETCHER, J. 1992. Refuge Cay, Kingston Harbour. Gosse Bird Club Broads. No. 59:14.

FLETCHER, J. 1994. White–tailed Tropicbirds. Gosse Bird Club Broads. No. 62:11–12.

FRIEDMAN, R. 1948. Black Skimmer and White Pelicans in the Bahamas. Auk 65(1):142.

FULLER, M. R., H. H. OBRECHT III, C. J. PENNYCUICK, AND F. C. SCHAFFNER. 1989. Aerial tracking of radio–marked White–tailed Tropicbirds over the Caribbean Sea. Pages 133–138 *in* Biotelemetry X: Proceedings of the Tenth International Symposium on Biotelemetry (C. J. Amlaner, Jr., Ed.). University of Arkansas Press, Fayetteville.

FURNISS, S. 1981. Birds of Puerto Rico and the U. S. Virgin Islands. Unpublished checklist, U. S. Fish and Wildlife Service, Caribbean Islands National Wildlife Refuge, Boquerón, Puerto Rico.

FURNISS, S. 1983. Status of the seabirds of the Culebra Archipelago, Puerto Rico. Colon. Waterbirds 6:121–125.

FURNISS, S., AND J. COLLAZO. 1983. Recent avian records for the Culebra Archipelago, Puerto Rico. Pages 115–121 *in* Memorias del Cuarto Simposio sobre la Fauna de Puerto Rico y el Caribe (R. A. Pérez–Rivera, L. O. Nieves–Rivera, and E. Ortiz–Corp's, Eds.). Universidad de Puerto Rico, Humacao.

FURNISS, S., J. TAYLOR, AND M. GRIFFEN–TAYLOR. 1984. Preliminary report on the nesting biology of White-tailed Tropicbirds at Cayo Luis Peña, Puerto Rico. Colon. Waterbirds Group Newsl. 8:38.

GARCIA, I., R. ALAYO, N. NOVOA, A. NICHOLAS, R. GONZALEZ, L. F. de ARMAS, D. DOMINGUEZ, C. SOMOZA, A. de la OSA, J. de la CRUZ, O. H. GARRIDO, J. RAMON CUEVAS, AND J. FONTAINES. 1973. Lista de los anfibios, reptiles, aves y mamiferos collectados en el Plan Jibacoa–Cayajabos. Informe del Trabajo faunístico realizado en el plan Jibacoa–Cayajabos. Serie Biol., Inst. Zool., A. C. C. 43:1–25.

GARCIA MONTAÑA, F., AND O. H. GARRIDO. 1965. Catalogo de las aves de Cuba. *In* Catalogo de la fauna cubana. XIII. Trab. Divulg. Mus. "Felipe Poey," Acad. Cienc. Cuba 27:82.

GARCIA MONTAÑA, F., AND O. H. GARRIDO. 1965. Nuevos registros de nidificacion de aves en Cuba. Poeyana No. 9:1–3.

GARCIA ROMERO, M. E., A. TORRES LEYVA, R. M. ABREU, AND J. de la CRUZ LORENZO. 1989. Datos sobre la nidificacion de *Pelecanus occidentalis, Phalacrocorax auritus* y *Nycticorax nycticorax* (Aves; Pelicanidae, Phalacrocoridae, Ardeidae) en Cayos Sevilla, Cuba. Cienc. Biol. Acad. Cienc. Cuba No. 21–22:179–181.

GARDENER, A., S. BINGHAM, AND M. BINGHAM. 1995. Birds at Malvern, St. Elizabeth. Gosse Bird Club Broads. No. 64:17–18.

GARRIDO, O. H. 1973. Anfibios, reptiles y aves del Archipiélago de Sabana–Camagüey, Cuba. Torreia (Havana) ser. nueva 27:1–72.

GARRIDO, O. H. 1973. Anfibios, reptiles y aves de Cayo Real (Cayos de San Felipe), Cuba. Poeyana No. 119:1–50.

GARRIDO, O. H. 1980. Adiciones a la fauna de vertebrados de la Península de Guanahacabibes. Misc. Zool., Inst. Zool. Acad. Cienc. Cuba 10:2–4.

GARRIDO, O. H. 1980. Los vertebrados terrestres de la Península de Zapata. Poeyana No. 203:1–49.

GARRIDO, O. H. 1985. Cuban endangered birds. Pages 992–999 *in* Neotropical ornithology, Ornithological Monograph No. 36 (P. A. Buckley, M. S. Foster, E. S. Morton, R. S. Ridgely, and F. G. Buckley, Eds.). American Ornithologists' Union, Washington, D. C.

GARRIDO, O. H. 1988. La migración de las aves en Cuba. Publicaciones de la Asociacion de Amigos de Doñana, [Graficas Mirte S.A.], Sevilla, España.

GARRIDO, O. H. 1988. Nueva gaviota (Aves: Laridae) para Cuba. Misc. Zool., Inst. Zool. Acad. Cienc. Cuba 37:3–4.

GARRIDO, O. H., A. R. ESTRADA, AND A. LLANES SOSA. 1986. Anfibios, reptiles y aves de Cayo Guajaba, Archipiélago de Sabana–Camagüey, Cuba. Poeyana No. 328:1–34.

GARRIDO, O. H., AND F. GARCIA MONTAÑA. 1975. Catálogo de las Aves de Cuba. Academia de Ciencias de Cuba, La Habana.

GARRIDO, O. H., AND F. GARCIA MONTAÑA. 1965. Aves nuevas para Cuba. Poeyana No. 10:1–6.

GARRIDO, O. H., AND F. GARCIA MONTAÑA. 1967. Nuevo *Oceanodroma* (Aves: Hydrobatidae) para las Antillas. Trab. Divulg. Mus. "Felipe Poey," Acad. Cienc. Cuba 48:1–4.

GARRIDO,ORLANDO H; GARCÍA MONTAÑA,FLORENTINO (1968): Nuevos reportes de aves para Cuba. Torreia (Havana), ser. nueva 4, 3-13.

GARRIDO, O. H., AND J. A. MORALES. In press. Nuevo estercorarino (Aves: Laridae) para Cuba. Misc. Zool., Inst. Zool. Acad. Cienc. Cuba.

GARRIDO, O. H., AND A. SILVA LEE. 1990. Seabirds nesting in southern Cuba. Pitirre 3(3):7.

GARRIDO, O. H., AND A. SCHWARTZ. 1968. Anfibios, reptiles y aves de la península de Guanahacabibes, Cuba. Poeyana No. A 53:1–68.

GARRIDO, O. H., AND A. SCHWARTZ. 1969. Anfibios, reptiles y aves de Cayo Cantiles. Poeyana No. A 67:1–44.

GOCHFELD, M. 1983. The Roseate Tern: world distribution and status of a threatened species. Biol. Conserv. 25:103–125.

GOCHFELD, M., J. BURGER, J. E. SALIVA, AND D. GOCHFELD. 1988. Herald Petrel new to the West Indies. Am. Birds 42(5):1254–1258.

GOCHFELD, M., D. O. HILL, AND G. TUDOR. 1973. A second population of the recently described Elfin Woods Warbler and other bird records from the West Indies. Caribb. J. Sci. 13:231–235.

GODMAN, F. du C. 1907–1910. A monograph of the petrels (order Tubinares). Witherby & Co., London.

GOLDING, P. 1985. Birding around Jamaica in 1984. Gosse Bird Club Broads. No. 44:11.

GOLDING, P. 1987. At Mona Reservoir on March 20, 6.00–8.30 a.m. with A. Downer and Catherine Levy. Gosse Bird Club Broads. No. 49:9–10.

GOLDING, P. 1995. Mona Reservoir, St. Andrew. Gosse Bird Club Broads. No. 64:17.

GOLDING, P. 1996. Brown Pelican. Gosse Bird Club Broads. No. 66:31.

GONZALEZ, A., J. ALVAREZ, AND A. KIRKCONNELL. 1992. Aves observadas en Cayo Cruz, Archipiélago Sabana–Camagüey, Cuba. Pages 25–26 in Comunicaciones Breves de Zoologia. Instituto de Ecología y Sistemática, Academia de Ciencias de Cuba, La Habana.

GOSSE, P. H., AND E. [Assisted by RICHARD HILL of Spanish Town]. 1847. The birds of Jamaica. John Van Voorst, Paternoster Row, London.

GRANGER, S. 1976. White–tailed Tropicbird. Gosse Bird Club Broads. No. 26:16.

GRIEVE, S. 1906. Notes upon the island of Dominica. Adam and Charles Black, London.

GRIEVE, S. 1925. Notes on some Dominican birds. Proc. Royal Physical Soc. 21:19–28.

GRAHAM, D. J. 1984. A sighting of a Black–legged Kittiwake in Saint Lucia. Am. Birds 38(2):256.

GRAHAM, R. 1971. White–tailed Tropic Birds. Gosse Bird Club Broads. No. 16:17–18.

GRAHAM, R. 1973. White–tailed Tropicbird. Gosse Bird Club Broads. No. 21:17–18.

GRAYCE, R. L. 1957. Range extensions in Puerto Rico. Auk 74(1):106.

GRISCOM, L. 1937. Herring Gull at Barbados. Auk 54(4):539.

GROSS, A. O. 1940. The migration of Kent Island Herring Gulls. Bird–Banding 11:129–155.

GUNDLACH, J. 1857. Beiträge zur ornithologie Cuba's. Nach mittheilungen des reisenden an Hr. Bez.—Dir. Sezekorn in Cassel; von Letzterem zusammengestellt. Mit zusatzen und anmerkungen geordnet vom herausgeber. J. Ornithol. 5(28):225–242.

GUNDLACH, J. 1859. Ornithologisches aus briefen von Cuba. J. Ornithol. 7(40):294–299.

GUNDLACH, J. 1859. Ornithologisches aus briefen von Cuba. J. Ornithol. 7(41):347–351.

GUNDLACH, J. 1861. Tabellarische uebersicht aller bisher auf Cuba beobachteten vögel. J. Ornithol. 9(53):321–349.

GUNDLACH, J. 1862. Zusätze und berichtigungen zu den "Beiträgen zur ornithologie Cuba's." J. Ornithol. 10(56):81–96.

GUNDLACH, J. 1862. Zusätze und berichtigungen zu den "Beiträgen zur ornithologie Cuba's." J. Ornithol. 10(57):177–191.

GUNDLACH, J. 1865–1866. Revista y catálogo de las aves Cubanas. Pages 165–180 in Repertorio Fisico Natural de la Isla de Cuba, Vol. 1 (F. Poey, Ed.). Imprenta del Gobierno y Capitanía General, La Habana.

GUNDLACH, J. 1865–1866. Revista y catálogo de las Aves Cubanas. Pages 386–403 in Repertorio Fisico–Natural Capitanía General, Vol. 1 (F. Poey, Ed.). Imprenta del Gobierno y Capitanía General, La Habana.

GUNDLACH, J. 1871. Neue beiträge zur ornithologie Cubas, nach eigenen 30 jährigen beobachtungen zusammengestellt. J. Ornithol. 19(112):265–295.

GUNDLACH, J. 1873–1876. Contribución á la ornitología cubana. Imprenta "La Antilla" de N. Cacho–Negrette, La Habana.

GUNDLACH, J. 1873. Catálogo de las aves Cubanas. An. Soc. Española Hist. Nat., Madrid 2:81–191.

GUNDLACH, J. 1874. Beiträg zur ornithologie der insel Portorico. J. Ornithol. 22(127):304–315.

GUNDLACH, J. 1875. Neue beiträge zur ornithologie Cubas. Nach eigenen 30 jährigen beobachtungen zusammengestellt. J. Ornithol. 23(132):353–407.

GUNDLACH, J. 1876. Contribución á la ornitología cubana. Imprenta "La Antilla" de N. Cacho–Negrette, La Habana.

GUNDLACH, J. 1878. Apuntes para la fauna Puerto-Riquena. Segunda parte (Aves). An. Soc. Española Hist. Nat., Madrid 7:343–422.

GUNDLACH, J. 1878. Neue beiträge zur ornithologie der insel Portorico. J. Ornithol. 26(142):157–194.

GUNDLACH, J. 1878. Briefliches über eine neue Dysporus–art auf Cuba. J. Ornithol. 26(143):298.

GUNDLACH, J. 1881. Nachträge zur ornithologie Cuba's. J. Ornithol. 29(156):400–401.

GUNDLACH, J. 1891. Notes on some species of birds of the island of Cuba. Auk 8(2):187–191.

GUNDLACH, J. 1893. Ornithología cubana ó catálogo descriptivo de todas las especies de aves tanto indígenas como de paso anual o accidental observadas en 53 años. Archivos de la policlínica ed. Imprenta "La Moderna," La Habana.

GRISDALE, T. 1882. On the birds of Montserrat. Ibis 6:485–493.

[GURNEY, J. J.] 1841. Mr. J. J. Gurney on Santa Cruz, St. Thomas, and Dominica. Ann. Mag. Nat. Hist. 6:527–529.

HAMILTON, J. 1981. Recoveries of wintering Roseate Terns. J. Field Ornithol. 52:36–42.

HANEY, J. C. 1986. Seabird patchiness in tropical oceanic waters: The influence of Sargassum "reefs." Auk 103(1):141–151.

HANEY, J. C. 1987. Aspects of the pelagic ecology and behavior of the Black–capped Petrel (Pterodroma hasitata). Wilson Bull. 99:153–168.

HANLON, R. 1955. Notes on some birds of Long and Great Inagua Islands, Bahamas. Flicker 27:98–104.

HARKNESS, A. 1994. Birds at (A) Hermitage Dam and (B) Stony Hill. Gosse Bird Club Broads. No. 62:17.

HARRINGTON, M. W. 1899. Fauna and flora of Puerto Rico. Science (NY), new series 10:286–288.

HARRIS, A. 1988. Identification of adult Sooty and Bridled terns. Br. Birds 81:525–530.

HART, P. 1965. Was this the last of the line? Gosse Bird Club Broads. No. 5:6–7.

HARTLAUB, G. 1847. Den heutigen zustand unserer kenntnisse von Westindiens ornithologie. Isis (Oken) 1847:604–615.

HARVEY, J. 1966. Of pelicans and frigate birds. Gosse Bird Club Broads. No. 7:15.

HAWKES, A. D. 1971. Sea birds at Savanna–La–Mar. Gosse Bird Club Broads. No. 16:15–16.

HAWKES, A. D. 1971. Frigatebirds. Gosse Bird Club Broads. No. 16:22.

HAWKES, A. D. 1971. Birds at Paradise, Westmoreland. Gosse Bird Club Broads. No. 17:18–19.

HAWKES, A. D. 1973. Birds at Naggo Head Beach. Gosse Bird Club Broads. No. 20:12–13.

HAWKES, A. D. 1975. Magnificent Frigatebird. Gosse Bird Club Broads. No. 25:20.

HAYMES, G. T., AND H. BLOKPOEL. 1978. Seasonal distribution and site tenacity of the Great Lakes Common Tern. Bird–Banding 49:142–151.

HAYNES, A. 1983. Conservation and ecology of *Sterna fuscata* and *Anous stolidus* in Jamaica. Pages 92–100 *in* Memorias del cuarto simposio sobre la fauna de Puerto Rico y el Caribe (R. A. Pérez–Rivera, L. O. Nieves–Rivera, and E. Ortiz–Corp's, Eds.). Universidad de Puerto Rico, Humacao. (121pp)

HAYNES, A. M. 1986. Preliminary report on status & conservation of 'booby' terns at Morant Cays, Jamaica 1982–1985, Vol. 2. Report to the Natural Resources Conservation Division, Kingston, Jamaica.

HAYNES, A. M. 1986. Report on a visit to Pedro Cays, October 1986. Unpublished report, Natural Resources Conservation Department, Kingston, Jamaica.

HAYNES, A. 1986. Masked Boobies nesting at Pedro Cays. Gosse Bird Club Broads. No. 47:2–3.

HAYNES, A. M. 1987. Human exploitation of seabirds in Jamaica. Biol. Conserv. 41:99–124.

HAYNES, A. M., AND R. L. SUTTON. 1988. Bird banding recoveries. Gosse Bird Club Broads. No. 50:11–12.

HAYNES, A. M., R. L. SUTTON, AND K. D. HARVEY. 1989. Conservation trends, and the threats to endemic birds in Jamaica. Pages 827–838 *in* Biogeography in the West Indies. Past, present, & future (C. A. Woods, Ed.). Sandhill Crane Press, Gainesville, Florida.

HAYNES–SUTTON, A. M. 1987. The value of seabirds as a socio–economic resource in Jamaica. International Council for Bird Preservation Technical Publication No. 6, Cambridge.

HAYNES–SUTTON, A. 1989. Banding and recaptures of Sooty Terns and Brown Noddies at Morant Cays, Jamaica. Pitirre 2(2):7.

HENRARD, L. 1995. Mona Reservoir, St. Andrew. Gosse Bird Club Broads. No. 64:17.

HILDER, P. 1989. The birds of Nevis. The Nevis Historical and Conservation Society, Charlestown, Nevis.

HILL, M. 1970. White–tailed tropic birds. Gosse Bird Club Broads. No. 15:17.

HOBLEY, C. W. 1932. Rediscovery of Dominica diablotin. J. Soc. Preserv. Fauna Empire, new ser. 17:17–20.

HODGES, M. 1993. Visit to the Morant Cays, May 1993. Gosse Bird Club Broads. No. 61:12.

HODGSON, M. 1974. Black Tern. Gosse Bird Club Broads. No. 23:23.

HOLMAN, J. P. 1952. West Indian Black–capped Petrel, *Pterodroma hasitata*, picked up on Fairfield Beach, Connecticut. Auk 69(4):459–460.

HOOGERWERF, A. 1977. Notes on the birds of St. Martin, Saba and St. Eustatius. Stud. Fauna Curaçao Other Caribb. Isl. 54(176):60–123.

HOUSTON, W. H. 1968. Some notes on the birds of the U.S. Virgin Islands. Gosse Bird Club Broads. No. 11:9–11.

HOUSTON, W. H. 1963. Laughing Gull and Caspian Tern. Gosse Bird Club Broads. No. 1:7.

HOUSTON, W. H., AND T. DAVIS. 1967. Forster's Tern. Gosse Bird Club Broads. No. 8:16.

HOUSTON, W. H., AND T. DAVIS. 1967. Black Tern. Gosse Bird Club Broads. No. 8:16.

HOWE, W. H., D. M. TAYLOR, AND D. A. JETT. 1989. Additional records of birds from Cat Island, Bahamas. Wilson Bull. 101:115–117.

HOWES, P. G. 1917. Bird collecting in eastern Colombia. Oölogist 34:95–98.

HUNDLEY, M. H., AND C. R. MASON. 1963. Field check list of the birds of the Bahama Islands. Florida Audubon Society, Maitland, Florida.

HUMMELINCK, P. W. 1953. Islote Aves, een vogeleiland in de Caraibische Zee. J. West–Indische Gids 33:23–34.

HOUSTON, W. H. 1968. Some notes on the birds of the U.S. Virgin Islands. Gosse Bird Club Broads. No. 11:9–11.

HOUSTON, W. H., AND T. DAVIS. 1967. Sandwich Tern. Gosse Bird Club Broads. No. 8:16.

HOUSTON, W. H., AND E. R. G. KIDD. 1964. Laughing Gull. Gosse Bird Club Broads. No. 2:19.

HUDSON, R. 1968. The Great Skua in the Caribbean. Bird Study 15:33–34.

HURST, L. 1980. Magnificent Frigatebird. Gosse Bird Club Broads. No. 35:13.

ICBP. 1988. Report of the 1978 University of East Anglia–ICBP St Lucia expedition. International Council for Bird Preservation, Cambridge, U. K.

IMBER, M. J. 1991. The Jamaican Petrel – dead or alive? Gosse Bird Club Broads. No. 57:4–9.

IMBER, M. J. 1991. The Jamaican Petrel – dead or alive? Page 481 in Acta XX Congressus Internationalis Ornithologici, Christchurch, New Zealand, 2–9 December 1990 (B. D. Bell, Ed.). New Zealand Ornithological Congrest Trust Board, Wellington.

JEFFREY–SMITH, M. T. 1947. [White Ibis and Sandwich Tern]. Nat. Hist. Notes Nat. Hist. Soc. Jamaica 3:116.

JEFFREY–SMITH, M. 1956. Bird–watching in Jamaica. Pioneer Press, Kingston, Jamaica.

JEFFREY–SMITH, M. 1966. Magnificent Frigate Bird. Gosse Bird Club Broads. No. 7:16.

JENNINGS, A. H. 1888. List of birds observed at New Providence, Bahama Islands, March–June, 1887. Johns Hopkins Univ. Circulars 7:39.

JOHNSON, T. H. 1988. Biodiversity and conservation in the Caribbean: Profiles of selected islands. International Council for Bird Preservation, Monograph No. 1, Cambridge, United Kingdom.

JOHNSTON, D. W. 1965. Grand Cayman Island in early May. Gosse Bird Club Broads. No. 5:4–5.

JOHNSTON, D. W. 1975. Ecological analysis of the Cayman Island avifauna. Bull. Fl. State Mus., Biol. Sci. 19:235–300.

JOHNSTON, D. W., C. H. BLAKE, AND D. W. BUDEN. 1971. Avifauna of the Cayman Islands. Q. J. Florida Acad. Sci. 34:141–156.

JOHNSON, T. H., AND A. J. STATTERSFIELD. 1990. A global review of island endemic birds. Ibis 132:167–180.

JONES, M. A. J. 1991. Beach tar pollution: a threat to nesting sites? Gosse Bird Club Broads. No. 56:9–11.

JOUANIN, C. 1962. Inventaire des oiseaux éteints ou en voie d'extinction conservés au Museum de Paris. Terre Vie 109:257–301.

KELLY, J. B., AND E. ROY. 1989. The status of Antigua's and Barbuda's wildlife, a mixed bag in habitat. Pages 14–18 in Wildlife management in the Caribbean islands. Proceedings of the Fourth Meeting of Caribbean Foresters (A. E. Lugo and L. B. Ford, Eds.). Institute of Tropical Forestry and Caribbean National Forest, Río Piedras, Puerto Rico.

KEPLER, C. B. 1971. Bird survey of St. Thomas (offshore islands) and St. John, Virgin Islands. Unpublished report, Patuxent Wildlife Research Center, Laurel, Maryland.

KEPLER, C. B. 1978. The breeding ecology of sea birds on Monito Island, Puerto Rico. Condor 80:72–87.

KEPLER, C. B., AND A. K. KEPLER. 1978. The sea–birds of Culebra and its adjacent islands, Puerto Rico. Living Bird 16:21–50.

KIDD, E. R. G. 1963. Black Tern. Gosse Bird Club Broads. No. 1:7.

KIDD, E. R. G. 1965. Brown Noddy. Gosse Bird Club Broads. No. 4:18.

KIDD, E. R. G. 1965. Sooty Tern. Gosse Bird Club Broads. No. 4:18.

KING, W. B., G. V. BYRD, J. J. HICKEY, C. B. KEPLER, W. POST, H. A. RAFFAELE, P. F. SPRINGER, H. F. SNYDER, C. M. WHITE, AND J. W. WILEY. 1976. Report of the American Ornithologists' Union Committee on Conservation 1975—76. Auk 93(4, Suppl.):1DD–19DD.

KING, W. B., AND A. T. FENN. 1967. A short Jamaican bird–watching tour. Gosse Bird Club Broads. No. 9:9–10.

KIRKCONNELL, A., O. H. GARRIDO, R. M. POSADA RODRIGUEZ, AND S. O. CUBILLAS. 1992. Los grupos tróficos en la avifauna cubana. Poeyana No. 415:1–21.

KIRKCONNELL, A., AND R. M. POSADA RODRIGUEZ. 1988. Adiciones a la fauna de Cayo Romano, Cuba. Misc. Zool., Inst. Zool. Acad. Cienc. Cuba 37:4.

KIRKCONNELL, A., R. M. POSADA RODRIGUEZ, V. BEROVIDES ALVAREZ, AND J. A. MORALES. 1993. Aves de Cayo Guillermo, Archipiélago Sabana–Camagüey, Cuba. Poeyana No. 430:1–7.

KNAPP, C. 1995. A flora and fauna survey of Guana Cay, with an emphasis on its rock iguana. Bahamas J. Sci. 2:2–7.

KNOX, J. P. 1852. A historical account of St. Thomas, West Indies, with ... incidental notices of St. Croix and St. Johns, etc. C. Scribner, New York.

KOHLER, B. F. 1964. Brown Pelican. Gosse Bird Club Broads. No. 2:16.

KOHLER, B. F. 1967. Behavior of some Jamaican birds. Gosse Bird Club Broads. No. 8:12.

LABASTILLE, A., AND M. RICHMOND. 1973. Birds and mammals of Anegada Island, British Virgin Islands. Caribb. J. Sci. 13:91–109.

LABAT, J. B. 1722. Nouveau voyage aux îsles de l'Amérique. Contenant l'histoire naturelle de ces pays, l'origine, les moeurs, la réligion & le gouvernement des habitants anciens & modernes: les guerres & les évènements singuliers qui y sont arrivez pendant le long séjour que l'auteur y a fait. Le commerce et les manufactures quey sont établies, 7 les moyens de les augmenter. Ouvrage enrichi d'un grand nombre de cartes, plans & figures en taille–douce. La Haye, P. Husson, Paris.

LACK, P. C., C. D. TAYLOR, AND E. K. DUNN [OXFORD UNIVERSITY EXPLORATION CLUB]. 1973. The Oxford expedition to Montserrat, 1973. Unpublished report, Oxford University, England.

LAFRESNAYE, F. de. 1844. Description de quelques oiseaux de la Guadeloupe. Rev. Zool. 7:167–169.

LABASTILLE, A., AND M. RICHMOND. 1973. Birds and mammals of Anegada Island, British Virgin Islands. Caribb. J. Sci. 13:91–109.

LAMB, G. R. 1957. On the endangered species of birds of the U. S. Virgin Islands. Research Report No. 2. Pan–American Section, International Committee for Bird Preservation, New York, NY.

LAMB, G. R. 1958. On the endangered species of birds in the U. S. Virgin Islands. Bull. Intern. Council Bird Preserv. 7:144–148.

LAWRENCE, G. N. 1862. Description of a new species of bird of the genus *Phaeton*, also of a new species of humming bird of the genus *Heliopaedica*. Ann. Lyceum Nat. Hist. N. Y. 7:142–145.

LAWRENCE, G. N. 1862. Notes on some Cuban birds, with descriptions of new species. Ann. Lyceum Nat. Hist. N. Y. 7:247–275.

LAWRENCE, G. N. 1867. Catalogue of birds collected at the island of Sombrero, W.I., with observations by A.A. Julien. Ann. Lyceum Nat. Hist. N. Y. 8:92–106.

LAWRENCE, G. N. 1877. A provisional list of the birds procured and noticed by Mr. Fred. A. Ober in the island of Dominica. For. Stream, New York 9:345.

LAWRENCE, G. N. 1879. Catalogue of the birds of Dominica from collections made for the Smithsonian Institution by Frederick A. Ober, together with his notes and observations. Proc. U. S. Nat. Mus. (1878) 1:48–69.

LAWRENCE, G. N. 1879. Catalogue of the birds of St. Vincent, from collections made by Mr. Fred. A. Ober, under the directions of the Smithsonian Institution, with his notes thereon. Proc. U. S. Nat. Mus. (1878) 1:185–198.

LAWRENCE, G. N. 1879. Catalogue of the birds of Antigua and Barbuda, from collections made for the Smithsonian Institution, by Mr. Fred A. Ober, with his observations. Proc. U. S. Nat. Mus. (1878) 1:232–242.

LAWRENCE, G. N. 1879. Catalogue of the birds of Grenada, from a collection made by Mr. Fred. A. Ober for the Smithsonian Institution, including others seen by him, but not obtained. Proc. U. S. Nat. Mus. (1878) 1:265–278.

LAWRENCE, G. N. 1879. Catalogue of the birds collected in Martinique by Mr. Fred. A. Ober for the Smithsonian Institution. Proc. U. S. Nat. Mus. (1878) 1:349–360.

LAWRENCE, G. N. 1879. Catalogue of a collection of birds obtained in Guadeloupe for the Smithsonian Institution, by Mr. Fred. A. Ober. Proc. U. S. Nat. Mus. (1878) 1:449–462.

LAWRENCE, G. N. 1879. A general catalogue of the birds noted from the islands of the Lesser Antilles visited by Mr. Fred. A. Ober; with a table showing their distribution, and those found in the United States. Proc. U. S. Nat. Mus. (1878) 1:486–488.

LAWRENCE, G. N. 1886. List of a few species of birds new to the fauna of Guadeloupe, West Indies, with a description of a new species of *Ceryle*. Proc. U. S. Nat. Mus. (1885) 8:621–625.

LAWRENCE, G. N. 1891. Description of a new subspecies of Cypselidae of the genus *Chaetura*, with a note on the diablotin. Auk 8(1):59–62.

LAZELL, J. D., Jr. 1967. The ternery on Aves Island in March. Condor 69:87–88.

LAZELL, J. D., Jr. 1964. The reptiles of Sombrero, West Indies. Copeia 1964:716–718.

LAZELL, J. D., Jr. 1981. Tropic birds. Virgin Islands 6:23.

LAZELL, J. 1986. A Guana guide: wildlife and natural history. The Conservation Agency and Guana Island Wildlife Sanctuary, Jamestown, Rhode Island.

LAZELL, J. 1989. Guana. A natural history guide. The Conservation Agency, Jamestown, Rhode Island.

LECK, C. F. 1972. U. S. Virgin Islands, St. Croix. Birding 4:281.

LECK, C. F. 1974. Avifauna of St. Croix. Pages 245–255 *in* Guidebook to the geology and ecology of some marine and terrestrial environments, St. Croix, U. S. Virgin Islands. Special Publication No. 5, West Indies Laboratory (H. G. Multer and L. C. Gerhard, Eds.). Fairleigh Dickinson University, Madison, New Jersey.

LECK, C. F. 1975. Notes on unusual and rare birds of St. Croix. Condor 77:107.

LECK, C. F., AND R. L. NORTON. 1991. An annotated checklist of the birds of the U. S. Virgin Islands. Antilles Press, Christiansted, St. Croix.

LEE, D. S., AND M. K. CLARK. 1994. Seabirds of the Exuma Land and Sea Park. Bahamas J. Sci. 2:2–9.

LEE, D. S., AND M. K. CLARK. 1995. Seabirds of the Bahamas Land and Sea Park, Part 2. Bahamas J. Sci. 2:15–21.

LEE, D. S., O. H. GARRIDO, R. W. DICKERMAN, AND J. C. HANEY. 1993. Reassessment of Black–capped Petrel in Cuba. Pitirre 6(1):4.

LEE, D. S., AND N. VINA. 1993. A re-evaluation of the status of the endangered Black–capped Petrel, *Pterodroma hasitata*, in Cuba. Ornitol. Neotrop. 4:99–101.

LEE, G. C. 1990. Puerto Rico's Least Tern status survey. Pitirre 3(3):8.

LE FAUCHEUX, O. 1953. Quelques observations ornithologiques dans l'océan Atlantique. Oiseau Rev. Fr. Ornithol. 23:303–304.

LEMBEYE, J. 1850. Aves de la isla de Cuba. Imprenta del Tiempo, La Habana.

LESSON, R. P. 1828. Manuel d'ornithologie ou description des genres et des principales espèces d'oiseaux. Roret, Paris.

LESSON, R. P. 1847. Oeuvres Complètes de Buffon aves la nomenclatum linnéenne et la classification de Cuvier. Revues sur l'édition in –4o de l'Imprimerie royale annotées par M. Flourens. Vol. 20. Garnier Frères, Paris.

LEVY, C. 1987. 1987 diary of nests & juveniles. Gosse Bird Club Broads. No. 49:2–6.

LEVY, C. 1988. Observations on the effects of Hurricane Gilbert on bird–life in Jamaica: St. Andrew (Seymour Lands). Gosse Bird Club Broads. No. 51:3–5.

LEVY, C. 1988. Birds at Treasure Beach, Mar. 26–29, 1988. Gosse Bird Club Broads. No. 51:10–11.

LEVY, C. 1990. Laughing Gulls. Gosse Bird Club Broads. No. 54:20.

LEVY, C. 1991. Christmas bird count – 1990. Gosse Bird Club Broads. No. 56:5–8.

LEVY, C. 1991. Goat Island. Gosse Bird Club Broads. No. 56:20.

LEVY, C. 1992. Christmas count 1991. Gosse Bird Club Broads. No. 58:4–6.

LEVY, C. 1993. Christmas Bird Count – 1992. Gosse Bird Club Broads. No. 60:18–19.

LEVY, C. [Editor]. 1993. [Recoveries and recaptures in Jamaica]. Gosse Bird Club Broads. No. 60:24.

[LEVY, C.] 1994. Christmas Bird Count 1993. Gosse Bird Club Broads. No. 62:13.

LEVY, C., AND L. DOUGLAS. 1996. Christmas Bird Count 1995. Gosse Bird Club Broads. No. 66:18–19.

LEVY, C. 1990. Report on recent activities made to the Inaugural Meeting November 15, 1989. Gosse Bird Club Broads. No. 54:2–5.

LEWIS, C. B. 1940. Report on the decline in the yield of booby eggs on Pedro and Morant cays, with recommendations for conservation. Institute of Jamaica internal report, Kingston.

LEWIS, C. B. 1942. Booby eggs. Nat. Hist. Notes Nat. Hist. Soc. Jamaica 1:4–5.

LEWIS, C. B. 1947. A trip to the Morant and Pedro cays. Nat. Hist. Notes Nat. Hist. Soc. Jamaica 3:105–108.

LEWIS, C. B. 1948. [Terns]. Nat. Hist. Notes Nat. Hist. Soc. Jamaica 3:203.

LEWIS, C. B. 1948. The history of the Pedro and Morant Cays. Jamaica Hist. Review 1:302–309.

LEWIS, C. B. 1949. Booby eggs. Pages 34–36 in Glimpses of Jamaican Natural History (C. B. Lewis and C. Swabey, Eds.). Institute of Jamaica, Kingston. (vol. 1)

[LEWIS, C. B.] 1951. The Cahow. Nat. Hist. Notes Nat. Hist. Soc. Jamaica 5:6,8.

LEWIS, C. B. 1954. Bird notes. Nat. Hist. Notes Nat. Hist. Soc. Jamaica 6:155.

LEWIS, C. B. 1961. Caspian Terns in Jamaica. Auk 78(2):264–265.

LEWIS, C. B. 1970. Brown Pelican. Gosse Bird Club Broads. No. 14:22–23

LIGON, R. 1673. A True & Exact History of the Island of Barbadoes. Illustrated with a Map of the Island, as also the Principal Trees and Plants there, set forth in their due Proportions and Shapes, drawn out by their several and respective Scales. Together with the Ingenio that makes the Sugar, with the Plots of the several Houses, Rooms, and other places, that are used in the whole process of Sugar–making; viz the Grinding–room, the Boyling–room, the Filling–room, the Curing–house, Still–house, and Furnaces; All cut in Copper. P. Parker and T. Guy, London.

LINCOLN, F. C. 1936. Returns of banded birds: third paper (Some recoveries of water birds from Latin America). Bird–Banding 7:139–148.

LINCOLN, F. C. 1940. Caspian Tern in Haiti. Auk 57(4):569.

LLANES SOSA, A., A. KIRKCONNELL, R. M. POSADA RODRIGUEZ, AND S. CUBILLAS. 1987. Aves de Cayo Saetía, archipiélago de Camagüey, Cuba. Misc. Zool., Inst. Zool. Acad. Cienc. Cuba 35:3–4.

LÖNNBERG, E. 1929. Några ord om en samling fåglar från Haiti. Fauna Flora (Stockh.) 3:97–112.

LOWE, P. R. 1909. Notes on some birds collected during a cruise in the Caribbean Sea. Ibis 3:304–347.

LOWE, P. R. 1911. On the birds of the Cayman Islands, West Indies. Ibis 9 5:137–161.

LOWERY, G. H., Jr., AND R. J. NEWMAN. 1954. The birds of the Gulf of Mexico. Pages 519–540 in Gulf of Mexico, its origin, waters and marine life (P. S. Gatesoff, Ed.). Fishery Bulletin 89. U. S. Department of the Interior, Fishery Bulletin of the Fish and Wildlife Service, Vol. 55, Washington, D. C.

LUDWIG, F. E. 1942. Migration of Caspian Terns banded in the Great Lakes area. Bird–Banding 13:1–9.

LUDWIG, J. P. 1965. Biology and structure of the Caspian Tern (Hydroprogne caspia) population of the Great Lakes from 1896–1964. Bird–Banding 36:217–233.

MACHADO, J. G. 1972. Magnificent Frigatebird. Gosse Bird Club Broads. No. 19:22.

MADDISON, P. R. 1977. White–tailed Tropicbirds at Hector's River. Gosse Bird Club Broads. No. 28:17–18.

MADDISON, P., AND A. MADDISON. 1977. White–tailed Tropicbird. Gosse Bird Club Broads. No. 28:23.

MADDISON, P, AND A. MADDISON. 1977. Bridled Tern. Gosse Bird Club Broads. No. 28:25.

MADDISON, P., AND A. MADDISON. 1977. Common Tern. Gosse Bird Club Broads. No. 28:25.

MADDISON, P., AND A. MADDISON. 1977. Laughing Gull. Gosse Bird Club Broads. No. 28:25.

MADDISON, P., AND A. MADDISON. 1977. Sandwich Tern. Gosse Bird Club Broads. No. 28:25.

MADDISON, P., AND A. MADDISON. 1977. Sooty Tern. Gosse Bird Club Broads. No. 28:25.

MADDISON, P., AND A. MADDISON. 1977. Least Tern. Gosse Bird Club Broads. No. 29:14.

MANNING, C. J. 1896. Ueber den vogelzug auf Barbados im jahre 1886. Ornis Int. z. gesam. Ornithol. 8:365–372.

MANON ARREDONDO, M. de J. 1968. Gaviotas y ratas. Listin Diario, supl. del 12 Mayo 1968.

MANSER, P. 1990. White–tailed Tropicbird. Gosse Bird Club Broads. No. 56:21.

MARCH, E. W. 1948. [Magnificent Frigatebird]. Nat. Hist. Notes Nat. Hist. Soc. Jamaica 3:172.

MARSDEN, H. W. 1887. Nidification of the noddy and sooty terns in the West Indies. Zoologist 3 11:429–430.

MASON, C. R. 1945. Pelican travels. Bird–Banding 16:134–143.

MASON, C. R. 1964. Grand Bahama Island. Fl. Nat. 37:116.

MATHEWS, G. M. 1915. Phaëthon catesbyi Brandt. Auk 32(2):195–197.

MAYNARD, C. J. 1889. Notes on certain West Indian birds. Bull. Newton Nat. Hist. Soc. 1:35–46.

MAYNARD, C. J. 1889. Description of a supposed new species of gannet (Sula coryi) from Little Cayman. Contr. Sci. 1:40–48.

MAYNARD, C. J. 1889. Description of a supposed new species of gannet (Sula coryi) from Little Cayman. Contr. Sci. 1:51–57.

MAYNARD, C. J. 1889. On the probable evolution of the totipalmate birds, pelicans, gannets, etc. Contr. Sci. 1:82–88.

MAYNARD, C. J. 1889. Breeding habits of the Bridled Tern. Oölogist 6:7–8.

MAYNARD, C. J. 1889. Description of a supposed new species of gannet. Ornitholog. Oologist 14:40–41.

MAYNARD, C. J. 1889. Observations on Cory's Gannet. Ornitholog. Oologist 14:59.

MAYNARD, C. J. 1890. Notes on West Indian birds. Contr. Sci. 1:171–181.

MAYNARD, C. J. 1896. The birds of eastern North America; with original descriptions of all the species which occur east of the Mississippi River, between the Arctic Circle and the Gulf of Mexico, with full notes upon their habits, etc, Revised ed. C. J. Maynard & Co., Newtonville, Massachussets.

MAYNARD, C. J. 1898. A catalogue of the birds of the West Indies which do not occur elsewhere in North America north of Mexico. Published by the author, Newtonville, Massachussetts.

MAYNARD, C. J. 1899. The man–of–war bird and Cory's gannet. Nat. Study Schools 1:229–243.

MAYNARD, C. J. 1918. Notes on some remarkable birds. Records Walks Talks Nature 10:20–25, 34–38, 40–46, 48–51.

MAYNARD, C. J. 1919. Some remarkable birds. Records Walks Talks Nature 11:4–7, 10–16, 19–20, 49–53, 55–57, 153–156.

MAYNARD, C. J. 1920. Bahama gulls and terns. Records Walks Talks Nature 12:155–157.

MAYR, E. 1953. Additional notes on the birds of Bimini, Bahamas. Auk 70(4):499–501.

MCATEE, W. L. 1945. Catesby's Tropic–bird. Auk 62(1):137–139.

MCCANDLESS, J. B. 1961. Bird life in southwestern Puerto Rico. I. Fall migration. Caribb. J. Sci. 1:3–12.

MCCANDLESS, J. B. 1962. Birdlife in southwestern Puerto Rico. II. The winter season. Caribb. J. Sci. 2:27–39.

MCKENZIE, P. M., W. C. BARROW, Jr., J. COLLAZO, AND C. A. STAICER. 1990. First summer record of the Common Black–headed Gull for Puerto Rico. Am. Birds 44(5):1092–1093.

MEIER, A. J., R. E. NOBLE, AND H. A. RAFFAELE. 1989. The birds of Desecheo Island, Puerto Rico, including a new record for Puerto Rican territory. Caribb. J. Sci. 25:24–29.

MELZER, J. P. 1935. Another Common Tern recovery in Puerto Rico. Bird–Banding 6:69.

MILLER, J. R. 1978. Notes on birds of San Salvador Island (Watlings), the Bahamas. Auk 95(2):281–287.

MILLS, H. N. 1989. Wildlife management in St. Kitts. Pages 53–62 in Wildlife management in the Caribbean islands. Proceedings of the Fourth Meeting of Caribbean Foresters (A. E. Lugo and L. B. Ford, Eds.). Institute of Tropical Forestry and Caribbean National Forest, Río Piedras, Puerto Rico.

MIRECKI, D. N., J. M. HUTTON, C. M. PANNELL, T. J. STOWE, AND R. W. UNITE. 1977. Report of the Cambridge Ornithological Expedition to the British Virgin Islands 1976. Churchill College, Cambridge.

MOFFATT, E. M. 1972. Magnificent Frigatebird. Gosse Bird Club Broads. No. 19:22.

MOHAN, D. 1982. Birdwatching at Yallahs Pond. Gosse Bird Club Broads. No. 39:9.

MOLTONI, E. 1929. Primo Elenco degli Uccelli dell'Isola di Haiti. Atti Soc. Ital. Sci. Nat. Mus. Civ. Stor. Nat. Milano 68:306–326.

MONTAÑEZ HUGUEZ, L., V. BEROVIDES ALVAREZ, A. SAMPEDRO MARIN, AND L. MUGICA VALDÉS. 1985. Vertebrados del embalse "Leonero", Provincia Granma. Misc. Zool., Inst. Zool. Acad. Cienc. Cuba 25:1–2.

MOODY, C. 1991. Least Tern. Gosse Bird Club Broads. No. 57:21.

MOORE, A. G. 1985. Winter status of birds on Grand Cayman Island. Bull. Br. Ornithol. Club 105:8–17.

MOORE, N. B. 1878. List of birds, chiefly visitors from N. America, seen and killed in the Bahamas in July, Aug., Oct., Nov., and Dec., 1876. Proc. Boston Soc. Nat. Hist. 19:241–243.

MOHAN, D. 1982. Birdwatching at Yallahs Pond. Gosse Bird Club Broads. No. 39:9.

MORALES LEAL, J., AND O. H. GARRIDO. 1988. Nuevo estercorario (Aves: Stercorariinae) para Cuba. Misc. Zool., Inst. Zool. Acad. Cienc. Cuba 39:3–4.

MORALES LEAL, J. de la C., AND O. H. GARRIDO. 1996. Aves y reptiles de Cayo Sabinal, Archipiélago de Sabana–Camagüey, Cuba. Pitirre 9(3):9–11.

MORALES LEAL, J. de la C., E. SUARES FALCON, A. CARDONA FUENTES, AND V. BEROVIDES ALVAREZ. 1991. Conducta reproductiva y nidificacion del Rabihorcado (*Fregata magnificens*). Rev. Biol. 5:3–8.

MOREAU DE SAINT–MÉRY, M. L. E. 1796. Description topographique et politique de la partie Espagnole de l'île de Saint–Domingue; avec des observations générales sur le climat, la population, les productions, le caractere & les moeurs des habitans de cette colonie, & un tableau raisonné des differentes parties de son administration; acccompagnée d'une nouvelle carte de la totalité de l'île. Printed and sold by the author, Philadelphia.

MOREAU DE SAINT–MÉRY, M. L. E. 1797–1798. Description topographique, physique, civile, politique et historique de la partie Française de l'île Saint–Dominigue. avec des observations générales sur sa population, sur le caractère & les moeurs de ses divers habitans; sur son climat, sa culture, ses productions, son administration, &c. &c. Accompagnées des détails les plus propres à faire connaître l'état de cette colonie à l'epoque du 18 Octobre 1789; et d'une nouvelle carte de la totalité de l'île. Chez DuPont/Soc. Francaise d'Histoire d'Outre–mer, Paris.

MORENO, J. A., N. I. PEREZ, AND A. GARCIA–MOLL. 1980. Management plan for the seabirds and shorebirds of Puerto Rico. Division of Coastal Resources and Wildlife Planning, San Juan.

MORENO, J. A. 1980. Wildlife management considerations for La Cordillera with recommendations for other areas in northeast Puerto Rico. Department of Natural Resources, San Juan, Puerto Rico.

MORENO BONILLA, A. 1946. Notas ornitologicas. Mem. Soc. Cubana Hist. Nat. "Felipe Poey" 18:185–188.

MORGAN, A. 1993. Effects of habitat manipulation on the waterbird populations of Hellshire. Gosse Bird Club Broads. No. 60:16–17.

MORGAN, A. 1993. Black Tern. Gosse Bird Club Broads. No. 61:18.

MORGAN, G. S. 1977. Late Pleistocene fossil vertebrates from the Cayman Islands, British West Indies. Master's Thesis, University of Florida, Gainseville.

MORGAN, G. S. 1985. Taxonomic status and relationships of the Swan Island hutia, *Geocapromys thoracatus* (Mammalia: Rodentia: Capromyidae), and the zoogeography of the Swan Island vertebrate fauna. Proc. Biol. Soc. Wash. 98:29–46.

MORITZ, C. 1836. Notizen zur fauna der insel Puertorico. Wiegmann's Arch. für Naturg. 2:373–392.

MORRIS, S. 1967. The birds of South Cay. Gosse Bird Club Broads. No. 9:5–6.

MORRIS, M. M. J., AND R. E. LEMON. 1982. The effects of development on the avifauna of St. Kitts, W. I. Report prepared for the Sub–committee on Wildlife and Natural History of the St. Kitts – Nevis National Heritage Trust, by McGill University, Montreal, Quebec.

MORRIS, R. D., AND J. W. CHARDINE. 1989. Some preliminary observations on age of first breeding, survival rates, and mate/site fidelity in a tropical seabird: the Brown Noody. Colon. Waterbird Soc. Newsl. 13:25.

MORRIS, R. D., AND J. W. CHARDINE. 1990. The breeding biology and feeding ecology of Brown Noddies. 20th International Ornithological Congress, Christchurch, New Zealand.

MORRIS, R. D., AND J. W. CHARDINE. 1990. Costs of parental neglect in the Brown Noddy (*Anous stolidus*). Can. J. Zool. 68:2025–2027.

MORRIS, R. D., AND J. W. CHARDINE. 1990. Brown Noddies in Culebra: trends in breeding biology 1985–1990. Colon. Waterbird Soc. Newsl. 14:22.

MORRIS, R. D., AND J. W. CHARDINE. 1991. Recent trends in breeding and survival of Brown Noddies nesting near Culebra, PR. Colon. Waterbird Soc. Newsl. 15:32.

MORRIS, R. D., AND J. W. CHARDINE. 1992. The breeding biology and aspects of the feeding ecology of Brown Noddies *Anous stolidus* nesting near Culebra, Puerto Rico, 1985–1989. J. Zool. (Lond.) 226:65–79.

MORRIS, R. D., AND J. W. CHARDINE. 1995. Brown Noddies on Cayo Noroeste, Culebra, Puerto Rico: what happened in 1990? Auk 112(2):326–334.

MORTENSEN, T. N. 1909. Dyrelivet Dansk Vestindien. Atlanten Medlemsblan fur Foreningen. Dan. Atlanterhavsuer. 5:639–651.

MORTENSEN, T. 1910. Fuglelivet paa de Dansk–Vestindiske Oer. Dan. Ornithol. Foren. Tidsskr. 3:151–161.

MORTIMER, C. 1732. A continuation of an account of an Essay towards a natural history of Carolina and the Bahama Islands, by Mark Catesby, F.R.S. with some extracts out of the fifth set. Philos. Trans. (Royal Soc. Lond.) 37:447–450.

MÖRZER BRUYNS, W. F. J. 1967. Black–capped Petrels (*Pterodroma hasitata*) in the Caribbean. Ardea 55:144–145.

MOTT, S. 1977. St. John, Virgin Islands. Birding 9:264(w).

MUDD, S. H., AND M. H. MUDD. 1973. White–tailed Tropic Bird colony near Ocho Rios. Gosse Bird Club Broads. No. 21:6–8.

MUDD, S. H., AND M. H. MUDD. 1974. White–tailed Tropicbird colony revisited. Gosse Bird Club Broads. No. 23:12–13.

MUGICA VALDÉS, L., AND M. ACOSTA CRUZ. 1992. Breve caracterización de la comunidad de aves de Cayo Largo y Cayo Hicacos (grupo insular de los Canarreos). Cienc. Biol. Acad. Cienc. Cuba No. 25:20–29.

MURPHY, R. C. 1915. The Atlantic range of Leach's Petrel (*Oceanodroma leucorhoa* (Vieillot)). Auk 32(2):170–173.

MURPHY, R. C., AND W. VOGT. 1933. The Dovekie influx of 1932. Auk 50(3):325–349.

NARANJO, L. G. 1979. Las aves marinas del Caribe colombiano: taxonomía, zoogeografía y anotaciones ecológicas. Tesis de grado inédita, Universidad de Bogotá Jorege Tadeo Lozano thesis, Bogotá.

NATURAL HISTORY SOCIETY OF JAMAICA. 1945. Glimpses of Jamaican natural history. Institute of Jamaica, Kingston.

NATURAL HISTORY SOCIETY OF JAMAICA. VOL. I. 1949. Glimpses of Jamaican Natural History, Second ed. Institute of Jamaica, Kingston.

NEGRON GONZALEZ, L., R. A. PÉREZ–RIVERA, AND F. CUEVAS VERGARA. 1984. Evaluacion ecologica del sistema estuarino–lagunar de Humacao como habitaculo de Vida Silvestre. Pages 63–89 in Memorias del quinto simposio de la fauna de Puerto Rico y El Caribe (E. Ortiz Corp's, R. A. Pérez–Rivera, M. E. Rivera Rosa, and A. M. del Llano, Eds.). Universidad de Puerto Rico, Humacao.

NELLIS, D. W. 1984. Status of the breeding pelicaniformes in the U. S. Virgin Islands. Colon. Waterbirds Group Newsl. 8:28.

[NELLIS, D.] 1985. Breeding age and recruitment of Sooty Terns (*Sterna fuscata fuscata*) on the Eastern Puerto Rico Bank. Unpublished report, Virgin Islands Division of Fish and Wildlife, St. Thomas.

NELLIS, D., AND R. H. BOULON. 1985 [?]. Nest habitat manipulation of the Blue–faced Booby. Unpublished report, Virgin Islands Division of Fish and Wildlife, Study FW–3–IIG 1981–1985, St. Thomas.

NELLIS, D. W., AND J. PIERCE. 1990. Brown Booby nesting 1 October 1985 – 30 September 1990. Final report, Virgin Islands Wildlife Restoration Project W–5, Study II, St. Thomas, U. S. Virgin Islands.

NELLIS, D. W., J. PIERCE, AND C. AMRANI. 1989. Brown Booby (*Sula leucogaster*) nesting habitat preference and reproductive success at Frenchcap Cay, US Virgin Islands. Colon. Waterbird Soc. Newsl. 13:25.

NEWTON, A., AND E. NEWTON. 1859. Observations on the birds of St. Croix, West Indies, made between February 20th and August 6th, 1857 by Alfred Newton, and, between March 4th and September 28th, 1858 by Edward Newton. Ibis 1:365–379.

NEWTON, I., AND L. C. DALE. 1996. Bird migration at different latitudes in eastern North America. Auk 113(3):626–635.

NEWTON, R. 1953. Terns (various). Nat. Hist. Notes Nat. Hist. Soc. Jamaica 6:36.

NICHOLS, J. T. 1913. Notes on offshore birds. Auk 30(4):505–511.

NICHOLS, J. T. 1916. Limicolae at Porto Rico in July. Auk 33(3):320–321.

NICHOLS, R. A. 1943. The breeding birds of St. Thomas and St. John, Virgin Islands. Mem. Soc. Cubana Hist. Nat. "Felipe Poey" 17:23–37.

NICOLL, M. J. 1904. On a collection of birds made during the cruise of the 'Valhalla,' R.Y.S., in the West Indies (1903–4). Ibis 4:555–591.

NISBET, I. C. T. 1980. Status and trends of the Roseate Tern *Sterna dougallii*) in North America and the Caribbean, Vol. 3. Unpublished report to U. S. Fish and Wildlife Service, Office of Endangered Species, Massachusetts Audubon Society, Lincoln, Massachusetts.

NISBET, I. C. T. 1981. Biological characteristics of the Roseate Tern *Sterna dougallii*. U. S. Fish and Wildlife Service.

NISBET, I. C. T. 1984. Migration and winter quarters of North American Roseate Terns as shown by banding recoveries. J. Field Ornithol. 55:1–17.

NOBLE, G. K. 1916. The resident birds of Guadeloupe. Bull. Mus. Comp. Zool. 60:359–396.

NORTHROP, J. I. 1891. The birds of Andros Island, Bahamas. Auk 8(1):64–80.

NORTHROP, J. I. 1910. A naturalist in the Bahamas. October 12, 1861–June 25, 1891. A memorial volume edited with a biographical introduction by Henry Fairfield Osborn. Columbia University Press, New York.

NORTON, R. L. 1979. New records of birds for the Virgin Islands. Am. Birds 33(2):145–146.

NORTON, R. L. 1984. Cayene x Sandwich terns nesting in Virgin Islands, Greater Antilles. J. Field Ornithol. 55:243–246.

NORTON, R. L. 1984. Distribution and population status of Sterninae in the American Virgin Islands. Colon. Waterbirds Group Newsl. 8:39.

NORTON, R. L. 1985. Effects of habitat manipulation on Sooty Terns (*Sterna fuscata*) in the Virgin Islands. Unpublished report, Virgin Islands Division of Fish and Wildlife, St. Thomas.

NORTON, R. L. 1986. United States Virgin Islands. Pages 585–586 *in* A directory of neotropical wetlands (D. A. Scott and M. Carbonell, Eds.). Conservation Monitoring Service, International Union for Conservation of Nature and Natural Resources, Cambridge, and International Wildfowl Research Bureau, Slimbridge, United Kingdom.

NORTON, R. L. 1986. Case of botulism in Laughing Gulls at a landfill in the Virgin Islands, Greater Antilles. Fl. Field Nat. 14:97–98.

NORTON, R. L. 1986. Recoveries of Sooty Terns (*Sterna fuscata*) on Saba Cay, St. Thomas, U. S. Virgin Islands. J. Field Ornithol. 57:226–228.

NORTON, R. L. 1986. Climatic influences on seabird populations of the tropical Western Atlantic. Pac. Seabird Group Bull. 13:44.

NORTON, R. L. 1987. Climate influences on breeding seabirds of the eastern Puerto Rico Bank. Proc. Segundo Simposio Anual de la Sociedad Ornitologia de Puerto Rico.

NORTON, R. L. 1988. The density and relative abundance of Pelecaniformes on the eastern Puerto Rico Bank in December 1982. Caribb. J. Sci. 24:28–31.

NORTON, R. L. 1988. Extra–egg clutches and interspecific egg–dumping of the Roseate Tern (*Sterna dougallii*) in the West Indies. Fl. Field Nat. 16:67–70.

NORTON, R. L. 1989. First West Indian record of the Black Noddy and nesting of Masked Booby at Sombrero Island, Lesser Antilles. Colon. Waterbirds 12:120–122.

NORTON, R. L. 1993. Avifauna of Little San Salvador, Bahamas. Fl. Field Nat. 21:16–17.

NORTON, R. L., R. M. CHIPLEY, AND J. D. LAZELL, Jr. 1989. A contribution to the ornithology of the British Virgin Islands. Caribb. J. Sci. 25:115–118.

NORTON, R. L., AND N. V. CLARKE. 1989. Additions to the birds of the Turks and Caicos Islands. Fl. Field Nat. 17:32–39.

NORTON, R. L., AND R. TEYTAUN. 1992. Bird study on St. John, U. S. Virgin Islands. Ornitol. Caribeña 3:4–9.

NOSEL, J. 1994. Parc Naturel Regional de la Martinique. Pitirre 7(3):11.

NUTTING, C. C. 1895. Narrative and preliminary report of Bahama Expedition. Bull. Lab. Nat. Hist. State Univ. Iowa 3:1–251.

OBER, F. A. 1880. Camps in the Caribbees. Lee and Shepard, Publishers, Boston.

OBER, F. A. 1899. Camps in the Caribbees: the adventures of a naturalist in the Lesser Antilles, 2nd ed. Lee and Shepard, Publishers, Boston.

OEXMELIN, A.–O. 1775. Histoire des aventuriers filibustiers qui se sont signalés dans les Indes, contenant ce qu'ils y ont fait de remarquable, avec la vie, les moeurs & les coutumes des boucaniers, & des habitans de St. Domingue & de la Tortue; une description exacte de ces lieux, & un état des offices, tant ecclésiastiques que séculiers, & ce que les grands princes de l'Europe y possèdent. Nouvelle ed. Atrevoux, par la Compagnie.

OGDEN, N. B., W. B. GLADFELTER, J. C. OGDEN, AND E. H. GLADFELTER. 1985. Marine and terrestrial flora and fauna notes on Sombrero Island in the Caribbean. Atoll Res. Bull. No. 292:61–74.

OGILVIE–GRANT, W. R. 1898. [Remarks on tropicbirds]. Bull. Br. Ornithol. Club 7:23–24.

OLSON, S. L. 1978. A paleontological perspective of West Indian birds and mammals. Pages 99–117 *in* Special Publication, No. 13: Zoogeography in the Caribbean (F. B. Gill, Ed.). Academy of Natural Science of Philadelphia, Philadelphia.

OLSON, S. L. 1982. Biological archeology in the West Indies. Fl. Anthropol. 35:162–168.

OLSON, S. L., AND W. B. HILGARTNER. 1982. Fossil and subfossil birds from the Bahamas. Pages 22–56 *in* Fossil vertebrates from the Bahamas. Smithsonian Contributions in Paleobiology 48 (S. L. Olson, Ed.). Smithsonian Institution Press, Washington, D. C.

OLSON, S. L., H. F. JAMES, AND C. A. MEISTER. 1981. Winter field notes and specimen weights of Cayman Island birds. Bull. Br. Ornithol. Club 101:339–346.

OLSON, S. L., G. K. PREGILL, AND W. B. HILGARTNER. 1990. Studies on fossil and extant vertebrates from San Salvador (Watling's) Island, Bahamas. Smithson. Contrib. Zool. 508:1–15.

ORBIGNY, A. D. d'. 1839. [Mamiferos y] Aves [de la Isla de Cuba]. Page 220 *in* Historia fisica politica y natural de la isla de Cuba. Segunda parte. Historia natural, Vol. 3 (R. de la Sagra, Ed.). Arthus Bertrand, Librero de la Sociedad de Geografia, Paris.

ORBIGNY, A. D. d'. 1839. Ornithologie [de l'île de Cuba]. Page 336 *in* Histoire physique, politique et naturelle de l'Ile de Cuba. 1839–56 [i.e., 1857], Vol. 3 (R. de la Sagra, Ed.). Arthus Bertrand, Paris. (32 color plates).

ORTEGA RICAURTE, D. 1941. Los cayos colombianos de Caribe. Bol. Soc. Geograf. Colombia 7:279–291.

OSBORNE, D. R. 1993. Nest site selection in Least Terns (*Sterna antillarum*). Pages 97–102 *in* Proceedings of the fourth symposium on the natural history of the Bahamas (W. H. Eshbaugh, Ed.). Bahamian Field Station, Ltd., San Salvador, Bahama Islands.

OTTENWALDER, J. A. 1979. Aves de la Isla Alto Velo. Pages 161–162 *in* Naturalista Postal 1976–1979, NP–15/79, Carta Ocasional del Herbario USD (J. Cicero, Ed.). Universidad Autonoma de Santo Domingo, Santo Domingo.

OTTENWALDER, J. A. 1979. Una visita a la Isla Alto Velo. Zoodom 3:20–31.

OTTENWALDER, J. A. 1982. Primer reistro del Rabijunco de Pico Rojo, *Phaeton aethereus*, (Phaethontidae: Pelecaniformes) en la Republica Dominicana. Nat. Postal 82:1–2.

OTTENWALDER, J. A. 1992. Recovery plan for the Black–capped Petrel (*Pterodroma hasitata*) in southern Haiti. Prepared for the Macaya National Park Project/University of Florida, MacArthur Foundation, and USAID/Haiti, Gainesville, Florida.

OTTENWALDER, J. A., AND T. A. VARGAS MORA. 1981. Nueva localidad para el Diabotin en la Republica Dominicana. Pages 185–186 *in* Naturalista Postal 1976–1979, NP–36/79, Carta Ocasional del Herbario USDA (E. de J. Marcano F. and J. Cicero, Eds.). Universidad Autonoma de Santo Domingo, Santo Domingo.

OVIEDO Y VALDÉS, G. F. de. 1526. De la natural hystoria de las Indias. Remón de Petras, Toledo.

OVIEDO Y VALDÉS, G. F. de. 1851–55. Historia general y natural de las Indias, islas y tierra firme del Mar Océano. Imprenta de la Real Academia de la Historia, Madrid, Spain.

PARKES, K. C. 1952. Taxonomic notes on the Laughing Gull. Proc. Biol. Soc. Wash. 65:193–195.

PATERSON, A. 1968. The birds of Fresh Creek. Fl. Nat. 41:117–118, 120.

PATERSON, A. 1968. New species records for the Bahamas. Bull. Br. Ornithol. Club 88:109–110.

PAULSON, D. R. 1966. New records of birds from the Bahama Islands. Notulae Naturae, Acad. Nat. Sci. Philadelphia 394:1–15.

PAULSON, D. R., G. H. ORIANS, AND C. F. LECK. 1969. Notes on birds of Isla San Andrés. Auk 86(4):755–758.

PAYNTER, R. A., Jr. 1947. The fate of banded Kent Island Herring Gulls. Bird–Banding 18:156–170.

PAYNTER, R. A., Jr. 1956. Birds of the Swan Islands. Wilson Bull. 68:103–110.

PEÑA FRANJUL, M. 1978. Investigacion de seis (6) habitats de la fauna autoctoma Dominicana. III. Laguna Salada. Zoodom 1:51–98.

PENNYCUICK, C. J., F. C. SCHAFFNER, M. R. FULLER, H. H. OBRECHT III, AND L. STERNBERG. 1990. Foraging flights of the White–tailed Tropicbird (*Phaethon lepturus*): radiotracking and doubly–labelled water. Colon. Waterbirds 13:96–102.

PÉREZ–RIVERA, R. A. 1979. Lista revisada de los animales vulnerables, amenazados o en peligro de extinción en Puerto Rico. Cuadernos de La Revista Cayey No. 3, Universidad de Puerto Rico, Cayey.

PÉREZ–RIVERA, R. A. 1981. Algunos de los problemas que podrían causar los exóticos que han alcanzado el estado silvestre en Puerto Rico. Pages 35–46 *in* Memorias del Segundo Coloquio sobre la Fauna de Puerto Rico (L. O. Nieves Rivera, R. A. Pérez–Rivera, G. Malavé Gutiérrez, C. Goenaga Portela, and M. E. Rivera Rosa, Eds.). Colegio Universitario dc Humacao, Humacao, Puerto Rico.

PÉREZ–RIVERA, R. A. 1983. Nuevos informes y comentarios sobre las aves de la Isla de Mona. Science–Ciencia 10:97–101.

PÉREZ–RIVERA, R. A. 1984. Aspects of the reproductive ecology of the White–tailed Tropicbird on Mona Island. Colon. Waterbirds Group Newsl. 8:38.

PÉREZ–RIVERA, R. A. 1987. Additional records and notes on migratory water birds in Puerto Rico, West Indies. Caribb. J. Sci. 23:368–372.

PÉREZ–RIVERA, R. A., AND G. BONILLA. 1982. Los huracanes: algunos de sus efectos sobre aves en Puerto Rico, incluyendo sus patrones de comportamiento. Pages 123–135 *in* Memorias del Tercer Simposio sobre la Fauna de Puerto Rico (L. O. Nievas Rivera and R. A. Pérez–Rivera, Eds.). Universidad de Puerto Rico, Humacao.

PÉREZ–RIVERA, R. A., AND L. MIRANDA. 1994. Corroboración de algunos registros de aves para Puerto Rico. Pitirre 7(1):2–3.

PETERS, J. L. 1917. Birds of the northern coast of the Dominican Republic. Bull. Mus. Comp. Zool. 61:391–426.

PETERS, J. L. 1927. Birds of the island of Anguilla, West Indies. Auk 44(4):532–538.

PHILIBOSIAN, R. 1975. Census of nesting birds in the Virgin Islands. Unpublished report, St. Croix.

PHILIPON, A. 1931. Note sur une Fregate marine. Oiseau Rev. Fr. Ornithol. 1:724.

PHILIPSON, W. R. 1940. Notes on birds seen on a voyage to the West Indies and back. Br. Birds 33:245–247.

PIERCE, J. 1990. Effects of Hurricane Hugo on cay–nesting avifauna in the U. S. Virgin Islands. Colon. Waterbird Soc. Newsl. 14:23.

PIERCE, J. 1991. Red–billed Tropicbird breeding in the United States Virgin Islands. Colon. Waterbird Soc. Newsl. 15:33.

PINCHON, P. R. 1953. Aperçu sur l'avifaune de la Désirade (Dépendence de la Guadeloupe). Oiseau Rev. Fr. Ornithol. 23:161–170.

PINCHON, P. R. 1961. Deuxième note complémentaire sur l'avifaune des Antilles Françaises. Oiseau Rev. Fr. Ornithol. 31:85–99.

PINCHON, P. R. 1963. Faune des Antilles Françaises.–Les oiseaux. Muséum National d'Histoire Naturelle, Fort–de–France, Martinique.

PINCHON, P. R., AND M. BON SAINT–COME. 1951. Notes et observations sur les oiseaux des Antilles Françaises. Oiseau Rev. Fr. Ornithol. 21:229–277.

PINCHON, P. R., AND M. BON SAINT–COME. 1952. Note complémentaire sur l'avifaune des Antilles Française. Oiseau Rev. Fr. Ornithol. 22:113–119.

POEY, F. 1851–1858. Memorias sobre la historia natural de la Isla de Cuba, acompañadas de sumarios latinos y extractos en francés. Imprenta de Barcina, Habana.

POEY, F. 1851–1855. Apuntes sobre la fauna de la Isla de Piños. Pages 424–431 in Memorias sobre la Historia Natural de la Isla de Cuba, acompañadas de sumarios Latinos y extractos en Frances, Vol. I. Imprenta de Barcina, Habana.

POEY Y AGUIRRE, A. 1848. Catalogo Metodico de las Aves de la Isla de Cuba. Mem. Real Soc. Econ., La Habana, ser. 2, 6:97–108.

PORTER, S. 1930. Notes on the birds of Dominica. Avicult. Mag. 8:114–126.

PORTER, S. 1930. Notes on the birds of Dominica. Avicult. Mag. 8:146–158.

PORTER, S. 1936. A West Indian diary. Avicult. Mag. 1:96–112.

POSADA RODRIGUEZ, R. M., A. KIRKCONNELL, F. DE ARAZOZA, AND A. LLANES SOSA. 1989. Ornitocenosis de los cayos Campos, Avalos y Cantiles, Archipiélago de los Canarreos, Cuba. Poeyana No. 365:1–9.

PREGILL, G. K., D. W. STEADMAN, AND D. R. WATTERS. 1994. Late Quaternary vertebrate faunas of the Lesser Antilles: historical components of Caribbean biogeography. Bull. Carnegie Mus. Nat. Hist. No. 30:1–51.

RABIÉ, M. René–G. de. [1773–1784]. [Histoire naturelle de St. Domingo]. [Fabrique toutes sortes de Registres & Portfeu], Paris.

RAFFAELE, H. A. 1973. Assessment of Mona Island avifauna. Apéndice: K. Pages K1–K32 in Mona and Monito islands. An assessment of their natural and historical resources, Vol. 2. Estado Libre Asociado de Puerto Rico Oficina del Gobernador, Junta de Calidad Ambiental, San Juan.

RAFFAELE, H. A. 1973. The fauna of Vieques Island. Unpublished report, Puerto Rico Department of Natural Resources, San Juan.

RAFFAELE, H. A. 1975. Important natural wildlife areas. Unpublished report, Puerto Rico Department of Natural Resources, San Juan.

RAFFAELE, H. A. 1977. La fauna de vertebrados de Puerto Rico. Pages 261–303 in El Gran Enciclopedia de Puerto Rico, Vol. 9. Tome lo Editorial Obre, San Juan, Puerto Rico.

RAFFAELE, H. A. 1981. New records of bird species for Puerto Rico and one for the West Indies. Am. Birds 35(2):142–143.

RAFFAELE, H. A., J. M. DUFFIELD, AND J. A. MORENO. 1979. Critical wildlife areas of Puerto Rico. Federal Aid Project PW–1–7, Department of Natural Resources Commonwealth of Puerto Rico, Area of Planning and Resource Analysis, San Juan.

RAMS BECEÑA, A. 1987. Segundo reporte para Cuba de Phaeton aethereus mesonauta Peters, Rabijunco de Pico Rojo. Garciana 2:3–4.

RAMS BECEÑA, A., A. COY OTERO, AND J. ESPINOSA. 1987. Contribucion al conocimeinto de la fauna de Cayo Fragoso, costa norte de Cuba, Parte III: Vertebrados. Garciana 5:2–3.

RAMSDEN, C. T. 1911. Nesting of Man–o'–war–bird (Fregata aquila) in Cuba. Auk 28(2):254.

RAMSDEN, C. T. 1912. Phœtusa magnirostris Licht. in Cuba. Auk 29(1):100.

RAPPOLE, J. H., E. S. MORTON, T. E. LOVEJOY III, AND J. L. RUOS. 1983. Nearctic avian migrants in the neotropics. With an appendix on Latin American laws by Byron Swift. U. S. Department of the Interior, Fish and Wildlilfe Service, Washington, D. C.

RAPPOLE, J. H., E. S. MORTON, T. E. LOVEJOY III, AND J. L. RUOS. 1993. Aves migratorias nearticas en los neotropicos. Conservation and Research Center, National Zoological Park, Smithsonian Institution, Front Royal, Virginia.

READ, A. C. 1912. Birds observed on the Isle of Pines, Cuba, 1912. Oölogist 30:130–131.

READ, A. C. 1913. Birds seen on a long journey. Oölogist 30:264–268.

[RICHARDSON, J.] 1993. Tern, Roseate. Gosse Bird Club Broads. No. 61:18.

[RICHARDSON, J.] 1993. Bridled Tern. Gosse Bird Club Broads. No. 61:18.

RICHMOND, C. W. 1899. Pelecanus occidentalis vs. P. fuscus. Auk 16(2):178.

RIDGWAY, R. 1888. Catalogue of a collection of birds made by Mr. Chas. H. Townsend, on islands in the Caribbean Sea and in Honduras. Proc. U. S. Nat. Mus. (1887) 10:572–597.

RIDGWAY, R. 1891. List of birds collected on the Bahama Islands by the naturalists of the Fish Commission steamer *Albatross*. Auk 8(4):333–339.

RILEY, J. H. 1904. Catalogue of a collection of birds from Barbuda and Antigua, British West Indies. Smithson. Misc. Coll. 47:277–291.

RILEY, J. H. 1905. Birds of the Bahama Islands. Pages 347–368 *in* The Bahama Islands (G. B. Shattuck, Ed.). The Geographic Society of Baltimore, The Macmillan Company, New York.

RILEY, J. H. 1905. List of birds collected or observed during the Bahama Expedition of the Geographic Society of Baltimore. Auk 22(4):349–360.

RIPLEY, S. D., AND G. E. WATSON, III. 1956. Cuban bird notes. Postilla No. 26:1–6.

RITTER, K. 1920. Voyage d'histoire naturelle et d'études botaniques dans les Indes Occidentales, île d'Haiti. Collection bibliotheque Edmond Mangones deposited at Bibliotheque de Saint Louis de Gonzague, Port–au–Prince, Haiti.

RITTER, K. 1836. Naturhistorische Reise nach der Westindieschen Insel Hayti, Auf Kosten Sr. Majestät des Kaisers von Oesterreich. Hallberger, Stuttgart.

ROBINSON, K. L. 1986. Culebra National Wildlife Refuge, Puerto Rico. Am. Birds 40(2):217–223.

ROBERTSON, W. B., Jr. 1960. Observations on the birds of St. John, Virgin Islands. Project completion report to the National Park Service, U. S. Department of the Interior.

ROBERTSON, W. B., Jr. 1962. Observations on the birds of St. John, Virgin Islands. Auk 79(1):44–76.

ROBERTSON, W. B., Jr. 1969. Transatlantic migration of juvenile Sooty Terns. Nature 222:632–634.

[ROCHEFORT, C. C. de]. 1657. Histoire naturelle et morale des îles Antilles de L'Amérique. A. Lyon, Chez Christophe Fourmy.

[ROCHEFORT, C. C. de]. 1666. The history of the Caribby–Islands, viz. Barbados, St. Christophers, St. Vincents, Martinico, Dominico, Barbouthos, Montserrat, Mevis, Antego, &c. in all XXVIII. In two books. The first containing the natural; the second, the moral history of those islands. Illustrated with several pieces of sculpture, representing the most considerable rarities therein described. With a Caribbian–vocabulary. Rendred into English by John Davies of Kidwelly. Thomas Dring and John Starkey, London.

[ROCHEFORT, C. C. de]. 1681. Histoire Naturelle et Morale des îles Antilles de l'Amérique, Enrichie d'un grand nombre de belles figures en taille douce, qui représentent au naturel les places, & les Raretéz les plus considérables qui y sont d'écrites. Avec un Vocabulaire Caraïbe. Dernière ed. Reinier Leers, Rotterdam.

RODRIGUEZ BATISTA, D., AND M. E. GARCIA ROMERO. 1987. Ornitocenosis de una vegetación litoral al norte de La Habana. Poeyana No. 347:1–7.

RODRIGUEZ FERRER, M. 1876. Naturaleza y civilización de la grandiosa Isla de Cuba, ó estudios variados y científicos, al alcance de todos, y otros históricos, estadísticos y políticos. Parte primera.–Naturaleza. Imprenta de J. Noguera á Cargo de M. Martinez, Madrid.

ROLLE, F. J. 1961. The avifauna of Mona Island, Puerto Rico. Fl. Nat. 34:195–202.

ROLLE, F. J. 1961. Notes and records of little–known species of birds from Puerto Rico. J. Agric. Univ. P. R. 45:333–341.

ROLLE, F. J. 1966. Notes on birds from some West Indian islands. Stahlia 7:1–4.

ROLLE, F. J., H. HEATWOLE, R. LEVINS, AND F. TORRES. 1964. Fauna notes on Monito Island, Puerto Rico. Caribb. J. Sci. 4:321–322.

ROTHSCHILD, L. W. 1907. Extinct Birds. An attempt to unite in one volume a short account of those birds which have become extinct in historical times—that is, within the last six or seven hundred years. To which are added a few which still exist, but are on the verge of extinction. With 45 colored plates, embracing 63 subjects and other illustrations. Hutchinson & Co., London.

ROTHSCHILD, W. 1907. On extinct and vanishing birds. Pages 191–217 *in* Proceedings of the Fourth International Ornithological Congress (1905) (E. J. O. Hartert and J. L. Bonhote, Eds.). Dulan & Co., London.

ROTHSCHILD, L. W. 1907. On the genus *Fregata*. Novit. Zool. 22:145–146.

RUSSELL, S. M., J. C. BARLOW, AND D. W. LAMM. 1979. Status of some birds on Isla San Andres and Isla Providencia, Colombia. Condor 81:98–100.

RUTTEN, M. 1934. Observations on Cuban birds. Ardea 23:109–126.

SAGRA, R. de la. 1842. Album de aves cubanas reunidas durante el viage de D. Ramon de la Sagra. Imprenta y Litografia de Maulde y Renou, Paris.

SAGRA, R. de la. 1842. Album d'oiseaux de Cuba réunis pendant le voyage de M. Ramonde la Sagra dédié à S. M. la Reine Isabelle II. Imprimerie et lithographie de Maulde et Renou, Paris.

SALIVA, J. E. 1989. Possible effects of Hurricane Hugo on the seabird populations of Culebra Island. Colon. Waterbird Soc. Newsl. 13:33.

SALIVA, J. E. 1989. Behavioral thermoregulation of breeding Sooty Terns. Colon. Waterbird Soc. Newsl. 13:26.

SALIVA, J. E. 1990. El rol de la vegetación en los habitos de anidaje de la Gaviota Oscura. Pages 130–134 *in* XVI Simposio de los Recursos Naturales Departamento de Recursos Naturales de Puerto Rico, San Juan.

SALIVA, J. E. 1990. Laughing Gull foraging technique at a Sooty Tern colony. Colon. Waterbird Soc. Newsl. 14:24.

SALIVA, J. E. 1994. Vieques y su fauna. Vieques wildlife manual. U. S. Department of the Interior – U. S. Fish and Wildlife Service, Boquerón, Puerto Rico.

SALIVA, J. E., AND J. BURGER. 1988. Dense vegetation as a nesting habitat of Sooty Terns (*Sterna fuscata*). Bull. Ecol. Soc. Am. 69:284.

SALIVA, J. E., AND J. BURGER. 1989. Effect of experimental manipulation of vegetation density on nest–site selection in Sooty Terns. Condor 91:689–698.

SALIVA, J. E., AND J. BURGER. 1995. Thermal stress and behavior of Sooty Terns nesting under variable vegetation density. Colon. Waterbird Soc. Bull. 19:62.

SALIVA, J. E., AND J. PIERCE. 1993. Distribution of Roseate Tern colonies in the Puerto Rico Bank. Colon. Waterbird Soc. Bull. 17:53.

SALIVA, J. E., AND D. A. SHEALER. 1991. Factors influencing reproductive success and colony site fidelity of Roseate Terns in the Caribbean. Colon. Waterbird Soc. Newsl. 15:34.

SALIVA, J. E., AND D. A. SHEALER. 1991. Aspects of the breeding biology of Roseate Terns in Puerto Rico. Pitirre 4(3):8.

SALLÉ, M. A. 1857. Liste des Oiseaux Rapportés et Observés dans la République Dominicaine (Ancienne Partie Espagnole de l'île St. Domingue ou d'Haiti), pendant son voyage de 1849 à 1851. Proc. Zool. Soc. London 25:230–237.

SALMON, L. 1965. Caspian Tern. Gosse Bird Club Broads. No. 5:22.

SALMON, L. 1967. Black Tern. Gosse Bird Club Broads. No. 8:16.

SALMON, L. 1970. White–tailed tropic birds. Gosse Bird Club Broads. No. 15:18.

SANCHEZ, B., V. BEROVIDES ALVAREZ, AND A. GONZALEZ. 1992. Aspectos ecológicos de la avifauna de la Reserva Natural Cayo Caguanes provincia de Sancti Spíritus, Cuba. Rep. Invest. Inst. Ecol. Sistem. No. Diciembre:1–16.

SANCHEZ, B., M. E. GARCIA ROMERO, AND D. RODRIGUEZ BATISTA. 1991. Aves de Cayo Levisa, Archipiélago de los Colorados, Pinar del Río, Cuba. Invest. Mar. CICIMAR 6:247–249.

SANCHEZ FALCON, C. 1940. Nuevo hallazgo del "Dovekie" (*Alle alle*) en Cuba. Mem. Soc. Cubana Hist. Nat. "Felipe Poey" 14:98.

SANDERSON, D. J. 1982. Birds of the Turks and Caicos Islands. Turks and Caicos Current 1982:35–42.

SCHAFFNER, F. C. 1984. White–tailed Tropicbird breeding at Culebra, Puerto Rico in 1984. Colon. Waterbirds Group Newsl. 8:30.

SCHAFFNER, F. C. 1985. White–tailed Tropicbird (*Phaethon lepturus*) breeding at Culebra, Puerto Rico: report for 1984–1985 and outline of continued study. Unpublished report to U. S. Fish and Wildlife Service, Coral Gables, Florida.

SCHAFFNER, F. C. 1986. White–tailed Tropicbird breeding at Cayo Luis Peña, Puerto Rico. Colon. Waterbird Soc. Newsl. 10:36.

SCHAFFNER, F. C. 1987. White–tailed Tropicbird (*Phaethon lepturus*) breeding at Cayo Luis Peña, Culebra National Wildlife Refuge, Puerto Rico: Report for 1984–1986. Report to the U. S. Fish and Wildlife Service, Cabo Rojo, Puerto Rico.

SCHAFFNER, F. C., Jr. 1988. The breeding biology and energetics of the White–tailed Tropicbird (*Phaethon lepturus*) at Culebra, Puerto Rico. Ph.D. thesis, University of Miami, Coral Gables, Florida.

SCHAFFNER, F. C. 1989. Regulation of food provisioning patterns of White–tailed Tropicbirds. Colon. Waterbird Soc. Newsl. 13:26.

SCHAFFNER, F. C. 1990. Feed size and feeding periodicity in pelagic birds: notes on methodology. Colon. Waterbirds 13:7–15.

SCHAFFNER, F. C. 1990. Food provisioning by White–tailed Tropicbirds: effects on the developmental pattern of chicks. Ecology 71:375–390.

SCHAFFNER, F. C. 1991. Nest–site selection and nesting success of White–tailed Tropicbirds (*Phaethon lepturus*) at Cayo Luís Peña, Puerto Rico. Auk 108(4):911–922.

SCHAFFNER, F. C., M. R. FULLER, C. J. PENNYCUICK, AND H. H. OBRECHT, III. 1989. Radio tracking of White–tailed Tropicbirds over the Caribbean Sea. Pac. Seabird Group Bull. 16:41.

SCHAFFNER, F. C., R. L. NORTON, AND J. TAYLOR. 1986. Range extension of Cayenne Terns on the Puerto Rico Bank. Wilson Bull. 98:317–318.

SCHAFFNER, F. C., AND P. K. SWART. 1991. Influence of diet and environmental water on the carbon and oxygen isotopic signatures of seabird eggshell carbonate. Bull. Mar. Sci. 48:23–38.

SCHMIDT, K. P. 1926. The amphibians and reptiles of Mona Island, West Indies. Field Mus. Nat. Hist. Zoology Series, 12:147–163.

SCHREIBER, R. W., D. W. BELITSKY, AND B. A. SORRIE. 1981. Notes on Brown Pelicans in Puerto Rico. Wilson Bull. 93:397–400.

SCHREIBER, R. W., AND P. J. MOCK. 1988. Eastern Brown Pelicans: what does 60 years of banding tell us? J. Field Ornithol. 59:171–182.

SCHWARTZ, A. 1969. Land birds of Isla Saona, República Dominicana. Q. J. Florida Acad. Sci. 32:291–306.

SCHWARTZ, A., AND R. F. KLINIKOWSKI. 1963. Observations on West Indian birds. Proc. Acad. Nat. Sci. Philadelphia 115:53–77.

SCHWARTZ, A., AND R. F. KLINIKOWSKI. 1965. Additional observations on West Indian birds. Notulae Naturae, Acad. Nat. Sci. Philadelphia 376:1–16.

SCLATER, P. L. 1910. Revised list of the birds of Jamaica. Pages 596–619 in The Handbook of Jamaica for 1910. Comprising historical, statistical and general information concerning the island, compiled from official and other reliable records (J. C. Ford and F. Cundall, Eds.). The Institute of Jamaica, Kingston.

SCOTT, W. E. D. 1891. Observations on the birds of Jamaica, West Indies. I. Notes on the habits of the Yellow–billed Tropic Bird (Phaëthon flavirostris). Auk 8(3):249–256.

SCOTT, W. E. D. 1891. Observations on the birds of Jamaica, West Indies. II. A list of the birds recorded from the island, with annotations. Auk 8(4):353–365.

SEA/DVS. 1992. Reconocimiento y evaluación de los recursos naturales de la zona costera del este. Secretaria de Estado de Agricultura, Secretaría de vida Silvestre, Santo Domingo, Dominican Republic.

SEAMAN, G. A. 1951. Wildlife resources survey of the Virgin Islands. Pittman–Robertson Quart. 11:110–111.

SEAMAN, G. A. 1961. Wildlife resources survey of the Virgin Islands No. 4–R: Quarterly Rcpt., June. Unpublished Report, St. Croix.

SEAMAN, G. A., AND J. E. RANDALL. 1962. The mongoose as a predator in the Virgin Islands. J. Mammal. 43:544–546.

SHEALER, D. A. 1996. Foraging habitat use and profitability in tropical Roseate Terns and Sandwich Terns. Auk 113(1):209–217.

SHEALER, D. A., AND J. BURGER. 1991. Comparative foraging success between adult and immature Roseate and Sandwich terns. Colon. Waterbird Soc. Newsl. 15:35.

SHEALER, D. A., AND J. BURGER. 1992. A "good" versus a "bad" year for Roseate Terns breeding in Puerto Rico. Colon. Waterbird Soc. Bull. 16:56–57.

SHEALER, D. A., AND J. BURGER. 1992. Differential responses of tropical Roseate Terns to aerial intruders throughout the nesting cycle. Condor 94:712–719.

SHEALER, D. A., AND J. BURGER. 1993. Effects of interference competition on the foraging activity of tropical Roseate Terns. Condor 95:322–329.

SHEALER, D. A., AND J. BURGER. 1993. Prey selection by tropical Roseate and Sandwich terns during years of food abundance and food stress. Colon. Waterbird Soc. Bull. 17:43.

SHEALER, D. A., AND J. BURGER. 1995. Comparative foraging success between adult and one–year–old Roseate and Sandwich terns. Colon. Waterbirds 18:93–99.

SHEALER, D. A., AND J. E. SALIVA. 1992. Northeastern Roseate Terns seen at Puerto Rican colony during breeding season. Colon. Waterbirds 15:152–154.

SHEALER, D. A., AND J. G. ZUROVCHAK. 1995. Three extremely large clutches of Roseate Tern eggs in the Caribbean. Colon. Waterbirds 18:105–107.

SIEGEL, A. 1983. Birds of Montserrat. Montserrat National Trust, Montserrat, West Indies.

SIPHRON, J. 1973. Reef birds. Gosse Bird Club Broads. No. 21:14.

SIPHRON, J. 1976. Tropicbirds. Gosse Bird Club Broads. No. 27:13–14.

SIRI NUÑEZ, D. 1986. Reportes de aves anilladas: Plegadis falcinellus (Linnaeus) y Sterna maximus (Boddaert). Hispaniolana, Publ. Ocas. 1:13–14.

SLADEN, F. W., AND R. H. WAUER. 1992. Third record of White–winged Tern for the West Indies. Ornitol. Caribeña 3:49–50.

SLADEN, F. W. 1988. Some new records and observations of birds in the Virgin Islands. Am. Birds 42(5):1227–1231.

SLADEN, F. W. 1988. Checklist of birds of St. Croix, U. S. Virgin Islands. Revised 1988 ed. Published by author, Christiansted, U. S. Virgin Islands.

SLADEN, F. W. 1992. Abundance and distribution of waterbirds in two types of wetlands on St. Croix, U. S. Virgin Islands. Ornitol. Caribeña 3:35–42.

SLOANE, H. 1707. A voyage to the islands Madera, Barbados, Nieves, S. Christophers and Jamaica, with the natural history of the herbs and trees, four–footed beasts, fishes, birds, insects, reptiles, &c. of the last of those islands; to which is prefix'd an introduction, wherein is an account of the inhabitants, air, waters, diseases, trace, &c of that place, with some relations concerning the neighbouring continent, and islands of America. Illustrated with the figures of the things described, which have not been heretofore engraved; in large copper=plates as big as the life. Printed by B. M. for the author, London.

SMITH, D. 1994. Brown Pelican. Gosse Bird Club Broads. No. 62:19.

SMITH, D. 1994. Herring Gull. Gosse Bird Club Broads. No. 62:21.

SMITH, D., AND C. KELLER. 1995. Birds at mouth of the Black River, St. Elizabeth. Gosse Bird Club Broads. No. 65:16.

SMITH, P. W., AND S. A. SMITH. 1993. Tern, Sandwich. Gosse Bird Club Broads. No. 61:17.

SMITH, R. W. 1964. Bird banding in Jamaica. Gosse Bird Club Broads. No. 2:4–5.

SMITH, R. W. 1964. Bird banding: January to June 1964. Gosse Bird Club Broads. No. 3:5–6.

SMITH, R. W. 1964. Black Tern. Gosse Bird Club Broads. No. 3:16.

SMITH, R. W. 1965. Bird banding, 1964. Gosse Bird Club Broads. No. 4:5–7.

SMITH, R. W. 1965. Bird banding. Gosse Bird Club Broads. No. 5:7–9.

SMITH, R. W. 1966. A trip to Morant Cays. Gosse Bird Club Broads. No. 6:5–6.

SMITH, R. W. 1966. Bird banding. Gosse Bird Club Broads. No. 6:7–10.

SMITH, R. W. 1966. Colour–marked Sooty Terns. Gosse Bird Club Broads. No. 6:10.

SMITH, R. W. 1967. Bird banding. Gosse Bird Club Broads. No. 8:4–6.

SMITH, R. W. 1967. Bird banding. Gosse Bird Club Broads. No. 9:15.

SMITH, R. W. 1969. Informal conversations on Jamaican birds. Gosse Bird Club Broads. No. 12:22–23.

SMITH, R. W. 1969. Further searches for the Blue Mountain Duck. Gosse Bird Club Broads. No. 12:11–15.

SMITH, R. W. 1970. Tropic birds in Jamaica. Gosse Bird Club Broads. No. 14:3–7.

SMITH, R. W. 1970. White–tailed Tropic Bird. Gosse Bird Club Broads. No. 14:23.

SMITH, R. W. 1970. White–tailed tropic birds. Gosse Bird Club Broads. No. 15:18.

SMITH, R. W. 1970. Birds of Port Henderson – 1894. Gosse Bird Club Broads. No. 15:22–23.

SMITH, R. W. 1971. Recovery of a banded noddy. Gosse Bird Club Broads. No. 16:13.

SMITH, R. W. 1971. White–tailed Tropic Bird. Gosse Bird Club Broads. No. 17:26.

SMITH, R. W. 1972. White–tailed Tropic Bird. Gosse Bird Club Broads. No. 18:19.

SMITH, R. W. 1972. Conservation areas – birds – April 1969. Gosse Bird Club Broads. No. 19:2–4.

SMITH, R. W. 1973. Conservation areas – birds (Contd.) April 1969. Gosse Bird Club Broads. No. 20:2–4.

SMITH, R. W., AND N. AGAR. 1967. Common Tern. Gosse Bird Club Broads. No. 8:16.

SMITH, R. W., N. AGAR, AND P. M. SMITH [Editors]. 1967. Distribution of Jamaican species. Gosse Bird Club Broads. No. 8:9.

SMITH, R. W., AND M. GOCHFELD. 1965. Black–capped Petrel (*Pteradroma hasitata*). Gosse Bird Club Broads. No. 4:14.

SMITH, R. W., AND W. H. HOUSTON. 1964. Parasitic Jaeger. Gosse Bird Club Broads. No. 3:15.

SMITH, D., AND C. KELLER. 1995. Common Tern. Gosse Bird Club Broads. No. 65:20.

SMITH, D., AND C. KELLER. 1995. Birds at mouth of the Black River, St. Elizabeth. Gosse Bird Club Broads. No. 65:16.

SMITH, D., AND C. KELLER. 1995. Black Skimmer. Gosse Bird Club Broads. No. 65:20.

SORRIE, B. A. 1975. Observations on the birds of Vieques Island, Puerto Rico. Caribb. J. Sci. 15:89–103.

SOUTHERN, W. E. 1974. Florida distribution of Ring–billed Gulls from the Great Lakes regions. Bird–Banding 45:341–352.

SOY, J. P., AND S. O. CUBILLAS. 1991. Conducta de asociacion de varias especies de aves como factor de supervivencia. Page 67 *in* Preservar la Biodiversidad, Premisa del Verdadero Desarrollo. II Simposio de Zoologia, 18–23 de junio 1991. La Habana, Cuba.

SOY, J. P., AND S. O. CUBILLAS. 1991. Conducta de asociacion de varias especies de aves como factor de supervivencia. Pitirre 4(2):7.

SPENCE, S. 1973. Magnificent Frigatebird. Gosse Bird Club Broads. No. 20:20.

SPENCE, S. 1974. Sooty Shearwater. Gosse Bird Club Broads. No. 23:20.

SPENCER, W. 1981. A guide to the birds of Antigua. Privately published, Antigua.

SPRUNT, A., IV. 1984. Some aspects of breeding seabirds in the Bahamas. Colon. Waterbirds Group Newsl. 8:37.

SPRUNT, A., IV. 1984. The status and conservation of seabirds of the Bahama Islands. Pages 157–168 *in* Status and conservation of the world's seabirds (J. P. Croxall, P. G. H. Evans, and R. W. Schreiber, Eds.). ICBP Tech. Publ. No. 2, Cambridge, U.K.

STAHL, A. 1882. Fauna de Puerto–Rico. Clasificacion sistemática de los animales que corresponden á esta fauna y catálogo del gabinete zoológico del Dr. A. Stahl en Bayamon. Imprenta del "Boletin Mercantil," 37 Calle de la Fortaleza, Bayamon, Puerto Rico.

STAHL, A. 1887. Beitrag zur Vogelfauna von Portorico. Ornis 3:448–453.

STARRETT, W. C., AND K. L. DIXON. 1947. Notes on the Pomarine Jaeger in the Atlantic and Caribbean. Auk 64(2):320.

STODDART, D. R., AND M. E. C. GIGLIOLI. 1980. Geography and ecology of Little Cayman. Atoll Res. Bull. No. 241:181.

STRONG, A. 1996. Brown Booby. Gosse Bird Club Broads. No. 66:31.

STRONG, A. 1996. Black Tern. Gosse Bird Club Broads. No. 66:33.

STRUTHERS, P. H. 1923. Observations on the bird life of Porto Rico. Auk 40(3):469–478.

STRUTHERS, P. H. 1927. Notes on the bird–life of Mona and Desecheo Islands. Auk 44(4):539–544.

SUNDEVALL, C. J. 1869. Foglarne på ön S:t Barthelemy, efter de af Dr. A. von Goës hemsända samlingarna bestämde. Öfvers. af K. Vetensk. Ak. Förhandl., Stockholm 25:579–591.

SUNDEVALL, C. J. 1869. Foglarne på ön Porto Rico, efter Hr Hjalmarsons insamlingar framställda. Öfvers. af K. Vetensk. Ak. Förhandl., Stockholm 1869:593–603.

SUTTON, R. L. 1976. Morant Cays. Gosse Bird Club Broads. No. 27:15.

SUTTON, R. L. 1979. Bird recoveries. Gosse Bird Club Broads. No. 32:11–12.

SUTTON, R. 1979. Visit to south coast areas. Gosse Bird Club Broads. No. 32:11.

SUTTON, R. L. 1991. Banded birds recaptured or recovered in Jamaica – Returns from US Fish & Wildlife Service for 3rd quater 1990/91. Gosse Bird Club Broads. No. 57:3.

SUTTON, R. L., AND J. SIPHRON. 1976. White–tailed Tropicbird. Gosse Bird Club Broads. No. 27:20.

SUTTON, A. M., AND R. L. SUTTON. 1988. Bird banding recoveries. Gosse Bird Club Broads. No. 50:11–12.

SUTTON, R. L., AND A. SUTTON. 1989. Recent recoveries in Jamaica of birds banded elscwhere. Gosse Bird Club Broads. No. 53:22.

SWANK, W. G., AND C. R. JULIEN. 1975. Wildlife management and protection. Dominica. Distribution and status of wildlife in Dominica. Project Working Document No. 1, Food and Agriculture Organization of the United Nations, Rome, Italy.

TAYLOR, E. C. 1864. Five months in the West Indies. Part II.–Martinique, Dominica, and Porto Rico. Ibis 6:157–173.

TAYLOR, J. P. 1984. Nesting habitat improvement for Sandwich Terns. Colon. Waterbirds Group Newsl. 8:39.

TAYLOR, J. P. 1985. [Status and management of seabirds in the Culebra National Wildlife Refuge]. Colon. Waterbirds Group Newsl. 9:23–24.

TAYLOR, R. G. T. 1970. White–tailed Tropic Birds. Gosse Bird Club Broads. No. 15:18.

TERBORGH, J., AND J. FAABORG. 1973. Turnover and ecological release in the avifauna of Mona Island, Puerto Rico. Auk 90(4):759–779.

TERRILL, S. B. 1990. Field notes from San Salvador, Bahamas. Unpublished list, Siena College, Loudonville, New York.

THALY, D. 1934. The re–discovery of the diablotin. Country Life 76:286.

THIENEMANN, F. A. L. 1857. Ueber die von Dr. Gundlach eingesendeten Eier und Nester cubanischer Vögel. J. Ornithol. 5(27):145–159.

THRELFALL, W. 1978. Dispersal of Herring Gulls from the Witless Bay Sea Bird Sanctuary, Newfoundland. Bird–Banding 49:116–124.

THWAITES, P. 1991. Brown Pelican. Gosse Bird Club Broads. No. 57:21.

TIPPENHAUER, L. G. 1892. Die Insel Haiti. Leipzig.

TIPPENHAUER, L. G. 1893. Die Insel Haiti. Vol. 3–4. F. H. Brodhaus, Leipzig.

TODD, W. E. C. 1916. The birds of the Isle of Pines. Incorporating the substance of field–notes by Gustav A. Link. Ann. Carnegie Mus. 10:146–296.

TODD, W. E. C., AND W. W. WORTHINGTON. 1911. A contribution to the ornithology of the Bahama Islands. Ann. Carnegie Mus. 7:388–464.

TORRES, A. 1994. Listado de las aves observadas dentro del corredor migratorio de Gibara, Provincia Holguín, Cuba. Garciana 22:1–4.

TORRES LEYVA, A., C. PEÑA, AND A. RAMS BECEÑA. 1989. Aves observadas en las cienagas de Birama, Cauto Norte y Carena, Provincia Granma, Cuba. Garciana 20:1–2.

TYE, A., AND H. TYE. 1991. Bird species on St. Andrew and Old Providence Islands, West Caribbean. Wilson Bull. 103:493–497.

U. S. DEPARTMENT OF THE INTERIOR. 1981. Final environmental impact statement. Proposed disposition and administration of lands declared excess by the U. S. Navy on the islands of Culebra and Culebrita in Puerto Rico. U. S. Department of the Interior, Atlanta, Georgia.

VALDÉS MIRO, V. 1984. Datos de nidificación sobre las aves que crían en Cuba. Poeyana No. 282:1–27.

VAN BARNEVELD, R. 1993. White–tailed Tropicbird. Gosse Bird Club Broads. No. 60:29.

VAN HALEWYN, R., AND R. L. NORTON. 1984. The status and conservation of seabirds in the Caribbean. Pages 169–222 in Status and conservation of the world's seabirds (J. P. Croxall, P. G. H. Evans, and R. W. Schreiber, Eds.). ICBP Technical Publication No. 2, Cambridge, United Kingdom.

VARGAS MORA, T. A. 1984. Informe sobre las aves acuaticas y ribereñas del Lago Enriquillo. Seccion de Ornitologia, Departamento de Vida Silvestre, Secretaria de Estado de Agricultura, Santo Domingo.

VARGAS MORA, T. A. 1984. Contribucion al conocimiento del estado actual de las aves acuaticas en el Lago Enriquillo. Pages 168–169 in Memoria de la Segunda Jornada Cientifica: Medio Ambiente y Recursos Naturales. Acadamia de Ciencias, Santo Domingo.

VARGAS MORA, T. A., AND M. GONZALEZ CASTILLO. 1984. Informe sobre la avifauna de la Peninsula de Barahona e Isla Beata. Pages 225–253 in Estudios en las areas silvestres de la Peninsula de Barahona e Isla Beata. Propuesta para la creacion de una zona protegida (parque nacional). Departamento de Vida Silvestre, Secretaria de Estado de Agricultura, Santo Domingo.

VARONA, L. S., AND O. H. GARRIDO. 1970. Vertebrados de los Cayos de San Felipe, Cuba, incluyendo una nueva especie de jutia. Poeyana No. A 75:1–26.

VAURIE, C. 1953. Observations and new records of birds from the Biminis, northwestern Bahamas. Auk 70(1):38–48.

VAURIE, C. 1961. List of and notes on the birds of the Iles des Saintes, French West Indies. Auk 78(1):57–62.

VERMEIJ, G. J. 1993. Biogeography of recently extinct marine species: implications for conservation. Conserv. Biol. 7:391–397.

VERRILL, A. E., AND A. H. VERRILL. 1909. Notes on the birds of San Domingo, with a list of the species, including a new hawk. Proc. Acad. Nat. Sci. Philadelphia 61:352–366.

VERRILL, A. H. about 1905. Additions to the avifauna of Dominica. Notes on species hitherto unrecorded with descriptions of three new species and a list of all birds known to occur on the island. Privately printed, Barbados.

VERRILL, G. E. 1892. Notes on the fauna of the island of Dominica, British West Indies, with lists of the species obtained and observed by G. E. and A. H. Verrill. Trans. Conn. Acad. Arts Sci. 8:315–355.

VIEILLOT, L. J. P., AND M. P. OUDART. 1825. La galérie des oiseaux, dédiée à son Altesse Royale Madame, Duchesse de Berri. (Continuateur de l'Histoire des Oiseaux dorés, auteur de celles des Oiseaux chanteurs de la Zone Torride et de l'Amérique septentrionale, de l'Ornithologie française, l'un des savans collaborateurs des deux éditions du nouveau Dictionnaire d'Histoire naturelle et du Tableau encyclopédique et méthodique des trois Règnes de la Nature, etc.). Constant–Chantpie, Paris.

VIEILLOT, L. J. P., AND M. P. OUDART. 1834. La galérie des oiseaux. Tome Primier. Carpentier–Mericourt, Paris.

VINCENTE, V. P. 1979. The occurrence of a nesting colony of the Royal Tern, Sterna Thalasseus maxima on the south coast of Puerto Rico. Am. Birds 33(2):147.

VIVALDI, J. L. 1986. La conservacion de la ornitofauna y el desarollo de Puerto Rico. Ornitol. Caribeña 2:3–8.

VOOUS, K. H. 1955. The birds of St. Martin, Saba, and St. Eustatius. Stud. Fauna Curaçao Other Caribb. Isl. 6(25):1–82.

VOOUS, K. H. 1957. The birds of Aruba, Curaçao, and Bonaire. Studies of the fauna of Curaçao and other Caribbean islands: No. 29, The Hague.

VOOUS, K. H., AND H. J. KOELERS. 1967. Check–list of the birds of St. Martin, Saba, and St. Eustatius. Ardea 55:115–137.

WALLACE, G. E., AND D. R. FILLMAN. 1994. Sighting of a Northern Gannet in Cuba. Fl. Field Nat. 22:114–117.

WARHAM, J. 1990. The petrels: their ecology and breeding systems. Academic Press, London.

WATSON, G. E. 1966. Seabirds of the tropical Atlantic Ocean. Smithsonian Press, Washington, D. C.

WAUER, R. H., AND J. M. WUNDERLE, Jr. 1992. The effect of Hurricane Hugo on bird populations on St. Croix, U. S. Virgin Islands. Wilson Bull. 104:656–673.

WEAVER, J. D., H. HEATWOLE, J. R. GOREHAM, AND F. J. ROLLE. 1961. Institute of Caribbean Studies field excursion to Isla Mona. Ornithology (5th. – 7th. November 1960). Caribb. J. Sci. 1:30–35.

WELLS, J. G. 1887. A catalogue of the birds of Grenada, West Indies, with observations thereon. [Ed. by George N. Lawrence]. Proc. U. S. Nat. Mus. (1886) 9:609–633.

WELLS, J. G. 1902. Birds of the island of Carriacou. Part I. Water birds. Auk 19(3):237–246.

WESTERMANN, J. H. 1953. Nature preservation in the Caribbean. A review of literature on the destruction and preservation of flora and fauna in the Caribbean area. Stud. Fauna Curaçao Other Caribb. Isl. 9:1–106.

WETMORE, A. 1916. Birds of Porto Rico. U. S. Dept. Agric. Bull. 326:1–140.

WETMORE, A. 1916. The birds of Vieques Island, Porto Rico. Auk 33(4):403–419.

WETMORE, A. 1917. The birds of Culebra Island, Porto Rico. Auk 34(1):51–62.

WETMORE, A. 1918. The birds of Desecheo Island, Porto Rico. Auk 35(3):333–340.

WETMORE, A. 1927. Birds of Porto Rico and the Virgin Islands. New York Academy of Science Scientific Survey of Porto Rico and the Virgin Islands. Vol. 9, parts 3 & 4. Pages 245–406. New York Academy of Science, New York.

WETMORE, A. 1930. The Rabie paintings of Haitian birds. Auk 47(4):481–486.

WETMORE, A. 1932. Birds collected in Cuba and Haiti by the Parrish–Smithsonian Expedition of 1930. Proc. U. S. Nat. Mus. 81:1–40.

WETMORE, A. 1932. Notes from Dr. R. Ciferri on the birds of Hispaniola. Auk 49(1):107–108.

WETMORE, A. 1932. The breeding of the Brown Booby in Porto Rican territory. Auk 49(3):341.

WETMORE, A. 1932. The diablotin in Dominica. Auk 49(4):456–457.

WETMORE, A. 1937. Ancient records of birds from the island of St. Croix with observations on extinct and living birds of Puerto Rico. J. Agric. Univ. P. R. 21:5–16.

WETMORE, A. 1938. A skua in the Caribbean Sea. Auk 55(2):277.

WETMORE, A. 1938. Bird remains from the West Indies. Auk 55(1):51–55.

WETMORE, A. 1939. A record of the Black–capped Petrel from Haiti. Auk 56(1):73.

WETMORE, A. 1940. A specimen of the Black–capped Petrel. Auk 57(1):105.

WETMORE, A. 1944. The subspecific characters and distribution of the New World skimmers (*Rynchops nigra*). Caldasia 3:111–118.

WETMORE, A. 1945. A review of the forms of the Brown Pelican. Auk 62(4):577–586.

WETMORE, A. 1952. A record for the Black–capped Petrel, *Pterodroma hasitata* in Martinique. Auk 69(4):460.

WETMORE, A., AND F. C. LINCOLN. 1933. Additional notes on the birds of Haiti and the Dominican Republic. Proc. U. S. Nat. Mus. 82:1–68.

WETMORE, A., AND W. M. PERRYGO. 1931. The cruise of the *Esperanza* to Haiti. Pages 59–66 *in* Exploration and Field Work of the Smithsonian Institute in 1930, Smithsonian Publication No. 3111. Smithsonian Institution, Washington, D. C.

WETMORE, A., AND B. H. SWALES. 1931. The birds of Haiti and the Dominican Republic. U. S. Nat. Mus. Bull. 155.

WHITE, A. W., B. HALLETT, AND A. M. BAINTON. 1996. Red–footed Boobies nest on White Cay, San Salvador. Bahamas J. Sci. 3:33–34.

WHITE, B. 1991. Common birds of San Salvador Island, Bahamas. Bahamian Field Station, Ltd., San Salvador, Bahamas.

WILEY, J. W. 1985. Bird conservation in the United States Caribbean. Pages 107–159 *in* Bird Conservation 2 (S. A. Temple, Ed.). University of Wisconsin Press for International Council for Bird Preservation, Madison.

WILEY, J. W. 1996. Ornithology in Puerto Rico and the Virgin Islands. Pages 149–179 *in* The Scientific Survey of Puerto Rico and the Virgin Islands. An eighty–year reassessment of the islands' natural history (J. C. Figueroa Colón, Ed.). Annals of the New York Academy of Sciences Volume 776, New York.

WILEY, J. W., AND J. A. OTTENWALDER. 1990. Birds of Islas Beata and Alto Velo, Dominican Republic. Stud. Neotrop. Fauna Environ. 25:65–88.

WILEY, J. W., AND J. M. WUNDERLE, Jr. 1993. The effects of hurricanes on birds, with special reference to Caribbean islands. Bird Conserv. Intern. 3:319–349.

WILLIAMS, E. H., Jr., L. BUNKLEY–WILLIAMS, AND I. LOPEZ–IRIZARRY. 1992. Die–off of Brown Pelicans in Puerto Rico and the United States Virgin Islands. Am. Birds 46(5):1106–1108.

WILLMANN, P. 1970. Black Skimmer, *Rynchops nigra*, on Puerto Rico. Fl. Nat. 43:180.

WILLMANN, P. A. 1971. Birding in southwest Puerto Rico. Birding 3:Unpaginated insert between pages 22–23.

WILLIAMS, E. H., Jr., AND L. BUNKLEY–WILLIAMS. 1992. Two unusual sea bird records from Puerto Rico. Caribb. J. Sci. 28:105.

WILLIAMS, R. S. R., G. M. KIRWAN, AND C. G. BRADSHAW. 1996. The status of the Black–capped Petrel *Pterodroma hasitata* in the Dominican Republic. Cotinga 6:29–30.

WING, E. S. 1969. Vertebrate remains excavated from San Salvador Island, Bahamas. Caribb. J. Sci. 9:25–29.

WING, E. S., C. A. HOFFMAN, Jr., AND C. E. RAY. 1968. Vertebrate remains from Indian sites on Antigua, West Indies. Caribb. J. Sci. 8:123–139.

WINGATE, D. B. 1964. Discovery of breeding Black–capped Petrels on Hispaniola. Auk 81(2):147–159.

WINGATE, D. B. 1964. Does the Blue Mountain Duck of Jamaica survive? Gosse Bird Club Broads. No. 2:1–2.

WINGATE, D. 1975. White–tailed Tropicbirds. Gosse Bird Club Broads. No. 24:6–7.

WITT, H.–H. 1978. Black Tern. Gosse Bird Club Broads. No. 30:13.

WITT, H.–H. 1978. Least Tern. Gosse Bird Club Broads. No. 30:13.

WOOD, P., S. BABBS, S. LING, AND P. ROBERTSON. 1987. Report of the 1986 University of East Anglia Martinique Oriole Expedition. International Council for Bird Preservation, Study Report No. 23, Cambridge, England.

WOODBURY, R. C., L. F. MARTORELL, AND J. C. GARCIA TUDURI. 1971. The flora of Desecheo Island, Puerto Rico. J. Agric. Univ. P. R. 55:478–505.

WOODS, C. A. 1987. The threatened and endangered birds of Haiti: lost horizons and new hopes. Pages 385–429 *in* Proceedings of the Jean Delacour Symposium on Breeding Birds in Captivity (A. C. Risser, Ed.). International Foundation for the Conservation of Birds, Los Angeles.

WOODS, C. A., AND J. A. OTTENWALDER. 1983. The montane avifauna of Haiti. Pages 607–622, 576–590 *in* Proceedings of the Jean Delacour/IFCB Symposium on Breeding Birds in Captivity (A. C. Risser, Jr., and F. S. Todd; Eds.). International Foundation for the Conservation of Birds, Los Angeles.

WOODS, C. A., AND J. A. OTTENWALDER. 1992. The natural history of southern Haiti. Florida Museum of Natural History, University of Florida, Gainesville.

WORTH, C. B., AND W. G. DOWNS. 1962. Recoveries in the West Indian Region of birds banded in North America, 1951–1960, and their possible relationship to the transport of arthropod–borne viruses. Wildl. Dis. no. 24:17.

YARRELL, W. 1871–1885. A history of British Birds, fourth ed., Vol. 3. John Van Voorst, London.

YATES, G. S. 1955. Notes on the Diablotin and Saffron Finch. Nat. Hist. Notes Nat. Hist. Soc. Jamaica 6:216.

YATES, G. S. 1977. Notes on the Diablotin and Saffron Finch. Nat. Hist. Notes Nat. Hist. Soc. Jamaica, new ser. 1:21–22.

ZULOAGA, G. 1955. The Isla de Aves story. Geogr. Rev. 45:172–180.